THE CLASSICAL
PARTHENON

The Classical Parthenon

Recovering the Strangeness
of the Ancient World

William St Clair

OpenBook
Publishers

https://www.openbookpublishers.com

©2022 William St Clair. ©2022 Preface by Paul Cartledge.

This work is licensed under a Creative Commons Attribution-NonCommercial-NoDerivatives (CC BY-NC-ND) license. This license allows you to share, copy, distribute, and transmit the work providing you do not modify the work, you do not use the work for commercial purposes, you attribute the work to the authors, and you provide a link to the license. Attribution should not in any way suggest that the authors endorse you or your use of the work and should include the following information:

William St Clair, *The Classical Parthenon: Recovering the Strangeness of the Ancient World*. Cambridge, UK: Open Book Publishers, 2022, https://doi.org/10.11647/OBP.0279

Copyright and permissions for the reuse of many of the images included in this publication differ from the above. This information is provided in the captions and in the list of illustrations.

In order to access detailed and updated information on the license, please visit https://doi.org/10.11647/OBP.0279#copyright. Further details about the Creative Commons licenses are available at http://creativecommons.org/licenses/

All external links were active at the time of publication unless otherwise stated and have been archived via the Internet Archive Wayback Machine at https://archive.org/web

Digital material and resources associated with this volume are available at https://doi.org/10.11647/OBP.0279#resources

Every effort has been made to identify and contact copyright holders and any omission or error will be corrected if notification is made to the publisher.

ISBN Paperback: 9781800643444
ISBN Hardback: 9781800643451
ISBN Digital (PDF): 9781800643468
ISBN Digital ebook (EPUB): 9781800643475
ISBN Digital ebook (AZW3): 9781800643482
ISBN XML: 9781800643499
ISBN HTML: 9781800646780
DOI: 10.11647/OBP.0279

Cover image: Aristophanes, *Lysistrata*, transl. C. Zevort (Paris: Librarie Charpentier et Fasquelle, 1898), pp. 20–21. Cover design by Anna Gatti.

Contents

Reports on the stonework of the Parthenon by well-qualified observers before the rapid expansion of the population of Athens, the extensive burning of coal, and the arrival of air pollution.

The clean dry air had preserved the marble surfaces of the ancient buildings to an astonishing extent, with the carved edges as sharp and crisp as they had evidently been in ancient times, as was noticed by Stuart and Revett in the 1750s when they examined the soon-to-be-demolished classical-era Ionic temple on the Illysos. As they wrote:

> It should be observed, that most of the ancient Structures in Athens, of which there are any Remains, were entirely built of an excellent white Marble, on which the Weather has very little Effect; whatever Part therefore of these Antiquities, has not been impaired by Violence, is by no means in that mouldering State of Decay, to which the dissolvent Quality of the Air, reduces the ordinary Buildings of common Stone: from which Cause it is, that, notwithstanding great Part of this Temple has long since been thrown down, and destroyed, whatever remains of it is still in good Preservation.

The exactitude and resultant durability was noted by Charles Robert Cockerell, one of the few on-the-spot observers who understood that the effect on the viewer was among the primary considerations of those who had commissioned and built the classical Parthenon. [...] In May 1814, when a party of the western community in Athens, including Cockerell, examined pieces on the ground, including those thrown from the building by Elgin's agents and were 'lost in admiration' at the 'incredible precision' with which the columns of the Parthenon had been constructed, they concluded from their specialist knowledge, that 'the marble was first reduced to its proper shape with the chisel after which the two pieces were rubbed one upon the other, and sand and water thrown into the centre of friction' so that, even at ground level, the joins presented 'a mark no thicker than a thread'.[1]

---

1   Taken from St Clair, William, *Who Saved the Parthenon? A New History of the Acropolis Before, During and After the Greek Revolution* (Cambridge: Open Book Publishers, 2022) [hereafter *WStP*], https://doi.org/10.11647/OBP.0136, Chapter 4, https://doi.org/10.11647/obp.0136.04, that also notes numerous comments by others with less specialist expertise.

Editors' Note

The Classical Parthenon and its companion volume, *Who Saved the Parthenon?* are the culmination of decades of immersion in its material and years of meticulous scholarship. Sadly the author, William St Clair, died in 2021 shortly before they were planned to go into production. He left behind electronic folders filled with his most recent drafts of the book's many chapters. It was our task, together with all the staff at Open Book Publishers, the academic press of which William St Clair was chairman, to make the book ready for publication.

Although the whole magnum opus could have been published as a single book, we decided to publish it as two separate volumes. It had always been William St Clair's plan to publish the contents of *The Classical Parthenon* on their own, in what he called a customised edition. The majority of readers of this latter volume, he thought would be classical scholars who might be less interested in the modern Parthenon during the Romantic era, the Greek Revolution, and up to the present day. Fortunately, in contrast to *Who Saved the Parthenon?*, the main chapters one to five of this volume were in a polished state and required no significant revisions. As the author intended, 'Heritage', the final chapter of *Who Saved the Parthenon?*, also concludes the present book. We have made only minor modifications for editorial purposes to the text of this chapter compared to that used in *Who Saved the Parthenon*.

Every effort has been made to find any information that was missing from the references and captions, but inevitably, without the author to lay his hand on the required volume or to interpret a cryptic note, the occasional gap may remain.

We would like to thank Paul Cartledge and Roderick Beaton for their input and invaluable guidance. We would also like to thank Sam Noble, who assisted with the first proofs of this book, and Christina

Sarigiannidou, who cast her expert eye over the Greek text in both this volume and its companion.

We hope that our efforts as editors have helped to make this second of two books about the Parthenon a superb literary legacy from an outstanding scholar with a lifelong interest in the Parthenon and all its meanings.

Lucy Barnes and David St Clair, June 2022.

Preface

Rather than repeating—all—the excellent and apposite remarks and items of information of Professor Beaton in his Preface to the companion volume *Who Saved the Parthenon?*, I shall begin by repeating just one of them: 'remarkable richness'.[1] Readers who wish to know more of the late William St Clair's (1937–2021) life trajectory and academic career, especially since 1967 (*Lord Elgin and the Marbles*), are referred at once to that lapidary Foreword, and to Beaton's *Memoir* of St Clair published in *Proceedings of the British Academy*.[2] But those who wish to sample and savour St Clair's *Classical Parthenon* chapters on their own terms of 'milky fertility' (*lactea ubertas*), the memorable phrase once used by an ancient critic of Livy's Roman history, should simply read on here!

The Parthenon, the original building constructed on the Acropolis of Athens between 447 and 432 BCE, is, to essay a for once legitimate use of the metaphor, an icon. An image, a metaphoric as well as a literal construct, it has stood the test of two and a half millennia to continue to cast a long cultural shadow, however much its physical fabric may have been depleted by the depredations of both non-human and inhuman agencies. It is also in many respects and for many reasons something of a puzzle. Or, as St Clair nicely puts it, 'a case where questions about the representative quality of the evidence are central to any attempt to understand why and how it came into existence'. He rightly makes no bones about it: the Parthenon's history is affected and afflicted by 'huge evidential gaps'.

It is a puzzle, for example, that the Parthenon—not the temple's ancient name, but just that of the main room that housed the cult-statue

---

1   Beaton, Roderick, 'Preface', in St Clair, *WStP*, https://doi.org/10.11647/OBP.0136.32
2   *Biographical Memoirs of Fellows of the British Academy*, 20, 24 May 2022, 179–199, https://www.thebritishacademy.ac.uk/documents/4099/20-Memoirs-09-StClair.pdf

          https://doi.org/10.11647/OBP.0279.07

of Athena the Virgin (Parthenos) by Pheidias—had no unique dedicated altar. Another puzzle is that the building is often thought of today as peculiarly democratic, and that the great democratic statesman Pericles probably had a major hand in bringing the project to fruition, although contemporaries seem to have seen it as not so much democratic as imperialist, and not so much to Pericles's credit as a bid for unseemly personal glory. St Clair well captures these rather jarring peculiarities when he writes that educated Athenians of the mid-fifth century BCE were 'both conscious of their deep past and aware of how little they knew about it'. Implying—if they knew so little, how could we possibly today know more?

To address that uncertainty, St Clair resorts to—or rather boldly embraces—the expedient of a kind of thought experiment. To avoid the sin of 'presentism', he writes the sort of speech that Thucydides—a contemporary Athenian historian—might have put into the mouth of the official Board of Commissioners (for the rebuilding of the post-480 Acropolis) when addressing the democratic Athenian Assembly in a later fifth-century annual report. Why the Acropolis had to be rebuilt, following the Persian sacks of 480 and 479 BCE, and why it was rebuilt when and how it was, is of course a larger story than just that of the Parthenon, though the Parthenon certainly was thought of as central to it despite its not being the principal temple of the Athenian state. That was the Erechtheum, the temple of Athena Polias with Poseidon Erechtheus, rebuilt even later than the Parthenon and not finished until the concluding decade of the fifth century. For that, see Chapter 2, replete with characteristic learning (349 notes!): Prof. Beaton rightly hails St Clair's 'meticulous archival research' and 'formidable intellectual underpinning'.

In Chapter 3 St Clair resumes what he calls 'the normal authorial voice'—stating and assessing what we can recover of how the Parthenon was regarded and used in fifth-century Athens. Which doesn't exactly prepare us for Chapter 4, in which he offers a new analysis of a very old chestnut indeed: namely, what exactly is represented on and by the 160-metre-long Parthenon frieze with its 378 personages, both (putatively) human and superhuman, and 245 edible animals? Probably the modern scholarly consensus view is that it represents some version of a Panathenaic procession, that is, the procession (*pompê*) annually marking the supposed birthday of Athens's patron goddess Athena Polias. But St Clair will have none of that: to him, the frieze scenario is nothing to do with the Panathenaea. And to be fair, he does have an initial point: Athena Parthenos and Athena Polias were two quite separate and distinct divinities, so why should the latter be so celebrated on a temple dedicated to the former? But readers will have to make up their own minds—or re-make them up—after a reading of St Clair's typically penetrating arguments.

Chapter 5—and we must remember that St Clair died before he was able to apply the finishing touch to this or the other chapters—offers a 'rhetorical discourse' or 'exercise' that revisits some of the earlier material, while Chapter 6 discourses briefly on still often vexed questions of the Parthenon's legacy and heritage.

Finally, it would be wrong not to point out in conclusion that William St Clair was a stalwart supporter of the cause of the return of the Parthenon Marbles, of which most of those now outside Athens are held or imprisoned in the British Museum, London. St Clair was for many years indeed a member of the British Committee for the Reunification of the Parthenon Marbles (BCRPM), for which he acted as a leading academic spokesman. *The Classical Parthenon* thus takes its worthy place in a chain of being inaugurated by his *Lord Elgin and the Marbles* and made unbreakable by *That Greece Might Still be Free* (the title a quotation from Lord Byron, a devoted early opponent of Elgin), first published in 1972 and reissued, with much new visual material, in 2008 by Open Book Publishers—just before the triumphant opening of the new Acropolis Museum with its dedicated upper Parthenon gallery looking out upon what remains, most impressively and suggestively, of the building itself.

The interested reader may wish to consult any or all of the following, which in their different ways complement or otherwise illuminate aspects of the arguments of this book:

Roderick Beaton, 'Memoir of William Linn St Clair', *Biographical Memoirs of Fellows of the British Academy*, 20, 24 May 2022, 179–199, https://www.thebritishacademy.ac.uk/documents/4099/20-Memoirs-09-StClair.pdf

Paul Cartledge et al., 'The Case for The Return', BCRPM website: https://www.parthenonuk.com/the-case-for-the-return

Christopher Hitchens, *The Parthenon Marbles: The Case for Reunification*, new edn (London: Verso, 2008).

Paulina Kravasili, (no title), https://greekcitytimes.com/2020/11/07/greek-sculptures-away-motherland/

Jenifer Neils, *The Parthenon Frieze* (Cambridge: Cambridge University Press, 2011).

William St Clair, *Lord Elgin and the Marbles* (Oxford: Oxford University Press, 1967; 2nd edn 1983; 3rd much enlarged edition, with new subtitle *The Controversial History of the Parthenon Sculptures*, 1998).

William St Clair, *That Greece Might Still be Free* (Cambridge: Open Book Publishers, 2008).

Paul Cartledge
Clare College, Cambridge
May 2022

1. Recovering the Strangeness

This book poses a question: since, in encounters between the present and the past, the present always wins, how might we in the present recover the strangeness of a society that flourished two-and-a-half millennia ago? Can we find ways of throwing off our mind-forged manacles, and instead make an attempt, without preconceptions or agendas, to re-enfranchise those who commissioned, designed, received and used the Parthenon in the classical era by removing the weight of modern practices and traditions? In the chapters that follow, I explore such apparently simple questions as: Why was the classical Parthenon built? What was its purpose or purposes? Why did it take the form that it did? Why, as the eighteenth-century travellers noticed, was it over-engineered?[1] Can we do more to release ourselves from traditions, whether admiring and co-opting ('the highest point of civilization ever reached by humanity'; 'men-like-ourselves'; 'our debt to Greece and Rome') or indignant ('not all dead white men')?[2] Can we set to one side

---

1   The question that bothered the eighteenth-century western architects, such as Cockerell, was discussed in St Clair, *WStP*, Chapter 6, https://doi.org/10.11647/obp.0136.06.

2   An example of 'highest point' was offered by de Moüy, Cte Charles de, Ambassadeur de France à Rome, *Lettres Athéniennes* (Paris: Plon, 1887), ii, and innumerable others, especially in the late nineteenth century. Like others, de Moüy regarded the changing light and colours as intrinsic to his experience of six years sitting at the foot of the Acropolis and to his opinion on the falsity inflicted on the experience when objects were placed in museums. The phrase, 'men like ourselves' had been popularized by J. P. Mahaffy, whose intervention in the debate on removing the Frankish Tower was noted in St Clair, *WStP*, Chapter 21, https://doi.org/10.11647/obp.0136.21, whose numerous popular and scholarly books dominated perceptions of ancient Hellas in the anglophone world for around half a century: 'The Greek classics are writings of men of like culture with ourselves, who argue with the same logic, who reflect with kindred feelings [...] In a word they are thoroughly modern, more modern than the epochs quite proximate to our own'. Mahaffy, Rev. J. P., *Social Life in Greece from Homer to Menander* (London: Macmillan, 1874), unnumbered page at beginning of Chapter 1. Perhaps under the influence of his pupil Oscar

    https://doi.org/10.11647/OBP.0279.01

the influence of modern master narratives, whether they take the form
of the arrival of evidence-based Enlightenment ideas or, more recently,
of post-colonial theories that present local peoples as being deprived of
'indigeneous' ways of interacting with the monuments? Can we clear
our minds of the suggestion that the Parthenon is 'the very symbol of
democracy itself'?[3]

These enquiries grew from the research and writing of a book to
which the present volume is a companion: *Who Saved the Parthenon? A
New History of the Acropolis Before, During and After the Greek Revolution*
(Cambridge: Open Book Publishers, 2022). That volume considered
the meanings conferred on the Parthenon by opinion-formers in
modern centuries, beginning at the moment when the bringing to
bear of a knowledge of the ancient classical texts began.[4] Only in the
late seventeenth century, with at most a handful of exceptions, do we
see attempts to understand the building within its ancient contexts.
We see too that for centuries later, both locally and among foreigners,
the older ways of seeing, mainly hostility and indifference, were not
displaced, but overlaid, with older traditions remaining active even
amongst some of the most highly privileged and well-educated men
and women of the nineteenth century.[5] We can appreciate more fully the

---

Wilde, Mahaffy confronted many of the differences, including what he called 'that
strange and to us revolting perversion' pederasty, as well as homoerotic practices,
enslavement and routine killing of prisoners. In later editions, perhaps responding
to public opinion or pressure from publishers, he rowed back on these passages
while maintaining his 'men like ourselves' claim, in effect crossing the line between
applying his knowledge as a scholar and historian, and telling a bland story, which,
by selective omission and reassurance, allowed him to continue his career as public
intellectual, offering, for example, many comments on Irish politics. Wilde found an
opportunity to retaliate at what he regarded as a betrayal when, in reviewing one
of Mahaffy's later works in the *Pall Mall Gazette* of 9 November 1887, he described
his former teacher's vision of ancient Greece as 'Tipperary writ large'. The tradition
of 'our debt to Greece and Rome' is discussed by Hanink, Johanna, *The Classical
Debt: Greek Antiquity in an Era of Austerity* (Cambridge, Massachusetts; London,
Harvard University Press, 2017), https://doi.org/10.4159/9780674978249, and in
Zuckerberg, Donna, *Not All Dead White Men: Classics and Misogyny in the Digital Age*
(Cambridge, MA: Harvard University Press, 2018).

3   Connelly, *Parthenon Enigma*, x.

4   Discussed in St Clair, *WStP*, Chapter 5, https://doi.org/10.11647/obp.0136.05
     and following, including the still unanswered question of why it had not begun
     centuries earlier during the Frankish period when the Acropolis was frequently
     visited by eminent classical scholars from Italy.

5   Discussed in St Clair, *WStP*, Chapter 7, https://doi.org/10.11647/obp.0136.07 and
     Chapter 22, https://doi.org/10.11647/obp.0136.22.

extent to which changes in the meanings attributed to the building were driven by ideas, of which some were recent at the time they were first applied, others very ancient, but all framed within imagined pasts and aspired-to futures. We realise, too, how dependent we are on a number of would-be opinion-formers from elites for recovering even a scanty and patchy understanding of those from non-elite groups who saw the building, with the ever-present risk of assuming that the real reader or viewer can be derived from the implied reader/viewer of the works of opinion-formers. This is the case even for those readers or viewers of modern centuries, let alone those from earlier epochs. The responses of most actual viewers or reader can usually only be found from scattered mentions.[6]

And although, during the Greek Revolution, as an exceptionally well-constructed and over-engineered building, the Parthenon sheltered those besieged in the Acropolis from artillery bombardment, and some of its marble was turned into cannon balls, it was the attributed symbolic, rather than the physical, characteristics that gave the building its power. During the Revolution, the Parthenon and the other ancient monuments had come to be regarded as ambassadors of a fourth party in the conflict, the famous ancient Greeks of the classical period, and it was that symbolic power which, when converted into the real resources of armaments, military volunteers, money, loans, guarantees, and eventually direct foreign military intervention, ultimately brought success to the Greek Revolutionary cause and enabled an agreement to be made that framed the post-Revolutionary settlement.[7]

All three of the active participants in the Revolution mobilized the symbolic power of the building, with threats to destroy it by both the Ottomans and the Greeks, as well as negotiations and bargains to save it from further destruction. And the representatives of at least two of the European 'great powers' offered, in the event that the building was deliberately destroyed, to harvest selected broken pieces and export

---

6   Discussed, for example, in St Clair, *WStP*, Chapter 14, https://doi.org/10.11647/obp.0136.14 that pieces together information about those who were enslaved. Chapter 22, https://doi.org/10.11647/obp.0136.22, which offers responses from a much wider, though still unrepresentative sample, shows what is normally missing.

7   As discussed in St Clair, *WStP*, Chapters 16, https://doi.org/10.11647/obp.0136.16, 17, https://doi.org/10.11647/obp.0136.17, 18, https://doi.org/10.11647/obp.0136.18, and 19, https://doi.org/10.11647/obp.0136.19.

them to their own countries in return for immediate direct benefits.[8] Indeed, it was at that moment in 1826 and 1827 when both sides, the Greek revolutionaries and the Ottoman high command, were themselves confronting a choice between destroying or not destroying the building, in a trade-off between its military and its contested symbolic power, that what remained of the building was put at the greatest risk it had faced since Elgin's day.[9]

And it was the visible presence of the Parthenon and the other monuments of Athens in the landscape at a time when there were few other ancient buildings to be seen in Greece, as well as the many pictures that circulated abroad, that enabled the ancient Hellenes to influence policy-makers and decision-takers during the Revolution. After Independence, they continued to influence the many authors, image makers, street planners and street re-namers, as well as conservationists, restorers, and monument cleansers, who together present the Greek Revolution as a rebirth, regeneration, and resumption of the glories of ancient 'ancestors'. The moderns had appropriated ('colonized') the ancients, but the ancients had also colonized the moderns.

But were those who claimed, during recent centuries, that they had the authority and knowledge, as well as the opportunities, to make the mute stones speak, as aware of the difficulties as our generation has learned to be? With over three hundred years of experience of the new science, including an increasingly reliable understanding of cognition, of speech acts, of visual invitations to perceive the outside world in certain ways, of the techniques of rhetoric, and of many other insights, now available, the chances of being seduced into a simplistic fantasy land, ('the glory that was Greece') are themselves better understood.

The risks of imputing modern ideas to the ancients and of judging them against modern criteria ('presentism') are, of course, now well understood, and a rapidly growing literature unpicks the characteristics,

---

8   The 1801 firman, more properly the vizieral letter that provided Elgin's agents with some cover for their depredations, and the 1806 firman that ordered a cessation, are discussed in Appendix A, *WStP*.

9   As discussed in St Clair, *WStP*, Chapter 12, https://doi.org/10.11647/obp.0136.12, and 13 https://doi.org/10.11647/obp.0136.13. Another incidental effect of the saving of the monument during the Revolution was to destabilize the narrative of 'saving' that had been applied to the damage done to the building by Lord Elgin and his agents a generation before, and that led to the attempts to patch up the narrative as discussed in *WStP*, Chapter 20, https://doi.org/10.11647/obp.0136.20.

'slippery, amorphous and polyvalent', as Robin Osborne has warned.[10] Indeed, the story of the modern quest to understand classical Athens can be told as a series of warnings against accepting the assumptions and practices of previous epochs. I need not emphasize that there is no good reason why a modern investigator should not turn to modern categories as well as to those used in various pasts, provided he or she consciously and explicitly differentiates between them, and accepts that present day categories are likely in their turn to become an episode that will need to be situated within wider contexts, just as the monument cleansing and romanticism of the nineteenth century, that appeared modern, forward-looking, and normal at the time, can now be seen as interludes.

Studying a Strange World

So how can we, in our own time, attempt to be fair to the ancient Athenians who built the Parthenon? Such an extraordinary and influential episode in the world's past as classical Athens, I suggest, deserves to have its history told within its own cultural discourses, practices, and norms as well as within others invented later. Although the task of composing such a history is necessarily confined within what is knowable and thinkable in our age, a sincere attempt to prepare such an account is not only a re-enfranchisement of the past from the condescension of the present, but a contribution to an understanding of what used to be called 'our debt to Greece and Rome'.

The difficulties are numerous and formidable. One difference between ancient Athens and the modern world that is seldom explicitly mentioned in modern writings on the Parthenon, let alone integrated into explanations, is what occurs during the act of cognition itself. Although we can be sure that cognitive processes have remained much the same for most of human existence, they have been overlaid with theories and cultural practices that may reinforce misunderstandings and therefore affect the decisions taken. It follows that, if we wish to understand the aims of those who designed, built, and used the classical Parthenon, we are obliged to take account of the assumptions that were

---

10   Osborne, Robin, 'Classical Presentism' in *Past and Present*, Vol. 234 (1) (2017), 217–226, https://doi.org/10.1093/pastj/gtw055.

present in the minds of both the producers and the consumers of the building, that is, of the shared civic discourse.

How, for example, can we restore the notions of 'extramission' that are seldom mentioned in modern works, but were almost universally accepted, and therefore likely to have been applied, in the ancient?[11] The attention paid to the sightlines of vision of characters pictured on vase painting becomes more understandable if we historicize the ancient viewer as imagining a cognitive transaction in which something, often a story of a mythic event with a moral, is transferred into the body and may lodge there, especially if the experience is regularly repeated in a context of high communal excitement, such as at a festival. And underpinning extramission was the then generally accepted theory of four elements, earth, air, fire, and water, that postulated that the beams of light emitted from the eyes derived from a preponderance of heat in the makeup of the body, a component of the cognitive transaction that could be influenced by education, as is explained in, for example, the works of Theophrastus and Hippocrates.[12] An alternative theory favoured by Epicurus and repeated in ancient writings over a similarly long period, which postulated that objects emitted atomic particles that caused changes in the viewer's own atomic make-up, carries many of the same implications.[13]

---

11   As summarized in St Clair, *WStP*, Chapter 22, https://doi.org/10.11647/obp.0136.22. The notion of the eyes as carriers of light, as postulated by the mainstream theory of extramission, is referred to explicitly in Plat. Tim. 45b; and as φωσφόρους κόρας in Eur. Cycl. 611, a play in which the putting out of the light-bearing cognition of the one-eyed Cyclops by a fire-bearing torch is central to the story, and of which the usual translation, 'shining', that is, a quality conferred by an external observer, loses part of the context that an ancient viewer/listener/reader would recognize. Indeed, the numerous references in ancient Greek literature to actual torches as light-bearing, and their frequent use in ritual and in visual presentations of ritual processions (as on the Parthenon frieze) may have carried an implication that, metaphorically, they were like eyes, rather than that, as may also have been true, extramission was derived from the experience of torches.

12   The modern science-based understanding, with its vocabulary of 'saccades' and 'salience' was discussed in St Clair, *WStP*, Chapter 1, https://doi.org/10.11647/obp.0136.01.

13   Smith, Martin Ferguson, 'New Fragments of Diogenes of Oenoanda' in *American Journal of Archaeology*, Vol. 75 (4) (Oct. 1971), 360, where he quotes 'an exposition of the Epicurean theory that visions, thoughts, and dreams are caused by effluences from objects [...] fine atomic films, similar in shape to the objects from which they emanate, which are emitted in consequence of the vibration of each object's component atoms.' I am grateful to Voula Tsouna at whose seminar 'The Method of

And we have examples of how these ancient theories, in whose validity many of the ancients were heavily invested, led to consequences not only for abstract philosophical debate but for the lives of real people. For it was misunderstandings about cognition that led not only to the destruction and mutilation of images, including many of those presented on the Parthenon, but to the targeted oppression of those whom Paul of Tarsus and his emerging imagined community condemned, often with demands for severe punishments, for having accepted and acted upon the invitations to respond to texts and images in ways that were already built into their minds.[14]

The strangeness of ancient theories of what occurs in cognition cannot be easily grafted on to current understandings, or treated as a matter of aesthetic response. The Greek word for seeing, 'opsis', for example, seems normally to have connoted more than the physiological act of looking with the eyes. The authority given to the sense of sight compared with the others made it more like 'knowing', a perception that gave rise to an extensive ancient literature on the extent to which things seen, 'appearances', could be trusted to be truthful. The primacy given to sight can also help to explain the frequent resort to the rhetorical device of 'enargeia', in which a speaker or writer tries to conjure up images in the mind of the listener or reader by presenting events as occurring in real time before their very eyes, when they are actually reports in words of events that occurred in the past.[15] Even Isocrates who, during the late classical era, composed model rhetorical speeches that were admired and applied, and who argued that listening to stories, whether, in modern terms, 'historical' or 'mythic', was a more reliable way of obtaining truthful knowledge about the past than looking at visual presentations, admitted that, in his privileging the sense of hearing, he was departing from a norm.[16] Until the discoveries made by Isaac Newton about the

---

Multiple Explanations in Epicureanism' at the Institute of Classical Studies London, 9 November 2020, the topic was discussed.

14   As discussed in St Clair, *WStP*, Chapter 22, https://doi.org/10.11647/obp.0136.22. An example of how we can identify the presence of such misunderstandings, and use that knowledge to offset their effects, is in Chapter 4 and its discussion of the Parthenon frieze.

15   An example is given in Chapter 3.

16   Isocrates, *Panathenaicus*, 149 and 150. Isocrates, unlike Thucydides, is willing to give credence to stories told by poets, including those stories explored in the tragic drama, but he appears to invoke them as examples of moral questions being

nature of light were first given wide currency in early eighteenth-century
Europe, all theories of what occurs in cognition were incorrect. How can
we find ways of actively distrusting our modern ways of seeing and the
modern viewing genres that depend on them?[17] Can we historicize the
other human senses, touch, smell, and taste, and the role that, in ancient
times, they were believed to play in the making of meaning?

Another modern category that, partly as a result, may be more of a
hindrance than a help in understanding ancient ways of seeing is the non-
ancient notion of 'art.' Some champions of the object-centred traditions
of western romanticism profess to value the Parthenon and its detached
pieces for their 'aesthetic' qualities and for their 'beauty', often offered as
universal and timeless categories rather than as historically contingent
imputations.[18] To some, operating within the same tradition, it may be
enough that ancient objects have survived through to our times so they
can be contemplated through modern eyes in new contexts. And some
unashamedly accept, if not in these words, that 'art', conceptually and
institutionally separated from 'non-art' as well as from 'propaganda', is a
colonization, and often also a commodification and commercialization,
of the culture of the past and the role that ancient objects, including the
Parthenon, played in the customs and performances of that civilization.
Such ideas continue to encourage the looting of archaeological sites,
feeding the vast illicit international antiquities trade with rich customers
far from Greece stoking the demand, and the destruction of knowledge
about the societies that produced the objects. Many who support such
ideologies might prefer to align themselves with the late Bernard

---

debated, not as factual accounts, which no-one familiar with the huge variety of
plots, as he was, could seriously believe or expect his audience to believe. Isocrates
himself rarely if ever resorted to enargeia.

17   Discussed further in relationship to the stories in stone presented on the Parthenon
in Chapter 3, where, for example, to modern eyes, even those used to notions of
maintaining critical distance, the metopes offer embarrassing scenes of gruesome
interracial violence, but may to ancient eyes have been regarded either as a warning,
or as a beneficial projection of the civic values ('arete') of classical Athens. The
contemporary evidence for how the men and women of the classical era engaged
with the stories in stone presented on temples, although not extensive, is fuller than
is generally realized, and is discussed in Chapter 3.

18   The rhetorics of western romanticism are discussed in St Clair, *WStP*, Chapter 9,
https://doi.org/10.11647/obp.0136.09. A recent example is the justification offered
by the British Museum authorities in 2014 for sending a piece of the west pediment
to Russia, as discussed in the same chapter.

Ashmole, who wrote of 'that unhappy term "work of art" with all its gruesome implications'.[19]

Some modern authors have criticised Plato, Aristotle, and indeed all the philosophers of ancient Hellas whose writings survive, even if only in fragments, for not accepting 'art' as 'an autonomous aesthetic domain'.[20] According to Jeremy Tanner, the ancients 'had not developed (or bothered to appropriate from contemporary artists) a vocabulary for visual analysis of comparable richness to that for literary analysis'.[21] However, it is not obvious why a modern person seeking to understand classical Athens in its own terms should regard western aesthetics, an academic 'discipline' invented in eighteenth-century western Europe, as a relevant conceptual framework for understanding classical Athens.[22]

In 2019, Daniel O'Quinn used the term 'pre-disciplinary' to describe the ways of seeing practised by western visitors to Ottoman lands during the long eighteenth century.[23] But this phrase too, besides its implied suggestion that 'disciplines' are the preferred way of studying a strange world in which such categories were unknown, excludes many forms of experience, and the categories into which these experiences were organised, that were actually used by classical Athenians. Their practice of including the natural environment, landscape, seascape, skyscape, and non-human living creatures and plants, within their cognitive frame, for example, was far closer to their actual ancient experiences, cognitive practices, and explanations than the modern practice of

---

19 Ashmole, Bernard, *Architect and Sculptor in Classical Greece* (New York: NYU Press, 1972), 26. Ashmole, who was my teacher, was scarred by his experience of seeing the damage that had been caused to the historic surfaces of most of the sculptural pieces of the Parthenon held in trust in the British Museum, by the capitulation of the 1930s trustees to Duveen's demand that the Parthenon pieces should be scraped to make them appear more white, and by the 1909 decision, discussed in St Clair, *WStP*, Chapter 9, https://doi.org/10.11647/obp.0136.09, to display them as 'works of art'. He also resisted the consumerist practice of using spotlights in museums, wresting ancient objects that were designed to be seen in the open air into the conventions of an oil painting by Caravaggio.

20 Tanner, Jeremy, *The Invention of Art History in Ancient Greece: Religion, Society and Artistic Rationalisation* (Cambridge: CUP, 2006), 199.

21 *Ibid.*

22 As discussed in St Clair, *WStP*, Chapter 9, https://doi.org/10.11647/obp.0136.09.

23 '[P]re-disciplinary miscellanies.' O'Quinn, Daniel, *Engaging the Ottoman Empire, Vexed Mediations, 1690–1815* (Philadelphia: University of Pennsylvania Press, 2019), 14, https://doi.org/10.9783/9780812295535.

erecting barriers, both physical and conceptual, round the material art object.[24]

Plato was not the only classical-era Athenian who regarded what, in modern terms, is called 'art', as a deception. Nor was Thucydides unique in regarding poets, by which he meant writers of imaginative literature including dramatists and Homer, as well as composers of pictorial images, as obstacles that stand in the way of recovering truthful knowledge about the past. It was part of the explicitly-stated aim of Thucydides that his written work about the Peloponnesian War would be 'useful', a word that, with its cognates and synonyms, he frequently turned to in his aim of helping his own and future generations to distinguish between appearance and truth. And, as it happened, one of the cases where Thucydides foresaw that future generations were at risk of being deceived by visual rhetoric into a false view of the past was when they looked at the buildings of classical Athens, such as the Parthenon, that were still new or under construction in his time, and we can see looking back that events have proved his foresight to be well founded, and that he was destined to be a Cassandra, loved but unheeded.

Recovering Ancient Attitudes to Religion

If the modern notion of 'art' risks encouraging a decontextualizing and limiting attitude to ancient objects, the non-ancient category of 'religion', that was also absent from classical Greece, carries similar risks. The public discourse of classical Athens included a boast that the city paid more honours to more gods than did any other Hellenic city, a factual claim that contemporaries accepted which is amply confirmed by the literary and archaeological record.[25] This 'omnipresence' of the gods,

---

24 Discussed further later in this chapter.

25 I note, as examples, adding to previous lists, Sophocles, *Oedipus at Colonos*, 1006–1007; Isocrates *Panegyricus*, 33; Lycurgus *Against Leocrates* 1.15: 'For you must realize, Athenians, that you would be held to have neglected the virtues which chiefly distinguish you from the rest of mankind, piety towards the gods, reverence for your ancestors and ambition for your country, if this man were to escape punishment at your hands'; the call of the chorus in Aristophanes, *Clouds*, 299; for a complaint that because Athens held more festivals than any other city, they imposed unnecessary delays on day-to-day life, as well as direct costs, as well as many disputes, and without implying that 'the gods' were actually honoured or influenced, we have the

this 'taken-for-grantedness,' to use Robert Parker's phrases, was visible in the town, on the Acropolis summit, and in the caves and sanctuaries on the slopes where an almost continuous cycle of ceremonies, private as well as public, were observed and observable.[26] There could be no prayers without sacrifices, but also no sacrifices without processions.[27]

But the word 'religion' comes loaded with later associations. To be a 'priest' or a 'priestess', for example, was to be the holder of an office, some menial, most time-limited, whose duty it was to perform a range of functions relating to the ceremonial practices and the upkeep of the

---

remarks of the 'Old Oligarch.' Ps. Xen. Const. Ath. 3; Aelius Aristides, *Panathenaic* 4.32,39,46; Pausanias 1.17.1; 1.24.3, apparently repeating a claim by the lost author Polemo. Frazer, J. G., trans., *Pausanias's Description of Greece* (London: Macmillan, 1898), i, lxxxvi; Josephus, *Against Apion*, ii, 130. 'Apion, who hath no regard to the misfortunes of the Athenians, or of the Lacedemonians, the latter of whom were styled by all men the most courageous, and the former the most religious of the Grecians.' Hegesias of Magnesia, a lost author, third century BCE, quoted by Strabo, 9,1. 'I am unable to point them all out one by one [the temples and shrines of the Acropolis]; for Attica is the possession of the gods, who seized it as a sanctuary for themselves, and of the ancestral heroes.' We hear the same thought in the often-quoted verse by Pindar in praise of Athens, translated as: 'Oh You, olive shiny and violet-crowned glorious Athens, famous in songs, rampart of Greece, "daimoned" city' which is discussed also in Chapter 2. Noted also by Livy 45.27.11. 'Athenas inde, plenas quidem et ipsas vetustate famae, multa tamen visenda habentis, arcem, portus, muros Piraeum urbi iungentis, navalia, monumenta magnorum imperatorum, simulacra deorum hominumque, omni genere et materiae et artium insignia.' The trope that the people of Athens were more 'religious' than those of other cities, basing the statement on the number of ceremonies and festivals, was adopted by the incoming Christians, perhaps remembering the comment attributed to Paul of Tarsus in the Acts of the Apostles and misunderstood in the subsequent tradition, as discussed in St Clair, *WStP*, Chapter 22, https://doi.org/10.11647/obp.0136.22. Examples in Kaldellis, Anthony, *The Christian Parthenon, Classicism and Pilgrimage in Byzantine Athens* (Cambridge: CUP, 2009), 132. Nearly a thousand years after the ancient rites and festivals of Athens had been banned, a Byzantine writer, who was familiar with the works of some ancient authors now lost, repeated the commonplace that there had been too many festivals devoted to Athena. Noted by Kaldellis, Anthony, *Byzantine Readings of Ancient Historians: Texts in Translation with Introductions and Notes* (London and New York: Routledge, 2015), 83, https://doi.org/10.4324/9781315720067, from [Lehnerdt's Canabutzes] *Ioannis Canabutzae magistri Ad principem Aeni et Samothraces in Dionysium Halicarnassensem commentarium primum edidit atque praefatus est Maximilianus Lehnerdt* (Leipzig 'Lipsiae': Teubner, 1890), 63. The phrase is εἰς τὴν ὑπερβολήν. Many of the classical-era festivals occurred at night.

26 Parker, Robert, *Polytheism and Society at Athens* (Oxford: Oxford University Press, 2005), 1, so/9780199216116.001.0001.

27 'a procession to the sacrificial altar was an essential part of a sacrifice, even a private one', Dunbar, Nan, ed., *Aristophanes, Birds* (Oxford: Clarendon Press, 1995), 502, https://doi.org/10.1093/actrade/9780198150831.book.1.

sacred sites, not a permanent status. Nor was there any equivalent of claims to universalism whereby, in the early centuries after the Christian takeover of the eastern Roman empire, 'priests' were constituted into imperial ecclesiastical career services that attempted to impose uniformity of practice and of outward displays of belief. As with art, so with religion, the terms are so heavily weighed down with later accretions that it is hard to use them without appending an essay of explanation.[28]

Some modern authors, impatient with what they perceive as a tendency to impute too much rationality to ancient Hellenic civilization, which they attribute to the ideas of European Enlightenment, have drawn a picture of the men and women of classical Athens cowering in fear of chthonic forces in 'a spirit-saturated, anxious world, dominated by an egocentric sense of themselves and an overwhelming urgency to keep things right with the gods'.[29] And certainly much of what is recorded as occurring in festivals, with charms, amulets, a desperate search for comfort and hope, and a constant looking out for signs of supernatural interventions, resembles modern Lourdes. In ancient authors we are given word portraits of 'the superstitious man', not all comic exaggerations. And archaeology has brought to light 'curse tablets' that show that the officially recommended gods were not the only ones present in the imagination or in the practice of classical Athenians. We cannot, I suggest, therefore avoid addressing the question whether a belief in 'the gods' was embedded in the minds of the people who took part in the ceremonial displays and performances, or whether it would it be more fair to the real men and women of classical Athens, or at least to the mainly socially and economically privileged men and women of whose lives we have most records, to suggest that to many of them 'the gods' had become a set of customs, practices, visual presentations, and speech acts that, by repetition and performance, helped to meet other

---

28 As discussed by, for example, Connelly, Joan Breton, *Portrait of a Priestess, Women and Ritual in Ancient Greece* (Princeton: Princeton UP, 2007), pp. 17–25.

29 Connelly, Joan Breton, *The Parthenon Enigma, A New Understanding of the World's Most Iconic Building and the People Who Made It* (New York: Alfred A. Knopf, 2014), xxi. The process of reclaiming the ancient Greeks from an assumption that they were always rational can be traced back to the publication of Dodds, E. R., *The Greeks and the Irrational* (Berkeley: University of California Press, 1951).

objectives, such as maintaining social cohesiveness within the polity.[30] A collection of sayings attributed to Demetrius of Phaleron, who ruled Athens from 317 to 307 BCE, and a prolific author of whose writings little survives, notes as advice on rhetoric: 'About gods, say there are gods' and 'whatever good you do, give the gods the credit for it, not yourself'.[31]

Furthermore, in classical Athens, as has seldom been noticed, 'the gods' are absent from many occasions where we might have expected to find them. They are, for example, scarcely mentioned in the famous funeral oration of Pericles as presented by Thucydides.[32] Such references to the gods as occur in funerary orations not only appear perfunctory but are often used as metaphors for the reputation of the dead soldiers. Plutarch, for example, writing much later but quoting from Stesimbrotos of Thasos, a classical-era author, reported of one of Pericles's other funeral orations: 'Again, Stesimbrotos says that, in his funeral oration over those who had fallen in the Samian War, he declared that they had become immortal, like the gods, "The gods themselves," he said, "we cannot see, but from the honours which they receive, and the blessings which they bestow, we conclude that they are immortal." So it was, he said, with those who had given their lives for their country'.[33] The only mention of the gods in the funeral oration of Demosthenes acknowledges their arbitrariness in deciding who should die and who should live. And they are only mentioned in the funeral speech of Hyperides in two brief asides that repeat the advice to continue to honour the old Athenian gods with sacrifices and images. That speech, which follows the standard model, also implies that most of the audience believes that death is non-existence, and that the only 'immortality' is in maintaining memory by displaying and performing it.

In funeral orations, the most formal and solemn of public civic occasions, the citizen soldiers are praised for what they did out of their

---

30 To some, the gods had been invented at some intermediate stage between living like animals ('brutishness') and their own modernity, a mainstream narrative of the Athenian past to be discussed below and referred to in Chapter 2.

31 Fortenbaugh, William W. and Schütrumpf, Eckart, eds, *Demetrius of Phalerum, Text, Translation and Discussion* (Oxford: Routledge, 2018), 163, https://doi.org/10.4324/9781351326926.

32 Thuc. 2.34–46

33 Plut. Per. 8.6.

sense of duty to the imagined community of the city and to the continuity of its officially approved past and aspired-to future. 'Dionysius of Halicarnassus', the pseudonymous author of a brief advice manual on 'how to compose funeral speeches' written some centuries later, besides drawing on the most famous examples and on the Platonic *Menexenus*, lists other speeches, including some from the classical period now lost. In setting out the strict and long-lasting conventions of the genre, he only mentions the gods in one sentence in which he suggests that the speaker can round off his speech by saying that the dead are better off in the presence of the gods.[34] By silently withholding the opportunity to give a share of the credit or the glory to the gods, the words deployed keep the achievement of the dead undiluted.[35]

And there were other occasions when the gods were either absent or given only a passing mention. In the elegies and epitaphs composed by Simonides and others to commemorate those killed in war, including that for the Spartans at Thermopylae that was frequently relayed in the Second World War, the gods are not mentioned. Indeed, in this genre too, the absence of 'the gods' seems to have been a constant feature.[36] In Athenian funerary monuments also, whether public such as war memorials or private such as those erected by families, the gods are noticeably absent both from the iconography and from the accompanying words. Although architecturally the 'little temples' ('naiskoi') of many of the carved memorials follow the conventions of large public sacred buildings such as the Parthenon, we seldom find any mention of the gods. They are not present in the examples selected from databases by Marta González González in a study that attempts to set funerary epigrams in their societal, performative, rhetorical, and not just their modern art-historical contexts.[37] Indeed, those mentions we do find can be regarded

---

34   Race, William H., ed., *Menander Rhetor and Dionysius of Halicarnassus, Ars Rhetorica* (Harvard: Harvard UP Loeb editions, 2019), 417–429.

35   Discussed by Loraux, Nicole, *The Invention of Classical Athens, The Funeral Oration in the Classical City, translated by Alan Sheridan* (Cambridge Mass: Harvard UP, 1986), especially 132.

36   I draw this conclusion from the list given by Kowerski, Lawrence M., *Simonides on the Persian Wars: a study of the elegiac verses of the "new Simonides"* (New York; London: Routledge, 2005), 151–160, https://doi.org/10.4324/9780203958452. The few apparent exceptions relate to the sanctuaries in which memorials are dedicated.

37   González González, Marta, *Funerary Epigrams of Ancient Greece: Reflections on Literature, Society and Religion* (London: Bloomsbury Academic, 2019), http://doi.

as exceptions that prove the rule.[38] It is as if, by the classical period, some matters, such as death, were too important to be left to the conventions of the official theism of the city. Instead of offering comfort, a traditional function of religion in many cultures, the gods were presented in the stories told about them as arbitrary, unfair, unreliable, selfish, scheming, vindictive, morally worse than humans, and, in some cases, making no attempt to disguise their lack of scruple.[39] Nor, in classical Athens, was the absence of the gods a recent phenomenon that some might consider attributing to the influence of the philosophical schools that encouraged their pupils to treat all received and officially authorized ideas with scepticism. Even in the seventh and sixth centuries, of the dozens of inscribed archaic grave monuments erected in Attica, not one in a comprehensive list published in 1961 even mentions the gods.[40] A longer list published in 1962 is also almost completely silent about the gods.[41] Indeed one of the few exceptions, the inscription on the grave memorial to Phrasikeia, a statue in the round ('kore') that has survived in excellent condition seems almost to scold the gods for letting her die unmarried.[42] Although at funerals and on such occasions it is likely that processions, prayers, and sacrifices may have been performed, the gods, by being excluded from the permanent record of writing and reading, are given at best a secondary role.

---

38   For example, on the tomb of a non-Athenian settled in the city ('a metic') given in a Victorian-era verse translation:

> Few griefs and many joys my life has held,
> Out-lengthened to the utmost bounds of eld.
> My name is Symmachus, in Chios born,
> Which rich with grapes the branching vines adorn;
> But when I died, my bones were hidden here.
> In Attic land, to gods and men most dear.

From Gardner, Percy, *Sculptured Tombs of Hellas* (London: Macmillan, 1896), Preface, Gardner's translation.

39   A notable example is Aphrodite in the *Hippolytus* of Euripides.

40   This emerges from the Epigraphical Appendix to Richter, Gisela M. A., *The Archaic Gravestones of Attica ... and an Appendix with Epigraphical Notes by Margherita Guarducci* (London: Phaidon, 1961).

41   Jeffery, L. H., 'The Inscribed Gravestones of Archaic Attica', *The Annual of the British School at Athens*, Vol. 57 (1962), 115–153, https://doi.org/10.1017/S0068245400013666.

42   National Archaeological Museum, Athens 4889. The reconstructed inscription includes the phrase: 'ἀντὶ γάμο παρὰ θεον τοῦτο λαχοσ' ὄνομα›.

When we put the pieces of evidence together, classical Athens emerges as having many of the characteristics of what is now called a post-religious society, that is, one that attaches a value to adhering to the old forms but for the purposes of conserving identity and promoting social cohesion, not from intellectual conviction. By the time of the Panathenaic oration of Aelius Aristides, the most formal of all expressions of the official self-fashioning of the Athenian polis, delivered in 155 CE, the speaker leads with the theory, in modern terms the narrative ('logos') of the city, demoting the gods to second place. And another professional orator, Dio of Prusa, whose professional role and duty was also to uphold the public narratives of cities, felt obliged to tell audiences that they had to really believe in the gods and not just go through the motions.[43]

In Menander's comedy, the *Tyche*, in English 'Chance' or 'Fortune', the character of Tyche is presented as the only explanation for the unfairness of life. And when Tyche appears as the goddess from the machine who tidies everything up at the end of this and other plays, there is no need to dismiss her as a comic subversion.[44] In the world of the tragic drama, which was controlled, financed, and its content patrolled by the institutions of the city, and perhaps also by formal guilds, Tyche could be invoked in the same terms as a god.[45] And she was also to be seen on the stories in stone on the Acropolis. In 1839, among the first finds as the Acropolis was cleared after the Ottoman army left was a statue base dateable to *c.* 360 to 350 BCE that named 'Tyche' alongside Zeus.[46]

Tyche may have been imagined by some as a force that intervenes, a non-Olympian god, a personification of randomness or contingency, a disturbance to a normally ordered universe. But she appears mainly to have been perceived as an alternative to formal theism.[47] In a society

---

43   Dio, 3rd 5.

44   In *Aspis*, fragments 97, 147, in Arnott, W. G., ed., *Menander* (Cambridge, Mass. and London: Harvard University Press, 1979–2000), i, 25, 29.

45   For example, in Sophocles, *Searchers*, fragment 314. Other examples noted by Lefkowitz, Mary R., *Euripides and the Gods* (New York, NY: Oxford University Press, 2016), https://doi.org/10.1093/acprof:oso/9780199752058.001.0001, with plentiful references to predecessors who have explored the uses of the word.

46   Acropolis Museum. Full description at http://www.perseus.tufts.edu/hopper/artif act?name=Athens,+Acropolis+4069&object=sculpture

47   Discussed by Lefkowitz, *Euripides and the Gods*, https://doi.org/10.1093/acprof: oso/9780199752058.0001.0001, with plentiful references to predecessors who have

that, since the time of Homer, had given little weight to ideas of divine providentialism, Tyche offered a way of excusing the moral failings and the indifference of the gods.[48] 'Tyche' also performs a useful role in exonerating 'the gods' and theism generally from having to accept any blame for failing to protect a city, for example when a battle is lost or an earthquake strikes.[49] Tyche enabled 'the gods' to perform their societal role in classical Athens, without any need for them to exist, or even for them to be generally believed or deemed to exist. This understanding of the frailty and contingence of human experience is markedly different from the theistic providentialism, often presented as benevolent, and other forms of determinism that are built into the self-construction of all the imagined communities mentioned in the book so far, as well as into the self-fashioning of the many 'great men', including Stratford Canning and Adolf Hitler, who saw themselves as instruments of destiny. The concept of Tyche is among the components of the public discourse of classical Athens that many in recent times prefer to those still practised in their own societies.[50]

Myths, Origin Stories and the 'Emergence from Brutishness' Narrative

In attempting to recover an understanding of the ancient classical experiences of seeing, sightlines, conventions, and genres, we ought also, I suggest, give weight to what the eighteenth-century philosophers called 'Nature', not as a tiresome and unwanted 'pre-disciplinary' intrusion to be elided in the same way as eighteenth-century artists and engravers excluded the storks from their pictures of the Parthenon. On the contrary, they and other birds, animals, and insects, ought to be re-inserted. In ancient times, for example, an area of the Acropolis slopes was called 'the pelasgikon', a place that, according to a local myth, the Pelasgians, a pre-Hellenic people, had cultivated

---

explored the uses of the word.

48   Tyche as a figure on the official inscriptions that relate to the making of a statue is mentioned in Chapter 2.

49   As, for example, in Dem. 60 19 and in the whole tradition of funeral orations.

50   The contradictions of Christian providentialism and the contortions that its advocates found themselves resorting to were discussed in St Clair, *WStP*, Chapter 22, https://doi.org/10.11647/obp.0136.22.

in pre-historic times.[51] The Pelasgians were credited with having been the first to level the Acropolis summit and surround it with a defensive wall before the arrival of the Hellenes, although that story was to come up against another piece of Athenian myth-making, namely that they were autochthonous.[52] But the area was also called by a verbal slippage the 'pelargikon', 'the place of the storks', the birds being a common sight in and around the Acropolis until the Greek Revolution.[53] An Athenian inscription of the classical period records an official decree that forbids the setting up of altars in the Pelargikon, so called.[54] As a terrace high above ground level where olive trees and other crops could be grown and animals grazed, the Pelargikon/Pelasgikon was part of the Acropolis military defences. It was, as one clever translator has called it, 'a storkade'.[55]

During the recent centuries for which we have records, domestic animals, including dogs, goats, donkeys, mules, horses, and chickens were kept on the summit, all of which helped to fertilize and deepen the soil and to encourage the insects on which wild birds fed. In ancient times too, the Acropolis summit was evidently a green space, almost a garden town. In the *Ion* of Euripides, for example, the rocky slopes

---

51   The location of the Pelasgikon is not known for certain, but it seems to have included the part of the north-west slope near the Clepsydra. Camp, John M., *The Archaeology of Athens* (New Haven: Yale University Press, 2001), 254.

52   The sources are brought together and discussed by Harding, Phillip, editor and translator, *The Story of Athens: The Fragments of the Local Chronicles of Attika* (London: Routledge, 2008), 23–26, https://doi.org/10.4324/9780203448342, and in his Appendix 3, 'Notes on pelasgians', 196–198.

53   The destruction of the storks by the Christians in the Greek Revolution as part of a religious cleansing was discussed in St Clair, *WStP*, Chapter 15, https://doi.org/10.11647/obp.0136.15; and their role in the eighteenth-century Enlightenment search for a philosophy of history in Chapter 8, https://doi.org/10.11647/obp.0136.8.

54   Quoted by Iakovidis, Spyros E., *The Mycenaean Acropolis of Athens* (Athens: Archaeological Society of Athens, 2006, translated from the Greek edition of 1962), 266 from W. Dittenberger SIG 3, 83. It is dated to *c.* 433/2 BCE. The early mythography and historiography of the Pelasgians, including the storks, is discussed by Fowler (2013) 89–96. The ancient testimonia about the Pelasgians and the storks, including the jokes by Aristophanes, inscriptions, and later scholiasts, are usefully collected by Iakovidis 257–272. The verbal slip was already known to Hesychios who noted it in his dictionary of the fifth century CE, quoted by Iakovidis, *Mycenaean Acropolis*, 270. And to Strabo: 'The race of the Pelasgi clearly sojourned here too, and on account of their wanderings were called Pelargi.' Strabo, 9, i, 19. The point was discussed in some of the standard educational books in the eighteenth century, notably Potter, so was known to many visitors from the west.

55   Benjamin Bickley Rogers in the first Loeb edition of Aristophanes.

of the Acropolis by Pan's cave where the character of Kreousa claimed to have been raped by Apollo, are contrasted with the 'green acres' in front of the temples of Athena on the summit.[56] On and around the Acropolis, many species of birds, including storks, owls, pigeons, finches, and sparrows, shared with humans the natural environment for their food and the built environment for their nesting sites. In ancient times, dogs, as agents of both actual and of symbolic pollution, were not normally allowed.[57] However, in the numerous festivals, cows, sheep, and domestic fowls were ritually slaughtered, eaten, and their bones burned and thrown away. Grain, fruit, honey-cake, and other food were ritually scattered, and wined poured. So frequent were the rituals, and so inflexible the conventions of no prayers without sacrifice, no sacrifice without a ceremonial procession to the altar where the creature was to be killed, and no eating or drinking without scattering a share for the gods, that the ancient Acropolis, like Delphi and Delos, had developed its own micro-ecosystem of food chains, the hunted and the hunters, the eaten and the eaters, the natural world interacting with the human, the real with the symbolic.[58] Fresh water, whether it was drunk, poured, accidentally spilled, excreted, or used in washing rituals, benefited the insects, possibly causing buried eggs of the 'autochthonous' cicadas suddenly to hatch.[59] The insects benefitted the birds and other creatures that inhabited a local eco-niche higher up the food chain. And we can take it that similar results were encouraged by other scatterings and spillages, whether of dry foods, wine, oil, or the blood and innards of

---

56 στάδια χλοερὰ πρὸ Παλλάδος ναῶν. Eur. Ion 497. Literally 'stades', a measure of six hundred English feet, from which the modern word 'stadium' derives. The fact that the 'temples' are put in the plural is, in my view, further confirmation that the author is referring to the open ground at the east end of the Acropolis, where the main action of sacrificing took place and from where the scene offered on the east frieze of the Parthenon, to be discussed below, is most visible.

57 Noted by Harding, *Story of Athens*, 172, https://doi.org/10.4324/9780203448342, from Philochorus.

58 'A procession ... to the sacrificial altar was an essential part of a sacrifice, even a private one.' Discussed in Aristophanes, *Birds*, Dunbar edition, 502, https://doi.org/10.1093/actrade/9780198150831.book.1, where examples, mainly from the comic and tragic drama, are cited. Sometimes it appears to have been enough to have a female attendant or a slave to bring the water that was also always needed.

59 The 'golden grasshoppers' [cicadas], and Aristotle's thought that they were among the creatures that may have been spontaneously generated, as well as their symbolic use as markers of autochthony is noted in Chapter 3.

slaughtered animals. All were part of the festival experience.[60] Since, in order to be effective, outward conformity is required at least on formal occasions, we should not expect a single answer to the question of how ancient Athenians understood religion. We do, however, have plentiful evidence that the issue was constantly debated in classical Athens, as well as earlier and later, with some writers insisting that, measured against the justifications offered, the whole nexus of temples, shrines, processions, prayers, sacrifices, and feasts was ineffective and, to some, both absurd and dangerous. Indeed, many writers made little secret of the fact that 'the gods' were a useful fiction, a 'nomisma', something 'deemed' to have value, an institution conventionally established and customarily practised because it serves a useful social purpose, without having either to exist or even to be believed to exist.

In the tragic theatre, a public medium that was financed and its content vetted by the institutions of the classical city, gods appear and speak, and characters cast doubt on the existence of the gods. In a fragment of the *Bellerophon*, a play by Euripides, the character of Bellerophon declares: 'Does anyone say there are truly gods in heaven? There are not, there are not, unless a fool is willing to make use of the old story'.[61] The character of Bellerophon goes on to note the injustice of tyrants who break oaths, sack cities, and get off scot-free, and of small cities that fall victim to the armies of larger cities however much honour they pay to the gods.

The 'autochthony' claim, as was discussed in Chapter 16 of *Who Saved the Parthenon?*, an example of a backward-looking myth of origin or foundation as an event occurring at a specific moment in the past, is an 'aetiology' with many parallels in other ancient Greek cities, and still a staple rhetoric of modern nationalisms that thrive on othering. As an element in the discursive environment, it was given prominence in, for example, the west pediment of the Parthenon and other visual

---

60   Discussed, with evidence from classical-era authors, in Chapter 2.
61   Collard, C., Cropp, M. J. and Lee, K. H., eds, *Euripides, Selected Fragmentary Plays Volume I* (Warminster: Aris and Phillips, 1995), 104. Fragment 286. My translation. The passage is discussed, with useful contextualizing and plausible suggestions, by Whitmarsh, Tim, *Battling the Gods, Atheism in the Ancient World* (London: Faber, 2016), 109–113. The only counter argument available within Athenian theism was that the gods were sometimes slow to act, an idea that had its own difficulties in a region often struck by earthquakes and other geophysical disasters.

objects on the Acropolis, as a characteristic of 'Athena'.[62] We would be anachronistic, however, if we regarded such inventions or elaborations as mere antiquarian lore. They are, I suggest, better understood as a rhetorical reaffirmation of an 'aristocratic' ideology that, in classical Athens, had consequences both in dividing Athenians from non-Athenians and in privileging one group of Athenians over others. The autochthony claim, in literal terms nonsensical as Aristotle and others pointed out, was mocked by Antisthenes, a philosopher and contemporary of Plato, one of those who was disenfranchised by the Periclean translation of the myth into political action.[63] By promoting difference, whether silently or avowedly, it made claims to superiority, and therefore ultimately the legitimacy and necessity of threats, violence, and war, another omnipresent component of the discursive environment of classical Greece.

Then there is the Athenian conception of time. Besides the climate, the landscape, and the built environment, which the Athenians of the classical period and earlier had turned into a theatre of mythic stories about their past, they had also set their city's uniqueness within a chronological narrative that began at a remote time and ran to their present day. Together the 'storyscape' and the 'timescape' as we might call them, provided the co-ordinates for an explanation, within whose conceptual boundaries the Athenians of the classical era looked backward to a time when their world had first come into existence and forward to successive futures that, to an extent, lay within their own power to shape. This world view sometimes included looking upward to the clear sky, whether during the night or in daytime, where some heavenly objects appeared to be fixed and others to move, which ancient Greek writers had also recorded, turned into stories, and included in their explanations as a skyscape.[64] Those phenomena that did not follow obvious patterns, such as strikes of lightning, storms at sea and on land—often damaging and sometimes fatal to human societies and

---

62   The numerous presentations of autochthony in Athenian vase painting of the classical period are collected and discussed by Shapiro, H. Alan, 'Autochthony and the Visual Arts in Fifth-Century Athens', in Boedeker, Deborah Dickmann and Raaflaub, Kurt A., *Democracy, Empire, and the Arts in Fifth-Century Athens* (Cambridge, MA: Harvard University Press, 1998), 127–151.

63   Discussed in Chapter 3.

64   Notably in the competing ideas offered by the characters in the *Symposium* by Plato.

individuals—as well as earthquakes, floods, droughts, plagues, and other disasters that could not be reconciled with notions of benevolent, just, or even interested deities, also attracted a range of stories and explanations, mainly mythical and theistic, that enabled them to be fitted into an overarching, unified, world view. In the opening Preamble to the horrors enacted in *Trojan Women*, Euripides presents a verbatim conversation between Poseidon and Athena. The two principal deities of Athens come across as selfish, scheming, indifferent to human concerns, vengeful, and petty-minded.[65] Not only did *Trojan Women* obtain the approvals and financing needed to be accepted for production, but it won the prize in 415 BCE.

As for the origin of the universe, it was commonly claimed, not only in Athens but elsewhere in Greece, that there had been a time when only gods existed and they had engaged in a long struggle to bring about some order against the forces of chaos, personified as giants. The 'gigantomachy' seems to have become a shorthand for the arrival of a more stable, but always precarious, cosmos, and it was frequently given fixed visual form on Hellenic temples, including the Parthenon, and in the design of fabrics used in ceremonies, such as the peplos (a formal garment worn by both males and females and associated with the mythic age) that featured in the Great Panathenaic, a festival that had been instituted in Athens in the sixth century but that was presented, as with many other institutions, as having existed much earlier.

To explain the earliest stages of human existence, the classical Athenians had access to ancient 'theogonies' mainly in the form of lists of names that gave some shape to the past, of which one composed by Hesiod, which has survived, commanded almost as much respect as the epics of the Homeric cycles, of which the *Iliad* and the *Odyssey* were accorded primacy over others of which we only have fragments. The classical Athenians knew that these texts had been translated from oral live performance to written, and therefore more fixed, forms in their fairly recent past, and to judge from the numerous quotations, in the classical era it was the fixed forms that were performed at festivals and

---

65 Eur. Tro. 1–97. My suggestion that the audience was offered a subversive alterative to the official ideology presented on the west pediment of the Parthenon, just as in the *Ion* they were given an alternative to the central event pictured on the frieze, is discussed in Chapters 3 and 4.

in competitions. As it happens, the fullest, albeit fictional, account of how classical-era viewers engaged dynamically and collectively with the stories presented in fixed form on ancient temples refers to looking at a gigantomachy.[66] The main stages were summarized by the character of Protagoras in Plato's dialogue of that name, which purports to give the actual words of Protagoras of Abdera, who was born in the early fifth century and was therefore of an earlier generation than Plato. According to this version, no mortal creatures had existed until the gods instructed their servants Prometheus and Epimetheus to make humans, as well as animals and birds, by moulding them from earth and fire, regarded as the primary elements along with water and air.

Of the texts from the classical period that have survived through to our own time, the last and longest of the dialogues of Plato, the *Laws*, is set in Crete, a location where some of the struggles from which the gods had emerged victorious had allegedly taken place, in and around the terrifying volcanic Mount Ida. The *Prometheus Bound* by Aeschylus was set on a mountain in Scythia, the remote area north of the Black Sea, where the unrepentant Prometheus is being eternally punished by Zeus, regarded as the 'father', that is, the first god to have existed, for stealing from the domain of the gods a knowledge of fire and of how it could be tamed by humans.

As for the emergence of human beings, a variety of explanations were offered, some of which, such as that of a great flood overwhelming the Aegean basin, may also have been rooted in memories of actual occurrences carried, mainly orally, across generations.[67] According to the character of 'the Athenian', with whom the other characters in the dialogue seldom disagree, and who may record the views of Socrates or Plato himself, a great flood had overwhelmed the world, from which the only survivors were a few herders of goats and sheep living simple lives

---

66   In the *Ion* of Euripides discussed in Chapter 3.

67   As will be noted in Chapter 2, the Athenians did not however disdain taking such precautions as they could, of which the successful earthquake-proofing of the Parthenon columns, itself an example of the progressiveness of the narrative, is discussed. Crete was also the site of stories about an ancient civilization dependent on the sea, a kingdom of Minos that excavations in the late nineteenth century proved to be more than a legend.

on the tops of mountains, who were now cut off from one another. All that they knew of the past before the flood were a few names.[68]

When time reached the more recent past, the story took on a form that was supported by evidence, partly historiographical and anthropological, but also derived from observation of other living things, animals, birds, and insects, and more rarely of the fish and plants with which humans shared the physical environment. What is common to all is that humans moved from a solitary brutish state, as a first step to living together in extended families in an 'oikos', seen as a political as much as an economic institution, before, in some cases such as Athens, coming together as a 'polis' that enabled them to do more as a unit than they could do separately, including, in many cases, the building of defensive walls.

The emergence-from-brutishness narrative, though seldom pieced together or integrated into explanations, is to be found both as a description of what occurred in the past and as a framework within which choices about the future should be made, in some of the most formal occasions on which the official ideology of the state of Athens was performed. An account of the brute-to-oikos stage can be found in the brief Homeric *Hymn to Hephaistos*. To judge from other hymns in the collection, of which the attribution to Homer appears to have been accepted in the classical period, this hymn was probably ceremonially sung at festivals.[69] This brute-to-oikos narrative is employed or alluded to at least three times in the formal works of Isocrates.[70] As he declared on one occasion, he could add further proofs that 'no one would think of disbelieving' based on the creditworthiness of ancient traditions and on actions that were deemed to have occurred.[71] The Funeral Oration of Lysias that, unlike the one put into the mouth of Pericles by Thucydides,

---

68 At the beginning of book 3 of the *Laws*.

69 HH 20 4.

70 *Panegyricus* Isoc 4.28; *Antidosis* Isoc. 15 254; and in *Nicocles or the Cyprians*. Isoc. 3 6, all with the tell-tale θηριωδῶς or its cognates, the mention of which, I suggest, was enough by itself to remind audiences of the narrative and its role in the self-construction of Athens as an imagined community. It is also alluded to in his rhetorical exercise by Isocrates known as the *Busiris*, perhaps playfully. Isoc. 11 25.

71 καὶ τούτοις ἀπιστεῖν μικρῶν ἔτι προστεθέντων οὐδεὶς ἂν ἀξιώσειεν. πρῶτον μὲν γάρ, ἐξ ὧν ἄν τις καταφρονήσειε τῶν λεγομένων ὡς ἀρχαίων ὄντων, ἐκ τῶν αὐτῶν τούτων εἰκότως ἂν καὶ τὰς πράξεις γεγενῆσθαι νομίσειεν. Isoc. 4 30.

may have been delivered, declares: 'For they [our ancestors] deemed that it was the way of wild beasts to be held subject to one another by force, but the duty of men to delimit justice by law, to convince by reason, and to submit to the rule of law and the instruction of reason'.[72] The narrative occurs in the tragic drama, put, for example, into the mouth of the character of Theseus in the *Suppliants* by Euripides, speaking as the spirit of Athens at its best, in a passage that brings together acquired ability to think and to communicate with economic developments in agriculture and trade.[73]

The narrative is mocked in the comic drama. Aristophanes, for example, in reversing the roles of humans and birds in the *Birds*, has one bird sneer at another as 'a most cowardly brute', the joke being that his fellow bird, in flying away from the bird-catchers who frequented the slopes of the Acropolis and choosing to save himself by quitting the field, was not yet advanced enough to be a citizen-soldier of the polis.[74] In the *Cyclops* by Euripides, a burlesque satyr play, the unheroic character of Odysseus, in an ancient equivalent of the pot calling the kettle black, addresses his noisy, cowardly, and untrustworthy followers as 'brutes'.[75] The narrative is also set out, within a strong teleological assumption about fulfilling the purposes of 'nature', in the opening chapters of Aristotle's *Politics*.

The brutishness narrative continued to be deployed long after the classical period, and is found for example in the work of first-century-BCE historian Diodorus Siculus.[76] His description of the difference between the 'mused', who had already developed a civilized life, and the 'unmused' who needed more 'paideia', repeats features found in the authors of the classical era.[77] Later still, more than half a millennium after the building of the Parthenon, it is found in the Forty-Sixth Oration of Aelius Aristides, delivered in 156 CE, in which the earliest humans are presented as living like brutes, from day to

---

72 Lys. 2 19.
73 Eur. Supp. 195–215. The key phrase with the word 'brutish' that, with its cognates, is enough to signal that the development claim is being referred to when used by other authors, is εἰ μὴ γὰρ ἦν τόδ᾽, οὐκ ἂν ἦμεν ἐν φάει. αἰνῶ δ᾽ ὃς ἡμῖν βίοτον ἐκ πεφυρμένου καὶ θηριώδους θεῶν διεσταθμήσατο.
74 Βρε δειλότατο θηρίο! Aristophanes, *Birds*, 85.
75 Eur. Cycl. 650 and Eur. Cycl. 707.
76 For example, τῶν ἀνθρώπων φασὶν ἐν ἀτάκτῳ καὶ θηριώδει βίῳ. Diod. 1.8.
77 Diod. 4.7.

day, in holes and clefts in the ground and in trees.[78] Thucydides, who was distrustful of the truth value of mythic stories and of imaginative literature, offered a version that related the start of material and social improvement that he observed in Attica, and to a lesser extent in other regions, to the political economy of Hellas as a whole. The situation that he observed in his own time, and which he put into the mouth of Pericles in the Funeral Oration, was one where all the good things of the earth flowed into Athens, and where Athens was also able to gather the fruits of its own soil with as much security as other lands, two apparently separate points that are linked in the speech.[79] Thucydides wrote in his summary of the early history of Greece that elsewhere in the Hellenic world, the seas were cleared of pirates by the Corinthians and by the overseas Ionians, making it safe for others as well as for themselves to trade by sea. Thucydides did not need to tell his readership that, apart from live animals, prisoners, and slaves who could be compelled to walk, the landscape of mountains and gulfs made it prohibitively uneconomic to take other goods, including most agricultural products, from one city to another, even with the help of donkeys.[80]

The ability to trade by sea, Thucydides says, enabled Athens to move from a precarious oikos economy of self-sufficiency, household by household, to one that produced tradable crops for the growing of which the soil and climate of Attica was most suited, including olives and olive oil, which could then be exchanged, with the use of sea transport, for different products grown elsewhere. That move away from an inefficient use of the fixed capital, the land, enabled the Athenian economy to generate 'surpluses', a word familiar to modern students of economic development that Thucydides uses twice in his

---

78 I have amended the translation offered by Behr, in Behr, Charles A., ed., *P. Aelius Aristides, The Complete Works* (Leiden: Brill, 1986), ii, 271.

79 Thuc. 2.38. I have translated the word for 'everything' as 'good things' to include ideas and avoid implying that he meant only tradable goods, although they were the most obvious.

80 In St Clair, William, *The Reading Nation in the Romantic Period* (Cambridge: Cambridge University Press, 2004), 217, describing an age still dependent on human, animal, and wind power, I noted that in real resource, as well as in monetised terms, it cost much the same to send a packet of books from Edinburgh to the port of Leith—roughly the distance from Athens to Piraeus—as it did to send it from the quayside in Leith to the quayside in Philadelphia.

explanation.[81] Empirical data from a variety of studies recently collected tend to confirm the account.[82] Among the benefits Thucydides mentions are the reduction in the need for every oikos to employ guards, and for men to be normally armed, while the manufacturing and service industries needed to support them could be dispensed with altogether when replaced by social trust. The resulting net reduction in the human resources employed in exploiting the land, whether free or slave, then became available to be redeployed to other productive purposes. From the fragmentary records of Solon, a historic figure, it appears that the transition was managed, with, for example, restrictions on olive oil exports to preserve or slow the reduction of jobs. The change may have been aided by an increasing use of metal coinage, although Athens did not produce its own coinage in Solon's time, despite having deposits of silver in its territory. Nor is it clear whether Thucydides thought that the move to a polis with walls and political institutions preceded the economic change or was a result. But, in many Hellenic cities, including Athens, these developments ushered in the 'age of the tyrants', it being easier for a would-be usurper to extract resources from an economy when

---

81 Thuc.1.2. περιουσίαν χρημάτων. It is anachronistic to translate the phrase as 'a surplus of money'. The notion of surplus is also used in Thuc. 1.7. And the misunderstanding persists, such as, for example, when Charles Forster Smith, in his 1919 Loeb version of Thucydides (still probably the one most used by students and others dependent on translations) has Thucydides explain why it took ten years for the Greeks to win the war against Troy: 'The cause was not so much lack of men as lack of money' and again in the same passage, 'because of lack of money'; the translator was, in effect, accusing Thucydides of what generations of teachers of that time would have called a 'schoolboy howler'. Anyone with a knowledge of the bronze-age heroic world of Homeric epic, a category that included most of the potential readers at the time when Thucydides wrote, knew that, in the world described in the *Iliad* and the *Odyssey*, the institutions of money as denominated by metal coins, though possibly not by oral contracts, had not yet been invented. Thuc. 1.11. αἴτιον δ' ἦν οὐχ ἡ ὀλιγανθρωπία τοσοῦτον ὅσον ἡ ἀχρηματία. τῆς γὰρ and later in the paragraph ἀλλὰ δι' ἀχρηματίαν. As Thucydides goes on to explain, the Greek army had to devote time that could have been devoted to fighting to foraging for food and even to planting crops.

82 Izdebski, Adam, Słoczynski, Tymon, Bonnier, Anton, Koloch, Grzegorz and Kouli, Katerina, 'Landscape change and trade in ancient Greece: evidence from pollen data' *The Economic Journal*, 130 (November 2020), 2596–2618, https://doi.org/10.1093/ej/ueaa026. 'Both literary sources and inscriptions from the Classical period provide us with examples of grain transfers occurring over significant distances to major urban centres, such as Athens [...] Archaeological evidence also points to trade in food commodities (not just olive oil and wine) at quite long distances in the Classical period [...] presenting a possible case for market integration in a wide geographical context already in the fifth century BCE'. 2611.

they took the form of amphorae of oil, durable and exchangeable as a form of money, than to send his thugs round numerous semi-defended households to seize a goat here, a lump of cheese from somewhere else, and small quantities of grains. So successful was the change that the oil itself was credited by Aristotle, and others, not only with increasing the numbers of men that Athens could field as soldiers or ships of war that could be manned, but with making the men themselves militarily more effective.[83]

The importance of the olive tree to classical Athens was noted by the character of the Chorus, speaking as the voice of the imagined community, in the *Oedipus at Colonos* of Sophocles, which, at first sight, is puzzling: 'It is a tree, self-born, self grown, unaided by men's hands, a tree of terror to our enemies and their spears, a tree that grows best upon this very land. It is the grey-leaved olive tree, a tree that nurtures our youth, a tree that no youth nor aged citizen can damage or destroy because it is cared for and protected by ever-watching eyes of Zeus Morios and Athena of the grey eyes'.[84]

As another example, in their puzzling description of olive trees as a 'terror to our enemies and their spears', the Chorus may be alluding to the increase in useful manpower, such as those who built the ships and manned the fleet, that the shift to tradable crops made possible. And when, writing centuries later but within the same discursive conventions, Aelius Aristides imagines from afar his walks round the Acropolis of Athens, he mentions that 'when I considered that both trade and naval warfare were gifts of Athena', he may be confirming the story offered on the west pediment of the Parthenon that connects the naval success of Athens to the economic changes brought about by

---

83   The presentation of an olive tree on the most prominent part of the west pediment of the Parthenon is discussed in Chapter 3. How the decision to place it there was justified to the democratic assembly is discussed as part of the Thucydidean speech offered as an experiment in Chapter 2.

84   Soph. OC 699. The play is thought to have been first produced between 450 BCE and 430 BCE. 'Zeus Morios' alludes to an altar to 'Zeus of the [sacred olive] groves', a feature of the landscape that the audience of the play would recognize; we can be confident that part of its function when it was established was, by the regular (though not necessarily frequent) ceremonies conducted there, including animal and other sacrifices, to remind viewers of the importance of the groves to the city and the penalties faced by those who damaged or stole them.

the cultivation of olives and tradable olive oil.[85] The Chorus may also be alluding to the opinion of Aristotle that rubbing the body with oil mixed with water 'stops fatigue'.[86] Aristotle presents his comment as an observation for which he had no explanation, and he may have had in mind the exercising of the body in games that were preparations for war, which became a feature of classical Athens and are alluded to in the funeral oration put into the mouth of Pericles by Thucydides. From our own perspective, we can suggest that neither Aristotle nor his contemporaries appreciated the extent to which consuming olives or olive oil, even in small quantities, can improve the general heath of people whose main diet is grain. Although they were evidently not seen as the nutritious foodstuffs that they are, there are enough references to their being consumed in the classical period for them to have improved the diet, the health, and therefore, the effectiveness in war, of those who consumed them in any amount.[87] And it seems likely that, whatever the price that olives and olive oil may have fetched in final markets abroad, in Attica they may have been plentiful, cheap, and perhaps, for many, free for the picking or the gathering.[88] As was noted by Duris of Samos, a fourth-century author who knew Demetrius of Phaleron, but of whose works only a fragments have survived, before Demetrius rose to power and indulged himself with grand banquets, he had lived entirely on 'olives and island cheese'.[89]

None of the ancient authors whose works we know presented the progress-from-brutishness narrative as inevitable or even as systemically self-generating, as some authors of the European Enlightenment had claimed for their own theories. On the contrary, in the ancient Greek versions, all societies, including those such as Athens who thought of themselves as the most advanced along the trajectory, were always at risk of slipping back. As Plato wrote: 'Man is a tame animal, as we put

---

85 'Speeches prescribed by oracle XXXVII Athena.' Aristides, *Complete Works*, Behr edition, ii, 226, to be discussed in Chapter 3.

86 *Problems*, 5.6.

87 The evidence in Plato is collected in Skiadas, P. K., and Lascaratos, J. G. 'Dietetics in ancient Greek philosophy: Plato's concepts of healthy diet' in *European Journal of Clinical Nutrition*, Vol. 55 (2001), 532–537, https://doi.org/10.1038/sj.ejcn.1601179.

88 The evidence for diet, including olives and olive oil to be found in the works of Plato is collected in Skiadas, P. K., and Lascaratos, J. G. 'Dietetics in ancient Greek philosophy: Plato's concepts of healthy diet' in *European Journal of Clinical Nutrition*, Vol. 55 (2001), 532–537, https://doi.org/10.1038/sj.ejcn.1601179, and there are references to human consumption in Theophrastus and other authors.

89 παντοδαπὰς ἐλάας ἔχοντα καὶ τυρὸννησιωτικόν Ath.12.60.

it, and if he receives a good education and has the right disposition, he can be the most god-like and gentle living animal, but if his education in the civic values ['paideia' in 'arete'] is inadequate or misguided, he will become the wildest of all animals'.[90]

Viewing Light and Time

While every generation cannot avoid being influenced by its own time, can we actively hold in check the urge to ask whether the Parthenon 'resonates' with our modern experience? And can we put aside the alleged right of individuals to interpret, invent, and impute meanings to the cultural productions of the past as they choose – what the late Wolfgang Iser, the theorist of response to literary works, sardonically called 'the great adventure of the soul among masterpieces'?[91]

In many respects, our present can rightly claim to be better equipped than the intermediate pasts of the modern centuries for the task of unravelling and trying to understand the intertwined threads that make up ancient cultures. However, there are some respects in which the men and women of classical Athens had at their disposal a range of intellectual means to arrive at a surer understanding of the world in which they found themselves than many modern commentators. One is that, for the classical period and later, almost everyone who was educated at all was educated in rhetoric, meaning the arts of persuasion, which the tradition has tended to associate with the arts of speaking or 'oratory' but was evidently also applied to the arts of picturing with visual images. We have a body of excellent, and largely self-consistent, literature that sets out the do's and the don't's, as well as specialist tricks of the trade, including advice on how to make visual images speak as if they were alive. Those who had been trained in rhetoric were, as a result, able to understand, point out, respond to, and if necessary to discount, rhetorical devices when they heard them. Dio of Prusa, who

---

90   Plato, Laws 765e3–76a4, καὶ ἀγρίων καὶ ἀνθρώπων: ἄνθρωπος δέ, ὥς φαμεν, ἥμερον, ὅμως μὴν παιδείας μὲν ὀρθῆς τυχὸν καὶ φύσεως εὐτυχοῦς, θειότατον ἡμερώτατόν τε ζῷον γίγνεσθαι φιλεῖ, μὴ ἱκανῶς δὲ ἢ μὴ καλῶς τραφὲν ἀγριώτατον, ὁπόσα φύει γῆ. The phrase 'as we put it' shows that the thought was, or was becoming, a commonplace, or piece of useful wisdom, 'chreia', and that it can be regarded as part of the general discursive environment rather than an insight personal to Plato.

91   Iser, Wolfgang, *How to Do Theory* (Oxford: Blackwell, 2006), 3.

was both a theorist and a practitioner, spent much of the introductions to his public speeches claiming not to be using rhetoric, itself a form of rhetoric, and Dio earned the name 'Chrysostomos', the golden-mouthed, or, as a modern person might say, 'silver-tongued', which brings out the ambiguity with which the skill was regarded.

Much can be deduced about the classical world from the geographical environment and the sightlines it permitted. Those who commissioned, designed, and caused the Parthenon to be constructed were, for example, evidently concerned with how it appeared from the long and from the middle distances, including from particular viewing stations, some readily identifiable, as I discussed in the companion volume to this book.[92] However, apart from the full-frontal view from the west where the entrance was and is situated, the Parthenon could not be seen by those going about their daily business in the town. Nor could it be seen even by those who approached the entrance along the 'Sacred Way' along the Areopagus, or by those who approached or left by the peripatos, the road that encircled the Acropolis within the enclosure.

The Parthenon was within the sightlines of those who gathered to take part in the processions that began at a distance from the Acropolis, disappearing below the horizon of their sight as they came nearer. It was still out of sight as they reached the Areopagus, where some processions appear to have halted and where it is possible that at least some of the facilities of the modern frontier zone could be found. But, as now, the Parthenon did not open up to their view until they had passed through the entrance gates of the Acropolis summit, the Propylaia.[93]

The classical Athenians had lived mostly outdoors in a microclimate with highly unusual characteristics, as they themselves knew, a fact that was noted with surprise and delight as something to be experienced by the visitors from the west from the time of the encounter.[94] The light, which had evidently remained remarkably stable over the ancient centuries, was different, not only day by day, week by week, or season by season, but in the course of every day. This ever-changing light, an intrinsic feature of the exceptionalism and the geodeterminism claimed by classical Athens, could still be experienced in the long eighteenth

---

92 St Clair, *WStP*, https://doi.org/10.11647/obp.0136. See particularly Chapters 2 and 4.

93 As will be discussed in Chapter 3.

94 Examples of how the light was understood and included in the self-image of classical Athens are given in Chapters 2 and 3.

century and for many years afterwards.[95] However, for two centuries after the encounter with the classically educated westerners and their books, most images of Athens that were taken abroad were in monochrome, black ink on white paper, a translation of a moving phenomenon onto a fixed flat surface of the lines and dots carved into a metal plate. Even in ancient times, with the exception of designs on fabric, and a few ceramics specially prepared, the Athens that was presented outside Athens was also mainly a duochrome world, known elsewhere, if at all, from the painted images in red and black ceramic that were mostly allusive and allegorical, as befitted the uses they were designed for, such as grave goods containing the ashes of the dead, or as prizes in formal contests such as games and dramatic competitions.

The pre-industrial microclimate of Athens, and the extraordinarily long sightlines it makes possible, can still occasionally be experienced. However after air pollution caused by carbon emissions became a regional, indeed a global, phenomenon, it was only during a window between the late nineteenth century and the first half of the twentieth that there was a conjuncture between the non-polluted climate and the arrival of the technology of printing in colour. Our attempts to imagine of the ancient lightscape and the way that it impinged on real ancient Athenians as they used the Parthenon and other features of the cityscape therefore relies on the few coloured images made during that window.

It was also only with the advent of printing in colour in a few industrially developed countries in the later nineteenth century that sizable numbers of people were able visually to experience something of the phenomenon at a distance. Although many visitors experienced the microclimate, it could usually be described to others only by the use of words, as many tried to do. Many of the books that carried an allusion to the light in their titles either remained unillustrated or used only black and white.[96]

---

95 As discussed in St Clair, *WStP*, Chapter 6, https://doi.org/10.11647/obp.0136.06.

96 For example Ancey, George, *Athènes couronnée de Violettes* (Paris: Charpentier and Pasquelle, 1908) not illustrated; Rodd, Rennell, *The Violet Crown, and Songs of England* (London: D. Scott, 1891) and several subsequent editions; Butler, Howard Crosby, *The Story of Athens, A Record of the Life and Art of the City of the Violet Crown read in its Ruins and in the Lives of Great Athenians* (New York: Century Company, 1902); and Whiting, Lilian, *Athens the Violet-Crowned, Illustrated from Photographs* (Boston: Little Brown, 1913). The description of Athens as 'violet-crowned' long predated Pindar, the word being used in *Homeric Hymn To Aphrodite* 6, by Solon, and twice by Theognis. Noted by Owens, Ron, *Solon of Athens: Poet, Philosopher, Soldier, Statesman* (Brighton: Sussex Academic Press, 2010), 217.

And as the twentieth century advanced, and the air pollution gradually increased, what had once been normal gradually became ever more rare. Paradoxically, the ancient buildings that innumerable viewers of earlier times had described as made of white marble, assuming wrongly that this was their colour in ancient times, are now, as a result of the loss to air pollution of the thin topmost layer ('epidermis') of the stone, whiter than they have ever been. For centuries the buildings had presented themselves in a variety of browns, except where the marble had been chipped or struck by gunfire, where it was bright white.[97] And the colour experienced by the viewer changed with the changing light, morning and evening, sunlight or moonlight, summer or winter. Sometimes when the sun was strong the Parthenon appeared cream-coloured, at other times violet, almost black.[98] It was this effect of the changing light on the marble that the first colour photographers attempted to convey, as shown in the examples that follow. We can also recover something of what had been normal before, including in antiquity, by looking at images made by artists in the window from the 1890s to the 1920s, including the brightness of the light, the purpling mountains, the wild flowers, and the long clear sightlines, as in Figures 1.1, 1.2, and 1.3.

Figure 1.1. 'The Propylaia from within'. Print 'from a water-colour drawing by L. V. Hodgkin'.[99]

---

97   Discussed, with coloured illustrations, in St Clair, *WStP*, Chapter 8, https://doi. org/10.11647/obp.0136.08.

98   I use the language of inherent colour for convenience, although it has long been known that colour is constructed in the human brain, and everyone's experience may be different.

99   Bosanquet, Mrs R. C., *Days in Attica* (London: Methuen, 1914), frontispiece. In the List of Plates, the artist is named as 'Miss Hodgkin'.

Figure 1.2. 'The Solemn Majesty of the Parthenon'. Thought to be from a painting reproduced by the three-colour process.[100]

Figure 1.3. 'The Acropolis at Athens, Early Morning'. Print from a painting by Jules Guérin, 1912.[101]

---

100 Frontispiece to Greer, Carl Richard, *The Glories of Greece* (Philadelphia: Penn. Company, 1936), no date given nor artist named.

101 Hichens, Robert, *The Near East, Dalmatia, Greece, and Constantinople, illustrated By Jules Guérin and with photographs* (London and New York: Hodder and Stoughton,

Others attempted to carry to others something of the enveloping light as in Figure 1.3.

In Figure 1.4, we have an image of how the Parthenon appeared to those approaching in festival procession along the road from Eleusis. They first saw it from a distance as crowning the Acropolis with Hymettus behind, only to disappear from view as they came nearer, and reappear in part when they arrived in front of the entrance on the west side and saw the west pediment.[102]

Figure 1.4. 'Athens from the road to Eleusis'. Reproduction of a painting in watercolour, made by John Fulleylove, 1895, published in book form in 1906.[103]

By the end of the nineteenth century, however, there was already a sense that the era when it was possible to experience the same micro-climate as had existed in classical Athens was coming to an end. Athens was now a city of ever encroaching modernity, with industries that polluted the air. A glimpse of the change can be seen in the small photograph shown as Figure 1.5.

1913), opposite 93. Hichens and Guérin visited Athens in the late summer of 1912, at the time of the Greek declaration of war against the Ottoman Empire, when Hichens was briefly arrested.

102 The ancient encounter with the stories presented in the west pediment, by far the most often-seen part of the building, is discussed in Chapter 3.

103 Fulleylove, John, *Greece Painted by John Fulleylove Described by Right Rev. J. A. McClymont* (London: A. and C. Black, 1906), opposite 174.

Figure 1.5. 'The Street of Tombs'. Photograph, 1890s.[104]

The English novelist George Gissing invented a conversation between two friends that picked up their sense of superiority to the Greeks, appropriated from the Roman satirist Juvenal, concerning the changes to the microclimate and the lightscape. Paradoxically, it was at the very time when the pieces of the Parthenon in the British Museum were being scraped white at the behest of Lord Duveen that the then director Sir Frederick Kenyon, who had evidently not looked at them for some time, was praising one of the books that brought out the 'light and colour and wonderful atmosphere of Athens', and commending how 'the clear atmosphere blended and subdued the colours on the marble which in a picture looks exaggerated yet is after all within the truth'.[105]

It was William Ewart Gladstone, whose periods as British Prime Minister made him one of the most famous men of the nineteenth century, who had first pointed out how variable were the Homeric words for colour. The sky might, he noticed, be described in English translation as 'violet' as could the sea, and the hills as 'purple' and

104 Hall, Mrs. Herman J., *Two Travelers in Europe; A unique story told by one of them, What they saw and how they lived while traveling among the half-civilized People of Morocco, the peasants of Italy and France, as well as the educated classes of Spain, Greece, and other countries* (Springfield: Hampden Publishing Company, 1898), 133. Ellen S. Bosanquet, returning to Athens in 1930 after nearly twenty years, remarked on the many smoking factory chimneys, especially from cement works, that were then to be seen, as Athens rapidly expanded to cope with the influx of refugees whose ancestors had colonized Ionia thousands of years before. Bosanquet, *Story*, 186, 196.

105 Boyajian, Zabelle C., *In Greece with Pen and Palette, Illustrated by the Author and with a Preface by Sir Frederic Kenyon* (London: Dent, 1938). Preface dated 'April 1938'.

the sea as 'wine-coloured'. And what, the question arose, did Homer mean by describing sheep as violet? Were the animals being presented prophetically as carrying wool that would be turned into garments dyed in that colour? Gladstone, who visited Athens in December 1858, had from his knowledge of the Homeric epics already noticed that in these words, as in others, Homer was not concerned with colour as fixed 'descriptions of prismatic colours or their compounds', but with the impact of the light on the human who experienced it.[106] In northern countries, he wrote, colours in the external world, 'nature', mostly changed only slowly. But, in a phrase that showed that he understood that perception is also conditioned by prior consumption of images—in modern terms, by horizons of expectations—he attributed this anachronistic way of seeing to two British national stereotypes of his day, a literalist tendency to force complexity into countable categories, like 'an auditor in the accounts of some delinquent Joint-Stock Company'.[107] He noted that a similar oversimplification was applied to the colours of the Newtonian spectrum. His contemporaries regarded them as qualities fixed, not as events experienced.[108] Gladstone's key observation has since been carried forward, with further evidence, as a persuasive emerging theory, and examples are displayed in colour plates by Adeline Grand-Clément.[109] In the world of Homer, colour was, as Gladstone appreciated, an embodied experience, with no sharp boundary expected or experienced between the mind of human viewer and things viewed. And perception and cognition appear to have been regarded and encouraged in the same way during the

---

106 Gladstone, Right Hon. W. E., *Studies on Homer and the Homeric Age* (Oxford: OUP, 1858), iii, 457–499. An example, from the Platonic dialogue known as the *Menexenus* is picked up in Chapter 2.

107 In modern terms, a joint stock company is normally a public limited company or plc, but some joint stock companies even in Gladstone's time were not publicly quoted on stock exchanges.

108 'Next to the idea of number, there is none perhaps more definite to the modern mind generally, as well as in particular to the English mind, than that of colour. That our own country has some special aptitude in this respect, we may judge from the comparatively advantageous position, which the British painters have always held as colourists among other contemporary schools. Nothing seems more readily understood and retained by very young children among us, than the distinctions between the principal colours.' *Ibid.* iii, 446.

109 Grand-Clément, *La fabrique des couleurs*. At the time of writing, most museums that contain Greek antiquities, including the British Museum, employ fixed spotlights, sometimes tinted, that make it even harder to imagine the ancient experience.

classical period too. This is to be found, for example, in the images of seeing to be found on vase paintings, which cannot easily be made to fit into the categories of modern representational or allegorical art where a live viewer is assumed to encounter an inert—objectified—object.[110] The museum practice of using fixed, sometimes tinted, spotlights is therefore not only a relic of western romanticism and a usurpation of the visitor's choice, but an obstacle to attempts to look at, or even imagine, objects such as the 'marbles' from the Parthenon in the ways that the classical Athenians and their successors encountered them for many centuries.[111]

Besides the ancient lightscape, much of the visible timescape encountered in classical Athens had also survived into modern times. The Athenians of the classical era, we can be certain, did not regard themselves as living 'in the youth of the world', a thought common in the modern centuries.[112] Nor did they regard themselves as living in the 'morning lands of history'.[113] At the time that the classical Propylaia, with its astonishing lintel, was built in the classical age, there had been

---

110 Discussed by Tanner, Jeremy, 'Sight and painting: optical theory and pictorial poetics in Classical Greek art', in Squire, Michael, ed., *Sight and the Ancient Senses* (London: Routledge, 2016), 107–114, https://doi.org/10.4324/9781315719238, and other essays in that volume.

111 To be discussed further in Chapter 3.

112 'Tout s'est réuni pour fêter ici le jeunesse du monde. Qu'ils étaient heureux ces Athéniens qui avaient passer l'idéal dans la pratique de la vie, puisque nous, barbares qui ne contemplons que des ruines, nous palpitons encore au seul souffle du passé.' Beulé, E., *Journal de mes Fouilles* (Paris: Claye, 1872), 14. Extracted from *Gazette des Beaux Arts*, 1872. Beulé was especially struck by the clear air and changing colours of the landscape that, at the time he wrote (1852), could not yet be economically reproduced in a book, as discussed in this chapter. As another example, which rode on the stadial theory of the philosophers of history: 'By no hypothesis within my power of framing, can I account for that extraordinary excellence, in art and literature, which the Greeks so unquestionably attained, except by embracing the notion that the world has its stages of age like man; and supposing that the antients lived in the youth of the world, when all things were more fresh and beautiful than in the state in which we see them.' Galt, John, *Letters from the Levant* (London: Cadell and Davies, 1813), 131.

113 The 'Morning Lands of History', the title of the book by Hugh Price Hughes, was discussed in St Clair, *WStP*, Chapter 22, https://doi.org/10.11647/obp.0136.22. Other examples: 'Those who approach [Attica] … may still know the joy of being young in the world's youth.' Bosanquet, *Days in Attica*, 66. 'In the days of the world's youth', Hanson, Charles Henry, *The Land of Greece Described and Illustrated with 44 Illustrations and three maps* (London: Nelson, 1886), 14. In the writings of visitors from western countries there are innumerable references to cradles, birthplaces, and dawns.

a gateway on the site for around eight hundred years.[114] In a long era of almost constant war and internal dissension, they are unlikely to have thought that they had achieved a perfect balance between the body and the soul, the useful and the beautiful, the citizen and the state, and liberty with patriotism, as the archaeologist Ernest Beulé wrote in 1869.[115] Nor could they have thought of themselves as living in the 'dawn of every thing which adorned and ennobled Greece', as the Select Committee that recommended the purchase of Lord Elgin's collection of antiquities had declared.[116]

On the contrary, to judge from the writings of the classical era that have come down to us, they were well aware that they were inhabiting a time that was the outcome of a deep past of which they knew little. Within a day's march from Athens were the deserted acropolises of Mycenae and Tiryns, which had been built of large irregular blocks of masonry with astonishing skill in pre-historic times by people about whom they knew little. Remnants of the 'Cyclopean' structures, as the classical Greeks named them, after the Cyclops, the one-eyed, gentle, vegetarian though not lacto-vegetarian, giant in the *Odyssey*, were to be found over much of the world that they knew as far as Italy. Huge, well-built monuments, some ruinous, but others with their walls still standing, not only reminded the ancient Athenians of a civilization of which they knew little, but scolded them. How could mere Athenian mortals living in the modernity of the fifth and fourth centuries BCE hope to match the achievements of the predecessors who had performed such feats of building? And why had the men who had built these huge structures disappeared, leaving only the stones and stories of uncertain historicity? The Athenians of the classical era seem also to have had an explicit understanding of the loss even of remembrance, disasters

---

114 Dinsmoor, William B. and Dinsmoor, William B. Jr, *The Propylaia to the Athenian Akropolis* (Princeton: American School of Classical Studies at Athens, 1980 and 2004), i, 4.

115 Beulé, E., Membre de l'Institut, Secrétaire Perpétuel de l'Academie des Beaux Arts, *Phidias, Drame Antique* (Paris: Didier, second edition, 1869), ii. The Preface is not in the first publication in the *Revue des Deux Mondes*, 2e période, tome 32, 1861, 292–331, nor in the first edition in book form. Beulé's excavations on the Acropolis were described in St Clair, *WStP*, Chapters 15, https://doi.org/10.11647/obp.0136.15, and 21, https://doi.org/10.11647/obp.0136.21.

116 *Select Committee Report*, 8, as discussed in St Clair, *WStP*, Chapter 9, https://doi.org/10.11647/obp.0136.09, including the rebuttals made at the time.

that had struck whole peoples, not only as long-run slow trends of depopulation and abandonment, although they saw these too, but as catastrophes that had occurred at sudden moments in deep time.

Images of Cyclopean remains as they still existed in the long eighteenth century largely undisturbed since they had apparently been abandoned in some remote past, are given as Figures 1.6 and 1.7.

Figure 1.6. Cyclopean walls in Greece. Engraving dated 1829.[117]

---

117 Not identified. Noted as 'J. M. Knopp f[ecit]'.

Figure 1.7. 'Portal to one of the treasuries at Mycenae'. Hand-coloured lithograph.[118]

On the scale shown in the caption to the image, the portal was around fifteen English feet long. A glimpse of Edward Dodwell using a rod to measure Cyclopean ruins in Italy is shown in Figure 1.8.

Figure 1.8. Detail from 'Subterraneous gate at Alatrium'. Aquatint from a drawing by Edward Dodwell.[119]

---

118 From Dodwell, Edward, *Views and Descriptions of Cyclopean, or Pelasgic Remains, in Greece and Italy, with Constructions of a Later Period, Intended as a Supplement to his Classical and Topographical Tour through Greece during the Years 1801, 1805 and 1806* (London: Rodwell and Martin, 1834). Since most copies of the book show the views in monochrome, it is possible that the colouring was added later.

119 Dodwell, *Cyclopean Remains*, number 92.

The image incidentally preserves information not only about the skill of the construction but about the measuring rods that were commonly used, with little change until recent times. Although no ancient example has been found, the image enables us to reimagine what was amongst the commonest sights during the building of the classical Parthenon, and was commonly used as a simile not only for exactitude and reliability but for anchoring the imagined to the familiar, and as an image of what was believed and presented as occurring in the act of seeing itself.[120]

In Athens itself, a fragment of a Cyclopean wall remained to be seen despite the classical-era refashioning of the Acropolis, as was discovered in the nineteenth century. An amateur photograph of unknown date, but taken before the Acropolis summit was cleared, is shown as Figure 1.9.

Figure 1.9. Remains of a wall at the entrance to the Acropolis. Amateur photograph, nineteenth or early twentieth century.[121]

This Cyclopean wall is, in modern terms, 'polygonal' and 'hammer-dressed', in construction, although with smaller stones than is normal.[122]

---

120 To be discussed in Chapter 2.
121 Unidentified. Private collection.
122 Discussed, with illustrations, one from 1846, by Shear, Ione Mylonas, 'The western approach to the Athenian akropolis' in *Journal of Hellenic Studies*, Vol. 119 (1999), 86–127, https://doi.org/10.2307/632313.

Whether it was an accidental survival of the Mycenaean-era acropolis from before the Persian destruction of 480, or was purposely preserved as a commemoration or a demonstration of continuity, it anchored the stories to the site, giving credence, at least in the moment of encounter when the imagination was already engaged, to this claim: that the characters who populated the stories displayed on the buildings and re-performed in newly imagined variants in the tragic drama were not entirely fictional, but had actually walked the land.

Together the landscape, the built cityscape, and the lightscape made a storyscape that the western visitors from the seventeenth century onwards immediately recognised from their knowledge of the ancient authors. They also discovered that it had, for local people, been so completely covered over and repurposed by a millennium and a half of imperial Christianization that it had been almost entirely lost from memory. However, since the storyscape was a human construct it could easily be recovered and substituted, as happened apace locally as well as amongst visitors after the Greek Revolution.[123] The surviving works of ancient authors, especially the writers of dramatic and dialogic texts, are replete with examples of interactions with the storyscape, including descriptions of how it was used on ceremonial occasions, such as festival processions, as a component of attempts to persuade and to internalize. Visual presentations of the Athenian storyscape are rarer, perhaps because, for the local people who already knew and lived among them, there was no need for the stories to be mediated. An example, which, because it contains explanatory words, may have been intended for export to a place geographically distant from Athens, is shown on an unprovenanced item of ceramic ware ('skyphos') as Figure 1.10, flattened in the reproduction so that the whole image is visible to the modern viewer in two dimensions.

In this example, the mute stones are made to speak not only in words set beside the visual image but also by translation into performance, as the stories were listened to, retold, and repeated and the pictures were seen and re-seen as part of an iterative process of making, authenticating, and consolidating a storyscape. By showing mythical figures using measuring rods and lines, the image humanizes them, making it easier

---

123 As discussed in St Clair, *WStP*, Chapter 6, https://doi.org/10.11647/obp.0136.06.

Figure 1.10. Athena apparently directing a giant, Gigas, in the building of the walls of the Acropolis, and another giant, Phlegyas.[124]

for its viewers both to see what were to them familiar objects, and to connect the imagined and invisible world of the gods to the real material world that they experienced.

The educated classes of classical Athens, we can be confident from the remarks made by authors of the time, were both conscious of their deep past and aware of how little they knew about it. Many had some knowledge of what had actually happened ('anteriority'), although only for the short period that can be held in human family memory without becoming unreliable. Most too had a fairly complete, if patchy, reliable knowledge of a longer anteriority that had been gathered by researches that were undertaken, written up, and preserved by those scholars and historians who placed high value on evidence, observation, and critical reading of primary sources, including ancient inscriptions. However, in the classical period of the fifth and fourth centuries, despite much effort, they found that there was little that could be regularized into calendar time before 776 BCE, the date of the first Olympic games. But the Athenians were also aware of more remote anteriorities about which they knew little other than what might be discerned from a corpus of stories that they preserved, critiqued and queried, added to and subtracted from, and that they presented, performed, and re-performed, of which

---

124 From a fifth-century skyphos in the Louvre, Reproduced from Harrison, Jane Ellen, *Primitive Athens as Described by Thucydides* (Cambridge: CUP, 1906), 22–23. Discussed by Cromey, Robert D., 'The Penelope Painter's Akropolis (Louvre G372 and 480/79 BC): History and Image' in *Journal of Hellenic Studies* Vol. 111 (1991), 165–174, https://doi.org/10.2307/631894. Although the landscape offered many stories, presentations of the Acropolis in the visual, mainly ceramic, record is rare, and of the Parthenon even more so. Since the piece is unprovenanced, we know nothing of where, why, or for what purpose it was commissioned.

the story of the birth of Athena was one that they chose to preserve and curate both on the Parthenon, on images inscribed on pottery, in written stories, and perhaps in dramatic performance.

There were overlaps between the categories, especially when attempts were made to reconcile the variations among the stories about deep time and to regularize them into a single narrative within calendar time. Taken together, however, they may still be able to provide us with the conceptual framework that the ancient Athenians themselves, as well as modern evidence-based disciplines, have found most useful in understanding their situation in general and, more particularly, the aims of their own cultural production and consumption, including the Parthenon.

What the eighteenth-century travellers did not recognize, and even today is seldom explicitly noticed, is that alongside the stories of mythic gods and heroes was a modern progressive narrative of how human beings had emerged from brutishness through a series of economic and social step changes to the Athenian city-based democracy in which they lived, as described earlier in this chapter. And that spoke too of a projected future that, from their fifth-century baseline, had the potential to progress even further in specific identified ways.[125]

Looking In / Looking Out: Experiments in Recovering the Strangeness

I leave to last another problem that needs to be addressed face-on if we are to recover the strangeness of the ancient world. How can the modern investigator take proper account of the huge gaps in the evidence as it has come down to us? In the case of the Greek Revolution of 1821–1832, he or she can recover an understanding by joining up the vast quantities of evidence that we now have not only for the events but for the mentalities and discursive practices of the main participants. But in the case of classical Athens, the evidence that we have, although plentiful,

---

125 Discussed further in Chapter 2, with citations to the numerous mentions by classical-era authors, and a consideration of its implications for understanding both the Parthenon and the tragic drama in which its presence can be seen. A useful list of the common fauna and flora of Athens in classical times, and of the noises and the smells in the natural environment, with some quotations from ancient authors, is provided by Connelly, *Parthenon Enigma*, 8.

is systemically unrepresentative in ways that we can recognize, such as the loss of the materiality of all those items kept on perishable materials such as papyrus and parchment, including some recorded as having been held for safe keeping in the Parthenon.[126] Lost too are the many painted images in two dimensions, 'pictures' in the modern sense, some famous in their time, which were commissioned by the Athenian polis and others, which played their parts in constructing the meanings offered to viewers of the classical Parthenon.[127]

And the evidence that we have is also the result of other non-systemic contingencies that have resulted in some written texts having come down to us, but not others. Because money in the form of coins made from metal has survived in large numbers, whereas money in the form of bonds, IOUs, guarantees, and oral agreements has been entirely lost except for occasional references in ancient authors, we have another systemic bias in the evidence, but also an asystemic bias since the survival of coins has depended on innumerable other contingencies, including their having been used in some cases as grave goods and treated as 'works of art' in accordance with western romantic aesthetics.[128] Over a hundred financial documents in the form of inscriptions on marble are now known, including many fragments that relate to cash flows during the construction of the Parthenon and of the other buildings and statues on the Acropolis. Partly as a result of conjectures for how the numerous lost lines and unreadable words might be restored that came to be accepted as authoritative, there has been a tendency to infer more from them than is warranted.[129] They relate mainly to cash flows during the financial years of the physical construction of the Parthenon and of other buildings and cult statues on the Acropolis, prepared for the purpose of audit. The transcription of the texts onto marble is the last step, the

---

126 Discussed by Harris, Diane, *The Treasures of the Parthenon and Erechtheion* (Oxford: OUP, 1995). Some specific examples are noted in footnotes in Chapter 2. Discussed, summarized and added to by Wagner, Claudia. *Dedication Practices on the Athenian Acropolis*. D. Phil thesis, University of Oxford, 1997, https://ora.ox.ac.uk/objects/uuid:6f2e2c02-7bc0-43c0-843c-cc76217c1485.

127 For example, the word description of, and commentary on, a lost picture (ekphrasis) of 'the people of Athens' referred to in Chapter 4.

128 To be discussed further in Chapter 3. Much writing on coins has, as result, concentrated on their symbolic and iconographical functions.

129 Discussed by Foley, Elizabeth, and Stroud, Ronald S., 'A Reappraisal of the Athena Promachos Accounts from the Acropolis (IG I³ 435)', *Hesperia*, Vol. 88 (1) (2019), 87–153, https://doi.org/10.2972/hesperia.88.1.0087.

conclusion of a process that proclaims itself as already settled. Although informative for other reasons, they are of little use for establishing the considerations and justifications offered for the expenditures before choices were arrived at. The ancient Parthenon therefore offers a case where questions about the representative quality of the evidence are central to any attempt to understand why and how it came into existence. Since the work of collecting mentions in the ancient authors began with Meursius in the early seventeenth century, for example, many have been surprised to discover quite how few, how thin, how far between, and how incidental, are the references to the Parthenon, as distinct from those to the Acropolis, where there are many more.[130] And although many tens of thousands of visual images from the era survive on ceramic pottery, none featuring the Parthenon have been found. Among ancient written works, now lost, one on the Parthenon by the architect Karpion, which appears to have been concerned with professional architectural matters, is almost an exception that proves the general rule.[131] Is this paucity an accidental result of the contingencies of survival? Or does it suggest that the modern attention to the 'architecture' and the 'sculpture', and to the Parthenon as a building, has diverted attention both from ancient ways of seeing and from the uses for which it was intended in the life of the city?

Attempts to bring together all the evidence from the ancient world, fragments of artworks, actual later copies, and mentions in the corpus of ancient texts and inscriptions have been denounced as 'utopian', even where they are plentiful and focused, since all are dependent on the 'serendipities of survival'.[132] However it is not obvious that voluntary

---

130 The few references and allusions are noted and commented upon by Kondaratos, Savas, 'The Parthenon as Cultural Ideal', in Tournikiotis, Panayotis, ed., *The Parthenon and its Impact in Modern Times* (Athens: Melissa, 1994), 20–28.

131 Discussed by Beulé, E., *L'Acropole d'Athènes* (Paris: Firmin Didot, 1862), 24. Among the records of what has been lost, Heliodorus wrote fifteen books on the Acropolis; Polemon wrote four books on the votive offerings and a treatise on the pictures of the Propylaia; and there are mentions and occasional quotations from works by Menecles, Callistratus, and Hegesias, Collected by Pausanias, *Description of Greece*, Frazer edition, ii, 396.

132 Stewart, Andrew, 'Pheidias: The Sculptures & Ancient Sources', a review of Davison, in *American Journal of Archaeology*, Vol. 115 (3) (July 2011), https://doi. org/10.3764/ajaonline1153.Stewart. The fact that the problems of presentism and skewed evidence were linked was set out explicitly by the French scholar Toussaint-Bernard Emeric-David, as long ago as 1805. Emeric-David, T. B., *Recherches sur l'art statuaire, considéré chez les anciens et chez les modernes, ou Mémoire sur cette question*

self-isolation within the artificial and limiting conventions of, say, art history as first practised by Vasari in the Italian Renaissance, is to be preferred, especially when it is obliged by the same contingencies to focus on the produced work, at the risk of marginalizing, taking for granted, or assuming that the contribution of the consumer is already known. Nor is it obvious that joining the dots of the miscellaneous pieces of evidence that have come down to us can free us from the haphazardness of the sources themselves.

Without implying that other ways are illegitimate, I therefore propose in this book, as an experiment, to go direct to the primary evidence that has come down to us, working from the geographical landscape, the climate and the light, the natural world, overarching world views such as the brutishness narrative, and the ways in which experience was turned into words and images, with the shared assumptions and the rhetorical conventions within which they were presented. I widen the notion of 'culture' to include sightlines, the encounters, the viewing stations, the occasions of seeing, and the resulting construction of landscape, as well as the surviving materiality, both of the buildings themselves and the information they can still offer.

I will attempt to recover the practices and rhetorics that were shared between the ancient producers and consumers, within whose conventions meanings were offered and interpretations made: in other words, the discursive environment that coexisted with and interacted with the other environments. The experiment enables me to give full weight to what Bernd Steinbock has called 'meaningful' history, preserving a social memory that may be more 'real', and carry greater weight in the making of decisions than the evidence-based history of the Hellenic and modern European tradition that attempts to recover a knowledge of what actually happened.[133] Dense with intertextuality, itself a device that aims to co-opt and flatter by offering familiarity and recognition, the discursive environment allows for exhortations

---

proposée par l'Institut national de France: Quelles ont été les causes de la perfection de la Sculpture antique, et quels seroient les moyens d'y atteindre? (Paris: Nyon, an XIII, 1805), 4.

133 Quoted by Steinbock, Bernd, *Social Memory in Athenian Public Discourse: Uses and Meanings of the Past* (Ann Arbor: University of Michigan Press, 2013), 8, https:// doi.org/10.3998/mpub.1897162. Other terms he notes are 'usable past', 'imagined and remembered history', 'cultural memory', 'believed history', and 'intentional history'.

to a future while apparently discussing the past and the present. The rhetorical conventions, although flexible and open to modification, both preceded the events that caused them and also outlasted them. They were the means by which the long-lasting natural environment was turned into useful long-lasting literary and visual practices. My suggested experiment can therefore also be regarded as an attempt to extend an understanding of cognition beyond the mind/brain, as theorized recently as 'extended cognition', but that can also be understood as my historical observation that many of the ways of presenting acts of seeing and cognition in ancient Athens drew their analogies and their metaphors from the shared experience of the actual environments.

I suggest that our best hope of approaching nearer to the historicity of what occurred in decision-taking is to confront the incompleteness face on; to postpone the dot-joining of pieces of doubtfully representative evidence until we have recovered what I will call the 'discursive environment' as a whole and the interconnections between the components. In effect I propose to change the viewing station of the author, and of his potential readers, from that of an external observer looking in and down from the heights of the present to that of an insider looking out from within the many encircling environments, discursive as well as geographical, of classical Athens itself.

In offering this answer to the historiographical challenge of inadequate and skewed evidence, can we learn from Thucydides and other ancient authors on how they chose to deal with the incompleteness in their time? Can we present the debates about the building of the Parthenon in the long-lived genres that were used at the time but have since fallen into disuse?[134] As an experiment, in addition to the main narrative account, I offer two such alternatives to narrative, firstly a 'Thucydidean speech', such as might have been delivered during the years of consideration of

---

134 In the text of Thucydides there are fifty-two speeches in direct speech, eighty-five in indirect speech, and three in a mixture of the two. Stadter, Philip, ed., *The Speeches in Thucydides: A Collection of Original Studies, with a Bibliography* (Chapel Hill: University of North Carolina Press, 1973), 5. The main Athenian direct speeches have recently been newly translated and commented on by Hanink, Johanna, trans., *Thucydides. How to Think about War: An Ancient Guide to Foreign Policy* (Princeton: Princeton University Press, 2019), https://doi.org/10.2307/j.ctvc77gmj. She adds a warning to those contemporary politicians who draw on the Periclean speeches and appropriate their rhetoric in justification of modern wars to remember 'the ultimate fate of Thucydides' Athens'.

the aims, choice of design, and execution of the Parthenon; and secondly a 'rhetorical exercise' such as might have been composed at one of the philosophical schools in Athens around five hundred years later on the theme of ' historical lessons of the Parthenon'.

As for the Thucydidean speeches, we can be confident that the Athenians of the classical age had a strong sense of the visual cityscape of Athens and of Attica, not only as the cumulative result of innumerable decisions, public and private, but as a visual text in its own right that had, to a large extent, been composed, and was available to be added to and to be subtracted from. Some of the classical or post-classical expedients for anchoring the official memory to the built and natural landscape, such as the mark where Poseidon had allegedly struck the rock with his trident causing salt water to flow, can today scarcely be looked at, or even read about, without the thought that they must been deliberately contrived, and may therefore also have been discounted as inauthentic by those who encountered them in ancient times. However, even when we remember that they were devices put in place by the producers, we may be wise to think instead that the ancient consumer did not regard such contrivances as fakes aimed at deceiving the uncritical but as pictures in three-dimensional space that were brought to life by the imagination of the viewers. Pausanias, for example, appears at least on occasions to have so regarded them, willingly suspending of disbelief. But, if anyone in post-classical Athens ever thought that the stories of deep time, including the dramas, were just inventions, the Cyclopean stones provided incontrovertible evidence, evidenced by, and palpable to, all the senses, that the deep past was not just a useful fiction, and a starting point for locating mythic stories, although it performed these roles too, but that it had actually occurred.

Since the Acropolis was an official site, and everything built or displayed there required the approval of the institutions of the ancient city, we are able to assume intentionality.[135] And although the custom of scolding Pausanias for not thinking like a modern art historian may have come to an end, the baleful influence of western romanticism is still pervasive. It is sometimes suggested, for example, that Pheidias,

---

135 The usefulness of this fact, present without interruption at all periods in the history of the Acropolis from neolithic times to the present day, is discussed in St Clair, *WStP*, Chapter 1, https://doi.org/10.11647/obp.0136.01.

as the general manager of the Parthenon project, a famous and professionally successful man at the time, was given a free hand to do what he wanted. For example, according to Olga Palagia, Pheidias 'had control over everything'.[136] For the classical Acropolis, however, it happens that almost uniquely, we have direct, mainly epigraphic, contemporary evidence for the commissioning of public sacred buildings by the civic authorities of Athens, sometimes by competition; the evaluation of the submitted designs; and the processes of acceptance and building, including some relating to the Athena Nike temple on the Acropolis.[137] The formal contemporary documents are a resource of extraordinary potential explanatory value. But Palagia, influenced by modern romanticism, is forced to assume that the annually appointed supervisory committees of citizens, many of whose names are known from the marble inscriptions set up on the Acropolis, were mere puppets, and she scolds those citizens who prepared the reports on the state of progress, such as the accountants and the auditors, for not naming Pheidias, or 'the true authors'.[138] Palagia also dismisses as unimportant some of the details of the recorded expenditure, for example, on clay and horse-hair. If, however, as seems likely, these were materials used in making models, we may have a glimpse here not only of how the design of parts of the composition of the sculptural components was experimented with, before decisions were taken to move to the expense and near irreversibility of carving the marble, but also how the appointed representatives of the city and others might have been consulted.

Although, from the epigraphic record it seems that the Parthenon was built, with astonishing speed, between 447/6 and 433/2, a fact

---

136 Palagia, Olga, *The Pediments of the Parthenon*, second unrevised edition (Leiden: Brill, 1998), 7.

137 The evidence summarized by Tanner, Jeremy, in 'Social Structure, Cultural Rationalization and Aesthetic Judgment in Classical Greece', in Rutter, N. Keith, and Sparkes, Brian A., eds, *Word and Image In Ancient Greece* (Edinburgh: Edinburgh University Press, 2000), 183–205, fn 5.

138 The accounts for building the Parthenon are summarised, consolidating earlier work, by Pope, Spencer A., 'Financing and Design: The Development of the Parthenon Program and the Parthenon Building Accounts', in Holloway, R. Ross, ed., *Miscellanea Mediterranea* (Providence, R.I.: Center for Old World Archaeology and Art, Brown University, 2000), 61–69. He estimates, at page 62, that the extant fragments constitute less than ten per cent of what once existed, although there is no reason to think the lost parts ever included the information that Palagia thinks they ought to have recorded.

that has encouraged romantic-era notions of bursts of 'creativity', we have few immediately contemporary sources about the commissioning and selection of the designs; the arranging of the financing and the management structures; the gathering of the necessary resources, both human and material, some highly specialized that were only obtainable from outside Athens and Attica; and the processes of obtaining approvals, including decisions on financing, from the civic authorities, although they are plentiful for later centuries.

It was the institutions of the Athenian polis ('the city') that proposed, commissioned, voted the financing arrangements for, and drew up the specifications for the massive buildings. It was the institutions who negotiated and agreed the contracts, supervised the progress, decided whether or not to accept the modules of the work as and when they were completed and invoices presented for payment. And it was officers of the city's institutions who audited the results both against the contractual design obligations and the budget, paying especial attention to the opportunities for theft of precious materials, including gold and ivory, and fraud by over-reporting of expenditures. Furthermore, it was the responsibility of the whole citizen body to scrutinize and, if they agreed, to approve the accounts when they were presented by these formal auditors, and arrange for decisions and accounts to be translated into durable marble in inscriptions that were viewable by citizens and others on the Acropolis, often set up alongside the buildings to which they referred. Although classical Athens was a limited democracy in the sense that political decisions were taken by citizens, it was also a highly regulated society with a large number of citizen office-holders given responsibility for a wide range of functions, from ensuring the security of the water supply to determining the fate of individual orphans. It may be unfair and unhistorical, as well as condescending and at odds with their conception and practice of democracy, to imply that the men of classical Athens who eagerly debated political questions that affected the civic actuality became mere stooges when proposals on the civic imaginary were under discussion.

There is still the problem of the gaps that exist in the available evidence. No example survives from the time of the wooden 'white tablets' in which proposals, meeting notices, drafts, minutes of meetings, and other temporary and intermediate records were written and read before decisions were taken, although there are plentiful references to their existence and to their importance.[139] Nor is it only public documents that we lack. One of the *Characters* of Theophrastus, traditionally translated as 'The Shameless Man', turns up at court 'with a potful of papers in the breast of his cloak and satchels of note-books in his hands'.[140]

Although, besides a body of historical, literary, and philosophical writings that have survived as a result of successive copying from manuscript to manuscript over hundreds of years, we have another corpus of over a hundred financial documents in the form of inscriptions on marble that were produced almost immediately after the events to which they relate, including many fragments concerning cash flows during the construction of the Parthenon and of other buildings and statues on the Acropolis. The fact that they are of contemporaneous manufacture may have tempted some into exaggerating their potential usefulness as evidence compared with other texts, although if they can be situated in their own rhetorical environment, including identifying their implied readerships and intended purposes, they may indeed be useful. Partly because certain conjectures about how the numerous lost lines and unreadable words might be restored have become accepted as authoritative, there has been a tendency to draw more inferences from them that is warranted.[141] Although, in some cases but not in most others, the agencies of the Athenian state ordered that the results of decisions be inscribed, or re-inscribed, on permanent stone, such translations of a text from what was, to them as well as to us, a perishable to an imperishable material, only occurred at the very end of the deliberative and decision-taking processes. The inscriptions normally do not mention the considerations that informed the decisions nor choices not taken. Indeed, as part of their rhetorical function as public documents that

---

139 For example, Rhodes, P. J., *The Greek City States: A Source Book, Second Edition* (Cambridge: CUP, 2007), nos 190, 203, 211, https://doi.org/10.1017/CBO9780511818035. White tablets used as schoolbooks surviving from the third century CE are described in Hock, Ronald F., and O'Neil, Edward N., eds, The *Chreia and Ancient Rhetoric: Classroom Exercises* (Atlanta: Society of Biblical Literature, 2002), 56, 60, 62.

140 Theophrastus, Character 6, as translated by Jebb, except for my change from boxfull to potfull, which reflects the fact that documents in the form of scrolls were stored in jars.

141 Discussed by Foley and Stroud in 'Reappraisal of the Athena Promachos Accounts', 87–153, https://doi.org/10.2972/hesperia.88.1.0087.

record and publicly display what has already been decided and, in some cases, already carried out, inscriptions may imply a greater degree of prior consent than had actually occurred. Indeed, the loss of the contested and perhaps muddled processes of coming to the decisions that they record is likely to have itself been among the rhetorical purposes of the translation to durable stone, including especially to impute a unanimity to the decision and to bring the processes of consideration to a close.

Documents prepared for the purpose of *ex post facto* audit, although full of interest, cannot take us to the processes of making policy ['proairhesis'] that begin with the aims ['tela'], and proceed through rational consideration ['phronesis'] to options, choices, decisions, and actions, as they were described most fully by Aristotle.[142] They are of little help in recovering what Thucydides and others called the 'prophasis', usually translated as the cause, or the true or underlying cause, that retains within its etymology a notion that ancient hearers may have understood as something already spoken of beforehand, an underlying logic, still discoverable by investigation but that also requires the investigator to deal explicitly with the gaps.

There comes a point when so many qualifications have to be added to the modern terms such as 'art' and 'religion', and even 'inscriptions' and 'money' that the categories lose their explanatory usefulness. The risks are multiplied when, in an attempt to move from things to people, these modern categories are spun into other modern terms as 'the cultural life of the ancient city' as if that was easily, or usefully, separable from 'the political' or 'the religious', or even the 'social' or the 'economic'. In considering the society of classical Athens, it may therefore be a mistake to draw too sharp a distinction between the verbal and the visual technologies of inscription. When, for example, in his treatise on the government of a city, Aristotle mentions, almost as an aside, that reading and writing are necessary for conducting the city's business, we can be confident that he does not only mean the skills needed for reading the public marble inscriptions that displayed a record of what had already

---

142 *Eudemian Ethics*, ii, 9–11, in Kenny, Anthony, trans., *Aristotle: Eudemian Ethics, A New Translation* (Oxford: World's Classics, 2011), 30–36, https://doi.org/10.1093/actrade/9780199586431.book.1. I use Kenny's translation for the Greek word 'proairesis'. Although set in the context of a theory of ethics for an individual, since a city was personalized, it is reasonable, in my view, to apply the description to collective decision-taking.

been decided.[143] And when, in the same sentence, Aristotle remarks on the need for citizens to be able to understand visuality ('graphike') so as to be able to judge which works made by the craftsmen are to be preferred, we can be confident that he has in mind participating in the processes of consultation, of approval, and of decision-making on what should be displayed, not the passive 'aesthetic' pleasures that arose from looking at objects already manufactured such as an eighteenth-century collector and/or connoisseur of ancient 'art' might enjoy sitting in his armchair or showing off to his friends.[144] To draw a sharp distinction between the technologies of inscription and the technologies of performance and display, as exemplified by, for example, parades, processions, and ceremonies, may also be anachronistic. The apparently simple question 'why did the Athenians of the classical era decide to build the Parthenon in the form that it took?', on the surface simple, is therefore a case in which questions about the representative quality of the evidence and how it is categorized are inseparable from all attempts to re-enfranchize the classical Athenians from the contingencies of the intermediate centuries.

So how can we best set about recovering not only the immediate considerations that presented themselves to the institutions of the Athenian city in the classical era, but also address the problem of how, in the words of Francis Macdonald Cornford in his discussion of Thucydides, much of a conceptual nature was 'already inwrought into the very structure of the author's mind'.[145] Can we find ways not only of shedding modern assumptions and attributions but systematically recovering what Cornford called, 'the circumambient atmosphere of his place and time', the discursive environment? I have extended from an individual to a constituency, where, as an added advantage, the

---

143 Aristot. Pol. 8.1338a. The other normal benefits he mentions in this passage are, in modern terms, making business contracts, managing a household (oikos) and education. ὥσπερ τὰ γράμματα πρὸς χρηματισμὸν καὶ πρὸς οἰκονομίαν καὶ πρὸς μάθησιν καὶ πρὸς πολιτικὰς πράξεις πολλάς

144 *Ibid.* δοκεῖ δὲ καὶ γραφικὴ χρήσιμος εἶναι πρὸς τὸ κρίνειν τὰ τῶν τεχνιτῶν ἔργα κάλλιον

145 Cornford, Francis Macdonald, Fellow and Lecturer of Trinity College, Cambridge, *Thucydides Mythistoricus* (London: Arnold, 1907), vii. Although I quote Cornford's aims with approval, I do not wish to imply that he entirely succeeded in carrying them out. Indeed, some of his explanatory categories, as a man of his own time, such as 'the Oriental mind', exemplify the problem of presentism.

evidence has turned out to be plentiful. In using the word 'discourse' I aim to bring together the limits within which it was normal to debate public questions, to recover the publicly thinkable—or rather 'publicly sayable'—in approved contexts, not to present an argument as a proposition.[146] Nor do I wish to imply that the design of the Parthenon followed sequentially from the discourse, although that is also likely to have happened, nor that the arguments offered were necessarily internally coherent. I suggest instead that we regard the Parthenon, along with the ritual ceremonial events that occurred in its vicinity, as components of a wider public discourse that mutually interacted with other cultural activities. What we can, I suggest, say with confidence is that there was a high degree of overlap between and among the actual producers and consumers, and that since the classical Parthenon was built, documents or speeches such as the experimental reconstruction offered here were not only prepared and delivered but, in the event, they proved to be persuasive.

Among the resources for building the experiment already alluded to in this chapter are the longevity of the highly unusual microclimate, the geographical sightlines, and the natural environment of weather, flora, and fauna, which immediately struck the classically educated at the time of the encounter in the later seventeenth century, although many of these features have altered since the later nineteenth century.[147] Is it possible, I now ask, to use the longevity of what I will call the 'discursive environment' as another resource that, in the world of ancient Athens persisted for centuries, not unchanged but with remarkable stability, surviving through the ups and downs of mere events, as enduring as the marble, and itself riding on the longevity of the natural environment?

Traditionally, in the western tradition, the main solution to the problem of inadequate and skewed evidence has been the historical novel, using invention to fill the gaps. However, thorough and

---

146 The extent to which written texts, including those of plays, were pre-censored or self-censored in accordance with budgetary allocation or private donations ('liturgies' a form of 'charis') or, as is most probable, by guild-enforced conventions, is not known. Compared with the practice of most states until recent times the limits appear to have been unusually wide. There were, however, general laws and customs, notably those against blasphemy or disrespecting the local gods and their images ('asebeia') that were unpredictably applied, of which the judicial putting to death of Socrates is the best known.

147 As discussed in St Clair, *WStP*, Chapter 6, https://doi.org/10.11647/obp.0136.06.

scrupulous though some historical novelists may have been in their researches, modern fiction, with its traditions of concentrating on plot and individual character, is often open to the suspicion that, as a genre, it is more concerned with creating a literary object for modern readers than with explaining or exploring the strangeness of the past. It is a form of 'reception'.

Are there other, evidence-based ways of approaching the problem? Methods that enable the modern reader or scholar to engage critically with the components of the discourse? And can these components be employed to change the viewing station of the modern investigator from that of a detached, all-seeing, well-libraried, Olympian who looks downward and inward, of which there are many examples, to that of an involved fifth-century Athenian, trying to make sense of the situation in which he or she found himself or herself, with the knowledge and resources available at that time, looking upward and outward?[148]

As an experiment, I offer two candidates. On the arguments (proaerhesis, prophasis, etc), we have an example of a problem that Thucydides solved by turning to the literary device of the Thucydidean speech, seldom now used, although one highly successful later example has been mentioned.[149] The main characteristics were described and justified by Thucydides himself in a general passage that explained his approach, of which the following is an extract:

---

148 Among notable works devoted to recovering the discursive environment, I mention Steinbock, *Social Memory*, https://doi.org/10.3998/mpub.1897162; Swain, Simon, *Hellenism and Empire, Language, Classicism, and Power in the Greek World AD 50–250* (Oxford: Clarendon, 1996); and for political metaphors, Brock, Roger, *Greek political Imagery from Homer to Aristotle* (London; New York: Bloomsbury, 2013), http://doi.org/10.5040/9781472555694.

149 Notably the speech put into the mouths of the Ottoman authorities in Athens in 1821 composed by Andreas Staehelin, quoted and discussed in St Clair, *WStP*, Chapter 10, https://doi.org/10.11647/obp.0136.10, another occasion when, because the author faced the same problem, it was not only necessary but, in my view, it served its purpose well, and its veracity has since been validated by contemporaneous documentary evidence not available until recently. Another example: when it became clear that the tradition that Paul of Tarsus began his speech with an aggressive insult was the result of a concatenation of mistranslations, as noted in St Clair, *WStP*, Chapter 22, https://doi.org/10.11647/obp.0136.22, the Rev. E. F. Burr attempted to repair the damage by including an alternative speech to that reported in the Acts of the Apostles, by inventing the second speech that was trailed by the narrator of the Acts in the phrase 'We will hear thee again of this matter.' Burr, Rev. E. F., *Dio, the Athenian; or, From Olympus to Calvary* (New York: Phillips, 1880), 468.

> With reference to the speeches in this history, some were delivered before
> the war began, others while it was going on; some I heard myself, others I
> got from various quarters; it was in all cases difficult to carry them word
> for word in one's memory, so my habit has been to make the speakers say
> what was in my opinion demanded of them by the various occasions, of
> course adhering as closely as possible to the general sense of what they
> really said.[150]

Closely related to the Thucydidean speech is the Thucydidean letter,
a written report sent by an army commander to be read aloud to the
Assembly by an official clerk, the conventions of which are the same.[151]
Xenophon, who wrote a continuation of the account of the war by
Thucydides, did not compose a fully-formed Thucydidean speech
even on occasions that cried out for such a presentation, but soon
lapsed into chronicling.[152] The *Plataicus*, a speech that shares many of
the characteristics of the genre, is included among the surviving works
of Isocrates.[153] Like the speeches by Thucydides, it has already been
polished, and to an extent made predictable, and although purporting
to be a historiographical contribution to understanding the recent past,
in this case events of the 370s, as a composition it has already taken on
some of the characteristics of a rhetorical exercise, as will be discussed
in the experiment in Chapter 5.

As practised by Thucydides, the Thucydidean speech, as was noticed
by Christopher Pelling in his critique of the form, allowed on occasions

---

150 Thuc. 1.22. There are elements of the conventions of a Thucydidean speech in the
     work of his predecessor Herodotus, notably the speeches attributed to Xerxes and
     members of the Achmaenid leadership as they considered their strategy towards
     Greece, and towards Athens in particular, presented by Herodotus in book 7 of
     his *Histories*. Like those of Thucydides, they are primarily addressed to a later
     readership and include remarks such as the inability of the Hellenes to combine
     that were still being quoted by Ottoman commanders during the Greek Revolution
     and by the authors of guides to Greece intended for British soldiers in 1945. See also
     his account of the debates before the battle of Salamis, in book 8. Nowhere is the
     convention explicitly justified as a historiographical practice. It was also adopted
     by authors influenced by Thucydides, for example, in the speech attributed to the
     Rhodians presented by Polybius, Plb. 21.23.
151 For example the letter sent by Nikias from Sicily reported by Thucydides at Thuc.
     7.10. The reciter is called ὁ γραμματεὺς ὁ τῆς πόλεως, implying that there were
     others.
152 For example on the occasion in 408 when representatives of Greek cities conferred
     with the Great King of Persia, where his readers are only offered a plain chronicle
     of names. Among the few exceptions are Xen. Hell. 1.4.13–17; and Xen. Hell. 1.6.5.
153 Isoc. 14.

for a degree of prescience to be displayed that, even if it was not likely to have been available to the speaker, was useful to the reader.[154] And if, as Pelling noted, the arguments can, on occasion, be exposed as 'contradictory or self-masking', that too is part of a dialogic form that readers at the time were familiar with, and that they might have noticed and perhaps discounted.[155] Thucydides himself evidently had in mind a readership that went beyond his contemporary fellow Athenians, as when, for example, he explains the circumstances of a funeral oration that most such readers could have been expected to be familiar with, and when, on occasion, he recounts the mythic history that was deployed by his speakers. On at least one occasion too, the speakers admit that, under the pressure of events, they stretch the truth in hopes of persuading their opponents.[156] Since it is not normal for a magician to reveal the secrets of his tricks, we may have another example here of how Thucydides was educating his readership not only in the arts of rhetoric, but in how to recognize them, and if necessary, to make the necessary offsets.

The occasion for the experiment that I have chosen relates directly to the question of why the classical Parthenon was built, and why it took the form that it did. Each year Commissioners ('epistatai') were elected by lot by the Assembly ('demos') to supervise the rebuilding of the sacred places destroyed by the Persian army in 480/479 BCE, and were required to report on their progress. The secretaries of the Commission, with their supporting clerical staff, were formally tasked with the duties of being the official remembrancers and keepers of archives. It also appears to have been part of their duty to present the reports of the Commissions they served in oral form, many citizens not being able to receive them in any other way. They were therefore also professional reciters who had no responsibility for the text other than to convert it faithfully from words into oral performance.[157] Since it is recorded that these officials were elected, not chosen by lot, their office

---

154 Pelling, Christopher, *Literary Texts and the Greek Historian* (London: Routledge, 2000), 118.

155 The phrase used by Pelling, 115.

156 Notably in Thuc. 5.90 where the Melians are arguing for their lives, to be discussed further in Chapter 2.

157 Discussed by Rhodes 220, from [Aristotle] Ath. Pol. 54, v. χειροτονεῖ δὲ καὶ ὁ δῆμος γραμματέα, τὸν ἀναγνωσόμενον αὐτῷ καὶ τῇ βουλῇ, καὶ οὗτος οὐδενός ἐστι κύριος ἀλλ᾿ ἢ τοῦ ἀναγνῶναι.

was amongst a handful, another being the superintendent of the water supply, that, in the democracy, were regarded as requiring professional expertise. It was reported by Thucydides that, when Pericles delivered his Funeral Oration, he stood on a raised platform so that as many people as possible could hear, but whether this was a common practice with speeches delivered on other less formal occasions is not recorded.[158] Although the Greek word, 'grammateus' is often translated as 'scribe', for the present purpose I will use the word 'reciter'. It is conceivable that the reciters were drawn from the professional actors in the Athenian drama for which similar qualities of voice were needed.

The speeches, we can be confident, also existed in part at least in written form, probably on papyrus, not necessarily as a continuous text but in some material form from which the professional reciter could enact and enunciate an authoritative text. The thoughts, arguments, and policy recommendations, we can therefore say, travelled from the minds of the authors of the proposals to the materiality of writing, and then, back through the orality of delivery and discussion, to the minds of the decision takers. From them, it was passed by a mixture of orality and writing, as in contracts, to those who executed the work, with the thoughts not taking the form of durable material evidence until it was ordered that decisions and financial accounts should be inscribed on stone for public display in a prominent place.

The orally-delivered report of the Commissioners on the progress of the rebuilding was accompanied at around the same time by a financial statement made by the Council ('boule') also addressed to the Assembly on the budget that they proposed for the forthcoming year, and that followed a similar transmission from oral, through material, back to oral, and in some cases, back again to fixed material. As with the policy decisions, so with the financial options and choices too. Although we can readily accept that ancient Athens depended less on writing than some other societies, and that the arts of memory were taught and successfully practised, it would have been hard, even if there had not been plentiful evidence to the contrary, to believe that complex matters that involved the cooperation of the many dozens of citizens who served on the commissions, as well as the hundreds more who took oral delivery of the reports and who came to collective decisions that were

---

158 Thuc. 2.34.8. Modern visual presentations usually omit this feature.

then passed to thousands of agents to implement, could have occurred without the help of numerous written documents. These would have included successive drafts, and other forms of demonstration such as diagrams ('paradeigmata') that include within themselves notions of showing to others. And there is plentiful scattered evidence that this is indeed how public business was transacted in a culture that was literate to an extent difficult to measure, as well as oral and performative, both in the sense of the viewing of dramatic and sporting performances and in the sense of citizens and others performing in front of one another in festivals and in partly-scripted ceremonies, such as occurred on and around the Acropolis. Some would have taken place in the vicinity of the Parthenon and of the other public sacred buildings, and of the stories that were displayed upon them.

In Chapter 2, I offer my suggestion for what the Commissioners for the rebuilding of the post-480 Acropolis might have said to the Assembly in one of their annual reports prepared during the later fifth century.[159] What I offer is not a 'competition piece', to use the term adopted by Thucydides in defending his own Thucydidean speeches, in a passage in which he dismissed consumerist writing that aimed to please only on the occasion.[160] Like Thucydides, I only present claims that can be 'evidenced' ('tekmaironomenos'), either directly or by reasonable inference.[161]

---

159 According to the author of the Ath. Pol, Fragment 50, writing later, there were 'ten Commissioners for Repairs of Temples, elected by lot, who receive a sum of thirty minas from the Receivers-General, and therewith carry out the most necessary repairs in the temples.' But this may be a reference to commissioners responsible for the upkeep of buildings already completed, not those given the responsibility for preparing proposals for the first rebuilding and for seeing them through.

160 ὠφέλιμα κρίνειν αὐτὰ ἀρκούντως ἕξει. κτῆμά τε ἐς αἰεὶ μᾶλλον ἢ ἀγώνισμα ἐς τὸ παραχρῆμα ἀκούειν ξύγκειται. Thuc 1.22. The part of Thucydides's claim that he wanted his work to be 'a possession for ever' has frequently been interpreted as an assertion that he was writing a work of wisdom that would be perennially true, constructing him as a boastful prophet or romantic self-proclaimed seer. Put in its linguistic and discursive context, however, he was merely, if merely is not too ungenerous a word, distancing himself from those who resorted to the arts of rhetoric to mislead audiences. In describing his history as a 'useful' 'possession for ever', he was making a more limited claim that his work should be treated as a material capital item, like a farm, that would yield benefits over time, not as a delivered speech that is consumed as it occurs. My experiment in composing a rhetorical exercise of the kind from which Thucydides distances himself is in Chapter 5.

161 The crucial role of evidence in this sense is a theme of Euripides's play, the *Ion*, to be discussed in Chapter 3.

For the experiment, Tyche has provided an invaluable resource that enables an integration between the physical and the discursive to be attempted. Not only were the geophysical characteristics of Athens, (mild dry microclimate, rocky soil, shortage of potable water and so on) remarkably stable from antiquity to the long eighteenth century, but the discursive environment, including the storyscapes and metaphors that, to an extent derived from the geophysical, persisted, in essentials unchanged except at the margin, for around five hundred years after the Parthenon was first conceived of and brought into use. I have sometimes referred to later writings that illustrate the durability of the conventions.[162]

The aim of the experiment is not to champion one form of presentation over another, such as elevating the scientific above the mythic, or to revive schools of thought that dismissed myth as an absurd and barbaric frontier between the civilized and the primitive mind.[163] It is an attempt to recover a discursive environment in which myth was frequently deployed alongside other forms of explanation and techniques of persuasion. There have, of course, been others who have suggested that approaches based on western notions of aesthetics or semiotics, which assume that images are ways of encoding reality in accordance with conventions, are inadequate for understanding the world view prevalent in classical Athens. Tonio Hölscher, for example, has argued that such approaches exaggerate the extent to which 'images' can exist outside the social and temporal, and, we may add, the viewing contexts and consumption genres for which they were commissioned and made in classical Athens, rather than displaying a conceptual framework within whose presented rhetorics real human beings were encouraged to live their lives.[164] But I know of no attempt to recover the strangeness of that world view by describing it from within.

In calling the composition 'Thucydidean', I allude to the conventions of the reconstructed speeches as employed by Thucydides and other ancient authors, with no attempt to imitate his individual style, ideology,

---

162 I am grateful to Sarah Moroson for encouraging me to pursue this idea and for her comments on an early draft.

163 Many examples are of such comments are given by Detienne, Marcel, *L'invention de la mythologie* ([Paris]: Gallimard, 1981).

164 Notably, for example, Hölscher, Tonio, *Visual Power in Ancient Greece and Rome: Between Art and Social Reality* (Oakland, California: University of California Press, 2018), 12, https://doi.org/10.1525/california/9780520294936.001.0001.

or assumptions, including his frequent resort to personal motivation as explanation, which are irrelevant to the experiment. Instead the discourse employed words and metaphors derived from making the city straight again or righting a ship that has keeled over. For example, in the peroration to speech put into the mouth of Nikias by Thucydides, where the general urges his soldiers to give up the struggle against Syracuse and concentrate on making the great power straight again, he repeats the commonplace that it is men who make a city great, not walls or warships.[165] The words, which imply that disasters are to be expected, reaffirm that the city, through its men, is always capable of renewing itself through its own efforts, itself a constant of the discursive environment.

In the footnotes I have noted the evidence along with comments, so giving choices to my potential readers on the extent to which they want to follow up particular sentences. The evidence offered has, in many cases, been selected from texts that present themselves as expressions of mainstream opinion, notably the pieces of conventional wisdom known as 'chreia', for example by the choruses in the tragic drama, and others deployed by many authors of the time, sometimes signalled by phrases such as, for example, 'as the saying goes', some of which appear to have been deliberately invented in order to be brought into circulation as co-opting rhetorical devices. The songs of the choruses in surviving plays and fragments of plays often supply commentaries from the point of view of mainstream observers. Speeches attributed to gods and heroes frequently take the form of statements about essential Athenianness. The philosophical dialogues of Plato and others, although they often offer novel, non-mainstream, ideas, present themselves as composed within a range of what was reasonably thinkable that are put forward in the dialogues in order to be queried and their inadequacies exposed. In statements of the mainstream, highly speculative ideas are sometimes introduced within a convention of 'some say ... but I tell you'. The choice and deployment of this evidence is not, therefore, reverse-engineered from a known result, but as an experiment that, I claim, can yield new insights.

---

165 'οἱ Ἀθηναῖοι τὴν μεγάλην δύναμιν τῆς πόλεως καίπερ πεπτωκυῖαν ἐπανορθώσοντες: ἄνδρες γὰρ πόλις, καὶ οὐ τείχη οὐδὲ νῆες ἀνδρῶν κεναί.' Thuc. 7 77.

Other pieces of evidence that are used in the footnotes are taken from other works and fragments including speeches, plays, and dialogues, and the corpus of works written by Plato including those whose authenticity may be in doubt. Although these are much studied as windows into the minds and ideas of Socrates and Plato, they remain, as literary compositions, under the control of the author or compiler and, I suggest, without in any way disparaging their value, always serve the author's rhetorical purposes of hoping to convince. Since these purposes include limiting the boundaries of a debate to what would be regarded as acceptable limits by the audience or readership, they are of great value in attempting to recover the mainstream. At the risk of labouring the obvious, I refer throughout to 'a character in ...', a distinction that the classical Athenians did not themselves always observe, with many common sayings regarded as rhetorically useful attributed to famous men and women, and sentiments put into the mouths of characters in dialogues and dramas, whose purpose was to set out an argument being attributed to the authors of the compositions. Euripides especially, whose compositions contain many pithy sentences (Latin 'sententiae') that were usually answered by another character was often a victim of this unfairness.

In using the word 'discourse' I aim to set out the limits within which it was normal to debate public questions, to recover the thinkable, not to present an argument as a proposition. I therefore note alternative thinkables in the footnotes. Nor do I wish to imply that the design of the Parthenon followed sequentially from the construction of the discourse, although that is also likely to have happened, nor that the arguments offered were necessarily internally coherent. I suggest instead that we regard the Parthenon, along with the ritual ceremonial events that occurred in its vicinity, as components of a wider public discourse that mutually interacted with other components, just as the institutions of politics interacted with those of the drama. What we can say with confidence is that there was a high degree of overlap among the actual producers and consumers, and that since the classical Parthenon was in fact built, documents or speeches such as the reconstruction offered here were not only prepared but, in the event, proved to be persuasive.

The composition offered is a reconstruction of a speech delivered to the Assembly of the People by the Commissioners responsible for the rebuilding programme in the fifth and fourth centuries. Like the many proposed reconstructions of the physical Parthenon, this reconstruction of the discursive environment is assembled from scattered pieces of evidence as an experiment in recovering the mainstream mentalities, including the worldview, within whose assumptions and conventions the proposals to build the Parthenon were developed, discussed, approved, and carried into effect. The evidence turns out to be plentiful and since the discursive environment, like the climatic, was, to a large extent, consistent over centuries, it provides a stronger defence against unintended and unconscious presentisms than traditional approaches that depend upon the modern investigator looking in from the outside. Although the speech offers a sustained and apparently coherent argument, it has been drafted in modular form so that passages can be dropped if they are not regarded as sufficiently well evidenced without causing the rest of the edifice to collapse. It also permits those who may wish to take the experiment further, to add or substitute other modules if they choose.

The construction of the Parthenon as a building was said by Plutarch, writing more than half a millennium later, to have been carried out with remarkable speed between 447 and 432, a remark he is likely to have taken from authoritative authors who wrote earlier.[166] However, the period of time before the actual work could begin that was needed for generating ideas and options, for considering respective merits, for taking decisions, and for arranging for the skills, materials, and other real resources to be found, assembled, contracted for, and put in place at the required times, is likely to have occupied several years before 447. Those with experience of planning and executing large-scale building works have realized that it was only because much preparatory work had been done on the earlier phases of the project that the actual construction work was carried out so speedily. But it is only as a result of the researches carried out on the site during the current conservation and restoration programme that we know the extent to which the classical-era Parthenon used marble that had already been selected and cut in the quarries, transported to Athens, and made ready for the building of the so-called Pre-Parthenon, whose construction was already well advanced at the time of the Persian

---

166 Plut. Per. 13.7.

sack of 479/480; we can therefore appreciate the extent to which the huge building had been planned, designed, approved, and the work started years before, although with later modifications.[167]

From the surviving fragments of various accounts inscribed on marble, it appears that there was normally an annual commission of five 'epistatai' (ἐπίσταται) who supervised the work on a particular building during construction.[168] The commissioners who were responsible for the earlier processes of drawing up the proposals in writing and for securing the financing were known as 'suggrapheis' (συγγραφεῖς), the same word as was used to describe writers now called ‹historians›, including Thucydides, although the main ancient connotation of the word may have been to their other function as record-keepers.[169]

What purports to be a verbatim draft of a resolution that had to be put before the Assembly of the Demos for approval when there was a proposal to erect a statue in honour of an individual is given by Lucian in

---

167 Discussed by Korres, Manolis, 'Topographic Examination of the Acropolis at Athens', *Brewminate*, 1 June 2017, https://brewminate.com/topographic-examination-of-the-acropolis-at-athens/.

168 Burford, Alison, *The Greek Temple Builders at Epidauros, A Social and Economic Study of Building in the Asklepian Sanctuary, During the Fourth and Early Third Centuries B.C.* (Liverpool: Liverpool UP, 1969), 24. There also appear to have been commissioners for a whole site. An example from *c.* 450 from Eleusis is noted by Rous, Sarah A., *Reset in Stone: Memory and Reuse in Ancient Athens* (Madison: University of Wisconsin Press, 2019).

169 As discussed by Boersma, John S., *Athenian Building Policy from 561/0 to 405/4 B.C.* (Groningen: Wolters-Noordhoff, 1970), 4. The use of the same word to cover both forward-looking and backward-looking discourses suggests that the opening words of Thucydides's work, Θουκυδίδης Ἀθηναῖος ξυνέγραψε τὸν πόλεμον τῶν Πελοποννησίων καὶ Ἀθηναίων, signalled from the start that he intended to cover both, as part of his aim of being 'useful', and that for this purpose his Thucydidean speeches were to be at least as useful as his narratives of events. In expressing his hope later in his introduction that his work will be judged to be 'a benefit', Thucydides turns to another word for useful, possibly because in the previous section on the emergence from brutishness he has made plentiful use of the other more commonly used words, 'chrestos' and its cognates, including especially 'chremata', as useful things, including forms of money, and he did not want to confuse his readers. The newly introduced word 'ophelima' is more modest, as befits the polite style of Thucydides, but leaves little doubt that the purpose of his history is to be useful to his contemporaries for the foreseeable future, which he expected to be long (as indeed the Parthenon was planned to last in its then roles) not for a remote posterity. ὠφέλιμα κρίνειν αὐτὰ ἀρκούντως ἕξει. Thuc. 1.22. In this regard Thucydides differed from his predecessor Herodotus, whose stated aim in his opening words, besides his claimed wish to celebrate and memorialize great deeds, was to record the results of his inquiry into what happened and why, a claim whose sincerity was disputed in ancient times as discussed in Chapter 4.

his Timon.[170] Although included in a work written centuries later, which may be more rhetorical exercise than historical chronicle, the transcribed document may nevertheless preserve traditional formulae about the separate branches of the civic government whose consent was needed. Besides the Council and the Demos, it mentions those responsible for organizing a festival, as well as the 'tribes' and the 'demes'.[171]

The text is presented as it might have been compiled and edited later by a historian who, like Thucydides, was able to take account of documents now lost as well as of personal recollections by himself and others, and who, in order to avoid repetition, has condensed a number of speeches by cohorts of epistatai and suggrapheis into a single text attributed to 'the Commissioners'. As a result, the composition preserves indications of how the speech was received when delivered orally to an occasionally rumbustious live audience, such as might have been added by an ancient scholiast. Spoken in literary Attic Greek by a professional reciter on one of the many occasions during the planning and approvals processes in the fifth century BCE, it follows the conventions of polite rhetoric.

In Chapters 3 and 4, I revert to the normal authorial voice looking in to discuss how the Parthenon was regarded and used in classical Athens, making use of the results of the experiment, some of which comfortably match the evidence, but also others which are surprising and which help to understand which stories in stone, metal, paint, and other materials were presented on the building and why, including a suggestion for answering a three-hundred-year old question.

My experiment with a Thucydidean speech and its lessons is then followed, as Chapter 5, by another experiment in looking out, an attempt to revive and mobilize another ancient invention that was also used as a means of assembling complex arguments, namely, the 'rhetorical discourse', a genre that was taught, practised, and theorized in Athens and elsewhere over hundreds of years. As genres, both the Thucydidean speech and the rhetorical discourse explicitly look both backwards and

---

170 Luc. Tim. 50. The genre of the 'rhetorical exercise', much practised in ancient Greece for many centuries, with my experiment in reconstructing an actual example, is discussed in Chapter 5.

171 'ἔτι δὲ καὶ ψηφίσματα γράφων καὶ συμβουλεύων καὶ στρατηγῶν οὐ μικρὰ ὠφέλησε τὴν πόλιν ἐπὶ τούτοις ἅπασι δεδόχθω τῇ βουλῇ καὶ τῷ δήμῳ καὶ τῇ Ἡλιαίᾳ καὶ ταῖς φυλαῖς καὶ τοῖς δήμοις ἰδίᾳ καὶ κοινῇ ...' Luc. Tim. 51.

forwards in time, positioning their implied readership in a specific, unrepeatable, moment. In modern terms, when read together, the two historiographical forms of writing, here revived, provide the materials for piecing together both an ex-ante appraisal and an ex-post evaluation.

As non-professionals, both the Commissioners and the author of the rhetorical discourse may have insufficiently disguised their own rhetorical strategies, as was the universal advice given in ancient times by those who taught the arts of persuasion. They may also have alienated their audience by their lumbering, strained, and clichéd attempts to show off their knowledge and display their wit.

Even for a straightforward translation of the Thucydidean speeches of Thucydides into English, it is hard to avoid what a Victorian scholar called the 'portly pedantry of Bloomfield, the grotesque likeness of Hobbes, the hideous fidelity of Dale, and the slipshod paraphrase of Crawley', the 'pretentious bigotry of Colonel Mure'.[172] The Commissioners have not always have been successful in limiting the lavishness of antithesis 'which is the more remarkable in one who lay under no temptation to redeem poverty of thought by rhetorical embellishment'.[173] I would hope however that, for the modern reader, their very clumsiness may itself be of value.

---

172 Comments by Wilkins, Henry Musgrave, M.A., Fellow of Merton College, Oxford, *Speeches from Thucydides Third Edition Revised and Corrected* (London: Longman, 1881), xiii, xvii.

173 *Ibid.*

2. 'How do we set straight our sacred city?'[1]

Men of Athens. It is the proud boast of our city that we are governed not by kings nor by oligarchs, but by ourselves.[2] And it is as free Athenians addressing free citizens that your Commissioners exercise our duty to speak usefully and plainly, without fear, flattery, or sophistry, and without resort to any of the rhetorical tricks that others employ to ensnare and corrupt the unwary.[3] As the saying goes: [*The reciter notes*

---

1   The title picks up on the wide range of metaphors relating to ships and voyaging, some already dead or moribund, that were common in classical Athens, and brought together by, for example, Brock, Roger, *Greek Political Imagery from Homer to Aristotle* (London; New York: Bloomsbury, 2013), http://doi.org/10.5040/9781472555694. At the time of the Greek Revolution, the commonest words used to describe the building of the new nation were variations on 'rebirth' and 'regeneration'. In classical Athens, such concepts, which owe much to post-antique Christianity, seem scarcely to have existed.

2   Although classical Athens had many characteristics of direct democracy by those adult men who qualified for full citizenship, in practice in many respects it was an oligarchy, as pointed out in the Thucydidean speech put in the mouth of Athenagoras of Syracuse at Thuc 6. 39 1 and 2.

3   The claim to be avoiding rhetoric, or not to know about rhetoric, is a common figure of rhetoric, for example in the opening section of the *Panathenaicus* by Isocrates, and one that the Athenian audience would discount as a mere conventional courtesy. Even in the world of myth, the character of Hecuba in the play by Euripides of that name, in pleading at line 819 with the character of Agamemnon as she faces death or slavery for herself and her children, and the destruction of all that Troy meant, apologizes for not having learned the art of persuasion, 'the only tyrant', implying that if she, like other mortals, had been more willing to pay the fees, she would not be in her present situation. Hecuba's invoking of a visual image in the same speech in order to make vivid her situation both to Agamemnon and to the audience and readership is referred to in discussing Figure 2.3 below. The Commissioners' promise to confine their speech to what is 'useful' echoes the advice given by the character of Athena in the passage from Euripides's *Suppliants* discussed with reference to Milton's *Areopagitica* at the end of St Clair, William, *Who Saved the Parthenon? A New History of the Acropolis Before, During and After the Greek Revolution* (Cambridge: Open Book Publishers, 2022) [hereafter *WStP*], https://doi.org/10.11647/OBP.0136, Chapter 22, https://doi.org/10.1164/obp.0136.22. The Commissioners also echo the sentiment of the speech by the character of Ion in

        https://doi.org/10.11647/OBP.0279.02

by a change in voice that he is quoting] 'It is easy to praise the Athenians among the Athenians'.[4] Weak minds, we all know, can be misled by the arts of persuasion, but your Commissioners will never bend the measuring rod that we ourselves must use.[5] Men of Athens know the difference between words that are polished but unfair and those that may be rough on the surface but that tell the truth.[6]

So we give you our own words as plainly as you wish to see them.[7] And we know that however good we are in word, without your goodwill, we will not be useful in deed.[8]

Euripides's play of that name, in which he laments the rights to speak in Assembly the he would lose if it turned out that, as a result of an audit of the evidence for what happened at the time of his birth, he was disqualified from speaking under the law of 451/0, to be discussed in Chapter 3.

4   The Commissioners make a point that seems to have become a cliché, included in the Platonic dialogue the *Menexenus* at Plat. Menex. 235d and 236a as an example of how to anticipate an objection. The *Menexenus*, a dialogue in the style of Plato, may have been written by him or another author as a rhetorical exercise, not as a work intended to deceive. The saying was attributed to Antiphon who was regarded as the best public speaker in classical Athens.

5   An example of the many metaphors drawn from the building industry, following, in this case, Aristotle in his treatise on rhetoric. Aristot. Rh. 1.1.5, An image of a measuring rod as used in the long eighteenth century, which matches what is known of actual ancient measuring rods and the metaphors they attracted, is at Figure 1.8.

6   A common rhetorical device, of which there are at least three examples in the plays of Euripides. Noted with references to the surviving plays and fragments by Karamanou, Ioanna, 'Fragments of Euripidean Rhetoric', in Markantonatos, Andreas and Volonaki, Eleni, eds, *Poet and Orator: A Symbiotic Relationship in Democratic Athens* (Berlin; Boston: De Gruyter, 2019), 90–91, https://doi.org/10.1515/9783110629729.

7   The Commissioners try to forestall the suspicion that they are just going to repeat well-rehearsed clichés, turning to the same comparison from the building industry as was used in the *Phaedrus*, the Platonic dialogue in which the role of editing as the enemy of spontaneity is discussed. Plat. Phaedrus 234e ἀκριβῶς ἕκαστα τῶν ὀνομάτων ἀποτετόρνευται. Noted by Kennerly, Michele, *Editorial Bodies: Perfection and Rejection in Ancient Rhetoric and Poetics. Studies in Rhetoric/Communication* (Columbia, S.C.: University of South Carolina Press, 2018), 37, along with other examples of the classical period, taken mainly from Old Comedy and from Alcidamas, who mentions the use of manuscripts and wax tablets. By appealing to 'seeing' rather than 'hearing', the Commissioners signal not only that they accept the primacy of the visual in cognition as discussed in Chapter 1, but that they will be encouraging the audience to imagine the words as 'opsis' by the rhetorical device of 'enargeia', of which examples follow. In practice the Commissioners use, indeed some would say they have already overused, many of the rhetorical devices that writers on the arts of persuasion, such as Aristotle, discuss and recommend as useful in moderation, as is picked out in later footnotes.

8   The Commissioners show, as does Demosthenes explicitly, with similar words in his funeral speech, Dem 30 14, that they understand that speaking is a speech act

Today we discuss the refloating of our foundered city, a matter that is, for all of us [*the reciter again notes by his tone of voice that a quotation follows*] 'above all time-consuming business', as the poet sings.[9] Our fortunes have been shaken, and now is the time to again set them straight.[10] As your Commissioners, ours is a heavy burden, but, although we are as unworthy in our own judgement as we are in yours, we accept the duty to obey that our laws lay upon us all.[11]

---

    intended to persuade and that its effectiveness is dependent upon the context, the shared and often familiar conventions, and the active participation of listeners in the making of meanings. Although at one level the remark is a rhetorical courtesy, the Commissioners show that they have a sophisticated understanding of the non-referential nature of language, and of the specific occasion, as we would expect from their plentiful experience of how speeches are received by live audiences. The binary between word and deed, common in all ancient Greek literary genres, is offered almost as a reassurance that conventions are being followed.

9   The Commissioners quote from Pindar, *First Isthmian*, 2, as the character of Socrates does in Plato's *Phaedrus*, 227b, in what had perhaps become a cliché for stressing the importance of the matter at the beginning of a speech as rhetorical handbooks recommend. The practice of quoting long passages from 'good and useful poets' [ἀγαθοὺς καὶ χρηστοὺς ποιητάς] in the theatre or the law courts was explicitly defended by Aeschines, Aeschin. 1 141. Although, in the surviving corpus, the practice is most often found in three of the ten fourth-century canonical Attic Orators, and it is to them that we are indebted for preserving some long fragments, such as that from the *Erechtheus* of Euripides, the practice of citing shorter phrases, as a chreia, is found earlier. In the full version of the Pindar quotation, which some members of the audience may have remembered, the speaking character addresses his city, Thebes, as his mother, so the quotation is well chosen by the Commissioners as an exhortation to put their duty to Athens as a set of obligations above any private concerns. Throughout, by their choice of words, the Commissioners say that a continuity is being maintained, not that buildings are being repaired or rebuilt after a disaster, itself a performance of what they wish the audience to think. An invocation of Mother Earth and the mutual obligation of children and mothers, including the duties put on both women in the household ('oikos') and men to fight, is offered by the character of Eteocles at the opening of *The Seven Against Thebes* by Aeschylus, in an example of how the Athenian tragic drama used the experience of other cities to set examples for Athens, sometimes as a contrast and at other times approvingly.

10 The Commissioners, abandoning the ships of state metaphors, which were overused to the extent that they had largely lost their primary meaning, turn to the earthquake metaphor used by the character of Creon in the *Antigone* of Sophocles. τὰ μὲν δὴ πόλεος ἀσφαλῶς θεοὶ/πολλῷ σάλῳ σείσαντες ὥρθωσαν πάλιν. Soph. Ant. 162 and 163. The context and the general 'things of the city' make clear that Creon was not referring to physical rebuilding.

11 Conventional, as in the Periclean Funeral Oration, Thuc. ii, 35. In contrast with modern political rhetoric in which practitioners like to draw attention to their own alleged personal qualifications, sometimes by claiming to have suffered as much as the unfortunates in the audience, ['we share your pain'], which is frequently discounted as a mere courtesy, ancient practice prefers to imply that the speaker

In preparing our proposals, we have, in accordance with the ancient customs of our city, sought the advice of the god, and all that we say accords with the oracles of Delphi, that you can read if you wish.[12] There may be a few here today who may have heard foolish stories that the gods take no interest in the affairs of men, but they are wrong.[13] Sometimes the gods are careless.[14] Since they know everything, they do not need the images that we dedicate to them nor the sacrifices that we make in their honour and of which we always give a share to the gods, but the more we show the sincere piety with which these gifts are offered, the

---

is merely acting as the medium for a message that is already agreed. One effect is to appear to treat the audience with respect as equals, but with the corollary that speakers may appear to be heartless, lacking in emotion, or cynical, as is a common modern reaction among readers of Thucydidean speeches.

12   The Commissioners follow a procedure described by Dio of Prusa, in his thirteenth oration in Athens, as 'an ancient custom of the Athenians'. As is normal, they leave 'the god' unidentified, but is likely to be a reference to seeking the advice of the oracle at Delphi of which the reports, probably written on papyrus, were archived on the Acropolis, probably in due course held in the closed chamber of the Parthenon along with the other valuables of the city, as will be discussed using epigraphic evidence in Chapter 3. Since the Commissioners speak as a collective, they assume a conventional position as if it were uncontested, itself a form of building consensus. However at least some of the Commissioners, and many others in their audiences, knew that there were many men in Athens, both individuals and members of the philosophical schools, who did not believe that the gods existed at all, or took the view that, if they did exist, they paid no attention to human affairs, and yet others, such as Prodikos, who taught openly that gods were inventions of human minds, 'nomismatic' like the coinage, whose usefulness depended upon the trust put in them, not on any intrinsic value, and who did not have to exist to be useful, as discussed in Chapter 1. The cognate word, without the -ize, was put in the mouths of the Athenians in the Melian dialogue, as part of their claim that they were acting in accordance with pan-Hellenic practice: 'οὐδὲν γὰρ ἔξω τῆς ἀνθρωπείας τῶν μὲν ἐς τὸ θεῖον νομίσεως, τῶν δ' ἐς σφᾶς αὐτοὺς βουλήσεως δικαιοῦμεν ἢ πράσσομεν.' Thuc. 5.105.1. On the Parthenon frieze, the gods are presented as taking an occasional interest in human affairs, as they do in the Homeric epics, as discussed in Chapter 4.

13   The Commissioners adopt the rhetorical device of acknowledging that there are opposing views, so that they can sweep away the objections by having their answer ready.

14   The Commissioners include the remark as part of the normal understanding, not as an aberration, as does Isocrates in the Panathenaicus Isoc. 12 186. Given the evident arbitrariness of life, with devastating lightning strikes, storms, and earthquakes, and innumerable unfair human contingencies, the Athenians found it impossible to devise theist explanations. However, they did adopt pragmatic solutions, some of which reveal an understanding of physics, as, for example, in the plugs in columns discussed in St Clair, *WStP*, Chapter 21, https://doi.org/10.1164/obp.0136.21.

greater the delight that the gods take in our gifts.[15] We Athenians will always be dear to the gods and, as our poets sing, in time the gods bring everything to a conclusion, even if they are slow.[16]

We have listened to the spirit ('daimon') of our rivers, of our hills, of our winds, and to the whispers of our olive trees.[17] We have journeyed over our land of Attica, to our towns, to our frontier forts, to our harbours, and to the rocky walls that defend us from robbers from the sea.[18]

---

15   The Commissioners adopt the point of view put into the mouth of Socrates by Xenophon in his account of his sentiments, in which he argued, as a believer himself, that it was as a demonstration of individual belief that justified these cultural practices, and that a small gift, if made in the right spirit by someone who could not afford a large one, was equally effective. Xen. Mem. 1.3.3. The sentiment is in line with the general aim of building community. It also encourages participants in festivals, whatever their 'true' motives, if such a concept is tenable, to exaggerate their performances in the knowledge that they are impressing the gods as well as their fellow celebrants. By the time of Dio of Prusa, a famous orator of the first century CE who participated in the discourse, and who accepted commissions from many cities, it was possible to pick out this effect publicly without being thought out of line. As he told the Rhodians, whom he scolded for their innovations: 'perhaps the god requires no images-to-be-wondered-at' ('agalmata'), often translated as statues, losing the implied role of the viewer. The mainstream defence of the practice of sacrificing to the gods was repeated by Dio of Prusa, centuries later: 'But in any event these acts are not ineffectual, because we thereby show our zeal and our disposition towards the gods'. D.Chr. 31.17. This component of the discourse adds further confirmation that the modern tendency to separate the buildings, the stories they offered, and the uses to which they were put in collective cultural activities may be anachronistic.

16   The Commissioners repeat the common response to those who doubt the existence or usefulness of gods, found, for example, in Euripides fragments 800, 915b and 948; and in the *Ion* 1615. Since the long term is not knowable, and sometimes we hear of sons having to suffer for the misdeeds of the fathers, invoking the long term is a neat way of rhetorically avoiding the question.

17   The Commissioners repeat ideas in Plato's *Phaedrus* 229b, attributed to the character of Socrates, that mention non-Olympian chthonic gods, the practice at the oracle of Dodona of listening to the oak trees, and the story of Oreithyia, daughter of Erechtheus, being carried off by Boreas, the North Wind. Besides, they forestall any suspicion that they are only interested in the metropolitan city of Athens. As in the *Phaedrus*, the sentence also enables the Commissioners to claim that they are modest receivers of ideas that are already present in the storyscape.

18   In their phrase 'rocky walls' the Commissioners remind the audience that historic Attica had few landing places from the seaward, other than its defended harbours, a geographical feature that was still vital during the Greek Revolution and in the Second World War. By mentioning that they have been to the country as well as the town, the Commissioners claim not only to have covered the geographical area of Attica, but that they have consulted across an ideological spectrum—it being a tag that the city dwellers were soft and the country dwellers were illiberal. This tag, possibly containing a hint of a suggestion that the emancipation from brutishness still has some way to go even in Attica, was caught by the thought offered by a

But enough of woods and rocks.[19] As the saying goes, for all matters that are dark, the teacher needs the light of evidence and of likelihood.[20] Under the watchful eyes of the gods, we are able steadfastly to follow the course and capture: [*quoting*] 'the pure light shining from afar'.[21]

In asking the Assembly to approve the plans, your Commissioners speak on behalf of the whole polis.[22] As Homer teaches us [*quotes*] 'two good men are better than one', and, like Agamemnon, we too wish we had ten of such fellow councillors.[23] And we speak especially for those citizens who are recovering from wounds or from sickness, who have been absent on campaign or working to secure the cities of our overseas kinsmen, or who have been on sea voyages bringing the fruits of other lands to our Attic shores.[24] On the knowledge and wisdom of these men the greatness of Athens is built and just as a huntsman selects his dogs

---

character in Henderson, Jeffrey, ed., *Aristophanes, Fragments* (London: Harvard UP, 2007), fragment 706.

19   The audience may have recognized that the Commissioners were repeating a phrase that Hesiod had used to signal a change of topic, especially if the reciter mimicked a Theban accent. ἀλλὰ τί ἦ μοι ταῦτα περὶ δρῦν ἢ περὶ πέτρην. Hes. Th. 35. If we give credence to the document quoted by Lucian in the note of introduction, visits around Attica may have been part of the consultation process.

20   The Commissioners turn to, and reinforce the usage of, what appears to be a 'chreia', with its trope of 'revelation', used and, as a result, preserved by Clement of Alexandria in advancing a Christian agenda. It has been thought by some to have been derived from Hyperides and is noted among his works as fragment D1, but he may himself be quoting.

21   The Commissioners turn to a phrase used by Pindar in his *Pythian Odes*, iii, 75, which was used as a piece of entrenched wisdom ('chreia') for taking a long-term view by Dionysius of Halicarnassus, Usher, Stephen, trans., *Dionysius of Halicarnassus, Critical Essays* (London: Harvard UP, 1974, 1985), i, 9, in pointing out what he presented as a weakness in the work of Thucydides. The phrase is apposite in the context of the speech, encapsulating the micro-climate of Attica, the stories with which it was associated, the apparently perpetual durability of the main materials that will be used in the physical rebuilding such as marble, gold, and bronze, as well the main features of the discursive environment to which the proposals themselves and the resulting Parthenon were a contribution within an aspired-to indefinite continuity of past through present to future, as did indeed happen for many centuries.

22   The Commissioners, presenting themselves as *suggrapheis,* employ the rhetorical device of claiming to speak on behalf of the whole citizen body, even although the occasion is formally intended to discover the range of opinions, confident that their claim to know what the result will be will not be taken at face value.

23   The Commissioners refer to remarks quoted from the *Iliad*, Hom. Il. 10.224 and 2.372, as a chreia, by Aristotle, Aristot. Pol. 3.1287b, planting the thought that the Parthenon will celebrate the values of the Homeric era.

24   The merchant mariners, and their willingness to take risks, are praised by a character in the lost play by Sophocles, *The Men of Scyros,* fragment 555.

and horses for how eager they are in the chase and not for their lineage, so too good birth does not always make for useful men.[25]

We speak too for those with little education, such as those who pull the oars of our ships of war, those who steer and act as lookouts, those who build the ships, and others who work tirelessly for our city for pay.[26]

We do not speak at length of what is already known.[27] Those who have served as commissioners already know more than we do. Others

---

25 This point, though presented as generally agreed, itself a rhetorical device, was not universally accepted in classical Greece. Theognis of Megara, for example, with experience of the eugenics of animal breeding in mind, warned of the effects on the human race if 'the best' bred with the 'low born' for example in *Testimonia*, 6. On the other side, it is suggested by a character in a play by Euripides, fragment 232, that 'arete' is hereditary. The Commissioners deploy the example from folk wisdom used in Plut. Comp. Lys. Sull. 2.2 to slip out an acknowledgment that, even in its greatest crisis, the Athenians had not been united. Indeed, the sons of Peisistratus, whose father, although a tyrant, had accomplished much for Athens, had personally urged Xerxes to invade Greece and had accompanied the Persian army when it sacked Athens. The myths of an unchanging Athenianness required that exceptions, including the actions of traitors, should be rhetorically accommodated and re-integrated into the official story, or at least actively ignored, as shown by, for example, Steinbock, Bernd, *Social Memory in Athenian Public Discourse: Uses and Meanings of the Past* (Ann Arbor: University of Michigan Press, 2013), https://doi. org/10.3998/mpub.1897162. In their historical passages, the Commissioners were less concerned with presenting a true picture of the past than with giving their audience what Steinbock calls a 'usable past', 'imagined and remembered history', 'cultural memory', 'believed history', and 'intentional history'. The same device of selection and omission was also used, as Steinbock shows, to enable the cities to shift their alliances and their wars with other cities—as, for example, the fact that Thebes, like the Peisistratids, had medized—and it is a common feature in the rhetorical self-construction of imagined communities. The taint of being associated with the tyrant Peisistratus and the quisling Peisistratids is yet another argument for discounting the possibility that the scene pictured on the Parthenon frieze is the actual Panathenaic festival, which was founded, or refounded, by Peisistratus. Although there are many examples of giving authority to current customs by claiming that they existed in the mythic age, there are other objections as will be discussed in Chapter 4.

26 The Commissioners risk antagonizing some of the audience by referring to the sentiment of the so-called Old Oligarch, Ps. Xen. Const. Ath. 4–6, who said that these men were more deserving than the hoplites of the army who were drawn from classes of Athenian regarded as socially superior. As is common in the literature of the classical period, the word for 'useful', which is repeated several times in the passage, is presented as the opposite of the word used for morally or civically 'bad' (kakos). As suggested in Chapter 1, the building of a fleet may have been made possible by the surplus of manpower that became available to be deployed for other purposes, as a result of the productivity gain in the economy brought about by the shift from the economic autarky of the oikos to the cultivation of exchangeable specialist crops.

27 Conventional, as in the Periclean Funeral Oration, Thuc. ii, 36, where it is also used as a co-opting device.

have participated in our deliberations since the plans were first proposed in shadowy outline ('skiagraphia') or have talked with the members of the Commission or our secretaries. It is difficult to say neither too little nor too much; and even moderation is apt not to give the impression of truthfulness.[28]

Tomorrow we, the people, (Assembly of the 'Demos') will decide what is best after we have all heard the reasoning ('logos') for our proposals. Every man who has the right to speak and he who speaks in respectful words will be listened to.[29] But let each man recall that Athens wants to hear only from those who have something useful to contribute.[30] Anyone who makes a disturbance will be handed over to the Scythians, and if he forfeits his daily payment for attendance, his family will go hungry.[31] And let us remind ourselves too that, if you change the decisions already taken, you may feel the displeasure of those who have taken upon themselves and their heirs the responsibility for ensuring that the work is finished and that all the appropriate payments are made.[32] When things go well, citizens cannot claim to share in the

---

28 The Commissioners repeat a sentence in the exordium to the Periclean Funeral Oration as presented by Thucydides with its halting double negatives, reinforcing the speaker's rhetorical presentation of himself as modestly feeling his way.

29 The Commissioners use a formulaic proclamation as discussed, with instances, in Collard, C., Cropp, M. J. and Gibert, J., eds, *Euripides, Selected Fragmentary Plays Volume II* (Warminster: Aris and Phillips, 2004), 302.

30 The Commissioners, in giving a warning, recall the limitations noted by the character of Theseus in the *Suppliants* of Euripides, noted at the end of St Clair, *WStP*, Chapter 22, https://doi.org/10.1164/obp.0136.22 in the discussion of Milton's *Areopagitica*.

31 These sanctions are mentioned in Ar. Eccl 143 and 292.

32 The Commissioners refer to the system of guarantees, some of which extended for many years, without which the Parthenon could not have been constructed, which is well documented for the fourth century and which we can be confident must also have been in operation in the fifth. Discussed by Burford, Alison, *The Greek Temple Builders at Epidauros, A Social and Economic Study of Building in the Asklepian Sanctuary, During the Fourth and Early Third Centuries B.C.* (Liverpool: Liverpool UP, 1969), 104–109. What the guarantees covered in the case of the Parthenon is not directly recorded, but if it followed the model applied later, they covered all financial liabilities, including wages, fees, and fines. Since the fines were levied for late or inadequate work, the guarantees effectively covered all aspects of the design and construction, the work in progress, with staged payments, and the acceptance and final payment. The system of guarantees, we can say, effectively spread the liability across the richer members of the polis beyond the public treasury. Seldom mentioned in modern discussions of the Parthenon, they enable us to say that 'the Athenians' built the Parthenon, but only in the sense that Queen Victoria 'built' Balmoral Castle. What effect the guarantees had on the money supply and on the growth of the economy cannot be measured, but it is certain to have been huge, and possibly strongly positive, not only in enabling more real resources to be mobilized from outside as well as from inside Attica, but in quickening the long

credit for our good judgment, and if they go wrong, we cannot blame the unexpected.[33]

Everyone who speaks will also reflect carefully whether his words are in accordance with our ancient laws and customs. Today we see the Areopagus at work, keeping us safe, day and night. [*The reciter points to the hill*]. If ever our laws and customs are polluted by misuse, or godlessness ('asebeia') they become like water stained with filth, poisonous and unfit to drink.[34]

As is the custom, we begin with our ancestors, who alone of the Hellenes arose from the land of Attica, and who have passed it on unconquered, from generation to generation, to the present day.[35] When the gods divided the earth, Athena, who loves wisdom, and Hephaistos, who loves the arts of making, of whom we are the sons, fashioned our land of Attica to be a place whose very nature encourages good government and civic virtue ('arete').[36]

---

trend towards specialization. Burford, who notes that Moses Finley helped her with the interpretation of the inscriptions, appears to have thought that the economy functioned without modern instruments of credit. The shift in the language from 'we', where responsibility is shared, to 'you', which blames and threatens potential opponents in advance, is a common rhetorical device.

33   The Commissioners, as Pericles does in his first war speech as reported in accordance with his conventions by Thucydides at Thuc 1. 140, are simultaneously claiming to be mere spokesmen for the citizen body and laying the ground for future excuses and recriminations. As their subsequent words show, however, the Commissioners, while at this point in their speech rhetorically bidding to be regarded as democrats who are above resorting to such devices, rely on the short memories of the listeners and themselves invoke Tyche when it suits their argument.

34   The Commissioners repeat a sentiment put into the mouth of Athena in Aesch. Eum. 694–695. As is common in political rhetoric, although they celebrate an alleged continuity, they will soon also declare for innovation. They implicitly warn against proposing significant changes. Such oblique hints, and the frequent emphasis on 'usefulness' and its cognates, helps to explain how, despite opposition as will be discussed in Chapter 5, the building programme was carried through over decades of changing electorates.

35   The Commissioners signal that they have reached the end of their exordium and are moving towards the main argument. They deploy the same piece of mythic history as was used at the beginning of the Periclean Funeral Oration, Thuc 2.36. As must have been widely known to the listeners, the Athenians were not unique in claiming to be autochthonous. The claim that Athens had never been invaded in mythic times was also put into the mouths of the Chorus in the *Medea* of Euripides, when the people of Corinth chant these truisms: 'From ancient times the sons of Erechtheus have been favored; they are children of the blessed gods sprung from a holy land never pillaged by the enemy'. Eur. Med 825. Passages from the same speech are cited later in this chapter as examples of geodeterminism.

36   The Commissioners summarize thoughts set out in the *Critias* of Plato, one of the classical-age texts predicated on a theory of geodeterminism, of which autochthony

We have all heard our fathers speak of the never-to-be-forgotten year when Phainippides was archon [490 BCE] when alone of the cities in Hellas, our men of Marathon saved Hellas and Hellenism itself.[37] Our immortal dead we awarded with special honours that, like their fame, can never perish.[38] Others remember the year when Kalliades and then Xanthippos were archons [480/479 BCE] when the oriental barbarians invaded our land, treacherously captured our acropolis, destroyed our sacred buildings, killed those who stretched out their arms in supplication, and knocked down our family dedications with their savage hammers and axes. When Hellenes take possession of another Hellenic city and its holy places, we do not act like the barbarians but allow the rites and ceremonies to continue as far as is possible.[39] But, not

---

was a component. Ἥφαιστος δὲ κοινὴν καὶ Ἀθηνᾶ φύσιν ἔχοντες, ἅμα μὲν ἀδελφὴν ἐκ ταὐτοῦ πατρός, ἅμα δὲ φιλοσοφίᾳ φιλοτεχνίᾳ τε ἐπὶ τὰ αὐτὰ ἐλθόντες, οὕτω μίαν ἄμφω λῆξιν τήνδε τὴν χώραν εἰλήχατον ὡς οἰκείαν καὶ πρόσφορον ἀρετῇ. Plat. Criti. 109b. The thought involved in linking two forms of knowledge, and the wisdom and skill involved in applying it, both words prefaced by 'philo-', is that herding sheep and goats requires the same qualities as governing human beings, with the animals that cohabit with them in an oikos or polis, and that the potential future was designed into the geography from the earliest times. The Commissioners use the Greek word for nature (phusis and its cognates) not to refer to an unchanging characteristic, but in its ancient sense of well suited to its purpose. The same sentiment is found in the *Homeric Hymn to Hephaistos* HH 20 1. That text, including its reference to the brutishness narrative, fits so well with other examples of Athenian self-construction and discursive practice in the classical era that at least one scholar has raised the possibility that the hymn, with its archaized language, was composed in Athens in the fifth century and projected back to the mythic Homeric age so as to accord it greater authority. Shear, T. Leslie, Jnr., *Trophies of Victory: Public Building in Periklean Athens* (Princeton, N.J.: Department of Art and Archaeology, Princeton University in association with Princeton UP, 2016), 160.

37 τὸ Ἑλληνικὸν as used, for example in Hdt. 7.139.

38 The Commissioners refer to the mound raised over the Athenian dead at Marathon, instantiating the memory of the battle in the built landscape. They refer to the commissioning of a large picture of the battle that was seen in Athens for centuries into the future. The dates of the archonates is from Harding, *Atthidographers*, 102. For the rest of the speech, the editor has used the dates of the modern calendar.

39 The same sentiment is offered in Thuc 4.98, a Thucydidean speech put into the mouth of a herald from Athens in answering a complaint that the laws had been violated. As Rachel Kousser has pointed out, the differences in the customs regarding organized destruction and mutilation of images contributed to the rhetoric that mutilation was un-Hellenic and 'barbarian', the word now becoming almost synonymous with the modern 'barbarous'. Kousser, Rachel, *The Afterlives of Greek Sculpture, Interaction, Transformation and Destruction* (Cambridge: CUP, 2017), 107. The best documented example of mutilation of images in classical Athens is the episode in a single night in 415 when the so-called herms, many presenting male figures with erect penises, that dotted the Athenian cityscape, were deliberately

content with destruction, the hated orientals set fire to our holiest places and committed another crime against the gods. Our houses are burned to ashes, our life-giving wells are choked with our broken household possessions.[40]

Cast your eyes, men of Athens, on our sick old men and wounded youths spurting blood as their defenceless bodies are pierced by eastern spears. See our daughters to whom we entrusted our most sacred treasures, cling to our altars like ivy to an oak.[41] Hear them shriek as they are raped and killed by monsters screeching their pitiless chants.[42] Smell the blackening blood, swipe at the clouds of buzzing flies, tremble at the snarling dogs. Our daughters who have not yet been given to a husband shake their arms in vain at birds so glutted that they can no longer cry out their messages that tell our soothsayers what the future holds.[43] Shudder at the impiety of monsters who deny the dead the

---

damaged, for reasons that are hard to understand except in general terms as acts of resistance to the official ideology of the city. The mutilation was immediately condemned as 'asebeia', in modern terms a criminal blasphemy against the official supernatural, and the perpetrators were punished at least as severely as if they had murdered living people, for example by death, exile, and confiscation of their property. After the putting down of the outbreak of resistence, the Athenian authorities restored the landscape, and therefore the storyscape and the festival-scape, to its pre-mutilation visual condition, with some herms repaired and others buried. Kousser, *Afterlives*, 138. Conspicuous mutilation became common in the Roman period and was evidently a formal policy of the ecclesiastical leaderships of the Christian successors, a fact that, as will be discussed in Chapter 3, helps to validate my suggestion for what event was displayed on the central slab of the Parthenon frieze.

40   Miles, Margaret, M., *Art as Plunder: The Ancient Origins of Debate about Cultural Property* (Cambridge: CUP, 2008), 24–25, from archaeological evidence from the Agora excavations, including layers of burned wood, and in the wells, mud bricks, pieces of wood, and broken crockery.

41   The Commissioners use the vivid image offered by the character of Hecuba at Eur. Hec 397.

42   As with the other examples of enargeia in the speech, it is impossible to know whether the rhetoric actually conjured up pictures, phantasms, or mental enactments in the minds of the listeners, or indeed whether internal picturing is consistent with modern neuroscience or is a useful way of understanding mental processes. In calling the statues 'powerless', the Commissioners echo the character of Hecuba's lament in the *Trojan Women* by Euripides νεκύων ἀμενηνὸν ἄγαλμα Eur. Tro. 193, an example of the tradition of presenting the dedications of images made by human dedicators to gods, as images of gods.

43   The Commissioners recall the signs of disorder in the city noted by Teiresias in Sophocles' *Antigone*, Soph. Ant. 1015–1020. The detail that orphans were employed in the work of shooing away birds from sacred sites comes from the *Ion* of Euripides. The role of birds as harbingers of the future was also noted by the character of Ion in

ceremonies that they deserve that save them from the black night of oblivion.[44]

When your Commissioners first looked at our shining city on the hill of Cecrops, we saw death-dealing scorpions and serpents slithering on the paths along which our perfumed daughters used to dance and sing their joy-giving hymns. The city has already put to a stop to the burning of useless things and the dumping of dung.[45] But your Commissioners share with you the shame of our young men, when at the ceremony at which they become our warriors, they see not the moment of victory but that of the unmerited defeat. We weep to see our best youths drinking in taverns, gambling with dice, and spending time with flute girls when they should be making new citizens with their wives at home. Some spend time with Lydians, Phrygians, Syrians, and others from the lands of the great king, whose hordes our fathers twice drove from our land, and whose foreign customs, unless they too are driven out, will dilute both their love of country and our native blood.[46] It is not our custom that immigrants should set themselves above the autochthonous, that those who receive the benefits should think themselves superior to their benefactors, or that those who come as suppliants should lord it over those who have helped them.[47]

We heard Athenians who see a snake calling on a foreign god they call Sabazios.[48] We see them cooling their wineskins in the 'Nine Channels'

---

the *Ion* who, at that stage of the play, is presented as innocently simple, at Eur. Ion 178. Some species of birds were credited with being able to foresee the future, and not just because they can see what is likely to arrive over the horizon from being able to fly high, as noted, for example in the work by Theophrastus on weather signs, an example of their species-specific culture.

44   The Commissioners remind us of the importance of funeral ceremonies in a society that had, for the most part, only a metaphorical notion of an afterlife as a continuation of memory. Destroying memory was part of the charge made by Lycurgus against Leocrates, Lyc. 1 147. Members of the audience are likely to have known the story of Antigone, and her defiance of authority to ensure burial rites for her brothers, perhaps in the version as retold by Sophocles.

45   From a fragmentary inscription dated 485/4, summarized by Camp, John M., *The Archaeology of Athens* (New Haven: Yale UP, 2001), 52. It was made from a metope, recycled from one of the temples destroyed by the Persians.

46   The Commissioners repeat the thought and some of the exact words used by Xenophon in his treatise on public finance known as *Ways and Means*, Xen. Ways 2.3.

47   Sentiments expressed in Isocrates, *Panegyricus*, Isoc. Pan. 63.

48   The Commissioners repeat a story of hybridity in Athens noted by Theophrastus, *Characters* 16.4. Sabazios was a Phrygian god, whose cult was also mentioned by Demosthenes.

.... [*A member of the audience shouts out an obscenity that raises a laugh. The reciter then addresses the interrupter*] Will you tell me, you brute, where I can buy a stopped-up nose [*laughter*]. [*The reciter resumes*]. Camel dung is for your yokel theatres [*more laughter*].[49] Let us remind ourselves of the law of Solon that requires that speakers must not be interrupted or shouted down.[50] You are not at the Dionysia now.[51]

[*The reciter resumes his formal style*] Our beloved city, O men of Athens, is stretched out like a sacrificial black horned beast, bleeding, eviscerated, stinking, with nothing useful left but its skin.[52] And we hear again the voice of Solon, the founder of our Athenian constitution, cry

---

49   In the *Acharnians* of Aristophanes, 38, a character plans to interrupt the speakers in the Assembly and the Scythians are called to restore order. The reciter acknowledges that the interrupter has made an obscene joke worthy of Aristophanes and he retaliates by making his own joke as it was to be used in Aristophanes, *Peace*, 20, showing he is also at home with obscenity. Rhetorically the reciter regains the initiative, with an implied sneer that the interrupter has spent his life in oriental countries where camels were most often seen. Since the audience for Old Comedy, which may have included women, was wider than the demos, it is likely that overlaps were common, and obscenity was regarded at this time, although not later, as part of the working of the democracy. As Benjamin Jowett noted long ago in discussing the platonic-style *Menexenus*, 'Plato, both in the Symposium and elsewhere, is not slow to admit a sort of Aristophanic humour', and we should therefore expect to find instances in other forms of speaking and writing, not as an exception but, as here, as a component of the discursive environment.

50   The Commissioners resume the seriousness by repeating the sentiment later voiced by Aeschines in Aeschin. 3 2. Whether there was such a law in Solon's day or whether a custom was attributed back to a heroic founder as an invented tradition cannot be determined with certainty.

51   According to the character of 'the Athenian' in *The Laws*, by Plato, the audiences in the Assembly praised or blamed each speaker as loudly as if they were at the theatre. Plat. Laws 9.876B.

52   The Commissioners turn to a vivid comparison that is first used in a surviving written record in a letter written much later by Synesius of Cyrene available in English translation in FitzGerald, Augustine, ed., *The Letters of Synesius of Cyrene* (London: OUP, 1926), Letter 136, and which may have been a cliché much earlier. In the Homeric *Hymn to Demeter*, the skins of slaughtered cattle are left, presumably to dry them out, for some time after the sacrificial killing, burning, and eating of the animals had ended. Since the same custom was practised in the classical period, as seems certain given that animal parts as well as their skins were preserved to be sold or were given to festival and temple staff as part of their remuneration, the skins would have added to the sense of the Acropolis as a perpetual slaughterhouse-cum-cookhouse, giving off stinks long after a festival procession had left. Black cows seem to have been specially prized, indeed specially bred, and their horns were wreathed before they were slaughtered.

out in his immortal lament: 'How my breast fills with sorrow when I see Ionia's oldest land being done to death.'⁵³

But why, you may ask, do we [*changes tone to signify a quotation*] 'repeat the unspeakable'?⁵⁴ For we also remember the day when as the oracle foretold, the women of Cape Colias roasted their barley on fires made from broken Persian oars.⁵⁵ Our alliances with kindred cities fortify our

---

53 The quotation, γιγνώσκω, καί μοι φρενὸς ἔνδοθεν ἄλγεα κεῖται,/ πρεσβυτάτην ἐσορῶν γαῖαν Ἰαονίας κλινομένην, preserved by Aristot. Const. Ath. 5, reminds us that a strong sense of Athenians themselves being Ionian predated the Persian wars and their aftermath, when many cities, principally in Asia, but also among the islands and in many locations elsewhere, including some in the Black Sea, were formally or informally joined with Athens in a real, imagined, or hybrid kinship as 'Ionia'. In referring to Athens as Ionian, Solon was contributing to what was to become a standard commonplace in the classical period, but by his use of the archaic form Ἰαονίας, he was taking authority from Homer, *Iliad*, 13.673, where the old form with the alpha is also used to include the Athenians. As noted later, the involvement of the Athenians in the Trojan war was small, and the mention may possibly be a late addition. As was normal, the speakers slip from a narrative relation of a past event into the energeia of the present. They also claim a collective continuity with earlier generations of commissioners, emphasizing in their own words the continuity of the city. Herodotus, in listing the kinship origins of the cities that took part, not all on the same side, in the war against the Achaemenid forces ('the Persians'), remarks—in a passage that was written and publicly recited at the time when the classical Parthenon was being designed and built—that the Athenians only called themselves Ionians, from the time of Ion, son of Xuthus. Hdt. 8.44. Solon was said to have settled a long-running dispute about the island, which is geographically as close to Dorian Megara is it is to Athens, by obtaining a declaration from the Delphic oracle that Salamis was 'Ionian'. Plut. Sol. 10.4. My suggestion that the Parthenon frieze displays Xuthus in the act of naming the infant Ion is discussed in Chapter 4.

54 The Commissioners turn to a phrase used by the character of Electra in the *Orestes* of Euripides, τί τἄρρητ' ἀναμετρήσασθαί με δεῖ; Eur. Orest. 14. The phrase used was a chreia more than half a millennium later by the Emperor Julian in his *Letter to the Boule and Demos of Athens. 270d*, which, as with other works by Julian, contains elements from the classical-era discourse. The quotation is introduced there 'as if from some tragedy' (τί με δεῖ νῦν ὥσπερ ἐκ τραγῳδίας τὰ ἄρρητα ἀναμετρεῖσθαι'). Julian had tried, without lasting success, to reverse the Christianization of the ancient empire and its institutions started by the military coup of Constantine that achieved success at the battle of the Milvian Bridge in 312, the mythology of which was invoked at the Siege of Athens in 1822. The custom of quoting useful phrases from ancient 'pagan' authors was continued by Christian writers, to the extent that they became one of the largest sources of fragments of lost works.

55 The Commissioners, in referring to the battle of Salamis, repeat the story about women living on the coast on the bay of Salamis given by Herodotus. Hdt. 8.96. As spokesmen for the official ideology, they uphold the authority of oracles, although in this case, as in others, the oracle was ambiguous and could have been taken as warning of a defeat.

land with walls of brass and steel.[56] And now, every true Athenian is asking himself, what is to be done to make the ship of state fit to resume our journey and make our holy places live again in shining glory? Some say that we ought to build more warships, but as the poet tells us, the safety of a city does not depend upon its walls but upon its men.[57] The success of a city does not lie in its armies and navies, but in the wisdom of its rulers.[58]

---

56   The Commissioners turn to a phrase about the value of alliances that would be used in the law courts by Aeschines, but that is likely to have been conventional before his time, and here applied to the Delian league of mainly Ionian cities. Aeschin. 3.84.

57   The Commissioners refer to what Aelius Aristides in oration 23, 68 calls 'an old saying', attributing it to the archaic poet Alcaeus, reminding the audience of the Delphic oracle's description of the fleet as a 'wooden wall'. In a recent book, David Pritchard claims to have 'settled' the question raised by Augustus Boeckh and his ancient predecessors, such as Plutarch, by compiling estimates, mainly from records of the fourth century, of the amounts budgeted and spent on a number of headings—so much on festivals, so much on payments to officials and citizens— figures that can be compared with estimates of the annual cost of constructing and maintaining the buildings, including the Parthenon, arriving at the conclusion that the largest item was for war and war preparations. Pritchard, David, *Public Spending and Democracy in Classical Athens* (Austin: University of Texas Press, 2015), commenting on passages such as: 'To expend large sums on the fine arts, which appeared in the highest perfection at the sacred festivals, upon costly but lasting ornaments for the temples, upon choruses and musical entertainments, and upon a theatre, which was so perfect that it excelled equally in tragedy and comedy, were considered as acts of a liberal and noble mind. And while the Athenians were led by their religious obligations to these costly practices, the Spartans were satisfied to manifest their piety by offering small sacrifices to the gods. That the person who provides the sacrificial feast should receive a share of the offering, appears both natural and reasonable; but when the principal revenues of the State were wasted upon public banquets, and the sacrifices were maintained at the public expence not so much for the purposes of religion, as for the support of the poor, the policy of the Athenians was alike unjust and inexpedient, inasmuch as the continuance of it without oppressing the allies was impossible, and the State, being deprived of the means of self-defence in a most frivolous and unpardonable manner, was led on to certain destruction.' Boeckh, Augustus, *The public economy of Athens: in four books; To which is added, A dissertation on the silver-mines of Laurion, Translated from the German of Augustus Boeckh* (London: Murray, 1828), i, 279. However, although Pritchard's general conclusion is unexceptionable within its own terms, it would be a poor policymaker who considered, or proposed to others that they should consider, only the budgetary inputs to a policy without being persuaded of the benefits of the expected outputs and outcomes, and it would be a non-functioning democracy that gave approval in such circumstances. Neither of these conditions obtained in classical Athens. Hence the need for the present experiment.

58   The Commissioners repeat what was evidently in this case a common, not a specially invented, 'chreia', being found, for example, with variations, in Thucydides vii. 77 and Isocrates, *Areopagiticus*, 13. The members of the Assembly are again flattered by being called the rulers when they know that, in practice, the decision-making is weighted towards the rich 'aristocrats'.

If the great king [*spoken with a touch of contemptuous irony*] and the unforgivable medizers were mad enough to try to invade our land again, we are ready.[59] But in our city the flood of lawlessness and impiety cannot be held back by endlessly adding new laws to those that already fill our porches.[60] For our forefathers in the time of Solon and Cleisthenes, who drove out the tyrants and gave the power back to the people, it was enough to ensure that our ancient customs were taught to the young and that those who broke them were punished and dishonoured.[61]

When we visit other lands, some possessed by other Hellenes, and others by the barbarians, we see the members of each household working every day to produce just enough for its own needs, keeping sheep and goats for cheese, meat, and wool, and picking fruits from their trees, but always at the mercy of Tyche, wondering whether the rains will come and if there will be enough to eat in the winter.[62] We see wild men in the countryside afraid of their neighbours, carrying arms in case they are attacked when they are on land and afraid to venture on to the sea because of the sea-robbers.

It was because we are one people, united in our trust in the gods and in one another, that we Athenians were the first to go naked and now only carry arms when we are at war.[63]

---

59   The Commissioners, who lose no opportunity to condemn the Thebans and stir up the Athenians against them, refer not only to military and naval preparations but to plans to evacuate the women and other non-combatants to the island of Salamis and elsewhere, as was done during the Greek Revolution. The so-called 'Decree of Themistocles', an inscription that commemorated the evacuation is discussed by Hammond, N.G.L., 'The Narrative of Herodotus VII and the Decree of Themistocles at Troezen' in *Journal of Hellenic Studies*, Vol. 102 (1982), 75–93, https://doi.org/10.2307/631127.

60   Isocrates, *Areopagiticus*, 42. The Commissioners lay themselves open to a charge of contradiction since elsewhere in the speech they speak of the value of written laws.

61   The Commissioners summarize the conclusion that Isocrates set out, at greater length, in the same section of the *Areopagiticus*, and which was evidently standard fare in speeches on the need for 'arete' and 'paideia'.

62   The Commissioners repeat the phrase that differentiates them from, and implicitly claims superiority to, the rest of the world.

63   The Commissioners point to other real efficiency improvements that had already resulted from the monetization of much of the economy, including a reduction in the amount of working capital needed and in the resulting higher real incomes accruing to an oikos, as was explicitly noted by Aristot. Econ. 1. 1344b. Although not mentioned specifically here, the remarks of the Commissioners form part of the generally accepted long-run narrative of development from brutishness discussed in Chapter 1.

As we look out to Brilessos, that until the days of our grandfathers only supported grazing goats, we see men at work harvesting the gifts of shining marble that the gods have planted in our land.[64] All Hellas has seen the strength and beauty of our Athenian marble at Delphi, and we will sell our surpluses to other cities.[65] Hard, stoney, and difficult to work though our land is, we win prizes in the competitions in the four great festivals. Our winners wet the cloaks of the spectators with our olive oil as they rush among them.[66] [*Shouts of approval*]. Since the time of King Cranaos, son of Cekrops, we Athenians have been the 'men of the rocks'.[67] [*Shouts of approval*].

---

64   The Commissioners use the ancient name for Pentelikon, where the Pentelic marble used in building the Parthenon and other monuments was quarried. So slow was the rate of change in the surface that, in the late nineteenth century, Sir James Frazer was able to describe how, from the Acropolis, the hill looked like a pyramid or a pediment, and how 'through the clear air of Attica the unaided eye ... can distinguish the white line of the ancient quarry.' Frazer, J. G., trans., *Pausanias's Description of Greece* (London: Macmillan, 1898), ii, 418.

65   The Commissioners' prediction was proved true. An undated inscription perhaps as early as the fourth century, but more probably later, reports payments of duties of ten per cent and two per cent to 'Lamachos in Athens' for two consignments of Pentelic marble. Quoted and discussed by Burford, *Temple Builders*, 24. Another inscription records a heavy fine levied on Molossos of Athens for delays in delivering marble from the quarries to the port of Piraeus, among whose implied viewers intended by committing the record to stone, we may guess, were not only those who needed to check on historic precedents but members of the intercity marble trade. Burford, 189. Such details tend to confirm the suggestion by Thucydides that the main driver of change in the pre-classical times, was the freeing of the seas from pirates, as discussed in Chapter 1. The notion of 'beauty' as a general category applied to humans, usually boys and youths, and to inanimate objects that encourages feelings in the viewer, is occasionally found throughout the Hellenic centuries, and occasionally analyzed in works on rhetoric. As it happens, one of the earliest instances is on an inscription relating to the columns of a temple. Porter, James I., *The Origins of Aesthetic Thought in Ancient Greece: Matter, Sensation, and Experience* (Cambridge: CUP, 2010), especially 413–414, where a certain Kleomenes, who may be either the client or the contractor, is recorded in an inscription relating to the sixth-century temple to Apollo at Syracuse as calling the columns 'beautiful', evidently separating them from the temple itself.

66   The Commissioners generalize from Ode 10 by Bacchylides that celebrates multiple victories of an Athenian runner, unfortunately unnamed in the fragments of the Ode first printed in 1897 from a papyrus, but probably known to the audience. The Commissioners follow the rhetorical practice of encouraging crowds to identify with sporting champions as a form of community-building. The picturing of Homeric chariots on the Parthenon and their intended relationship with contemporary commemorative games is explored later when discussing the so-called peplos scene.

67   The Commissioners repeat a common play on the archaic Aeolic word κραναά, which links the eponymous king with the rocky landscape of Attica, repeating a

No enemy in ancient times tried to seize our land by war in hopes of expelling us and resettling our motherland with men of alien kin sent from their mother city, as Athenians do. And unlike other cities, Athens has never gone to war or exacted a sweet revenge except when our cause is just.[68] We Athenians have, as we all learned in childhood, always remained in possession of the land from which we sprang and have been shaped and kept pure by its excellences as if by another mother and another nurse.[69] Our land and our sea, from whom we are born, came to our aid as our kin when Darius in his arrogance

---

trope found, for example, in Herodotus 8. 44 and Strabo 9.1. 'Rocky Athens' is used by Pindar, in *Olympian* 7.82; 9.88; 13. 38; and *Nemean* 8. 4; 8.11; 19. 5 and 49 as a conventional compliment to the city and its victors. The references in Aristophanes, *Acharnians* 75; *Lysistrata,* 482; and *Birds,* 123 refer to the Athenian Acropolis. Many of the references in the ancient authors are collected by Harding, Phillip, editor and translator, *The Story of Athens: The Fragments of the Local Chronicles of Attika* (London: Routledge, 2008), 30–32, https://doi.org/10.4324/9780203448342. Since King Kranaos is said to have been present at the first trial on the Areopagus, he may have been among the figures presented in the packed composition on the west pediment of the Parthenon. And, as usual, as far as the names are concerned, we see a typical ancient attempt to use eponymns to impose a chronological historicity on mythic stories that are allowed to be fluid, depending upon the occasion in which they are deployed. Athena herself is presented as calling the people of Athens 'the children of Kranaus' in Aesch. Eum. 1011, a phrase that may imply in its highly formal context that only those Athenians whose families were accepted as 'autochthonous' are being addressed, an interpretation that might reasonably have been taken by some members of the audience who were thereby consigned, by official deeming ('nomisma'), to a secondary status.

68   The claim is also explicitly made, in fuller and stronger terms, in the Funeral Oration of Demosthenes, Dem. 60 5. The fact of a divergence between what was actually done and how deeds were rhetorically presented is debated between the character of Socrates and Alcibiades in the Platonic dialogue known as Alcibiades 1, in terms that may imply that everyone who heard such sentiments treated them as mere conventional rhetoric for an occasion. Examples of Athenian aggression contrary to Hellenic norms are given by Thucydides, including that of Naxos, but not Melos. While there are many examples, such as in Greece during the military occupation of 1941–1944, when readers were happy to consume what is called 'propaganda' openly presented as such (and we can see the value to certain constituencies of, say, funeral orations, as statements that they can themselves use) it is enough to repeat that we cannot assume that funeral orations cannot be taken as the values of historic Athenians of the classical period, any more than we should assume that they physically resembled the figures presented on the Parthenon frieze.

69   The Commissioners repeat part of the emergence-from-brutishness narrative in the version of Thucydides Thuc. 1.2, as discussed in Chapter 1, that emphasizes the economic purpose of war in what, to him, were ancient times. The Greek word 'arete', used for what is here translated as the 'best' land, was the same as that used for the 'best' men, a reference to geodeterminism and autochthony, not likely to have been lost on the ancient audience.

('hubris') had tasted the bitterness of defeat at immortal Marathon. See [*the reciter assumes a solemn tone usually heard in the theatre or a formal oration*] Amistres and Artaphrenes and Megabates, and Astaspes skilled in archery and horsemanship and Artembares, who fought from his chariot, and Masistres, and noble Imaeus, skilled with the bow, and Pharandaces, and Sosthanes, who urged on his doomed horses, and Susiscanes, and Pegastagon of Egyptian lineage, mighty Arsames, lord of sacred Memphis, and Ariomardus, governor of Egyptian Thebes, and the marsh-dwelling oarsmen. See those who held the cities of our kin in subjection redden our harbour with their noble blood.[70]

Today it becomes our duty to seek the truest causes both of the defeats and of our glorious victories. Your Commissioners had wished, men of Athens, to bring forward Hippocrates of Cos, skilled in the art of healing, as many can testify.[71] He has sent us a written papyrus, part of a longer work, in which he sets out the most modern knowledge on how differences among peoples arise, and especially the differences that have arisen between the Ionians of Athens and those Ionian kinsmen who live overseas in the cities of Asia and the islands. We will not weary you with theogonies that are tiresome to the ear.[72] But, as we all know, just as children owe a debt of mutual gratitude ('charis') to their parents and to their nurses, so too the men of today are bound to render to our fathers the honours which they have earned by their deeds.[73]

---

70   The Commissioners follow the convention that Aeschylus in the *Persians* took from Homer of listing names, emphasizing the variety and asserting that they were worthy opponents. They have, in error, given the list of those who set out, instead of the other list of those who died, which is given later in the play. Like Aeschylus, they refer to the fact that the Persian fleet contained contingents of overseas Ionians and, by implying that they had no choice, enable the cities and island concerned to be reintegrated into the Ionian family, as is made explicit in the play.

71   Since it was common in the law courts for pleaders to bring in live witnesses, it is likely that the same practice occurred at important political meetings, although there is no direct evidence.

72   The Commissioners adopt the explicit advice of Menander Rhetor in his section on 'how to praise cities' in Race, William H., ed., *Menander Rhetor and Dionysius of Halicarnassus, Ars Rhetorica* (Harvard: Harvard UP Loeb editions, 2019), i, 6. Although writing much later, Menander Rhetor is drawing on his knowledge of classical-era as well as of later practice, and of the extent to which it was rhetorically effective. As will emerge in Chapter 3, it was a neglect of genealogy that led to a contradiction in the status of the eponymous Ion as pointed out by Euripides in his play, the *Ion*.

73   The analogy of exchanging 'charis' with ancestors, on the analogy of the mutual obligations between parents and children, is used in the opening of the Panathenaic speech by Aristides. It can be regarded as an ancient Athenian equivalent of an

[*The reciter reads aloud the following deposition that is written and spoken in the Ionic dialect*: 'With regard to the lack of spirit and of courage among the inhabitants, the chief reason why Asiatics are less warlike and more gentle in character than Europeans is the uniformity of the seasons, which show no violent changes either towards heat or towards cold, but are equable. For there occur no mental shocks nor violent physical change, which are more likely to steel the temper and impart to it a fierce passion than is a monotonous sameness. For it is changes of all things that rouse the temper of man and prevent its stagnation. For these reasons, I think, Asiatics are feeble. Their institutions are a contributory cause, the greater part of Asia being governed by kings. Now, where men are not their own masters and independent, but are ruled by despots, they do not seek to be practised in war but on not appearing warlike.'[74]

---

imagined community, as developed by, for example, Benedict Anderson, and discussed in St Clair, *WStP*, Chapter 2, https://doi.org/10.1164/obp.0136.02. The Greek word for one's own young child ('tokos') is the same as that used for the interest payable on a debt denominated in monetary terms, the analogy being an increase in the productive capacity of the 'oikos', with 'children of children' used by Demosthenes to mean compound interest. The word is also used by Xenophon to mean the produce of the land, picking up another piece of rhetoric: that those receiving income from utilizing the land, or employing others to do so, deserve more respect than those whose income derives from trade, manufacture, or from providing financial services such as loans either as capital or as working capital.

74   Hp. Aer. 12. Although the Hippocratic Corpus includes works compiled over several centuries, the *Airs, Waters, Places*, which is written by an author who is well-read and well-travelled, and which reflects attitudes current after the Persian wars, is thought to have been composed in the later half of the fifth century, as is the recent view of Craik, Elizabeth M., *The 'Hippocratic' Corpus: Content and Context* (London: Routledge, 2015), 11, https://doi.org/10.4324/9781315736723. The text contains many other observations relating to the effects of the environment, including diet, different types of drinking water, exposure to the sun, physical exercise, and clothing, that may have influenced policy-making. A particular example, the custom of wrapping babies in tight swaddling bands, which is relevant to my suggestion of what is presented on the central scene of the Parthenon frieze, is noted in Chapter 4. The Commissioners adhere to a form of geodeterminism that pervades the literature of the classical period and was part of the discursive environment, and the advice of Hippocrates rests on assumptions about the four elements discussed in Chapter 1. However, although the apparent continuity of microclimates, including that of Athens and Attica, was used to support rhetorics of continuity in the characters of peoples, and of the stereotyping found, for example, in the Old Comedy, it seems always to have co-existed with rhetorics of the capacity to be changed for the better by paideia, as embodied in the myths of Anacharsis the Scythian, and never to have embraced the essentialism of modern European and American theories and rhetorics of 'race'. There is, for example, no mention of essentialist racial characteristics in the *Characters* of Theophrastus. However, what the Commissioners present as

[*The reciter resumes*] We Athenians have always treated both our Ionian kin and those who have come home to live in our city as our own children whom we love and educate, and who in their turn from their earliest childhood must again learn how to honour the parents who have adopted them.[75] And their minds and dispositions too will be improved as our city, that is their motherland, is restored to health by your wise decisions. The sons of Dorus like to say that they are the bravest of the Hellenes, but the sons of Ion know that we are the cleverest.[76] [*Laughter*].[77]

In the times through which we have lived, the stories of our united city have been damaged and we need to straighten them too.[78] Like the sacred buildings at Delphi built by others that are made from coarse

---

well-attested, received, in modern terms 'common-sense' knowledge, may not have been universally accepted. Theophrastus, for example, professed himself puzzled by 'the great variety to be found among men living under the same sky who have had the same upbringing'. Τί γὰρ δήποτε, τῆς Ἑλλάδος ὑπὸ τὸν αὐτὸν ἀέρα κειμένης καὶ πάντων τῶν Ἑλλήνων ὁμοίως παιδευομένων, συμβέβηκεν ἡμῖν οὐ τὴν αὐτὴν τάξιν τῶν τρόπων ἔχειν. Thphr. Char. 0. In opening his treatise with a question that presented itself to him as an empirical observation, Theophrastus undermines two of the pillars of official Athenian self-fashioning: geodeterminism, and the power of paideia to shape character and therefore conduct. He can, even from the evidence of this one passage, be regarded as among the 'resisting viewers' of the Parthenon, alongside the atheists, the 'cynics', the doubters and those who maintained an outward conformity mainly for the incidental benefits and the comforts of inclusion.

75 The vital importance of starting education at a very young age, for otherwise bad habits will continue throughout adult life, is emphasized by a character in a play by Euripides in fragment 1027. The steps by which the notion of charis (as offered, in, for example, the Periclean Funeral Oration) was extended from relationships among citizens within the polis of Athens to the wider community of the Ionians is discussed with references to ancient and modern authors, including Loraux, by Azoulay, Vincent, *Xenophon and the Graces of Power, A Greek Guide to Political Manipulation* (Swansea: Classical Press of Wales, 2018). Translated by Angela Krieger from the French edition of 2004, 43–44.

76 The Commissioners pick up the exact advice on how to praise a city for its origins, Menander Rhetor, i, 15, 5, and the almost identical advice in [Dionysius of Halicarnassus], *Ars Rhetorica*, in his advice on funeral orations, 6, 2, that appears to have been written at much the same time but independently.

77 The audience was invited to enjoy being complicit in the cliché, especially as they are all aware that the overseas Ionians were a staple of comic stereotyping in the 'old comedy' of Eupolis and Aristophanes for being lazy, addicted to luxury, effeminate, cowardly, sexually deviant, and speaking in funny dialects. The mocking fragments of Eupolis are discussed by Storey, Ian C., *Eupolis Poet of Old Comedy* (Oxford: OUP, 2003), https://doi.org/10.1093/acprof:oso/9780199259922.001.0001; and those in the Aristophanic corpus are collected by Storey, Ian C., *Aristophanes: Peace* (London: Bloomsbury Academic, 2019), http://doi.org/10.5040/9781350020252.

78 The Commissioners may have been influenced by the passage on the early history of Athens in Herodotus 5. 55 to 96, where his attempt to combine stories from myth with reports of contemporary events is hard to follow, and would have been so even

local tufa with a covering of smooth imported Parian marble, they do not persuade our eyes and are easy to destroy.[79] We need no songs that please only for the moment, and that will not bear the bright light of our Attic sun.[80] The clear aether that the gods have given us has always made us able to see the distant horizons by land and sea.[81] The air around enters us through our eyes, our noses, our mouths and other apertures of our bodies, subtly becoming part of the marrow of our bones, like an enchantment.[82] Our superiority in the arts of peace and war we owe to our mother, the land, and to our sky, our winds, and our encircling sea.[83]

---

at the time when Herodotus recited and wrote. The accounts by Thucydides and his suggested explanations, although patchy and disputable, are clearly presented.

79   The Commissioners refer to the description of a temple in Delphi in Hdt. 5.62.1, of which fragments that confirm the description were found in excavations. Although the association the Commissioners make is not specifically recorded in any known source, it is in line with what is known to have happened both with the building programme and with the general discursive environment that makes frequent use of metaphors from the building industry.

80   The Commissioners again follow the Periclean Funeral Oration, running together the two thoughts, first that building memory and ideology in physical form is more durable than words and performance, and secondly, that even Homer cannot be trusted as a chronicler of the past. That the Athenians played a larger role in the war against Troy than that presented in the Homeric epics is implied in the Prologue, uttered by the character of Poseidon in Euripides's tragedy, the *Trojan Women*, Eur. Tro. 31, but, in the context of that drama, mainly so that the Athenians become entitled to a larger share of the captured women, and questions relating to the treatment of enslaved women and refugees, a theme of several surviving plays, are discussed later in the speech in the passage beginning 'We Athenians will always…' They have adopted the geodeterminist trope of clear air leading to clear thinking, partly, we may guess, to avoid the blunt statement attributed to Pericles that Homer and poets do not tell the 'truth'. At this stage the Commissioners are at risk of exposing their own contradiction that they want to build an Acropolis in order to achieve certain rhetorical effects on viewers and users while, as is usual in rhetoric, disowning rhetoric as such.

81   Euripides, *Medea*, 825. ἀεί διὰ λαμπροτάτου βαίνοντες ἁβρῶς αἰθέρος. The remark paves the way for the geodeterminism that follows.

82   This explanation of how geodeterminism worked in practice was offered by a character in the *Aethiopica* of Heliodorus, III, 7.3. He also mentions the possibility of malignancy and ophthalmia, a common illness in Greece even now from the sand particles that blow in from the Sahara, and an occupational hazard for marble workers, and especially the men who polished the surfaces of the Parthenon and other buildings with emery, as was understood at the time and will be discussed in Chapter 4.

83   The Commissioners remind the audience of the geodeterminism that, taken with kinship, is among the central arguments by which they justify their proposals to take a long view of the future. The claim that Attica was geographically equivalent to an island is almost a standard and enduring component of the discursive environment,

It will next be judged useful to remind ourselves of the choices with which the city is confronted. And just as in a trial of criminals and traitors, in which many of you have been jurymen, those who have not been fully informed cannot give the right verdict, so too in matters of policy, the city requires its lawgivers to understand the situation in its entirety.[84] We have therefore decided to begin by setting forth the argument ['logos'], for if we had neglected to make this clear, our speech would appear to many as curious and strange.[85]

In our walks outside the walls, we saw the dutiful storks who arrived here, as they do every spring, twenty-two days after our Flower Festival ('Antherstia') [7 March] which our slaves celebrate with us. Some say that it is our slaves, who do not benefit much from other festivals, who like them most, having few other pleasures in their daily lives.[86] The storks have been faithfully repairing and rebuilding their nests, feeding their young, caring for their old, bathing the wounds of their injured kin in health-giving herbs, and sharing with us the benefits of living close to us in our houses.[87] Our citizens too follow the unceasing 'charis' of parents to children and of children to parents, in which the storks have reached the perfection of their nature. [*The reciter points to the nests that are always in sight even when the storks themselves have left for the winter*].[88]

---

being set out explicitly in, for example, Xenophon, *Ways and Means*, and in Aelius Aristides.

84 The speakers, in a typical binary of the kind that the ancient writers loved, pick up and labour a commonplace of the courts, as deployed by, for example, Lycurgus in his speech against Leocrates, Lyc.1. 13.

85 Almost a direct quotation from the Panathenaic speech of Isocrates in which, to our mind laboriously, but in Athenian terms respectfully, defends making a small change from what the audience might have expected, Isoc. 15.1.

86 Aristot. Econ. 1.1344b.

87 The many references in ancient authors to the regular lives of the storks, among which all the examples are noted, are collected in Arnott, W. Geoffrey, *Birds in the Ancient World from A to Z* (London: Routledge, 2007), 138–169, https://doi. org/10.4324/9780203946626. They are not examples of popular 'folklore' but the science of the day as collected, notably, by Aristotle and his school. The adoption of the ideas by Aristophanes in the *Birds* parodies the laws of Solon that insisted on intergenerational responsibility.

88 The Commissioners refer to the stories about the intergenerational reciprocal duties of storks celebrated by the character of Socrates in Plato's *Alcibiades*, and noted in Chapter 1, as examples of the emergence from brutishness narrative, and of the usefulness of cooperation with humans. We may also see a reference to the Parthenon frieze that, as will be discussed in Chapter 3, celebrates the role of women, and their role in the oikos in the imagined community of the polis, as discussed by Fehr, Burkhard, *Becoming Good Democrats and Wives: Civil Education*

Our daughters are as dutiful as the birds. [*Noises of approval*].[89] As we look up to the heavens through our matchlessly clear Athenian aether, we see the stars and the planets circling as in a dance, as our Ionian philosophers have explained.[90] And we all recognize those who are feigning as easily as if they have a bell round their necks.[91] When we hear the cries of the cranes ['geranoi'] overhead, we know it is time

---

and Female Socialization on the Parthenon Frieze. Hephaistos Sonderband. Kritische Zeitschrift zu Theorie und Praxis der Archäologie und angrenzender Gebiete (Berlin, Münster, Vienna, Zürich, London: Lit Verlag, 2011).

89 The storks, cranes, and some other waterbirds are commended as practising the womanly reciprocal duties ('charites') in the household. Such birds are pictured as companions of young women on vase painting, often regarded by modern viewers simply as pets. The example pictured in Fehr, *Good Democrats and Wives*, Fig. 87, a red-figure hydria *c.* 470, now in the Houston Museum of Fine Arts, 80.95, shows such a bird as almost a participant or monitor in a scene of women placing wool in a basket and performing other household tasks. An image of what may be a crane is shown with female dancers in Osborne, Robin, *The Transformation of Athens: Painted Pottery and the Creation of Classical Greece* (Princeton: Princeton UP, 2018), plate 6.13, from a red figure hydra in Copenhagen. An anecdote from a time before the catastrophic reduction in biodiversity of the last century illustrates how an ancient viewer, such as Aristotle, might have thought that his understanding was empirically observable. In 1828, Colonel Miller, sailing back from his philanthropic work in Greece, noted that: 'At ten o'clock, a young crane fell upon our deck. How or in what manner it reached the ship, still remains a mystery to all of us, unless it had been borne upon the back of another; it could not have flown the distance, being as yet unfledged'. Miller, Col. Jonathan P., of Vermont, *The condition of Greece, in 1827 and 1828; being an exposition of the poverty, distress, and misery, to which the inhabitants have been reduced by the destruction of their towns and villages and the ravages of their country, by a merciless Turkish foe ... As contained in his journal, kept by order of the Executive Greek Committee of the city of New-York; commencing with his departure from that place in the ship Chancellor, March, 1827, and terminating with his return in May, 1828; during which time he visited Greece, and acted as principal agent in the distribution of the several cargoes of clothing and provisions sent from the United States to the old men, women, children, and non-combatants of Greece; Embellished with plates* (New York: Harper, 1828), 29.

90 The Commissioners claim for Athens the intellectual achievements of the many philosophers now known as pre-Socratics, many of whom came from the cities of Ionia, of whose written works only fragments have survived, but whose ideas are referred to by later writers.

91 The Commissioners turn to what was probably an old saying about shaming and goat bells quoted by Demosthenes in referring to jurors in the law courts. Dem. 25.90. The passage goes on to describe the shaming power of the mutual gaze. To a modern eye, many of the images of festival goers found on vase paintings show them exaggerating their gestures of being transported into an emotional frenzy. The festival goers presented on the Parthenon frieze, being pictured as exemplars from the mythic world, show no vulgar histrionics.

to plough our land and to prepare for the winter rains.[92] Some say the birds learned their extraordinary dance from seeing us dancing our own geranos.[93] As we watch them fly over our land and sea, we see them formed into squadrons with the leader changing frequently, as in our democracy, but always maintaining their allotted place in the ranks.[94]

All who live here obey all the laws and customs, not only the ancient and the unwritten, but the newly enacted, that keep our city pure.[95] Men are fitted by their nature to govern the polis, and women the household ('oikos').[96] We will celebrate the tasks performed by our pure Athenian women, the best in all Hellas, and especially their faithfulness in performing their duty to produce useful Athenians.[97] For, as we all know, for human beings ('anthropoi' ungendered), as for all other animals and living plants, it is only when the first shoots are cultivated

---

92 The Commissioners pick up a point common since at least the eighth century when Hesiod wrote the phrase in *Works and Days*, passage beginning at line 448, that, because of the status of Hesiod, fixed it in the discursive environment for hundreds of years.

93 Arnott, *Birds in the Ancient World*, 52–54.

94 As modern wild-life studies have shown, the long V-shaped formations of migrating cranes, with the birds taking turns to be leader, conserves the energy of the whole flock by enabling it to maximize the benefits of the slipstream. In recent years, under the protection of laws agreed at regional level and wider, numerous species of birds, which once were plentiful and then were almost extinct in Athens, now winter in small numbers in the partial wilderness of the Acropolis slopes, as is noted on labels now displayed there that helpfully extend the visitor's understanding of the classical Acropolis and of the prevalence of bird metaphors.

95 As Burkhard Fehr has plausibly suggested, given that the two-parent Periclean decree of 451/50 was being considered and carried into effect at the same time and by the members of the same civic institutions as were considering the proposals for the rebuilding of the Parthenon, there is nothing surprising in finding that viewers of the Parthenon were reminded of what Fehr calls 'the importance of the Athenian extraction of Athenian [male] citizens on the maternal side, as prescribed by the citizenship law'. Fehr, *Good Democrats and Wives*, 143–144. The 'customs' referred to by the Commissioners include the practices by which legitimacy of birth is established, including the rejection of the unwanted by, for example, being abandoned and exposed to die. To be discussed in Chapter 3, drawing on the evidence of the *Ion* of Euripides and archaeological evidence.

96 That women had been disenfranchised was part of the earliest account of what was presented on the Parthenon, as discussed in Chapter 3.

97 In Athens, there is no word for 'Athenianness' although that linguistic formation was applied to women of other cities, a reminder that women, although allotted specific roles in the oikos, including the education of young children in civic, gendered, arete, were not citizens participating in the institutions of the polis.

properly that they develop towards their full potential of excellence.[98] Euripides, son of Mnesarchus, tells us that he would rather fight in three battles than give birth to even one child. [*Laughter*]. And it is easy for him to set himself up as your adviser for he knows nothing about either. [*Approving laughter, and a shout of 'neither do you'*].[99] We offer a sketch of how what we all desire might be pictured. [*The reciter passes round an outline as in Figure 2.1*].

---

98 The Commissioners offer the same thought, which is implicit in the brutishness narrative, as is set out extensively by the character of the man of Athens in Plato's *Laws*, especially παντὸς γὰρ δὴ φυτοῦ ἡ πρώτη βλάστη καλῶς ὁρμηθεῖσα, πρὸς ἀρετὴν τῆς αὐτοῦ φύσεως κυριωτάτη τέλος ἐπιθεῖναι τὸ πρόσφορον, τῶν τε ἄλλων φυτῶν καὶ τῶν ζῴων ἡμέρων Plat. Laws 6.765e. The Commissioners do not explicitly warn against the corollary that the character of the Athenian made explicit and whose validity appeared to be validated by occurrences during the Peloponnesian War, that, if paideia was not regularly applied right through life, men, like other creatures, could revert, a point picked up in the rhetorical exercise in Chapter 5.

99 The Commissioners repeat the general ideology that women exist to serve men, and even that childbirth is a matter in which the male contribution is determinative, to be found in the classical-era authors. Such information as survives about the life of Euripides and the stories told about him, collected in the edition of Euripides edited and translated by David Kovacs, include the sneer that, unlike Aeschylus and Sophocles, he had not experienced war, and that, as a form of put-down, his mother was a seller of vegetables. The main allusion is however to the speech put into the mouth of the character of Medea in Euripides's play of that name. Although first publicly performed in 431, striking thoughts in the play may have been known before then, as Euripides took his proposal through the stages of acceptance to be performed in the Festival and to obtain funding from private donors as part of their duty as 'charis'. Alternatively, we may have an example of the composer or editor of a Thucydidean speech showing some knowledge of the future, as Thucydides himself does occasionally. The remark, in the *Medea*, line 251, ὡς τρὶς ἂν παρ' ἀσπίδα στῆναι θέλοιμ' ἂν μᾶλλον ἢ τεκεῖν ἅπαξ, was later to become a ‹chreia' again attributed to Euripides, not to a character in a fictional work by Euripides, as in the work by Lucian known as *The Cock* where a slightly different version is quoted by the character of Mykillus: 'ἀλλὰ κἂν σὺ μὴ εἴπῃς, ἱκανῶς ὁ Εὐριπίδης διέκρινε τὸ τοιοῦτον, εἰπὼν ὡς τρὶς ἂν ἐθέλοι παρ' ἀσπίδα στῆναι ἢ ἅπαξ τεκεῖν. Luc. Gall. 19.

Figure 2.1. 'The stages of womanhood'. Engraving from a painted vase in Naples.[100]

---

100 Reinach, Salomon, *Peintures de vases antiques recueillies par Millin, 1808, et Millingen, 1813. Publiées et commentées par S. Reinach* (Paris: Firmin-Didot, 1891), unnumbered. From a painted vase in Naples. The stages appear to be, from right to left, as the vase might have been rotated when it was handled by its ancient owner, unmarried ('parthenos'), marriage ceremony, and motherhood. As for birds, none have been noticed pictured within the stories presented on the Parthenon for which there is evidence, but an image of a bird looking much like that shown in the Figure, shown as tending its nest in a tree, was carved in low relief on the fifth-century Asclepieion on the south slope. Noted by Mantis, Alexandros, Archaeologist of the 1st Ephorate of Prehistoric and Classical Antiquities, *Disjecta Membra. The Plunder and Dispersion of the Antiquities of the Acropolis, translated by Miriam Caskey* (Athens: Anthemion, 2000), figure 8a, in the Museo Civico in Padua. As the ages of woman ['bildung'] narrative implied by the Figure exemplifies, although women and children are honoured in all classical-era media, including the literary, the time gap between the change of a young woman's status brought about by the ceremony of marriage and the next change brought about by the ceremony of acceptance into the family of a healthy and legitimately conceived child is an interlude that is ignored. Of the tens of thousands of images painted on pottery to have survived, none has been found that shows a woman who is pregnant or in the immediate circumstances of giving birth. Lewis, Sian, *The Athenian Woman: An Iconographic Handbook* (London: Routledge, 2002), 13 and 15, https://doi.org/10.4324/9780203351192. Lewis's estimates, including on the preponderance of images relating to funerals and their rites, were given in St Clair, *WStP*, Chapter 4, https://doi.org/10.1164/obp.0136.04. It was a joke, derived from a comedy by 'Plato Comicus', that even the neighbours, who lived in flimsy houses, scarcely knew what was happening next door. Plat. Alc. 1 121d. It appears from the same passage that it was in these earliest days of life that the swaddling bands, to be discussed later in this chapter, were applied to the hapless infant. The large water bird in the image is another identity marker. Credited by Plato and Aristotle with having their own specific culture, such birds,

When we show mortals, we will not pick out the strongest or the fastest but show those that hold the mean position between opposites.[101] And only those, whether male or female, who lead blameless lives such as fit them to be guests at the ceremonies of marriage and acceptance of children will be pictured.[102]

In the mornings and in evenings of the springtime, we hear the laments of the nightingales, always remembering, always returning, never conquered by the sharp-eyed hawks. Some say that women who have been wronged by their families are transformed into nightingales so that they will never be forgotten and in due time will enjoy a sweet

---

storks, cranes, herons and others, are frequently found alongside images of young women. For example, Osborne, *Transformation*, plate 27, and 6.13, red-figure hydria from Athens, National Museum of Denmark 7359; Fehr, *Good Democrats and Wives*, fig. 87 at page 109, shows part of a red-figure hydria, unprovenanced. Another such bird is shown in the image of young women learning the arts of Athenian civilization practised at festivals reproduced on the cover of this book. Other examples are shown in Lewis, 21 and 26. A white-ground lekythos, a type of vessel used in the commemoration of the dead, whose manufacture is dated on stylistic grounds to *c.* 490, from a collection purchased in 1901, in the Hermitage Museum, St Petersburg, reproduced in Kaltsas, Nikolaos and Shapiro, Alan, eds, *Worshipping Women: Ritual and Reality in Classical Athens* (New York: Onassis Foundation, and Athens: Hellenic Ministry of Culture and National Archaeological Museum, 2008), no 36, shows a mythic crowned figure, with the attributes of Artemis, apparently feeding a swan and who is wearing the Athenian marker of snake bracelets on both wrists. It is mentioned in Chapter 3, where the significance of that marker, and its possible relevance to understanding the central scene of the Parthenon frieze are discussed.

101 The Commissioners pick up a point about the desirability of showing uniformity so as to reduce the temptations to rivalry made by the character of the Athenian in Plato's *Laws*. τίμιον εἶναι σῶμα οὐ τὸ καλὸν οὐδὲ ἰσχυρὸν οὐδὲ τάχος ἔχον οὐδὲ μέγα, οὐδέ γε τὸ ὑγιεινόν—καίτοι πολλοῖς ἂν τοῦτό γε δοκοῖ—καὶ μὴν οὐδὲ τὰ τούτων γ᾽ ἐναντία, τὰ δ᾽ ἐν τῷ μέσῳ ἁπάσης ταύτης τῆς ἕξεως ἐφαπτόμενα σωφρονέστατα ἅμα τε ἀσφαλέστατα εἶναι μακρῷ. Plat. Laws 5.728.

102 Following thoughts set out in the section of Plato's *Laws* that deals with the differences between desirable ('useful') Athenians and those who have committed irregularities, the Commissioners pick out the penalties of being excluded from the two most significant rites of passage. μήτε γὰρ εἰς γάμους ἴτω μήτε εἰς τὰς τῶν παίδων ἐπιτελειώσεις. Plat. Laws 6.784. In the same passage where the two penalties are mentioned again, the character of the Athenian adds that any man who tries to break the convention can be struck and expelled. In the *Laws*, the author does seem to be offering his own ideas, and the work contains little that is intellectually dialogic except in form—so it is fair to say that Plato envisages a corps of oikos inspectors who would check on whether young couples were performing their civic duty to have frequent sexual encounters in accordance with a strict and detailed code. At least some of the passage is relevant to my proposed new answer to the old question of what is the event pictured as a contribution to paideia on the Parthenon frieze, to be discussed in Chapter 4.

revenge.[103] But, on our walks, we also see the shameless and greedy kites whose arrival tells us that it is time to shear our sheep, but who snatch meat from the divine altars and the market stalls, who gobble the eggs and chicks of the other birds, and who even pick at our clothes for scraps to line their nests.[104] Among the cities of the birds the kites are the Achaeans, but we are the storks.[105] Our city is for Athenians, but it is also for our kin and our friends, always as welcoming as Delphi, Olympia, and Delos, as our birds, our birdcatchers, and our flocks of fatherless and cityless urchins know.[106]

---

103 The Commissioners, who at this point change to a coopting enargeia of the present tense, draw on a tradition stretching back to Homer that includes not only the *Oedipus at Colonos* by Sophocles but his *Tereus*, of which substantial fragments have survived. The numerous references from classical authors are collected by Suksi, Aara, 'The Poet at Colonus: Nightingales in Sophocles' in *Mnemosyne*, Vol. 54 (6) (2001), 646–658, https://doi.org/10.1163/15685250152952121, to which may be added Eur. Hec 337. The nightingales remind us too that in classical Athens the calendar date changed in the middle of the day, not during the night, but that many festivals occurred, at least in part, during the hours of morning and evening when the changing light of the unique natural environment was at its most colourful, most mutable, and most dramatic, and at night when the moon threw its own shadows.

104 Sophocles, unassigned fragment 767. In the *Birds* of Aristophanes, line 890, in a political parody of the way in which a new city [such as post-480 Athens] is invented, instituted with festivals, and named and governed by powerful men in their own interest, the character of Pisthetaerus, protesting at the suggestion that all the species of birds should be invited to the sacred feast that they are founding as part of city-building, remarks that a single kite could carry off everything. There are many other references in Arnott, *Birds in the Ancient* World, 76–78. The Commissioners, like Aristophanes, use the well-known rhetorical device of speaking in analogies as a way of avoiding criticizing their fellow citizens directly.

105 The Commissioners make a bold poetic claim based on the assumption that animals are also on a development path from individualism ('brutishness') to civilized cooperation, and repeat the thought in the version by Thucydides that western Greece was the least civilized region.

106 The implied comparison with pan-hellenic sacred sites where the local ecology was also influenced by the abundance of food for birds and other creatures, a consequence of the frequency of the festivals, is implied by the character of Ion in Euripides's play of that name, in which, when he is at Delphi, he shouts at the flocking birds to go instead to Delos, Olympia, or Nemea, all sites where festivals were frequent. Eur. Ion 167; 175–176. As an orphan, the young Ion had subsisted on scraps left over from the festivals. That Delphi was 'loved by birds' was also noted by Aeschylus. Aesch. Eum. 23. As the occasional references to bird catchers round the Acropolis suggest, although some species of birds appear to have been formally protected, others were killed and eaten. If the Commissioners appear to be insensitive to the plight of orphans who are without kin or city, that may be a fair inference, although they go on to suggest a humane policy towards refugees.

Our famous hills and places show us our democracy at work.[107] We are struck with awe as we look at the plain where Theseus saved the city from the bare-bosomed archers. Our eyes fill with tears when they meet the armour-makers on the nightingaled hill from where the child of the blind king of Thebes caught her first sight of our welcoming walls.[108] [*Here the reciter gestures to the Hill of Colonos*] Oh how unfortunate was that mortal family when it was deserted by Tyche.[109]

So how, we now ask you to consider, can we best restore the ancient customs of our city? How can we cure its many illnesses?[110] How do we help our friends and harm our enemies?[111] How can we again be sure that our women again know that the best service they make to our city is to see that the household (oikos') is well run, to look after the property

---

107 The Commissioners refer to the Areopagus and the Pnyx and the other 'famous hills'.

108 The Commissioners are pleasing and co-opting the audience by presuming that they would recognize the allusions to the Amazons who were defeated near the Areopagus Hill and to Oedipus at the Hill of Colonos. Sophocles, who came from a family of armour-makers whose workshop was at Colonos, was born there. By their allusions, the Commissioners sidle up to two points found in the civic rhetoric of the time, already discussed, namely that Athens had never been successfully invaded in mythic times, as in the *Medea* of Euripides, and that Athens was welcoming to foreigners and refugees, as in the Periclean Funeral Oration, a point returned to later in the speech when the Commissioners discuss the stories to be presented on the Parthenon.

109 The Commissioners imitate one of the conventions of the chorus in the tragic drama of saying the obvious in case some members of the audience may not have followed the allusions and the argument.

110 The misleading comparison that would-be political influencers make between their ideologically-driven rhetoric and a medical doctor using his specialist knowledge and experience to prescribe ways of curing sicknesses of the human body was used and developed by the character of Socrates in Plato's *Crito*. In the *Alcibiades*, the character of Socrates, in partial contrast, points out that his aristocratic education in 'writing and harping and wrestling' was of little value in fitting him to be a political leader. A related point is made by the author of the rhetorical discourse offered in Chapter 5.

111 The Commissioners adopt the opinion of the character of Polemarchus, one of the three mainstream views of what constitutes justice that the character of Socrates sets as his agenda to be challenged in Plato's *Republic*. The others are Cephalus, who defines justice as giving what is owed, and Thrasymachus who takes the view that justice is the interest of the stronger. That the view of Polemarchus was not that of a straw man invented for the purpose of the dialogue but was widely shared is shown by the fuller version offered by the fourth-century philosopher Alcidamas, noted in Muir, J. V., ed., *Alcidamas, The Works and Fragment* (London: Bristol Classical Press, 2001), 81. The opinion is also attributed to the rich and overbearing Meno who is said to have learned it from Gorgias by the character of Socrates in Plato's *Meno*, Plat. Meno 71d.

indoors, and to obey their husbands.[112] How can we strengthen all the duties of kinship.[113]

During the troubled times our city never ceased to pay due honours to the gods. While the danger persisted, we preserved and repaired as much as we could of our beloved city.[114] We repaired our walls and many of the sacred buildings knocked down and burned by the barbarians, and we maintained our ancestral customs and ceremonies.[115] It is the

---

112 The opinion is also attributed to the character of Meno in Plato's *Meno* Plat. Meno 71d. The suggestion that much of the Parthenon frieze displays the feminine sphere is discussed in Chapter 4.

113 I use the phrase 'on account of our kinship with' to convey the sense of κατὰ τὸ ξυγγενὲς as used by Thucydides in Book 1, Chapter 6, to include pan-Ionianism and the mutual obligations it entailed. This was a key feature of Athenian self-fashioning in the classical period, evidenced by many examples that emerge from the experiment, and is likely to have influenced the minds of those who commissioned the Parthenon, as will be suggested as an explanation for the central event pictured on the frieze in Chapter 4. Besides references in the main narrative, Thucydides has the speakers in six Thucydidean speeches invoke the bonds and obligations of their shared kinship or 'genos'. Thuc. 1.95.1; 1.71.4; 5.104; 6.6.2; 3.86.3; 6.44.3. Noted by Alty, John, 'Dorians and Ionians, in *The Journal of Hellenic Studies*, Vol. 102 (1982), 4, fn20, https://doi.org/10.2307/631122. And although, on occasion, Thucydides may have appeared to disdain the truth value of old myths and eponyms, he also gave his personal view, as an experienced military general, that in Sicily, the Athenians, as Ionians, went willingly to fight the Syracusans who were Dorians, a neat example of the general point that what people can be persuaded is true can improve their performance even in war. Thuc. 7. 57.

114 Described by Miles, Margaret M., 'Burnt temples in the landscape of the past', in Ker, James and Pieper, Christoph, *Valuing the Past in the Greco-Roman World: Proceedings from the Penn-Leiden Colloquia on Ancient Values VII* (Leiden, Boston: Brill, c 2014), 111—145, https://doi.org/10.1163/9789004274952_006. The Commissioners may be referring to the so-called Seated Athena that still survives, which asserted the Athenian claim that Endoios the sculptor had learned his craft from the mythic Daidalos, but even at the time of Pausanias, 'ancient statues' were to be seen.

115 In a recent book, Sarah A. Rous suggests that the Athenian authorities deliberately kept some material remains of the Acropolis that was sacked by the Persians, including the row of column drums from the pre-Parthenon shown in, for example Figure 24.17, Volume 1, as acts of what she calls 'upcycling', defined as 'an act of self-conscious re-use that involves attention not only to the materiality of the object but also to the visibility of the prior life of the object and of the act of re-use itself'. Rous, Sarah A., *Reset in Stone: Memory and Reuse in Ancient Athens* (Madison: University of Wisconsin Press, 2019), 6. The notion, which is a useful one and of which there are numerous modern examples, can help to explain the mutilation as well as the preservation of some objects, of which I offer an example from the Parthenon in Chapter 4. The use of the unused column drums in the hurried rebuilding of the walls, we can be confident, required a deliberate decision, but in this case, since meanings can later be attributed to 'upcycled' remains that were not present at the time of an emergency, the question of intention is, I suggest, more open. The earliest non-speculative relevant piece of evidence is in a remark of Isocrates, who in 380,

nature of our Attic olive trees to live well not only when the air is hot and when it is cold, but in the rain that wets and in the sun that dries.[116] And, as we all know, nature does nothing in vain.[117] As with our dogs, so with our trees, it takes time for them to become tame and give us their benefits, but even when they are forced to revert to their wild state, they return willingly to our households. When they are wounded, the gaps close.[118] If our enemies cut them down, they bring forth new shoots. Like our city, the trees renew themselves as one generation follows another as they have always done. Their fruit, each in its shield, that give us oil for cooking our meat, fuel for our lamps, and relish for our bread, bring to our blessed land the alien fruits that are, by nature, unsuited to our land.[119] It is not only our stinging and biting insects that our famous oil drives away but any enemy who sees our shining bodies [*laughter*].[120] The trees that spring from our land are the greatest of the gifts that Athena has conferred on the city that has taken her name, and we will

---

towards the end of the classical era as conventionally dated, suggested that the [overseas] Ionians left their temples un-rebuilt as a memorial to the impiety of their enemies, adding the forward-looking consideration, that those who saw the ruins would distrust those who broke the Hellenic convention of 'making war not only on our bodies but on our dedications' ἀλλὰ καὶ φυλάττωνται καὶ δεδίωσιν, ὁρῶντες αὐτοὺς οὐ μόνον τοῖς σώμασιν ἡμῶν ἀλλὰ καὶ τοῖς ἀναθήμασι πολεμήσαντας. Isoc. 4 156. To modern ears, the second reason strikes an anticlimactic note, but it can be regarded as an example of the strangeness of the public discourse as it applied to war and the sacking of cities, to be discussed later in the chapter.

116 As usual in the classical era, by 'natural' the Commissioners mean fit for purpose.

117 The examples in this passage are mainly taken from Book 5 in the work of Theophrastus commonly known as 'On the causes of plants' but that, in the Greek, also implies origins, which discusses the cultivation of olive trees. The parallel with domestic dogs is in *De Causis* 3.6. As usual in the classical period, both Theophrastus and the Commissioners regard 'nature' as fulfilling a purpose.

118 An illustration of the regeneration that occurred after the Greek Revolution was given as Figure 14.3, Volume 1. At Melos, which had suffered severely during the war, it was reported in 1838 by one of the many travellers obliged to spend time there, that grafting the local olive trees with cuttings improved both the rate of growth and the yield. Garston, Edgar, *Greece Revisited and Sketches in Lower Egypt in 1840, with Thirty-Six Hours of a Campaign in Greece in 1825* (London: Saunders and Ottley, 1842), i, 203. The claim by the Athenians of the classical era that they had discovered the benefits of grafting, and their celebration of the olive tree as the source of their prosperity on the west pediment of the Parthenon, is discussed in Chapters 1, 2, and 3.

119 A point made in the Funeral Oration as put by Thucydides into the mouth of Pericles.

120 The Commissioners repeat the one of the claims made by the Chorus in the *Oedipus at Colonus* of Sophocles, with the suggested explanation by Aristotle, quoted in Chapter 1.

never cease to return her charis in word and in deed.[121] And now is the time, men of Athens, for our city to yield new fruits of 'arete'.[122]

Even those philosophers who wish to undermine the ancestral wisdom of our city are united in their belief that civic morality ('arete') can be taught, and that the first step towards learning the good is to unlearn the bad.[123] Our young men are not like the stamped gold valuables that we keep in our acropolis, ready to be brought into use when needed, their nature unchanged.[124] Some of you keep your slaves fettered to stop them running away.[125] But other slaves have been so successfully educated into our Athenian laws and customs, written and unwritten, that they are trusted with our most precious possessions, and some take a part in the education of our children.

The time has come, the Assembly has already decided, to rebuild our city to make it fit not just for today and tomorrow but for all time.[126] The

---

121 The Commissioners refer to the story presented on the west pediment of the Parthenon to be discussed in Chapter 3.

122 That the domestication of trees was much like the domestication of animals, as indeed it is, is implied by the story that Orpheus could do both just by his music, which was recounted by Clement of Alexandria at the beginning of his *Protrepticus*. θηρία γυμνῇ τῇ ᾠδῇ καὶ δὴ τὰ δένδρα, τὰς φηγούς, μετεφύτευε τῇ μουσικῇ. In this context I prefer the interpretation that he could change the nature of trees to the usual meaning of the word that he could transplant them.

123 The Commissioners, reluctant to name those who were dismissively called 'Cynics' who were noted for their robust challenging of mainstream ideologies, draw credibility from the works of Antisthenes, now lost apart from fragments and reports, in this case items 87A, 87B and 87C in Price, Susan, ed., *Antisthenes of Athens: Texts, Translations, and Commentary* (Ann Arbor: University of Michigan Press, 2015), 312–313, https://doi.org/10.3998/mpub.5730060.

124 The Commissioners repeat the remarks of the character of Socrates in the *Meno* of Plato, Plat. Meno 89b, which gives another example of the utilitarian refrain of 'usefulness' noted in the quotation from *The Children of Heracles* by Euripides on the title page of the *Areopagitica* of Milton where the Greek word is used twice, as discussed in St Clair, *WStP*, Chapter 22, https://doi.org/10.1164/obp.0136.22. Like the character of Socrates in the *Meno*, the Commissioners appreciate the distinction between 'money' and real resources, and the modern distinction between fixed, i.e. material, resources and human resources that are not all the same, and neatly set the foundation for the need for paideia. Σωκράτης καὶ γὰρ ἄν που καὶ τόδ' ἦν: εἰ φύσει οἱ ἀγαθοὶ ἐγίγνοντο, ἦσάν που ἂν ἡμῖν οἳ ἐγίγνωσκον τῶν νέων τοὺς ἀγαθοὺς τὰς φύσεις, οὓς ἡμεῖς ἂν παραλαβόντες ἐκείνων ἀποφηνάντων ἐφυλάττομεν ἂν ἐν ἀκροπόλει, κατασημηνάμενοι πολὺ μᾶλλον ἢ τὸ χρυσίον, ἵνα μηδεὶς αὐτοὺς διέφθειρεν, ἀλλ' ἐπειδὴ ἀφίκοιντο εἰς τὴν ἡλικίαν, χρήσιμοι γίγνοιντο ταῖς πόλεσι. What 'useful things' consisted of was discussed in Chapter 1.

125 Xen. Ec. 3.

126 Unfortunately, the speech does not help to answer the much-debated question of whether there really was an 'oath of Plataea' under whose terms the Hellenic

tyrants, who only sought their own glory, were untrue to our ancient customs, and their sons, who accompanied the barbarous and cowardly Asiatics, will always be condemned as traitors by all right-thinking Athenians.[127] We Athenians will continue pull down the images set up by other cities in their holy places as we have always done since we punished the cursed city of Troy, but never again will any enemy be able to do the same to us.[128] We will ensure that any invader of our land, whether barbarian or Hellene, who looks at our Acropolis will know that he can never capture our holy places, and that he can never destroy or remove our idols, our memorials, or our tombs.[129] They cannot take away what is most precious to us, our nature as Athenians.[130] And we will always be able to guard and to keep safe the knowledge of who we

---

cities that had been desolated by the Persians agreed to postpone rebuilding for thirty years, or if it was a fourth-century rhetorical invention. Discussed by Kousser, *Afterlives*, 101.

127 The Commissioners acknowledge, without naming them, that Peisistratus and his sons undertook many building works that benefitted the city but that these works did not save it when the Persians invaded, with the Peisistratids among their local allies. They have come to the same conclusion as Boersma, who, in his 1970 study of the building works, concluded that: 'the buildings constructed by Peisistratus were modest and functional; they were intended to benefit his own generation and not posterity'. Boersma, John S., *Athenian Building Policy from 561/0 to 405/4 B.C.* (Groningen: Wolters-Noordhoff, 1970), 18. In translating the Greek word, eidolon, as 'idol', I do not imply that the Commissioners were being derogatory.

128 The Commissioners allude to the episode in the Athenian war against Aegina, when, as recounted by Herodotus, Hdt, 5.85, in an attempt to draw the Aeginetans into a sea battle, the Athenians tried to pull down the images with ropes, only for them to break. Herodotus adds that he does not believe the story that the images fell upon their knees and that they could still be seen in that position. The general point that large images were protected by their size was made in a memorable phrase by Cicero quoted in Chapter 5. Earlier the Athenians had sacked the city of Sardis, in the territory of the Great King, and the expeditions of 490 and 480/479 were, to an extent, likely to have been acts of revenge and precautions against a repetition— although all accounts are filtered through Greek authors.

129 The Commissioners use the Greek word for visual image (εἴδωλον) that does not carry the negative connotations later attached to 'idol' by others. They also allude to the role of the Parthenon as a secure storage facility, impervious even to fire, to be discussed in Chapter 3. In describing the duties of the official who had responsibility for the keys of the buildings in which the city's valuables were held, the Aristotelian *Ath Pol* couples the physical assets and the written records as complementary, not as opposed. οὗτος τάς τε κλεῖς τὰς τῶν ἱερῶν, ἐν οἷς τὰ χρήματ' ἐστὶν καὶ τὰ γράμματα τῇ πόλει, Aristot. Const. Ath. 44.1.

130 That the Thebans, whose role in the Persian wars was condemned by most other Greek cities as shameful, might decide, if they were given a chance, to remove the monuments in the built storyscape, and discontinue the associated ceremonial acts of commemoration, so changing the future narrative and threatening their

are and what we hold in common with the best men and women of our past, on which the future well-being of our city depends.[131]

With our excellence in the arts of writing, in which our children are becoming ever more skilled, our city need no longer rely solely on our memories, refreshed by our festivals, and the stories that our land tells that the best people will always remember.[132] And it is by bringing together the elements of Nature that our most marvellous visual images are made, gold with fire, stone [marble] with Athena's [olive] oil and water.[133] Our makers, who are inspired by the Muses, were already practising in the age of heroes.[134]

---

very identity, was suggested by the ambassador of the Plataeans in the *Plataicus* attributed to Isocrates. Isoc. 14 58.

131 The Commissioners, taking a ride on the injunction inscribed at Delphi, 'know thyself', will allude almost immediately to the need to preserve archives written on perishable materials, but here they put first the measures to preserve an approved version of the memory in visual images, in performance, and in combinations of the two.

132 The Commissioners refer to the previous sources of authority noted by Isocrates in his *Panegyricus*, especially 28, which is explicitly presented, even to the use of the word, as a step in the development-from-brutishness historical narrative, mentioning the particular role of festivals that initiate their members into 'mysteries'—that is, specialist knowledge—which they are given the responsibility of preserving.

133 The Commissioners, applying notions of the four elements, describe some of the manufacturing processes in much the same terms as they were later summarized by the elder Pliny in Plin. Nat. 30.33, and which, as noted in Chapter 1, pervaded the mainstream understanding in the classical era and earlier. Examples of materials used in the manufacture of images are also noted in the passage, but I omit them here, not only because some may have been introduced later, but to bring out the pervasiveness and longevity of the elements, and the purposiveness of 'Nature' in the discursive environment.

134 The Commissioners, in accordance with the usage of the time, make no sharp distinction between 'poets' whose medium was words presented in verse, and those 'artists' who worked in the visual arts; they draw attention to what can be regarded as anachronisms but can be regarded more plausibly as the invention of heritage, whereby the authority of current ideologies and practices is enhanced by giving them a longer pedigree than is warranted by evidence. All three of the tragedians of whom we have a few complete texts, use the device. Examples range from pushing back the founding of the Areopagus, the excluding of women from political affairs, the cultivation of the green olive, the custom of the funeral oration, and to the tight swaddling of infants. In modern terms, the presentations in 'literature' match those in 'art', for example in the stories displayed on the Parthenon. Since both media were employed to convince the same constituencies of consumers, such 'anachronisms' can be used to solve questions of what stories were presented on the Parthenon, including, in a few cases, the filling of gaps. I make use of the *Oedipus at Colonus*, the *Trojan Women*, and the *Ion*, all of which include references to stories presented on the Parthenon.

It is not our custom to inscribe the images of our gods and our heroes
with their names.[135] What need is there for words? From our childhood
we Athenians know them and their stories and we learn how to emulate
them.[136] Some say that images can only exercise their power in the cities
where they are set up, whereas stories of great men can be told in words
all over Hellas. But while words can be changed by our enemies, images
tell the same story for ever.[137]

---

135 The Commissioners repeat a sentiment offered by Dio of Prusa in the Rhodian
     oration, D.Chr. 31.91, where Dio notes that Rhodes followed the practice among
     the Athenians. This may be an example of Athenian claims to an exclusionary
     exceptionalism, The gods and mythic heroes presented on the sculptural battle of
     gods and giants (gigantomachy) on the archaic-era Treasury of the Siphnians at
     Delphi, a pan-hellenic site with a wide range of visitors, are named. The description
     of women visitors engaging with a gigantomachy at Delphi in the *Ion* of Euripides,
     as discussed in Chapter 3, is one of the few sources that enable us to understand
     how the ancient Athenians are likely to have engaged with the stories presented on
     the Parthenon.
     Much of the Rhodian oration is devoted to attacking the then-recent practice of
     refurbishing statues of now largely forgotten men by adding new nominal labels,
     not as an intentional rewriting of the city's history by altering the visible built
     heritage but as a way of saving on costs. The point is referred to by the author of the
     rhetorical discourse in Chapter 5.
136 D.Chr. 31.87 and 90. The local myths inscribed on the Parthenon, especially on
     the pediments and frieze, although complex, appear never to have been labelled.
     We need not take it that this custom implies that the viewer was already expert in
     all the stories, as some may have been, but that spoken guidance (especially in a
     participative collective festival context) was potentially more effective and inclusive
     as a means of disseminating the lessons of the stories as paideia. To judge from
     the innumerable vase paintings in which the names of the characters, including
     gods, are frequently included in the design, there was no objection to the naming of
     gods as such, although there are examples in other cultures. Many were evidently
     exported far from Athens, where their users could be expected to be less familiar.
     The same considerations may have applied to the frieze of the Treasury dedicated
     by the Siphnians at Delphi, a site visited by many from around Hellas and beyond,
     on which the names of the displayed characters were prominent.
137 The Commissioners aim to 'straighten' the story of Athens from the confusion of
     Herodotus, for example, and intervene in the debate about the relative effectiveness
     of the two main technologies in inscription, addressed in the *Encomium to Evagoras*
     by Isocrates Isoc. 9 73 and 74, using the word 'dunamis' to connote active agency,
     including agency of ideas, and couching the argument as a contrast, as is common
     in Greek literary writing, reinforced by particles, such as 'men' followed by 'de'.
     Isocrates, a professional speaker, favoured words. The Commissioners favour
     picking up the alternative view in the debate about the relative advantages of the
     visual and the verbal set out in the *Phaedrus* of Plato, especially Plat. Phaedrus 227
     d and e, where the character of Socrates argues that images cannot converse but
     continue tell the same story for ever, in contrast with words that get bandied about
     and become unstable. Although the character of Socrates uses the language of signs,
     as in modern semiotics, neither he nor Isocrates explicitly acknowledges that neither

And we have a well-tried medicine for that disease.[138] We see the bird of night with the other birds flocking round her in admiration.[139] It is her nature to serve the purposes of the gods.[140] Athena's living bird with her flashing eyes keep her divine presence in our minds day and night.[141] Our signed silver that leaves our mints show Athena with her owl and

---

    medium can be understood unless it has been mediated, as the Commissioners themselves were practising within the boundaries of the discursive environment— perhaps because it went without saying in a society in which making the mutes stones speak was a feature of cults and festivals.

138 A common metaphor in classical-era writings.

139 Dio of Prusa, known as Chrysostomos. D.Chr. 12.1. Although he was writing, or rather orating, perhaps with a standard speech before a panhellenic audience at Olympia half a millennium after the Parthenon and its cult statue were made, he makes use of parts of the long-lived discourse applied in Athens. Although, ornithologically, the other birds are mobbing the owl as a bird of prey that is a danger to them, the Commissioners present them in the same terms as in the Thucydidean funeral oration put into the mouth of Pericles, as examples of the wish of other cities to copy Athens, as the teacher of Hellas.

140 Why the little owl, which appears to have been plentiful in many localities besides Attica, came to be so closely associated with Athens has been much discussed, notably by Dunbar in her edition of the *Birds* of Aristophanes. To me the best explanation is the Greek name of the bird, 'glaux', being immediately connected by an ancient audience with the standard epithet, 'glaucopis', applied on dozens of occasions in both of the Homeric epics. The word itself was enough to identify Athena without the need to name her, for example at Hom. Il. 24.26. The name of the bird may be a back formation, akin to an eponym. As usual the Commissioners, following the conventions, present 'nature' as teleological and purposeful. Despite many suggestions for what colour is meant by 'glaucopis', of which 'blue-grey' has been much favoured, it may be that such attempts may be anachronistic. The study by Grand-Clément, Adeline, *La fabrique des couleurs: histoire du paysage sensible des Grecs anciens: VIIIe-début du Ve s. av. n. è.* (Paris: De Boccard, 2011), 399–403, suggests that, as discussed in Chapter 1, the classical-era experience of the little owls was that of their flashing eyes, as they darted here and there, as they were illuminated by the changing light, especially in moonlight.

141 Dio, in a passing remark at D.Chr. 12.6, preserves the only reference in the discourse to the level of detail exercised by the demos, in which he reports that Phidias, who had been commissioned to make the cult statue known as the Athena Promachos, as imagined by Schinkel in Figure 21.2, Volume 1, required specific approval of the people to make the small alteration of adding an image of the owl to the shield. The phrase, συνδοκοῦν τῷ δήμῳ, that is translated by Russell as 'with the consent of the demos' in Russell, D. A., ed., *Dio Chrysostom, Speeches. Selections. Orations VII, XII, and XXXVI* (Cambridge: CUP, 1992), 159. It may preserve the wording of a formal record of the democracy. The record of the episode undermines the notion associated with western romanticism that Phidias was a free artist able to decide what to compose, rather than a contractor commissioned to carry out a plan decided by others on which he might expect to be consulted. It is in line with the general thrust of the discourse that is to link Athenian theism to the land, the light, and the viewerships, to provide a dynamic storyscape.

olive, and for the benefit of those foreigners who can read or remember
a sign, we will proclaim that it was you, the people of Athens, who made
them from the purest silver dug from the underground riches of Athena's
land, and carried them, with the help of Poseidon all over the world
and back to us.[142] We will celebrate our kings, both those who sprang
from the earth and those who were sons of Poseidon.[143] We will tell the

---

142 The Commissioners may be referring to painted ceramic vases that were exported
     from Athens to many locations in the Hellenic world and beyond, as well as being
     put to use in Athens itself, which show episodes from myth as well as from real
     life. Most use words to help the viewer, reader, and/or performer, to understand
     the scene depicted. Since the majority of those now surviving were acquired by
     individuals and museums in accordance within the destructive western ideology
     of 'works of art' that cares little for provenance or recovering the uses to which the
     objects were put, notably as part of funerary rites, their potentiality for recovering
     the customs and practices of ancient life is lost; the same ideology encourages the
     destruction of knowledge brought about by a huge, mostly illegal, trade to continue.
     The point made by the Commissioners applies more directly to the coinage issued
     by the state of Athens from the sixth century that picture the head of Athena on the
     obverse with a big-eyed owl, a sprig of olive, and the identifying legend AΘE. As
     shown by Kraay, C. M., *The Coins of Ancient Athens* (Newcastle: Minerva Numismatic
     Handbooks, 1968), they continued to be produced with minor variations for many
     centuries to the extent that the coins can be regarded as one of the most stable, most
     long-lived, and most frequently encountered presentations of the officially approved
     discursive environment. Coins do, of course, also have an economic role, but in
     classical Athens, as was well understood by, for example, Aristotle, their value was
     'deemed'. Those modern authors who continue to regard coins made from select
     metals as having an 'intrinsic' value against which real goods and services were,
     can, and ought to be, denominated, rather than the other way round, suffer from a
     form of money illusion perpetrated, and often internalized, by its beneficiaries. The
     effects on the Athenian economy of the money creation brought about by loans,
     guarantees, and oral contracts, is hard to assess because of lack of data, but, as with
     the olive oil revolution, is likely to have increased the real productivity, the growth
     rate, and the gross product, while bringing about inequalities in real incomes and
     wealth that were only partially alleviated by the redistributive customs of 'charis'
     and festivals. Hence, the simmering discontent and the huge effort devoted to
     community building, making use of the discursive environment of the time, as here
     provisionally recovered.
143 The Commissioners refer to the Theseids who claimed descent from Poseidon,
     but also to the Neleids, especially Melanthos the Neleid who came to Athens as a
     refugee and, after the failure of the Theseids, founded the new dynasty of Codros.
     Noted by Hopper, R. J., 'Athena and the early Acropolis' in *Greece & Rome*, Vol.
     10, Supplement: Parthenos and Parthenon (1963), 12. We would expect to see the
     acceptance of a foreign dynasty, as obliquely referred to in the Periclean Funeral
     oration composed by Thucydides, featured on the west pediment of the Parthenon,
     mostly long since lost, where, under the valued symmetry, as discussed by Pollitt, J.
     J., *The Ancient View of Greek Art: Criticism, History, and Terminology* (New Haven: Yale
     UP, 1974), the stories connected with Poseidon and the sea, on the viewer's right,
     balanced those connected with Athena and the land, on the viewer's left. Discussed

histories of those who first ruled our land long ago when only Pelasgians lived here.[144] We remember the sons of Kecrops and Erechtheus, when we became Athenians, and when Ion, son of Xuthus, was made leader of our armies, when we became Ionians.[145] Our ancestors are always with us and we bear their names.[146]

We are warned by clever men not to trust what is written by others for that may discourage the arts of memory that lie within ourselves, so that some men may appear to be more wise than they are.[147] But, knowing the dangers we do not fear them, and we can also turn to the arts of today in which all Hellas knows we are the leaders and that they

---

further in Chapter 3. The story of the Neleids matched that of Xuthus, father of Ion, another foreigner who entered the Athenian mythic self-construction, both of whom, I suggest in Chapter 4, are likely to have been pictured on the Parthenon.

144 The Commissioners, as is normal, make no distinction between stories and histories. The translator has introduced a variant to avoid the modern convention of '[his]tories.'

145 The Commissioners repeat, almost word for word, the account given by Herodotus writing in the third person, as an outsider, at Hdt. 8.44.2. The name 'Pelasgians' that morphed with the word for stork 'pelargos' was used to connote the pre-Hellenic inhabitants, of whom a few traces remain in the names of geographical features such as the river Kephissus, personified and displayed as a reclining figure in the right corner of the west pediment, as a marker of location.

146 That the stories, when enacted, ['the Muses'], were among the means by which the claimed continuity between the past and the future was deliberately kept alive in the minds of young men as part of their education when they reached civic maturity is made explicit in Euripides, fragment 1028. The Commissioners encourage the thought that the myths to be pictured are part of the intrinsic identity of the Athenians, not objectified, or even imitated, say, by adopting the names, although they do that too, repeating the sentiment that Sophocles, himself a native of Colonus, put in the mouth of the native of the place when he is met by Oedipus in the *Oedipus at Colonus*. τοιαῦτά σοι ταῦτ' ἐστίν, ὦ ξέν', οὐ λόγοις τιμώμεν', ἀλλὰ τῇ ξυνουσίᾳ πλέον. Soph. OC 61. Much of the design of the Parthenon, with the choices of stories in stone that were displayed, as well as the festivals and collective performances that burgeoned during the classical period can be regarded as examples of what Eric Hobsbawm called 'The invention of Tradition', discussed in Hobsbawm, Eric, 'Inventing Traditions', in Hobsbawm, Eric and Ranger, Terence, *The Invention of Tradition* (Cambridge: CUP, Canto edition, 1992) where, on page 1, tradition is defined as 'a set of practices, normally governed by overtly or tacitly accepted rules and of a ritual and symbolic nature, which seek to inculcate certain values and norms of behaviour by repetition, which automatically implies continuity with the past'.

147 The Commissioners repeat the caution in Plato's *Phaedrus*, 275a, encouraging their audience to use their own critical skills as they look at look at the pictured stories, and providing legitimation both for the fluidity of the classical tragic drama and for the audience to take control of the meaning-making process, as discussed and exemplified in Chapter 3.

then follow. As our own inspired poet reminds us, when he warned of the dangers of tyranny: [*quotes*] 'when the laws are written, both the powerless and the rich have equal access to justice'.[148] And we will ensure that the new records are kept safe, even when they are made of perishable wood and wax, or written on skin with ink.[149]

As for what form the buildings should take, your Commissioners have been reading again the works of the great Ionian philosophers of the skills and instruments needed for successful architectony, Theodoros, Chersiphon, and his son Metagenes, who at the time of our grandfathers, helped to prepare the designs ('paradeigmata') and also to supervise the building of the largest, the most modern, and the most worthy-to-be-seen sanctuaries in all Hellas.[150] Also useful to us is the library of our kinsman, Euthydemos of Chios, whose collection of books is enough to prepare him to become an architecton himself if he ever chose to move from words to deeds.[151] [*Laughter*].

---

148 The Commissioners quote from line 433 of the same passage in the *Suppliants* of Euripides in which the character of Theseus, speaking as the spirit of essential Athenianness, commends, that is, the 'usefulness' of allowing citizens to speak, as discussed in St Clair, *WStP*, Chapter 22, https://doi.org/10.1164/obp.0136.22 and misquoted in Milton's *Areopagitica*. Although poets were regarded as skilled makers of words just as sculptors or painters were skilled makers of images, they were often described as being 'inspired'. This is the reverse of the rhetoric of 'creators' in modern western romantic terms that compares 'artists' with gods. Other examples of literacy being commended, notably by Aristotle, are noted in Thomas, Rosalind, *Literacy and Orality in Ancient Greece* (Cambridge: CUP, 1992), 130. The Commissioners present a shift in the balance from orality to literacy as part of the narrative of Athens taking the lead in the continuing progress-from-brutishness narrative. And, as many in the audience would have known, some rival cities, including Sparta and Corinth, made little use of inscriptions on stone until centuries later.

149 An example of the records of the Areopagus written on perishable material being preserved in the Parthenon is noted in Chapter 3.

150 The names of the builders of the sixth-century temples at Samos and Ephesos had near-mythic status, not least because their written works on the techniques of building appear to have been amongst the earliest to have been composed and circulated in prose. Discussed by Coulton, J. J., *Greek Architects at Work: Problems of Structure and Design* (London: Elek, 1977), 24 and 163 fn 52. The translator has retained the Greek word 'architectony' to avoid the modern word 'architecture' which, like 'artist' comes freighted with anachronism. As Coulton noted, the ancient architectons, whose expertise included the whole field of civil engineering, both practical and theoretical, appear to have been guildsmen and were not normally paid much more than the skilled workers whom they supervised.

151 The Commissioners anticipate the joke attributed to Socrates, himself a trained stone carver, in Xen. Mem. 4.2. 8–10, noted by Coulton, *Greek Architects at Work*, 25 and 163 fn 63. They add their own humorous twist by turning the clichéd trope of

Architectons are useful men, with useful skills in making useful things, and with experience of telling workmen what to do according to rules. We will pay them well for their help in returning our city to heath just as we pay our doctors. But their skills do not fit them to govern a city as you, men of Athens, have been called upon to do.[152]We will only employ sworn association members with long experience and knowledgeable masters. Only they can ensure the excellence ['arete'] of the work and keep it in good condition.[153] Our own Endoios, who made

---

deeds being better than words on its head, since for Euthydemos to have become an architecton would have involved a drastic loss of social status.

152 The Commissioners flatter the audience by denigrating the contribution of men with experience, picking up on a remark attributed to 'the Stranger', in conversation with the character of the young Socrates, in Plato's *Statesman*, 261e, 'καὶ γὰρ ἀρχιτέκτων γε πᾶς οὐκ αὐτὸς ἐργατικὸς ἀλλ᾿ ἐργατῶν ἄρχων' and even the admission that an architecton directs the work of others has to be dragged out of him.

153 The Commissioners appear to refer to the economic organizations, known in later times as guilds, in which responsibility for the training, management, and contracts for employing different skills were formally divided among brotherhoods. We have an example of a document that sets out the main features of a guild, in the work in the Hippocratic corpus known as 'the Oath' (Hp. Jusj) that has seldom, if ever, been regarded as an example of a guild document or statement of customary practice such as may have existed across the wider economy, and not only among medical practitioners. It commits members to swear to treat the children of their teachers as though they were brothers; to share their money in case of distress; to train only other guild members; never to encroach on the work of other guilds, even in emergencies; and to keep the secrets of the brotherhood. These are almost exactly the same as are found for all guilds that were the main form of economic management in European countries from the mediaeval period until the change to free competition in the later eighteenth century. There are various indications of the existence of guilds in the making of images in the ancient texts, especially those historians written later by, for example, Pliny, that often give the master under whom a famous maker learned his skills as a kind of patronymic. And there are references to family members pursuing the same skilled occupation, including a brother of Phidias, noted in Chapter 5. Some boundaries, such as those between makers/workers in stone and those in bronze are made necessary by the differences in skills. As Adam Smith showed, taking the silversmiths as a case in point, the guild system resulted in less silver being available within an economy than if entry to the craft was not restricted, and, under the guise of looking after widows and children, slipped into conspiracies to raise prices. However, for large multi-year projects such as building the Parthenon, the continuity of a corporate guild offered big advantages to the clients; for example, some contracts appear to have included responsibility for upkeep, such as one to the family of Phidias to maintain the chryselephantine cult state at Olympia. It seems likely that guilds existed in the literary sphere, which would help to explain the persistence of conventions in the tragic drama and the astonishing extent to which the complex texts of some authors, though not mythic stories, remained stable for hundreds of years. We also hear of organizations such as the Homeridae (descendants of Homer) that appear

the ancient dedication on the Acropolis that we have all seen, learned his craft from Daidalos himself.[154] We will preserve the old image of Athena seated on her throne that, although in a style that nobody would choose today, was made for Callias by Endoios of Athens, son of Metione, and grandson of our king Erechtheus. Endoios, who made images all over Ionia and elsewhere, learned his skill direct from Daidalos.[155]

We invite anyone who has knowledge of the designs ('paradeigmata') of the building that Libon of Elis is constructing for the Eleans at Olympia, to prove that he is a useful citizen.[156] How are the Eleans dealing with the visits of the Earthshaker to the new temple ('naos') that they are dedicating in replacement of the brick, timber, and terracotta structure that, all Hellenes agree, is a disgrace that hurts the eyes? The houses made for other gods in other cities, even when they are well made, always fall, but your Commissioners will make sure that Athena's male children will stand for ever.[157]

---

to have curated the texts of the Homeric corpus and perhaps the extent to which they could be altered as well as performed. Following this interpretation, when Alexander of Macedon left the 'house of Pindar' untouched when he ordered the destruction of Thebes, he was not preserving a building with famous associations, like a modern national trust, but ensuring that the works of Pindar would continue to be regulated.

154 The Commissioners refer to the 'Seated Athena' that either survived the Persian sack or was replaced, that can still be seen in the Acropolis Museum. Some guilds or, in modern terms, 'schools' of sculptors, calling themselves 'sons of Daidalos' traced their origins back to a mythic founder of that name, in accordance with the custom of eponymizing. One continuous pedigree with all the intermediate names is summarized from scattered mentions in Pausanias and other post-classical authors by Jones, H. Stuart, *Select Passages from Ancient Writers Illustrative of the History of Greek Sculpture*, edited with a translation and notes by H. Stuart Jones, M.A. [and other academic qualifications] (London, New York: Macmillan, 1895), 1–16. From the long lists of names of numerous tragedies, now lost, Daidalos was always presented as a character from the heroic mythic era.

155 The main accounts of the life of Daidalos found in the ancient authors were usefully collected by Falkener, Edward, *Daedalus; or The Causes and Principles of the Excellence of Greek Sculpture* by Edward Falkener, Member of the Academy of Bologna, and of the Archaeological Institutes of Rome and Berlin (London: Longman 1860), xvi. The Seated Athena by Endoios, and its later history are discussed by Marx, Patricia A., 'Acropolis 625 (Endoios Athena) and the Rediscovery of its Findspot' in *Hesperia*, Vol. 70 (2) (Apr.–Jun., 2001), 221–254.

156 Discussed by Ashmole, Bernard, *Architect and Sculptor in Classical Greece* (New York: NYU Press, 1972).

157 The Commissioners turn to the metaphor for the columns of temples used by the character of Iphigeneia, when, in Eur. IT 42–58, she describes her dream of the temple at her home city of Argos collapsing in an earthquake. The Commissioners may be referring to the plugs made from olive wood described in St Clair, *WStP*, Chapter 21,

As we rebuild our great temple with the stones that even the Persians could not destroy, every visitor will know that the immortal gods have never ceased to favour those who have served our city by land and by sea, and that they will continue to do so for ever. [*Shouts of approval*].[158]

The wise Solon will forever be remembered for reuniting Salamis with her Ionian motherland as the Delphic oracle decided.[159] Ionians and Dorians, though we have a common ancestor in Hellen, and together defeated the Barbarians in the immortal battle near the island, will always be enemies.[160] But we remember too how Solon, with the blessing of the gods, taught us how to use the fruits of the earth and how to share our knowledge with other men.[161] On our acropolis, we

---

https://doi.org/10.1164/obp.0136.21 that proofed the Parthenon against collapsing in an earthquake, but also to the gift of Athena in making the men of Athens clever and inventive enough to devise a scientific remedy, a variation on the reputation for innovation that was part of Athenian self-fashioning, and to other components of which much of the play is devoted.

158 The Commissioners in effect promise that what will be, by far, the most frequently seen presentation in the city (at least during festivals), the west pediment of the Parthenon, will give equal space to the land and the sea gods and heroes: a much-valued symmetry. By showing the contribution in mythic terms, as on the tragic stage, Athens is able to offer a timelessness to the viewers, or at least those who know their local mythology or who can have the stories retold by guides and temple servants. Since their understanding of the time that had passed since the beginning of the world was measured in centuries or millennia at most, and they were aware of the durability of marble in the microclimate, a promise to build 'for ever' was not incredible, although the Commissioners were wise enough to include a reference to the unforeseeable in their peroration. The questions that arise in recovering what was displayed and commended on the west pediment are discussed in Chapter 3.

159 In a long-running dispute over the ownership of the island, which is geographically as close to Megara is it is to Athens, Solon was said to have settled the issue by obtaining a declaration from the Delphic oracle that Salamis was 'Ionian'. Plut. Sol. 10.4.

160 A common trope. Examples are collected, including some from Thucydidean speeches by Figueira, Thomas and Soares, Carmen, eds., *Ethnicity and Identity in Herodotus* (London: Routledge, 2020), https://doi.org/10.4324/9781315209081. The Commissioners feel obliged to repeat it although the decision to build Ionian features on to a Doric building to an extent runs counter to the argument and is quickly passed over.

161 The Commissioners anticipate what was to become a standard claim made by Isocrates Isoc. 4 29, and picked up by successors, including the Romans as noted by Plat. Menex. 238a; Cicero, Flaccus 62: 'adsunt Athenienses unde humanitas, doctrina, religio, frugeres, iura'. Without saying so explicitly, the Commissioners give the credit to Solon for the agricultural revolution that featured the combination of the change from an oikos economy to a polis economy, facilitated by the partial economic shift from a subsistence economy to an economy of olive plantations and of exchangeable olive oil that produced a surplus of real resources, as explained in

celebrate the ancient olive tree that sprang up again the moment the enemies and the traitors left our land. And wood from our sacred tree always protects Athena's house from the Earthshaker.[162]

To achieve the useful is always difficult. But a man who can lift a heavy load can easily lift a light one. A good runner will always beat a laggard. But a spear-thrower or an archer who is not the best will die in a battle and lose the whole city.[163] We will build our new Propylaia and our new Parthenon to a colossal size.[164] And we will build them to such exactitude that they will appear to have been made from a single piece of flawless marble. The winds that blow secretly through narrow openings are sharper than those that are more diffused.[165] Any enemy considering laying siege to our acropolis will know that, however big his army, he can never succeed. And even if, as happened in the years of our shame, an enemy has found traitors, he will never be able to knock down our buildings or change our eternal story before the true Athenians return and cast them frothing into the dust.[166] To affirm our proud ancestry as Hellenes and as Ionians, we will build two temples that will both be in

---

the Thucydidean version of the brutishness narrative discussed in Chapter 1. Since Solon was, for the classical Athenians, a fully historical and not a mythic figure, there was no question of proposing him for a place among the stories presented on the Parthenon.

162 The olive tree is mythologized on the west pediment. The stories of the olive tree as symbol of resilience planted in the ground are noted St Clair, *WStP*, Chapter 21, https://doi.org/10.1164/obp.0136.21, as is the use of wood from the olive as an effective precaution against the columns of the Parthenon being thrown down in earthquakes.

163 The Commissioners use the argument deployed by Alcidamas, a fourth century author, in his treatise known as 'On the Sophists'.

164 Although other colossal temples were being planned and built in Sicily and what is now southern Italy ('Magna Graecia'), the Parthenon appeared bigger than it was, by, for example, having eight columns at each end instead of the more normal six. Discussed by Coulton, *Greek Architects at Work*, 74–96.

165 Plut. De Herod. 1. Although Plutarch is writing much later, he is offering a timeless general observation that may have been part of the discursive environment in the classical period. If so, it may have been used to justify the high specification to which the Parthenon was built, the lack of incipient gaps providing protection not only against the tools used by human invaders to destroy buildings but against natural erosion, seen as connected.

166 The Commissioners allude to the plans, which were carried into effect, of over-engineering the buildings as discussed in St Clair, *WStP*, Chapter 21, https://doi.org/10.1164/obp.0136.21, and the virtual impossibility, with the tools available at the time or foreseeable, of an enemy being able to knock down the buildings without an unaffordable cost in manpower, time, and risk.

sight when the processions come to a halt.[167] See, men of Athens, the single altar where the beasts are slaughtered and where we share the food and the smoke with the gods.

We Athenians give the honour to Butades and his daughter and to the effeminate Corinthians for being the first to use clay and fire to imitate a shadow thrown by a lamp.[168] And as befits our ancient custom of being a people who welcomes ideas that are just and useful, our Athenian potters soon learned how to do better. As we all know, our pottery is now admired and desired by all, and carries pictures of our Athens all over the world even to the wild Scythians beyond the Pontus.[169] But we Athenians are not slavish copiers, doing the same things again and again just because they are familiar. Even the divine Daidalos, who received the gift of image-making from the gods, and who taught the

---

167 Among other examples, in the Platonic dialogue, known as the *Ion*, the character of Socrates reminds the character of Ion of Ephesus that the Ephesians are Athenians, Plat. Ion 541. He also reminds Ion that the Athenians have often elected non-Athenians to be generals because they have demonstrated their military ability, and the two examples he gives are from cities regarded as overseas Ionian. Although the Athenians regarded themselves as Ionians, and descendants of the mythic eponymous Ion, they were also closely related to the Dorians since Ion was the grandson of Dorus. According to the complex genealogy that united the different branches of Hellenes through their eponyms, Hellen was the son of Deucalion, the first human after the Great Flood. His sons were Doros, eponymous founder of the Dorians, plus Xuthus and Aeolos, eponymous founder of the Aeolians. And the sons of Xuthus were Achaeos, eponymous founder of the Achaeans, and Ion, eponymous founder of the Ionians. It was this family tree that, in his play, the *Ion*, Euripides both assumes to be correct and shows is inconsistent with the Periclean citizenship law that confined voting rights to those men who could claim Athenian parentage on both sides, as will be discussed in Chapter 3.

168 The Commissioners refer to the story about an earthenware face made by Butades for his daughter who wanted a picture of a young man, which was exhibited at Corinth, as related by the Elder Pliny, xxxv.151, quoted by Güthenke, Constanze, *Feeling and Classical Philology: Knowing Antiquity in German Scholarship, 1770–1920* (Cambridge: CUP, 2020), 25, https://doi.org/10.1017/9781316219331, which influenced Winckelmann and Goethe to posit a feminine origin to 'art' as a *bildung*, or as the ancients called it, a paideia, to civility.

169 The Commissioners refer to the image of the seated Athena. By giving Endoios a local pedigree, the Commissioners claim the credit for all his work for Athens. By declaring him a pupil of Daidalos, a mythical figure, the authors of the dedicatory inscription anchor the image on the Acropolis to the world of myth. In the tragic drama there are reports of many plays that apparently include Daidalos as a character, so Endoios stands at the patrolled boundary, giving assurance to visitors to the Acropolis that the world of myth and of the tragic drama had once existed.

skill to our own Endoios, if he were to come back and make images of mortal men in the Daidalian style, would be laughed at.[170]

As far as is fitting, we will rebuild on the locations of the temples that were destroyed by the barbarians or were under construction at the time.[171] We will remind both Athenians and our Ionian kin who live both here and overseas that, unlike the Lacedaimonians, we do not disdain the cosmetic arts.[172] Our jewellery makers and pottery workers will prepare the golden beads, the coloured glass, and the precious stones that will capture the eyes as effectively as the ornaments worn by our women on special days, and with which we clothe and remember them on their memorials. We ask the best makers [in Greek 'poets'] to make proposals, to present preliminary models, and to come and work for us in Athens for good pay. We will proclaim our invitation to all

---

170 The Commissioners make a point attributed to Socrates in Plato, *Hippias Major*, 282a. A similar thought, that Daidalos only deserved to admired because his work was an early stage on a progression to Pheidias is in Aristides 2,118, Davison, Claire Cullen, with the collaboration of Birte Lundgreen, ed. by Geoffrey B. Waywell, *Pheidias: The Sculptures and Ancient Sources* (London: Institute of Classical Studies, 2009), ii, 675. How far other archaic dedications may have survived the 480 destruction of the Acropolis, or been replaced with replicas, cannot be reconstructed with confidence, but elsewhere in the town and the countryside, they were probably still seen in cemeteries. As late as the time of Pausanias, works allegedly made by Daidalos could be seen elsewhere in Greece. The use of the word τέχνη to mean an organised trade is well attested and there is a later epigraphic reference to a συντεχνία λινουργῶν.

171 The Commissioners refer to the Parthenon and the Erechtheion, of which the Parthenon is primarily Doric but with elements, notably the frieze, that are Ionic, and the Erechtheion extravagantly Ionic. It is sometimes assumed that Vitruvius, in attributing the origin of the Ionic order to the eponymous hero Ion, took his account from a source that made use of the *Ion*, the play by Euripides. However, the version that he recounts is more consistent with the pre-Euripidean version that the *Ion* subverts and whose explicit conclusion is that it has to be replaced, as will be discussed in Chapter 3. The conferring of the eponym of Ion on to the Ionic order of architecture is therefore likely go back to a time before the fifth century, perhaps made explicit in one of the many lost works on which Vitruvius drew. The passage in Vitruvius is as follows: Postea autem quam Athenienses ex responsis Apollinis Delphici, communi consilio totius Hellados, XIII colonias uno tempore in Asia deduxerunt ducesque singulis coloniis constituerunt et summam imperii potestatem Ioni, Xuthi et Creusae filio, dederunt, quem etiam Apollo Delphis suum filium in responsis est professus, isque eas colonias in Asiam deduxit et Cariae fines occupavit ibique civitates amplissimas constituit Vitr 4.1.4.

172 The Commissioners refer to the commonplace that the Ionians were soft and effeminate, but turn it into a justification.

Hellas by sending out heralds.[173] We will set up images in places where they can be seen and from where they can send their lessons into our minds both as we move around our city and on festival days.[174] But we will rearrange all the festivals for another day if the city is in danger. [*Laughter*].[175] We already have many useful images, including some dedicated long ago, such as those of the Tyrannicides, who protected our city, that will remain for ever as heralds for the eternal values of our city and of our democracy.[176] They will produce children, and children of children, for ever.[177]

Since the Tyrannicides and our other heroes show us how the life of the city is always more to be valued than that of any man, we propose that no citizen should be permitted to put up an image of himself nor

---

173 The remark of the Commissioners, with its use of 'poets', which in ancient usage included makers of visual art as well as fictions in words (including plays), is a reminder that neither the famous poets in verse, such as Pindar and Simonides, nor the statue makers, such as Pheidias, were 'creators' standing outside society, as rhetorics of romanticism are inclined to assume, but were fully integrated into the economy and reliant on pleasing those who commissioned them.

174 The Commissioners, as was normal, use the Greek word 'graphe' to include various types of images, not distinguishing 'painting' from 'sculpture' in cases where, since their focus was on the intended effects on the viewer, there was no need to mention the difference. Indeed, as far as the low relief of the Parthenon frieze are concerned, it would have been hard for the ancient viewer to tell the difference, even if he or she were interested, as will be discussed in Chapter 3, with the possible reference in Euripides's play, the *Ion*.

175 The audience pick up a coded attack on the Spartans, with whom war is expected, remembering that it was because the Spartans refused to interrupt a festival that an inadequate force was sent too late to Thermopylae, and a coded reference to the annihilation of Leonidas and his companions.

176 This was a rhetorical exaggeration, unlikely to have convinced the whole audience. The circumstances of the coup and of the killing of the tyrant were as much personal as political, as described by Monoson, S. Sara, *Plato's Democratic Entanglements: Athenian Politics and the Practice of Philosophy* (Princeton, N.J.: Princeton University Press, 2000), 21–50. And since this, and other coups, took place during a festival, a phenomenon that was well-known, noted in for example Aen. Tact. IV and others in Thucydides, including in the speeches, the Commissioners are, to an extent undermining their own proposals to have more festivals. The memory of the botched conspiracy also further weakens the already weak case that what was presented on the Parthenon frieze was the Panathenaic festival when the killing started, to be discussed in Chapter 3.

177 The Commissioners, in explaining in familiar terms the notion of moral progress as set out by Thucydides and the others, make use of the multiple meanings of the Greek word, *tokos*, that starting from a notion of a newly born baby is carried across to the produce of the land, and on through simple interest paid on a debt, that might not be denominated in monetary terms, to compound interest 'children of children' of which an example occurs in Aristoph. Thes. 830.

of any official, however famous, who is only holds his office for a short time on behalf of us all.[178] It will be for our grandchildren to decide who should be commemorated in perpetuity among our city's heroes. As the great Solon told us, we cannot judge men till after they are dead.

So what must we do? We must first encourage the practice of 'charis' that binds together the rich nobleman and the poor labourer. Your Commissioners welcome proposals from those who have useful knowledge for translating into stone the story ('logos') of this preliminary sketch ('paradeigma'). [*The reciter passes round an image as shown in Figure 2.2*].

This picture, when set out in a prominent place in imperishable stone at the entrance to the Acropolis, will draw the eager eyes of men and boys to the exciting bodies of the naked women as they dance, in a perpetual circle, each in her proper place.[179] And their eyes will follow the beams emitted by the eyes of the women to the fruits that they are holding out to us in their hands. Just as a well-managed farm, in which the master, the mistress, the slave, and the beast work together to produce all that is needed for the body, so too, just as harvest follows seeding, a city that practises 'charis' will always produce 'arete'.[180] And we, our sons, and their sons will commission more stories to be told in bronze and marble

---

178 The proposal of the Commissioners appears to have been accepted, there being no images of citizens, except possibly one of Pericles for over a hundred years. Monoson, *Plato's Entanglements*, 25. By forbidding the practice, as an unintended consequence, the Commissioners opened the way for accusations that the rule was being evaded as discussed in the rhetorical discourse in Chapter 5.

179 The erotic power of the Charites was acknowledged by the character of the Cyclops in the play by Euripides of that name, although he preferred boys. Eur. Cycl. 581.

180 An image of Hermes and the three Charites was seen outside the entrance to the Acropolis by Pausanias, and its existence noted by later writers who also say it was made by the father of Socrates, the philosopher. It is possible that the 'Three Charites' set up at the entrance to the Acropolis may have resembled the sketch. A two word fragment of the *Erechtheus* by Euripides 'three yoked maidens' ζεῦγος τριπάρθενον, to which some have suggested adding Χαρίτων, Sonnino edition fragment 21, would be in line with the custom, noted elsewhere in the Chapter, of making direct allusions to the classical era landscape, in plays set in mythic times, as a means of conferring on them the authority of having existed since time immemorial. Paus. 1.22.8. In mentioning elsewhere that the figures were draped, Pausanias admitted to being puzzled since, in his time, the Charites were presented as naked. In the classical period, although within the Acropolis, some males were presented as naked on, for example, the Parthenon frieze to signal that the events were set in the mythic heroic age, females were loosely draped, in what appear to be ankle-length 'Ionian' costumes. Discussed further in Chapter 3.

now and for ever in the future.[181] The men of Athens will look upon our beautiful city, day after day, and become her lovers.[182]

---

181 The Commissioners plan that the Acropolis authorities will continue to commission other images, and encourage others to seek permission to dedicate yet more, as happened, perhaps with some de-accessioning. Since, for what was approved and erected, we only have the account by Pausanias written long after and some archaeological traces, it is impossible at present to know the chronological order or the justifications offered at the time, especially as the credit for some statues appears to have been retrospectively attributed to famous sculptors including Phidias. Pausanias did not know what to make of 'a bull set up by the Council of the Areopagus', and in responding to his invitation to make guesses, I suggest that it reminded visitors that what were the most prized sacrificial animals, since most Athenians seldom ate beef, could be donated as 'charis' and that the sight encouraged the rich to do so, as well as breeding such animals to be purchased by the city or by the treasurers of festivals. Paus 1.14.2. Others were statue groups of two or more figures that offered moral stories in mythic terms. Discussed by Schanz, Holly Lee, *Greek Sculptural Groups Archaic and Classical* (New York: Garland, 1980). That of Apollo driving away an infestation of locusts reinforces the thought that the gods favour Athens. That of Apollo striking the satyr Marsyas, as punishment, materialised a story, already familiar in the classical period from the, now lost, work of the then highly-regarded fifth century lyric poet Melanippides of Melos. Marsyas was later said to have been flayed alive, in modern terms a disproportionate penalty for using the wrong type of flute, but in classical Athens a reminder that the songs were not to be altered, as discussed later. For a satyr, who is a leftover from the days before the emergence from brutishness to disobey the rules for festivals was not however a venial form of hybris. As will be discussed later in the speech when they declare that 'Even a change in our songs can hurt the whole city' they were reporting an opinion attributed to Socrates, the songs being more important than the static images, indeed the way their meaning was internalized and embodied. By the time of Hegesias of Magnesia, writing in the middle of the third century BCE, of whose works only fragments survive, the enterprise of turning the Acropolis into a mythic history in three dimensions, that the authorities could control and update as an apparently more durable statement of `Athenian self-fashioning as well as of paideia than any work consisting of words written on papyrus, even in multiple copies, was still under way. As he wrote, in a tantalising fragment: 'I am unable to point them all out one by one [the temples and shrines of the Acropolis]; for Attica is the possession of the gods, who seized it as a sanctuary for themselves, and of the ancestral heroes.' Around a century later, Polemon of Athens, by all accounts a more learned author than Pausanias, turned the comment of Hegesias into words, in a work devoted to the monuments and votive offerings on the Acropolis. Seldom has the precariousness of our modern understanding been more graphically exemplified. Had Polemon survived, even in a single copy as was the case with Pausanias, the whole tradition might have been more securely based on viewerly ways of seeing and on the intentions of the city's authorities as presented in accordance with prevailing norms of rhetoric rather than on the chatty anecdotes of the uncritical Pausanias. He might have saved the site from being regarded as 'art' and made the current experiment in retrieving the discursive environment less necessary.

182 The Commissioners turn to a metaphor deployed by the character of Pericles in the Thucydidean Funeral Oration at Thuc. 2.41. As has been shown by S. Sara

Figure 2.2. 'Paradeigma for an image of the three Charites'. Copper engraving.[183]

Since we Athenians rule ourselves, we have learned to distinguish what
is real from what are mere imaginings and attempts to deceive us.[184] Men

Monoson, the passage, that in the past has been regarded as a metaphor for selfless
devotion and willingness of individuals to die for their country, and that could
therefore be appropriately referred to in modern ceremonies of remembrance,
has as its comparator the Athenian social practice of free-born men pursuing free-
born boys in an elaborate sexual code, involving an exchange. It was a form of
reciprocity or 'charis.' The metaphor depended too for its potential effectiveness
on the extramission theory that the 'gaze' is itself an exchange. Since the practice
was available almost exclusively to elites not to the generality of citizens, the
allusion may therefore, both here and in the Periclean speech, have carried an
implied promise that the men in the audience had an opportunity of joining the
elites. As Monoson notes, Pericles had a reputation for speaking boldly, of which
the 'erastes/eromenenos' metaphor may be an example of first usage rather than
of first recorded usage. It is possible therefore that the sentence is an anachronistic
addition by a later editor. The word 'kalos' and its cognates, usually translated, as
here, as 'beautiful', seems not to have implied a general 'aesthetic' standard but to
be related to implied purpose – beautiful for what? It was commonly used, perhaps
coincidentally, to describe attractive young high-born men such as are pictured on
the Parthenon frieze.

183 [Naples Museum] *Raccolta delle più interessanti Dipinture e de'più belli Mosaici
rinvenuti negli scavi di Ercolano, di Pompei, e di Stabia che ammiransi nel Museo Reale
Borbonico* (Naples: n.p., 1840). One hundred and twenty one outline copper
engravings, untitled and unnumbered, although some copies have a manuscript
index.

184 The Commissioners make a plea for the education ('paideia') in the city's values,
both for adults and for those adults and young persons who are not yet educated,

who walk alone lazily feed their own imaginations without bothering to consider other possibilities.[185] We Athenians imitate our skilled midwives who, from their long experience in their art, know when they can bring forth the true and when they must abort the false.[186] And we will ensure that those who participate in our festivals obey the rules that our city lays down. [*Quoting*] In sound is our sight, [*unquoting*] as we all know.[187] Even a change in our songs can hurt the whole city.[188]

---

to include an understanding of dialectic, among other routes to reliable knowledge, as recommended by the character of Socrates in Plato's *Theaetetus*, Plat. Theaet. 143a and in the *Republic* Pl.R.536d. It can be taken too as a defence of the dialogic nature of Athenian tragedy and, as I will suggest in Chapter 3, a recommendation to look at visual images according to the same criteria.

185 A point made by the character of Socrates in Plato's *Republic* Plat. Rep. 5.458a referring to the opportunities of learning in conversations with friends as is the setting for the *Republic* as the characters walk to Piraeus to see a new festival, but it applies also to participating in a festival oneself.

186 This analogy was offered, and its implications developed, by the character of Socrates in the *Theaetetus*.

187 The Commissioners quote what is presented as a chreia or 'saying' in Soph. OC 139, but that may have been placed there by Sophocles in hopes that it would become a common saying. It is an example of what was then regarded as the primacy of sight over the other senses in the understanding of cognition, made more poignant in its first context by having been coined by the character of Oedipus who has destroyed his own eyesight. It also encourages listeners, who will soon themselves be processioners in festivals to embody their emotions that derive from all their senses together, just as Bacchylides uses a single verb, 'melpein' to refer to ritual song and dance as inseparable.

188 The Commissioners share the sentiment put into the mouth of Socrates in Plato's Republic 424cd, where I have, in line with the thought in the previous sentence, widened the usual translation 'music' that may tend to suggest that Socrates is referring only to music in a modern sense. The bringing together of two hundred and fifty inscriptions, some fragmentary, that relate to rituals in ancient Greek cities in the online database [CGRN] *A Collection of Greek Ritual Norms* edited by Carbon, Jan-Mathieu; Peels, Saskia; and Pirenne-Delforge, Vinciane, in 2017 (available at http://cgrn.ulg.ac.be/), a resource that includes some from the classical period in Athens, shows that rituals were regulated to a high degree of detail. They lay down, for example, the times of day, the costumes to be worn, specifying the colour, the animals to be killed, the division of the meat into animal parts, and the remuneration of the officials ('hieropoioi') that may include particular cuts of meat, sometimes with items individually costed along with the source of funds. Some include measures for fines and other penalties if the regulations are departed from, and set out strict criteria, relating, for example, to quorums, procedures, and voting that would have made it almost impossible to make changes. A few claim to lay down decisions 'for ever.' The Parthenon frieze pictures a large number of men usually called 'marshals' whose role, in the light of the inscriptions, is likely to have gone beyond keeping the procession moving along. Indeed they can be taken as part of the visual rhetoric of the stories presented of pushing back presentations of a well-run celebration into mythic times, as will be discussed in Chapter 3. The

We will commission the best musicians of Hellas to prepare the songs that we will sing at our festivals. The proxenos of misty Thebes, has already celebrated the uniqueness of our clear-air city. [*At this point, a section of the audience begins to chant an extract from a commissioned work of Pindar that had already become almost an Athenian civic anthem, inadequately rendered as 'shining and violet-crowned and celebrated-in-song bulwark of Hellas, famous Athens, god-favoured city'*].[189]

We will ensure that all who live here obey all the laws, both old and new, that, with the help of the gods, our city has enacted for our safety and for our benefit.[190] And we will show stories that celebrate our

---

rhetoric of the inscriptions, as set up in public spaces, is therefore not only to lay down rules but to give advice to viewers of the frieze and to reduce the need for its detail to be seeable.

189 Pindar fragment 76. 'Ὦ ταὶ λιπαραί καὶ ιοστέφανοι καὶ αοίδιμοι, Ελλάδος ἔρεισμα, κλειναί, Αθῆναι, δαιμόνιον πτολίεθρον.' The English word 'glittering' occurred to Perdicaris, the recently arrived Greek-American consul, in 1838, whose experience of the phenomenon was direct. Like some members of the audience of the speech, he may not have been aware that he was echoing Pindar who himself may have been turning a local oral tradition into the greater fixity of commemorative verse. Perdicaris, G.A., A.M., Late Consul of the United States at Athens, *The Greece of the Greeks* (Boston: Paine and Burgess, 1845), i, 27. The archaic word for city 'ptoliethron' conjures up the opening words of the *Iliad*. In Homer a ptoliethron is a city worth sacking, but being daimoned, Athens, according to the rhetoric, is protected by the gods. I am grateful to the late Martin West for his advice on this point. The first part of the phrase is quoted by the chorus in a slightly different version in Aristophanes, *Knights*, line 1329. ὦ ταὶ λιπαραὶ καὶ ιοστέφανοι καὶ ἀριζήλωτοι Ἀθῆναι. The same word is used by the Chorus in praising Athens in Eur. IT 1130, perhaps as a quotation from Pindar that the audience would recognize as such. It is possible that the word could be taken to include the olive-oil covered athletic young men as well as the gleaming marble and statue of Athena Promachos. Some, such as the editors of Disraeli's *Letters*, i, 175, have detected a pun on the eponymous hero, Ion, a suggestion that would conform with the discursive environment, including giving additional support to my suggestion for what was presented on the Parthenon frieze as discussed in Chapter 3, and there is a pun on the name in the *Ion* of Euripides, noted in that Chapter. However, if a joke is intended in the *Knights*, or was heard as such by the audience, the point is not developed. By mentioning the micro-climate of Thebes and Boeotia, the Commissioners remind the audience of the geodeterminism that Byron was to use in his attack on the character of Lord Elgin, as noted in St Clair, *WStP*, Chapter 19, https://doi.org/10.1164/obp.0136.19.

190 It has often been noticed that on the Parthenon frieze, young women are given almost as much picturing space as young men, both being presented as dutifully discharging their gendered roles. As Burkhard Fehr has suggested, given that the two-parent Periclean decree of 451/50 was being considered at the same time as proposals for the rebuilding of the Parthenon, there is nothing surprising in finding that viewers of the Parthenon were reminded 'of the importance of the Athenian extraction of Athenian [male] citizens on the maternal side, as prescribed by the citizenship law.' Fehr, *Good Democrats and Wives*, 143–144. In Chapter 3 I suggest

continuing progress from brutishness and our city as a school for all Hellas.[191] Our city will educate not only our own sons and daughters in the qualities that have made us great, but other Hellenes too.[192] On our sacred hill we will commemorate the moment when Athena taught us how to domesticate the grey olive tree.[193] We will remember the tasks performed by our women in the 'oikos', where we lived in the childhood of Athens before we became a 'polis'.[194] Our Athenianesses as much as our Athenians, all will see, are superior to those of all other Hellenes, as

---

that this observation, when put with the other evidence, enables us to identify the mythic scene that is presented.

191 The Commissioners, following the general narrative of economic and social progress from brutishness to its then current stage of Athenian democracy, suggest that the stories of the Athenian pasts to be presented, numerous though they are, should not be just an archive of local myths, but should be a selection made in accordance with the aims and claims of 'paideia' as frequently enunciated, most famously in the Funeral Oration of Pericles.

192 The Commissioners repeat the sentiment put into the mouth of Pericles in the Funeral Oration. τὴν πόλιν πᾶσαν τῆς Ἑλλάδος παίδευσιν εἶναι Thuc, 2.41. Often translated as the 'School of Hellas', a phrase that seems to me to risk implying too static a role, and to underplay that it is the specifically Athenian version of 'arete' that is commended for others to adopt.

193 The Commissioners use almost the same words as are spoken by the Chorus in the Trojan Women by Euripides. Eur. Tro. 801–803. ἵν' ἐλαίας/ πρῶτον ἔδειξε κλάδον γλαυκᾶς Ἀθάνα,/οὐράνιον στέφανον λιπαραῖσί τε κόσμον Ἀθήναις, Eur. The meaning of the various words, including 'teaching' is discussed by Kovacs, David, ed., Euripides: Troades. Edited with Introduction and Commentary (Oxford: OUP, 2018), 252, https://doi.org/10.1093/actrade/9780199296156.book.1. Despite the joke in the Acharnians of Aristophanes, that uses the common Greek word normally translated as 'shining' to mean 'oily' like a sardine, he suggests that it may not refer to oiled human bodies. What seems certain from the passage that lists the gifts of Athena, is that it is a reference to the actual olive tree and mark of Poseidon's trident pointed out on the Acropolis, and almost certainly to the story told on the west pediment of the Parthenon, where, as discussed in Chapter 3 the olive tree is given pride of place. The passage, with its reference to 'shoots' also confirms that it was a technology of grafting olive trees, and its application to the green variety, that precipitated the real-terms productivity gain that we may call the olive oil revolution, as suggested by Thucydides and as summarized in Chapter 1, not the harvesting of olives as appears to have been common long before and was not associated with Athena as innovator. What is know of the cultivation of olive trees round the Mediterranean basin, and the separation of the domestic from the wild variety, is discussed by Foxhall, Lin, Olive Cultivation in Ancient Greece: Seeking the Ancient Economy (Oxford: OUP, 2007).

194 The Commissioners run together the obvious point that children are born and brought up in the oikos during their early years with the metaphor that the oikos stage came before the polis stage in time, according to the brutishness narrative, but it was now less important than the polis.

mothers, as teachers of our children, and as makers of the useful things that we wear.

Theseus was a great hero who did great things for Athens in his time and we have his bones in our land where he will be remembered for ever.[195] See him rescuing unfortunate women fleeing the wrath of Ares who are being torn from altars by brutish monsters. Our new philanthropy, as you all know, has now become our custom, decided upon by the city with the consent of our citizens, and will always remain so. [*The reciter passes round an image as shown in Figure 2.3*].

Figure 2.3. Theseus as rescuer, as presented on the frieze of the classical-period temple at Phigaleia.[196]

Refugees are ambassadors for the generosity of your city, better speakers than any inscribed monument ('stele').[197] And it was the sons

---

195 In 476 BCE, for example, Kimon had established a temple in Athens to house the alleged bones of Theseus, specially brought from Delos, as part of a general agenda of building up a memorialising cult of Theseus as one of the founding heroes of Athens.

196 [British Museum] *A Description of the Collection of Ancient Marbles in the British Museum* (London: British Museum, 1818), iii, opposite 26.

197 A thought offered by Aelius Aristides in his Panathenaic oration. Pan 81. Although composing hundreds of years after the classical period, Aristides may have been incorporating into the self-celebratory discourse an episode recorded by Xenophon who was alive at the time. When, in 405, the Athenians feared, with good reason, that they would be subjected to ritual extermination ['andrapodizein', a technical term to be discussed in the passage on the Thebans elsewhere in the speech] by the Spartans. Xen. Hell. 2.2.14–20, where the word or its cognates occurs three times, Xenophon has them declare that they would not so treat a city who had done such good work in the greatest danger ever to have befallen Hellas. The episode as recorded, whatever its historicity, may be contributing some of the answer to

of Theseus, Demophon ('he who speaks for the people') and Akamas
('the untiring') who showed us by their deeds how greater works can
done by sons than by fathers, now and in the future.[198] Our temple will

the question of why the Parthenon and other classical era monuments on the
Acropolis were over-engineered. Not only could they be expected to be long lasting,
and physically difficult to destroy, but they provided a rhetorical defence against
those, notably Lysander, who in accordance with other pan-Hellenic conventions
need suffer no private or public scruples at putting unarmed enemies to death, and
frequently did so, but who decided, for other reasons, to try to achieve their aims by
negotiation as Lysander did.

198 Among the formal political constituencies of the Athenian democracy were the
Akamantidae, who are reminded of what Homer said of their having joined the
expedition to Troy in the Funeral Oration of Demosthenes, Dem. 60 29, although the
passage in the *Iliad* 3.144 does not fully support the claim. It is likely that Akamas
is among the 'Eponymous Heroes' pictured on the Parthenon frieze, and was, as
with the other Eponymous Heroes for their own constituents, pointed out as a
focus of attention and storytelling at certain festivals, especially those that included
boys. Demophon, in the tragedy by Euripides, *The Children of Heracles*, along with
Akamas who is referred to but does not speak, emphasized that he is a democrat
and is willing to take Athens to war against Argos/Mycenae, rather than return
refugees who have sought sanctuary. In the *Hecuba*, by contrast, the two sons of
Theseus are reported by the Chorus to have taken the illiberal side in the debate
whether the enslaved Cassandra should be put to death as a sacrifice at the tomb of
Achilles, perhaps implying that theirs was, or had been, a reasonable point of view,
although the character of Agamemnon describes as 'barbarian', a word becoming
synonymous with 'brutish', an attempt by Polymestor to seize the grieving Hecuba.
Eur. Hec 122–124, and 1129. In the *Medea*, the character of Medea who has killed
her children to spite their father Jason, in an act that he declares that no Hellenic
woman could ever have done, nevertheless expects to be given sanctuary in Athens,
and is not contradicted. Eur. Med 1339 and 1384. The Commissioners allude to the
fact that Theseus, although promoted by predecessors, notably Pisistratus, as part
of an Athenian continuity back to Homeric times, had many embarrassments on
his CV, for example that he had raped Ariadne, Antiope, Anaxo of Troezen, and
Helen when she still a child, that in classical Athens was below the marriageable age
of fourteen, as reported by Plutarch in his *Comparison of Theseus and Romulus*. The
presented contradictions, may not have been lost on audiences of the tragic drama
where the character of Theseus is presented as the spirit of all that is best in Athens,
as for example, in the *Suppliants* discussed at the end of St Clair, *WStP*, Chapter 22,
https://doi.org/10.1164/obp.0136.22 in connection with the title page of Milton's
Areopagitica. In the debate recorded in the surviving tragedies and fragments, the
case for welcoming refugees, or at least refugees from the leaderships of other cities,
appears to be recommended, but only if the people, usually in the tragic drama, the
same as the army agree, a form of democracy but also in some circumstances, an
abnegation of a duty to provide leadership. The evidence was gathered by Ducrey,
Pierre, *Le Traitement des prisonniers de guerre dans la Grèce antique: des origines à la
conquête romaine* (Paris: Boccard, 1968). Although there is evidence for codes of law
and practice relating to decisions to go to war and to its practices, especially between
cities regarded as fully Hellenic, those persons whose cities were conquered,
whether men, women, or children, appear to have been regarded as a form of

celebrate them too.[199] Since some who visit our acropolis, including our children, are not yet as mused as we are, we will not show gods and heroes when they are untrue to their divine nature.[200]

Some have suggested that Athenians cease from killing the men we capture when we seize a city or in battle.[201] But if enemies are permitted

---

booty, to be disposed of in whatever way the conqueror decided, including being put to death, enslaved, ransomed, or allowed to remain. Whether presentations in the tragic drama brought about any change in practice is impossible to judge from the evidence available. What is documented is that, by the time of the Panathenaic oration of Aelius Aristides many centuries later, the imagined city of Athens was presented as an example of welcome and generosity to refugees. Pan 48, with the example of Orestes quoted, perhaps from the drama, a thought also found in the Oration known as *Athena*, Behr, Charles A., ed., *P. Aelius Aristides, The Complete Works* (Leiden: Brill, 1986), ii, 223. It is possible that we have here an example of the brutishness narrative being employed to look forward to the future, as well as constructing a pleasing picture of a morally progressive past.

199 Whether Theseus, or his sons, were presented on the metopes of the Parthenon, and if so, in what form, cannot be judged given their mutilated state. In another example of the usefulness of genealogy and eponyms as recommended agents of change while claiming continuity, Menexenus, after whom the Platonic dialogue was named, is said in the *Lysis* and the *Phaedo*, to be the 'son of Demophon.' Although some have conjectured that Theseus is amongst the figures portrayed on the Parthenon pediments, and he may be there, the recumbent figure traditionally known as 'the Theseus', in the corner of the Parthenon east pediment is more likely to be a personification of one of the Attic rivers.

200 The Commissioners, alluding to the progress from brutishness narrative along whose trajectory Athens is the most advanced city, propose to exclude the portrayal of many myths that show the gods quarrelling or otherwise behaving in ways contrary to the city's official self presentation, as seems to have happened, open up a gap between what was allowable in the drama, to understand which a higher level of critical sophistication was required than looking at fixed images. They were anticipating the objections set out by, for example, Isocrates in his Rhetorical Discourse known as the *Busiris*, such as 'the calumnies of the poets, who declare that the offspring of the immortals have perpetrated as well as suffered things more atrocious than any perpetrated or suffered by the offspring of the most impious of mortals; aye, the poets have related about the gods themselves tales more outrageous than anyone would dare tell concerning their enemies. For not only have they imputed to them thefts and adulteries, and vassalage among men, but they have fabricated tales of the eating of children, the castrations of fathers, the fetterings of mothers, and many other crimes.' Isoc. 11. 38. Paradoxically, as we learn from Athenagoras of Athens, a second-century-CE author who composed a plea to the emperor Marcus Aurelius to accord the status of a tolerated religion to the Christians as a breakaway from the tolerated Jewish religion, picked out some of the same myths, including those of Thyestes and Oedipus, as examples of what was being unfairly said about the Christians. Schoedel, William R., ed., *Athenagoras, Legatio and De Resurrectione* (Oxford: OUP, 1972).

201 The Commissioners refer to an idea that is uniquely found in the surviving written record of the classical period in Euripides's play known as the *Heracleidae*, or *The Children of Heracles*. In two short passages Eur. Heraclid. 961–966 and 1009–1011, an

to live they will come back and attack us. Nor can they be turned into useful slaves. We must therefore continue to follow the ancient laws of Hellenes and barbarians.[202]

We proclaim our autochthony not only on the dedications to Athena but on the sacred buildings and at other places in our favoured land.[203] Just as when we are captivated by a well-prepared and multi-coloured funeral oration, we feel more noble and more tall, and our companions

---

attendant, tries to persuade the character of Alcmene that it is contrary to the laws of the Hellenes to put prisoners to death. The word used for attendant, 'therapon', gives the character much greater authority than a 'slave' who under the conventions of Athenian tragedy is allowed to say the unsayable but can be assumed not to be telling the truth. We have a glimpse here of a suggested next step in the progressivist advance from brutishness grand narrative.

202 The practice of killing the men and enslaving the women and girls is attested by Thucydides and Xenophon for the fifth, fourth, and later centuries. We may have some archaeological evidence from the cemetery at Phaleron by the sea where a mass grave of about eighty captives, still bound, has been. With only a few exceptions, the victims were aged between twenty and thirty-four years and had been deprived of water and beaten before being put to death. As discussed Chryssoulaki, Stella, 'The Excavations at Phaleron Cemetery 2012–2017: An Introduction', in Graml, Constanze, Doronzio, Annarita, and Capozzoli, Vincenzo, *Rethinking Athens before the Persian Wars: Proceedings of the International Workshop at the Ludwig-Maximilians-Universität München (Munich, 23rd-24th February 2017). Münchner Studien zur Alten Welt; Band 17* (München: Utzverlag, 2019), 103–113. If that age pattern was the norm, it helps to explain why, in many cities, including Melos, Lysander and others were able to restore the cities to their previous citizens, the boys who were spared being now grown up and joined by some older men who had found ways of surviving in exile. The many scenes of violence shown on the Parthenon are consistent with the view it is Homeric conventions that are offered, and the classical Athenians and Hellenes more generally had a strong sense of city and kinship, but little concept of what in modern terms is called 'human rights.'

203 This plan was carried out, notably on the west pediment of the Parthenon where part-human part snake figures are shown in the so-called Kekrops group, but also on the iconography of statues of Athena and on their bases that were encountered at eye-level. The discourse of autochthony, when decoded, opened up two internal divisions, first the normalizing ('nomismatizing') of a general sentiment against foreigners and immigrants of the kind described by Euripides in the *Erechtheus*, and secondly a normalizing of a division by social class within citizen families, autochthony being a status that only birth could confer. The discourse of autochthony in its first sense was carried into law by the Periclean era law of 450 that restricted the right to participate in public debates to those men, who could show that they were 'Athenian' by both parents, an example of a form of racism practised in recent centuries until the present day, and which runs counter to the Athenian self construction as set out in, for example, the Periclean Funeral Oration. Unusually we have contemporary records of opposition, notably by Antisthenes, one of those who was prevented from political participation and by the character of Ion in Euripides's play, the *Ion*, to be discussed in Chapter 3.

too feel that our whole city is ennobled, so we will be able to use our festivals to achieve the results we all desire.[204] It is not enough that we and our friends are given an occasional treat, like the nibble of a quince that our great Solon recommended to brides before they are first taken to bed, as a sign that the delights of lips and speech should be harmonious and pleasing from the first day.[205] As in our tragic drama, the number of ways in which our stories can be usefully told and usefully seen, told, and heard, to the benefit of our city, is limited only by the number of festivals and by the willingness of our citizens to show their 'charis'.

We will grant immunity to citizens from being seized for debt during a festival, so that these occasions become havens of peace in the stormy life of our city.'[206] And we will defend the gods against irreverence ('asebeia').[207] We have all been to festivals where some of those present

---

204 The Commissioners repeat, at the beginning of their sentence almost to the letter, the sentiments attributed to the character of Socrates at the start of the Platonic dialogue known as the *Menexenus*, a rare example of a description of the response of a real consumer, or certainly of the intended effects of the rhetorical aims of funeral orations. The use of the phrase 'those that are named multi-coloured' in the *Menexenus* (τοῖς ὀνόμασι ποικίλλοντες) also makes it an example of what Aristotle and others called 'aesthetics' a word not confined to visual 'art' in the modern usage but to the sensations felt by the consumer with all of his or her senses, including the assumption that William Gladstone was amongst the first to notice, that in Homer, the ever-changing light of Athens was itself better understood as a contributor to the sensation than as a mere externality to be elided, as discussed in Chapter 1. The usage of the Greek word 'aesthetica' and its cognates in the classical period, notably by Aristotle in his *Art of Rhetoric* and elsewhere, is discussed by Porter, *Origins of Aesthetic Thought*, 46–57. Although not written by Plato, the *Menexenus*, like the *Eryxias* mentioned in Chapter 1, is not a 'spurious work' intended to deceive, but an example of a rhetorical exercise, with elements of nudge-nudge playfulness and parody, into whose conventions the readership is invited to enter and become complicit. Its aims may include, as in the Old Comedy of Aristophanes (and others mostly lost except for fragments) a critique of the conventions of rhetoric itself. My experiment with the form is in Chapter 5.

205 The Commissioners adapt a requirement said to have formed part of the laws of Solon that regulated family, including sexual, relationships. Discussed with the associated ancient documents in Leão, Delfim F. and Rhodes, P. J., eds, *The Laws of Solon* (London: I. B. Tauris, 2015), fragment 52a, http://doi.org/10.5040/9780755626281. In the platonic discourse, *The Menexenus*, the character of Socrates notes that the ennobling effects of attending a funeral oration only lasted for three days at most.

206 Parker, Robert, 'Law and Religion' in Gagarin, Michael and Cohen, David, eds, *The Cambridge Companion to Ancient Greek Law*, (Cambridge: CUP, 2005), 64, https://doi.org/10.1017/CCOL0521818400.004, discussing Demosthenes against Meidias Dem.21.

207 The law under which Socrates was judicially put to death, an event that, by itself, should dispel the modern idea, discussed in the discussion of Milton's *Areopagitica*

say the right things about the gods and the city, who parade, sing, dance, and pray in unison, but then, when the food and drink run out, a few [*signifies contempt*] 'cynics' start sneering.[208] We will punish with death or exile, and with the confiscation of property, anyone who steals from our holy places. And we will accept the testimony of slaves, who often know what is happening within a household ('oikos') and grant them freedom, so that even the meanest can see the benefits of performing good citizenship.[209]

Our festivals will take place both at rosy-fingered dawn and at violet-crowned evening, not only in eye-dazzling summer but also in soft-shadowed winter when our mariners are at home with their families.[210] At no other times do our images reveal the gods more clearly to us than when the Earthshaker sends his life-giving watery tempests, on which our city depends, and when, to delight as well as to terrify us, for the gods like to be playful, he lights up the starry sky with his sudden silver rods.

There may be some who think that Athens already has too many festivals, that the crowds block the traffic, interrupt the life of the city, and slow down the work that many have to do.[211] And we hear the same

---

in St Clair, *WStP*, Chapter 22, https://doi.org/10.1164/obp.0136.22, that classical Athens protected or valued freedom of speech as such.

208 The Commissioners repeat a point made explicitly by, for example, Plut. *De Iside* 70. They also signal an assumption that the audience already shares that the main purpose of sacred sites and their buildings is to be a venue for festivals

209 *Ibid.* 65. The Commissioners, aware that speech acts do not necessarily represent what a speaker thinks, hasten to return to the easier ground of regulation. Contradicting an earlier part of their speech about mutual trust, they encourage slaves to make allegations against their masters and mistresses, even although they know that, with such incentives for men and women who had little reason to want to uphold the institutions of the city and its rhetorics, at least some allegations will be false.

210 In their attempt to maintain the elevated, poetic tone of this part of their discourse, the Commissioners refer to the old favourites, Homer and Pindar. Whether the references were still fresh or were clichés under construction cannot be judged, except to note that the allusions would have been instantly recognized by a high proportion of the citizenry and, as a result of their appearance in speeches such as the present one, become familiar to many who knew little of the historical occasions and contexts in which they first exercised their rhetorical power, but had encountered them in their own, to them modern, contexts, including reading them or listening to them being recited.

211 For a complaint that Athens already held more festivals than any other city and that they were an expensive nuisance that imposed unnecessary delays on day-to-day life, and costs on business, we have the remarks of the so-called 'Old Oligarch.' Ps.

men complaining that our metics and our slaves are dissolute and out of control, and by forgetting their proper place, are corrupting the whole city and even our language, with their foreign usages.[212] The duty to advise the city on how much of its useable resources ('chremata') the city should devote to meeting its many needs lies with other commissions, and today we will not go into the precise amounts either on the costs of our proposals or on how best to pay for them. It is however right for you to learn what is needed as early as is possible, not only so that we can decide on how best to manage our farms so that they will produce animals and other foods and wines that are needed at the right time, but also to give us time to consider how much the most fortunate will be able to afford to contribute as our duty and our obligation ('charis') require us.[213] Only a foolish steward agrees to buy a donkey on his master's behalf without knowing whether it is stubborn or biddable, how much food and water it will consume, and whether its labour will improve the income of the farm. And we remember the sheep who complained to the master that while they worked hard every day to produce milk, wool,

---

Xen. Const. Ath. 3. For a complaint that Athens already held more festivals than any other city and that they were an expensive nuisance that imposed unnecessary delays on day-to-day life, and costs on business, we have the remarks of the so-called 'Old Oligarch.' Ps. Xen. Const. Ath. 3.

212 This sentiment is also in Ps. Xen. Const. Ath. 3.

213 It should not be assumed that the Commissioners were being ironic, let alone sarcastic. The city was a large-scale purchaser of the farm products, grains, wines, and notably animals suitable for sacrifices, some of which had lead times of many months and required working capital over similarly long periods. And the expectation that citizens with large incomes would make voluntary contributions in accordance with 'charis' (including the unwritten laws of reciprocity and of honour), that is, make plans for their own forward-budgeting for the 'oikos', was an entirely reasonable one. We can take it too that the shift from 'you' to 'we' is not a result of lack of care but a rhetorical device aimed at consensus building and promoting notions of inevitability. The Commissioners have not taken the opportunity that Pericles is reputed to have done in his Thucydidean speech of the funeral oration, to criticize the free-loaders, in Greek 'idiotes', who selfishly take no part in public affairs while enjoying the benefits provided by the city. The fact that Thucydides felt able to include that criticism in what is otherwise a consensus-building rhetoric, may be an indication that some acknowledgement of the damage to civic cohesion done by the 'idiotes' could not be avoided if the whole speech was to achieve its broader purpose on the occasion. But for the historic Pericles to have introduced such a jarring and divisive political complaint on an occasion whose primary purpose was to pretend to unity is so unlikely that we may have here an example of how Thucydides was able to use a Thucydidean speech to address a wider audience, as already discussed.

and leather, his dog just lay around eating food from his master's table, and the master had to explain to the stupid sheep that it was the dog who guided them, guarded them, and kept them safe.[214]

Festivals bring us together, even those whose nature is to serve. And as the festivals become more frequent they drive out those gods that are not approved by the polis. We will take measures against men who set up their altars and slaughter sacrificial animals in the storkade.[215] And despite the best efforts of the Areopagus, foreigners from the east have brought their [*the reciter pauses and signifies contempt*] 'Magi' into our city and turn to magic practices to try to communicate with the gods directly. We swear by Zeus, by Athena, by all the gods of Olympus, and by those ancient gods who inhabited this land before them, that if these evil men or unchaste women use their despicable tricks to fix horse races, on which honour and money depend, and harm men and women whom they want to destroy, they will not succeed.[216] Their cursing tablets, often cunningly made from imperishable lead, have been found hidden in our most sacred places, including the abodes of the dead and among the bones of our babies.[217] When cursing is appropriate, it is our

---

214 Xen Mem 2.7.14. Discussed by Parsons, Mikeal C. and Martin, Michael Wade, *Ancient Rhetoric and the New Testament: The Influence of Elementary Greek Composition* (Waco: Baylor UP, 2018), 50, as an example of the use of animal fables in rhetoric. The Commissioners employ the device to remind the listeners in advance that money can be used to buy useful services and not just useful things, a point that they will return to later.

215 That this was done is proved by the inscription quoted by Iakovidis, Spyros E., *The Mycenaean Acropolis of Athens* (Athens: Archaeological Society of Athens, 2006, translated from the Greek edition of 1962), 266 from W. Dittenberger, SIG 3, 83. It is dated to *c.* 433/2 BCE. The use of the phrase 'storkade' in an official inscription shows that the memory that linked the site to the Pelasgians had been lost or was being cleansed.

216 By mentioning the chthonic gods whose cults continued to be practised in the caves of the Acropolis slopes and elsewhere, the Commissioners acknowledge, perhaps inadvertently, that the Olympian twelve had only assumed their primacy as a result of a human decision to deem them so by 'nomisma', although Athena is sometimes referred to as chthonic as part of the discourse of autochthony.

217 Discussed, with illustrations of actual examples found in archaeology, by Maggidis, Christofilis, 'ΜΑΓΙΚΟΙ ΚΑΤΑΔΕΣΜΟΙ or Binding Curse Tablets: A Journey on the Greek Dark Side', in Holloway, R. Ross, ed., *Miscellanea Mediterranea* (Providence, R.I.: Center for Old World Archaeology and Art, Brown University, 2000), 83–100. The character of the wise nurse in the *Hippolytus* of Euripides suggests to the character of Phaedra that her sexual obsession with Hippolytus may be due to the secret actions of some enemy, so implying that no well-brought up woman could even think of such an explanation but also that it was prevalent and recognizable as

city not individuals [*'idiotes'*] or nurses or slaves who will decide who must be cursed.[218] Our city is not a bar of iron or a slab of marble that looks strong at first sight but has a hidden seam that causes it to break up if it is ever put under strain.[219]

So what more must we now do? In a city, as in a human body, although disease may flow from the parts into the whole, the wholesome parts can also correct the whole.[220] Some measures to preserve ourselves from the effects of marriage with foreigners have been taken, at the behest of the wise Pericles.[221] But we need new regulations and new officers to enforce them.[222] And laws by themselves are not enough. As we all know, love ('φιλότης') brings together the four elements of which all nature is composed, and strife ('νεῖκος') causes them to separate.[223] And,

---

prevalent by the audience. Eur. Hipp. 318. We have what is presented as a verbatim version of the penalties called down by a public curse on individuals, on cities and on whole ethnic groups, in the later classical period in the model speech by Aeschines against Ctesiphon, Aeschin. 3 110, of which the following is an extract: 'That their land bear no fruit; that their wives bear children not like those who begat them, but monsters; that their flocks yield not their natural increase; that defeat await them in camp and court and market-place, and that they perish utterly, themselves, their houses, their whole family; "And never," it says, "may they offer pure sacrifice unto Apollo, nor to Artemis, nor to Leto, nor to Athena Pronaea ['the Athena who foresees and preempts'], and may the gods refuse to accept their offerings." For how a formal, unpublicized time period between a physical birth and an acceptance of a disabled baby as a legitimate member of a family was available to allow for the disposal of unwanted babies and, incidentally, to ward off stories that a family had been cursed, is discussed in Chapter 4.

218 Examples from outside Athens noted by Osborne, Robin, and Rhodes, P. J., *Greek Historical Inscriptions, 478–404 BC* (Oxford: OUP, 2017), 102.

219 Plut. Per. 11.3. The reference is to internal political divisions that lead to civil disorder, conspiracies, and coups, with another resort to a comparison with the tools of the building industry.

220 The medical metaphor drawn from ancient misunderstandings is used in, for example, Plut. Lys. 17.6.

221 The Commissioners refer to the law of 450 that limited full citizenship and political participation to those men who could claim that both parents were free-born Athenians, the 'two-parents rule', which is discussed further, with its implications for understanding what is presented on the Parthenon frieze, in Chapter 3.

222 Although classical Athens was proud of being free, meaning independent, it was also internally highly regulated, as can be seen from the large number of offices noted in the Aristotelian *Ath. Pol.*

223 The Commissioners refer to the cosmological theories of Empedocles of Akragas, then at the height of his fame, of which a fragment containing the quotation they allude to has been preserved. Empedocles was carrying forward the ideas of earlier philosopher/scientists in developing the theory of extramission that was mainstream at the time of the speech and whose main features were to be further reinforced by the work of Plato and Aristotle.

as the wise Anacharsis told Solon who thought he could bring about order in the city with written laws, 'these laws are like spiders' webs; they hold the weak in their meshes, but are torn to pieces by the rich and powerful'.[224] So what better measures, we ask every man of Athens to consider for himself, can we take to bring our city back together as strongly as we were when we faced the barbarians? And the answer your Commissioners give you is simple: Just as a farm, however small, when it well tended, will yield a harvest; just as the Scythian slaves that we have bought, when given their food and shelter, will contentedly keep order at disturbances; so too can our famous festivals continue to produce harvests of peace and harmony in our city.[225] And just as we must make our acropolis secure against any attack by an army and make sure that enemies can see with their own eyes that it is impregnable, so too we must protect our city's most valuable possessions against infiltrators, usurpers, and thieves.[226]

You, men of Athens, who share a lineage of unrivalled purity, do not need to be reminded that the aim of 'paideia' is to turn our young men into brave soldiers.[227] So how can we use our surplus of useful things to

---

224 The story is told in Plutarch's *Solon*, Plut. Sol.5.2.

225 The Commissioners take a moment to explain the economic concept of capital and streams of benefits as different from financial capital and the interest that money can earn if lent out. It was a distinction that, we can be confident, the Athenians were well aware of and that they practised in their personal as well as civic lives, although they do not appear to have had an overarching word for capital in this, its most important sense for any policy maker whether in ancient Athens or at other times. In the ancient Greek language, although there are words for money, and for useable money, as the Commissioners will come to in their speech, common usage did not always distinguish between wealth and income derived from the possession of assets, or between the real economy and the ways in which the operation of the real economy was financed.

226 The Commissioners point out the interdependence of the Propylaia and of the Parthenon, whose actual construction seems to have proceeded simultaneously, both in deterring any attack by being seen to be astonishingly well-constructed from large marble blocks and in making it hard, even if an enemy were to take over the site, for him, or her, to seize the valuables stored there. It was well known, for example, from the failed coup by Kylon that political conspirators usually tried to seize the treasuries where coined money and bullion were stored along with other precious objects that could be melted down, converted into physical money, and used to buy real resources, part of the plot of Aristophanes's comedy, the *Lysistrata*. The contents of the treasuries in the classical period were published and discussed by Harris, Diane, *The Treasures of the Parthenon and Erechtheion* (Oxford: OUP, 1995) and are briefly summarized in Chapter 4.

227 The Commissioners, in reminding the audience of the autochthonous myth and explaining the purpose of education in the stories of mythic and actual forebears,

produce useful men?[228] As we look out across Attica we see our groves of tame olive trees, that, as our poet sings [*signifies quotes*] 'are a terror to enemy spears' [*unquote*].[229] Since we can obtain whatever we want with the proceeds ('poroi') of what we exchange, our barns are no longer full of stocks of food, drink, and oil that are not yet needed and that attract the greedy eyes of tyrants and robbers.[230] As we look out to Brilessos,

---

follows almost exactly the conventional rhetoric of the words of the Funeral Speech of Hyperides, delivered in 322.

228 The Commissioners deploy the various usages and cognates of the Greek word for 'use' and 'useful' to associate the resources of the city, including 'chremata' [useful things including 'money'] to produce 'chrestoi' [useful men].

229 The Commissioners refer to a description put into the mouth of the Chorus, and therefore a commonplace, in the *Oedipus at Colonus* of Sophocles. ἐγχέων φόβημα δαΐων Soph. OC 699. As suggested in Chapter 1, the adoption of a tradeable crop almost as a monoculture may have been part of a real productivity improvement in the output of the land of Attica, compared with the poor quality of the land for producing agricultural crops for human consumption as in the oikos subsistence model. There are traces of an olive oil revolution in the fragments of the works of Solon that, whether genuinely by him or invented to preserve a memory, have him imposing limits on exports of oil, that is a measure to preserve jobs, and precautions, that were unsuccessful, to avert tyranny, it being easier for potential leaders of coups to seize cisterns full of oil than to tax or seize such little surpluses, a goat here or some barley there, that were available to be taxed or seized from the numerous semi-independent settlements of the oikos economy. Olive oil, a nutritious crop, appears to have been mainly valued as a way of cleansing and oiling the bodies of athletes, as is mentioned in the development account by Thucydides. Having the manpower available to the city well exercised would be an advantage in war, but scarcely enough to justify the word 'terror.' According to Plutarch's *Solon*, for which he claimed the authority of poems now lost, Solon wrote a law forbidding slaves to practise gymnastics, or to take boys as lovers, so dignifying these practices by confining them to 'the worthy.' Plut Sol 1.3. A direct claim for the military value of olive oil is made by Aristotle in *Problems* 5.6, where he says that rubbing the body with oil mixed with water 'stops fatigue.' And Aristotle may have been right. Olive oil includes lipids that are 'indispensable for human nutrition ... almost completely absence from cereals' even when olives are consumed in small quantities as a piece of fruit. Discussed by Bresson, Alain, *The Making of the Ancient Greek Economy: Institutions, Markets, and Growth in the City-States. Expanded and Updated English Edition, Translated by Steven Rendall; Originally Published in French 2007–2008* (Princeton; Oxford: Princeton UP, 2016), 128, https://doi.org/10.23943/princeton/9780691183411.001.0001. It is also possible that the audience for the *Oedipus at Colonus* and others appreciated that it was the releasing of manpower from inefficient farming that had enabled Athens to build its merchant fleet and navy. A discussion of the olive tree displayed on the most prominent place on the Parthenon, the west pediment, is in Chapter 3.

230 The Commissioners point to other real efficiency improvements that had already resulted from the monetization of much of the economy, including a reduction in the amount of working capital needed and in the resulting higher real incomes accruing to an oikos, as were explicitly noted by Aristot. Econ. 1. 1344b. Although

that once could only support a few goats, we see men at work harvesting other gifts that the gods have bestowed on our land of Attica.[231] It is fitting that, as our fathers decided, for our sacred sites, autochthonous men should use autochthonous stone.[232]

As for the stories that our great temples will tell now and for ever, our problem, men of Athens, has been how to choose which of our heroes to leave out than which to include.[233] None will be without signs.[234] We need no longer show the monsters by which our ancestors recalled that time using images made from unshining poros stone.[235] It is more useful

---

not mentioned specifically here their remarks form part of the generally accepted long run narrative of development from brutishness discussed in Chapter 1.

231   See note 64.

232   The reference to our fathers is to the decision to build what is now called the pre-Parthenon with local Pentelic marble.

233   Although this is a rhetorical device, found, for example, in the Periclean Funeral Oration, it was highly relevant and convincing in the present context. One of the features of both pediments of the Parthenon is that they are so overcrowded with figures from the mythic history of Athens that it is hard to imagine that any ancient viewer would have been able to identify them all just from their markers, as will be discussed further in Chapters 3, 4, and 5. The Commissioners make a substantial point about the intended content and viewership, but as the character of Socrates remarks in the *Gorgias*, listeners do not, in any case, like speeches that are tempered to suit foreigners. Plat. Gorg. 513c.

234   The Commissioners echo a phrase used by the character of the god Hermes in the Prologue to the *Ion* of Euripides where Athens as a city is referred to as 'not asemic', to coin a word from modern semiotics, the study of signs and how they are used to signal more than may be suggested by a literal reading of words or images. ἔστιν γὰρ οὐκ ἄσημος Ἑλλήνων πόλις, τῆς χρυσολόγχου Παλλάδος κεκλημένη, Eur. Ion 8 and 9. In the play, as here, the comment may be reminding the audience that it is legitimate to draw a range of meanings from looking at the images, including as in the play, parallels with contemporary experience, but that remains a speculation. Some modern scholars in referring to the stories presented on the Parthenon use the word 'polysemic' although the problem of recovering what the signs meant in the strange circumstances of classical Athens remains. As it happens, the *Ion* preserves one of the view descriptions from the classical era of how real viewers, albeit fictional, engaged with the stories in stone as will be discussed in Chapter 3.

235   The Commissioners refer to the custom of filling the awkward spaces of temple architecture with mythical creatures that are half human, half animal, from the many examples found in the Acropolis excavations in the later nineteenth century as described in St Clair, *WStP*, Chapter 21, https://doi.org/10.1164/obp.0136.21. A conspicuous exception was the picturing of autochthony in the so-called Kekrops group on the west pediment of the Parthenon. An example of how the displayed monsters had been used to teach 'arete' in the past was put into the mouth of the character of Prometheus, who struggles to overthrow the old order, in the *Prometheus Bound* of Aeschylus: 'Pity moved me, too, at the sight of the earth-born dweller of the Cilician caves curbed by violence, that destructive monster of a hundred heads, impetuous Typhon. He withstood all the gods, hissing out terror with horrid

to be reminded of the brutish life that those who first seized Attica and founded our city had to endure so that we today and in the future can live in a well-run city.[236] We will offer pictures that by their freshness nourish the sight and draw our minds to ancient deeds that deserve to be imitated.[237] Made from eternal marble, held with hard iron and gilded bronze, and easily renewed if their cosmetic paint is wiped or stained by rain, the images will draw the eyes of our people, causing them to remember, to re-tell, to imitate, and to relive.[238] We will make sure that no enemy of our city, either from Athens or from elsewhere, will destroy or deface them.[239] We will present the history of the war against the Trojans from the first sailing of our fleet to the glorious burning and sacking of that city.[240] As Homer sings, we Ionians, with our long flowing

---

jaws, while from his eyes lightened a hideous glare, as though he would storm by force the sovereignty of Zeus. But the unsleeping bolt of Zeus came upon him, the swooping lightning brand with breath of flame, which struck him, frightened, from his loud-mouthed boasts; then, stricken to the very heart, he was burnt to ashes and his strength blasted from him by the lightning bolt.' Aesch. PB, 355 to 365. That monsters were used to scare children is included by Aristides in his Panathenaic oration, 25, half a millennium later, an example of the long continuity.

236 The Commissioners defend the decision, on which they may have anticipated that their recommendation would be overruled by conservative forces in the Assembly, by enabling viewers to position the anomaly in the progress from brutishness narrative.

237 A point made in, for example, Plutarch's *Life of Pericles*, Plut. Per. 1.3, where it is presented as a direct result of extramission, adding notions of being drawn to 'the good.' To a Greek listener, the word translated as 'fresh' is cognate with 'flower.' In the immediately following passage readers are warned not to equate the work with the moral quality of the maker, a confusion encouraged by the rhetorics of western romanticism, but dismissed as an error as discussed in Chapter 4.

238 The Commissioners repeat a thought offered by the character of Helen in Euripides's play of that name, that if her attractiveness could have been wiped off as on a statue, the Greeks would have forgotten about her. Eur. Hel 260–264. I am grateful to David Kovacs for his advice on the meaning of the passage.

239 The Commissioners know that images are defaced as ways of performing opposition to the official ideology, sometimes, as in the case of the mutilation of the herms, apparently as a threat of terrorism. In practice the Commissioners knew that, as far as the stories presented on the Parthenon were concerned, it would have been impracticable, with minimal security, for anyone to get close enough to the sculptural images, whether to damage them or steal the metal. Mutilation at a distance only became practicable with the advent of firearms. Although there is not an exact correspondence, the officially authorized acts of mutilation of Christian times, discussed briefly in Chapter 3, appear to have been concentrated on the images that gave greatest offence to the new regime.

240 The Athenian audience did not need to be explicitly reminded that the sacking of cities and the taking of female slaves were among the attractions of war in their own time under their own conventions.

chitons, were among those who captured and sacked Troy, as we now celebrate and commemorate at our festival at Delos.[241] We will make our own Menestheus live again, wielding his death-dealing axe and seizing his deserved share of the spoils.[242] Our brave sailors were also there. As Homer tells us, when Ajax (Aias) brought twelve ships from our Salamis to Troy, he [*quotes*] 'halted them where the Athenian phalanxes were stationed'.[243] In those never-to-be-forgotten times, which we relive in our festivals, it was we Athenians who were the gallant Opuntian Locrians, doing more than anyone thought that we could, and leading all Hellas to victory.[244] We will show how our gods fought against the

---

241 The phrase appears to be directly quoted, even to the use of the archaic 'Iaones', by Thucydides 1.6., who is the source for the wearing of the distinctively Ionian dress in the Ionian festival at Delos that brought together Ionian Athens with the overseas Ionian settlements in the islands on the coast of Asia. That the phrase is a late insertion in the *Iliad*, designed to boost the claims of Athens to have played a larger role in the Trojan war than the earlier versions reported, has been suggested by scholars, not least because it is implausible that 'Ionians', who are only mentioned in the *Iliad* at this one place, could have actually have fought wearing such an inconvenient dress. In this case, Thucydides, like other authors of the classical age, regarded the information about the past embedded in formal performances of memory as of at least equal truth value as those carried by technologies of inscription, whether written in words or pictured in visual images. What we can say is that the phrase 'long chitoned Ionians' (ἑλκεχίτωνες Ἰάονες), whenever it was accepted into the *Iliad*, became part of the discursive environment of the classical era and was presented in visual form as a counter-ecphrasis, as worn by the 'Caryatids' on the Ionic Erechtheion, and on the frieze of the Parthenon as discussed in Chapter 4.

242 The Commissioners apply to the metopes of the Parthenon the practice of making stories in stone displayed on sacred buildings become alive in the imagination of their viewers as is described by Euripides in the *Ion*, the main source for ways of looking at stories presented on sacred buildings, as will be discussed in Chapter 3. The Commissioners also remind us that the metopes, bearing scenes of pitiless violence, rape, within a tradition of monstering non-Hellenes, were much more visible than the stories presented on the frieze.

243 Hom, Il. 2.558. The geographical encyclopedist suggested the verses had been inserted into the Homeric text either by Peisistratus or by Solon to boost the Athenian claim that Salamis had always been part of Attica, populated by Ionians, that is, by kinsmen of the Athenians who also called themselves Ionians. Strab. 9.11.

244 The Commissioners compare the catalogue of ships in Book 2 of the *Iliad* in which the small size of the Athenian contingent is mentioned with the catalogue of the ships at Salamis, noted by Herodotus at 8.1.1, that recalls the list in Homer, to remind the audience of how far Athens has come both militarily and in comparison with other cities since those days. At Salamis the Athenians are reported as having provided a hundred and twenty-seven ships, by far the largest contribution, whereas the Opuntian Locrians, the smallest contingent, could only manage seven fifty-oared 'penteconters', a smaller type of vessel. By their rhetorical device the Commissioners turn the small and undistinguished role that Athens was reported as having played in the war against Troy in the Homeric epics, from a matter of

Giants and our own ancient victories against oriental barbarism.[245] Every
good citizen of Athens knows the name of his ancestral father who lived
here in our ancestral land, the common possession of all Athenians.[246]

---

shame into one of pride. Another example of the complaint that Homer had been
unfair to the contribution of Athens to the conquest of Troy is in the speech put by
Herodotus into the mouths of the Athenians in which they claim the right to be
second to the Lacedaimonians at the forthcoming battle of Plataea 'in the hard days
of Troy we were second to none.' Hdt. 9.27.

245 Thanks to the careful work among the many small fragments by Alecos Mandis and
Katherine A. Schwab, some of the conjectures made earlier, have been confirmed.
Most of the metopes on the South side of the building appear to have been
deliberately and comprehensively mutilated, probably as part of the Christianization
of the building. Why others were left unmutilated remains unexplained, especially
as they included some pieces that were at least as visible. In the absence of any
plausible explanation related to visibility or ideology, we may be right to conjecture
a change of policy, motivated by a thought that it was wasteful to devote resources
to the expensive task of mounting scaffolds and chiselling out images, when
there was no longer much of a threat of a successful counter-revolution against
the Christianization. An alternative and cheaper strategy, that involved displaying
the act of successful mutilation itself, appears to have been applied, either as an
alternative, or more probably as an addition, to the central slab of the east frieze
as will be discussed in Chapter 3. As I have been informally advised by Professor
Yannis Lyzitzis of the University of the Aegean, to whom I record my thanks, a
technology already exists that will enable the dates of breakage and mutilation to
be estimated with greater precision, for example to the nearest century, and could,
I suggest, be proposed as a project to the authorities responsible for the site.

246 In justifying the stories to be presented on the Parthenon, many of which, in
the event, referred to eponyms of the various formal geographical and kinship
constituencies, the Commissioners turn to a sentiment put into the mouths
of the war dead in the Funeral Oration of Demosthenes. Dem. 60 1. On the first
part, different constituencies were taught to identify themselves by eponyms,
especially at festivals, such as at the pan-Attic Apatouria, one of the most inclusive
and, at three days, the longest-lasting of the annual festivals, when the young, or
occasionally adult, males who passed the various birth qualifications were inducted
and registered, and it is plausible that the designers of the Parthenon, chose such
stories to promote unity in difference as part of the general aim of producing
'useful' citizens. The Apaturia, on which there is much information recorded
over many ancient centuries, including on its rules for performing and displaying
induction, inclusion and exclusion, is described by Parker, Robert, *Polytheism and
Society at Athens* (Oxford: OUP, 2005), especially 371, 458–461, and 488–449, https://
doi.org/10.1093/acprof:oso/9780199216116.001.0001. On the second point, the
Commissioners risk encouraging an unfavourable reaction from at least some of
the audience. The land of Attica, all knew, was not a 'common possession' but was
privately and unequally owned and that the dead, who could not reply, were being
rhetorically deployed to help justify a political unity that they may or may not have
agreed with when they were alive. The apparently similar claim put into the mouth
of Pericles in his Funeral Oration as reported by Thucydides, namely that the whole
earth was their sepulchre, was less objectionable.

And of all our festival feasts, none gives more delight to Athenians than those in which we remember the ancestral heroes of our kin.[247] [*A member of the audience, foreseeing where the argument is leading, intervenes:* 'Can the Commissioners promise that we, the Anagyrasians, who are descended from Erechtheus, will be able to see and remember our ancestor Anagyrus?', *a remark that is met with shouts of assent and some knowing nods. The reciter, picking up the mood, responds*]. Our friend speaks well. Your Commissioners will show how all our demes and families came direct from the earth.[248] It would however be wrong for our temple to show insulting versions of our stories put about by a few malcontent and godless playwrights.[249] Some of us wish that some citizens would show their charis by donating a few black oxen to the festivals that bring us together as Athenians, or helping to pay for a warship, instead of confusing audiences with their clever honied words at the Dionysia.[250]

---

247 The Commissioners make a factual claim whose validity there is no reason to doubt. In a rhetorical exercise composed by Lucian, centuries later but within the continuing discursive tradition, known as *Anacharsis, or Athletics*, the character of Solon, often invoked as the originator of the best civic institutions, tries to persuade the character of the doubting Anacharsis that these occasions were amongst the greatest benefits the gods can bestow on a city, noting them in a list that includes, personal freedom, security, wealth and reputation. ἀλλ᾽ ὃς ἐν αὐτῷ συλλαβὼν ἔχει τὴν ἀνθρώπου εὐδαιμονίαν, οἷον ἐλευθερίαν λέγω αὐτοῦ τε ἑκάστου ἰδίᾳ καὶ κοινῇ τῆς πατρίδος καὶ πλοῦτον καὶ δόξαν καὶ ἑορτῶν πατρίων ἀπόλαυσιν καὶ οἰκείων σωτηρίαν, καὶ συνόλως τὰ κάλλιστα ὧν ἄν τις εὔξαιτο γενέσθαι οἱ παρὰ τῶν θεῶν. Luc. Anach. 15. The word for enjoyment, ἀπόλαυσις, as it was used by authors in the classical period retained the sense of actual consumption of fruits brought about by good government, although there is no need to suspect the Commissioners of appealing here to the bellies of the audience, the redistribution of real incomes being a well understood effect, as well as civic policy, of most communal feasts involving meat.

248 The reciter, who had been primed to expect opposition to the proposal to disallow references to the half-snake myth of autochthony, that was among the cornerstones of the power of certain families within Athens, concedes the point as a way of escaping having to make bigger concessions by including the so-called Kekrops group on the west pediment, where it struck the ancient viewer, Antisthenes, as it does most moderns, as so implausible as to be ridiculous and to attract ridicule.

249 An allusion to the extraordinary latitude allowed to classical era dramatists, especially Euripides, to tell old stories in new ways. In the *Phoenix* by Euripides for which there are testimonies and fragments, the character of Anagyrus revenges himself on a neighbour who had cut down his trees, by maddening one of his foreign girl friends to claim falsely that she had been abused by the neighbour's son, with the result that the father blinded his son and hanged himself and the girlfriend threw herself into a well.

250 The reciter presages an argument that later was made explicitly, and is still heard today, that enabling citizens to exercise critical judgement is not an optional extra

And we assure you that our people, including our women and children
will be able to look at the stories in complete safety just as when the
chorus watches a tragedy performed by actors in our festivals.[251]

Our citizens will call on the Sun and the Moon, on our swift-winged
breezes, on the sources of our rivers, and on the laughing waves of
ocean, by which our mother earth nourishes us.[252] All true citizens

---

to a civic education, but the best means of enabling a democracy to make informed
decisions. Here, as elsewhere, we are reminded that those who commissioned
the Parthenon were concerned to promote oligarchic values, and to an extent to
persuade the populace to accept such values, especially a liking for aggressive war
and imperial expansion, as if no alternatives were available. The extraordinary
freedom of the classical era drama was ended not long after.

251   The Commissioners encourage viewers, to whom by their choice of words they
reveal some condescension as leaders to followers, to imagine the images as able
to move like the actors in a play, as will be discussed, with examples of that way of
seeing from Euripides, in Chapter 3. The mention of 'safely' anticipates the objection
that, under the theory of cognition by extramission, the viewers may internalize
the actions of the dialogic actors rather than the moral and political lessons of the
dialogue itself. Because it became a 'chreia', that is, a useful piece of wisdom, by
good fortune, we have a surviving fragment of a dialogue that gives support to the
idea that this thought is present in the discursive environment. In the fragment,
the character of Antisthenes, a historic figure and friend of Plato, who was noted
for the boldness of his ideas, points out to the character of Socrates that, although
there is much violence in the tragic drams, 'no poet of tragedy has been so bold and
shameless as to bring into his drama a chorus being slaughtered.' *Antisthenes of
Athens*, Price edition, Chreia 16, 65, https://doi.org/10.3998/mpub.5730060. It has
been noticed that the chorus in Greek tragedies is sometimes part of the drama as
participating characters and sometimes stands outside as observers. For example,
Mastronarde, Donald J., *The Art of Euripides: Dramatic Technique and Social Context*
(Cambridge: CUP, 2010), 89, https://doi.org/10.1017/CBO9780511676437, where
the distinction is made between the 'intra-dramatic' and the 'extra-dramatic.' And
there is at least one case in a surviving tragedy in which a chorus scuttles from the
one to the other. In Aeschylus, Libation Bearers, 872–874, 'let us distance ourselves
from the deed, so that we may seem to be without responsibility for these evils' as
translated by Mastronarde, 100. Although in this case the chorus of slaves appears
to be presented as simply avoiding responsibility, they might also be avoiding the
pollution of being complicit in causing a death. The chreia of Antisthenes enables us
to claim with greater certainty that this convention was a general one that is likely
to have been enforced in advance of approval to perform, if that was ever needed,
by the city's institutions, including the institutions that supplied the financing. A
limitation, that may have been driven by other occasions, therefore gives the gnomic
statements of the chorus a particular authority as statements made within the limits
of the permissible, and therefore makes them especially useful in reconstructing
the discursive environment. In the stories presented on the Parthenon, there is no
equivalent of the external chorus, although there are many examples of the main
characters presented as observing the action.

252   The Commissioners quote from the invocation to the local climatic conditions
that in the *Prometheus Bound* of Aeschylus are brought together as gifts of the

will be able to point out their own ancestors and share in the glory of their great deeds.[253] The images we commission will help us to see the invisible gods who helped to give our city the glory that she now deserves, as well as all the other gods, known and now unknown, who have favoured our unity as citizens, as kinsmen, and as heroes held together in unbreakable bonds.[254]

---

land-as-mother metaphor already deployed and perhaps familiar and conventional, as necessary for the survival of the city. PB 88–91. All these features are pictured on the Parthenon, where the symbolic figures set in the corners of the pediments are normally understood as positioning the main events pictured in time and place, but without directly linking the land with the production of food. The vital importance of water both in defence and in food-production, by, for example, irrigating the olive groves and other crops, was never absent, and the references to the sea may have reminded the local audience of classical Athens both of fishing and of overseas trade. In one of he many twists in the *Ion* by Euripides that are soon reversed, the character of Ion, in what may be an allusion to the reclining figure in the pediment of the Parthenon, angrily invokes the eponymized Cephisos river as father of his true mother, in contrast to Kreousa, his stepmother, who has at this point in the play plotted to kill him. Eur. *Ion* 1261. Since the whole passage is hard to comprehend and Cephisos, a male character, is not mentioned elsewhere in the play, some scholars have seen it as an interpolation, as noted by Martin, Gunther, ed., *Euripides, Ion, Edition and Commentary* (Leiden: de Gruyter, 2018), 463, https://doi.org/10.1515/9783110523591. However, apart from breaching the general principle of preferring the more difficult reading, the contrast between a human genealogy and one emergent from the local geography and climate, an elaboration of autochthony, may not be too strained.

253 It is striking that the Commissioners do not begin with the gods, but as in funeral orations grant them only a subordinate walk-on role, when they are mentioned at all. Alongside the political and legal institutions, that were legitimated by having their date of foundation pushed back to the mythic time of the founding of the Areopagus, were the kinship associations, 'phratries', mentioned as existing at that time in Aesch. Eum. 656, and the 'phylai', conventionally translated as 'tribes.' Besides the numerous three-dimensional images of mythic characters that were displayed in the crowded pediments of the Parthenon, the frieze displays images in two dimensions of what appear to be the 'Eponymous Heroes.' In Chapter 3, I discuss how such images may have been engaged with by viewers in the classical era.

254 The Commissioners, picking up the familiar rhetoric of seeing and remembering, evidently refer to the two pediments of the Parthenon crammed with figures from the mythic history, that invite the non-mythic human generations both immediately and in the future to join them in a parade of 'arete' maintained. They seem also to refer to the images of the largely passive gods displayed on the east frieze of the Parthenon and who confer, by their presence as unseen spectators, their approval of the mythic events that are presented on the frieze as being enacted.

The mortals will be tall, straight, and perfect in limb from having been carefully moulded by their kin from the moment of their birth.[255] Our young men and women will never be fat, short, and flabby like wild Scythians.[256] Long ago we adopted a good custom from the noble

---

255 The socio-medical claim that, if babies were tightly wrapped in swaddling bands, they would grow up to be tall, lean, and straight, was a commonplace of the discursive environment during many ancient centuries. It is presented as normal by Hippocrates in the fifth century BCE work, Hp. Aer. 20, where the barbarous, ungainly, and ugly Scythians are alluded to as examples of what happens when swaddling is not practised. The advice given by the character of the 'Athenian stranger' in Plato's dialogue, the *Laws*, Plat. Laws 7.789E, was that a child should be kept swaddled till it is two years of age, and then physically carried everywhere by a strong nurse for another year as a precaution against distorting its legs by putting too much pressure on them. The 'stranger' who though not named, is thought, as in earlier dialogues, to represent, and speak for, the historic Socrates, who for most of his life had a closer physical resemblance to the flabby Scythians than to the young men presented on the Parthenon frieze, acknowledges that his proposal would be difficult to enforce and might incur ridicule. The stranger makes clear that he is arguing by analogy with moulding soft wax, and that he thought that babies were at their most brutish when young, for which he took the vocal and other protests made by babies at being controlled in this way as evidence. Swaddling bands feature in the *Alexandra*, one of the few post classical plays to survive, Hornblower, Simon, ed., *Lykophron: Alexandra: Greek Text, Translation, Commentary, and Introduction* (Oxford: OUP, 2015), line 1202; and frequently in the New Comedy of Menander, from where the themes of late recognition and reconciliation, and the defeat of Tyche, were adopted into comedy in Latin. As late as the first century CE, Luke of Antioch, (St Luke), the man with medical knowledge who may have written or compiled the Acts of the Apostles, uniquely among the authors of the four canonical Christian accounts ('gospels') of the life of Jesus of Nazareth, mentions that the infant at his birth was wrapped in swaddling bands, perhaps partly to signal a royal ancestry, but Luke goes on to imply that it was because Jesus was swaddled in infancy and because in boyhood he held conversations with medical doctors, that he grew up to have the qualities prized by Athenian paideia, tall, wise, and understanding the mutual obligations between humans and gods. Luke 2, and especially 52, where I have given the ancient meaning of 'charis.' Καὶ Ἰησοῦς προέκοπτεν σοφίᾳ καὶ ἡλικίᾳ καὶ χάριτι παρὰ θεῷ καὶ ἀνθρώποις. The numerous examples in the visual record are noted, with illustrations, in Chapter 4. I mention here, in anticipation of a question that may arise in the minds of readers, that I had come to that provisional thought before I decided to offer the Thucydidean speech that I have prepared as impartially as I could, without being swayed in the choice of topics by my knowledge of what is to come. In Chapter 4 I set out the evidence for swaddling more fully than for other components of the discursive and rhetorical environment. Although, in the event, the Thucydidean speech adds much weight to the suggestion, Chapter 2 has been drafted so as to preserve the potential value of the approach even for readers who may be unconvinced by the suggestion in Chapter 4.

256 The Commissioners allude to the opinion of Hippocrates, drawing on the standard theory of the four elements, that the main cause was that the Scythians did not use swaddling clothes. Hp. Aer. 20. They call them 'wild' to distinguish those who were nomadic, from the Scythians the audience were more familiar with, who were employed to keep order.

'long-heads' and soon all our sons and all who come later will be as the brave and wise general Pericles son of Xanthippos.[257]

Since everything is intended by nature to fulfil a purpose ('telos') all the men carrying jars or containers will use their left shoulder, as is needed when they defend themselves in battle.[258] With their horses too, it is hard to persuade them to keep their ranks in processions.[259] It was here in our land [*pointing to the hill of Colonus*] that Poseidon first gave men the horse-taming bridle and our horses, like our other beasts, will soon be as far advanced in their nature as their owners.[260]

257　The Commissioners, pursuing the theme of improving the physique and the moral qualities by swaddling refer to the description by Hippocrates of swaddling the head of infants to make it more elongated: '[I]mmediately after the child is born, and while its head is still tender, they fashion it with their hands, and constrain it to assume a lengthened shape by applying bonds and other suitable contrivances. The Ionic Greek: ἀναπλάσσουσι τῇσι χερσὶ καὶ ἀναγκάζουσιν ἐς τὸ μῆκος αὔξεσθαι δεσμά τεπροσφέροντες καὶ τεχνήματα ἐπιτήδεια shows that by 'bonds', Hippocrates meant forcible constraint such as was used on prisoners. They refer to the portrait of Pericles by Cresilas, of which many copies survive from ancient times, that show him with his helmet pushed back – to show he never ceases to be a warrior- and that emphasises his long head. Although Hippocrates says the custom is no longer practised, because, as he says, quoting examples of hereditary characteristics, the son of a father who has had his head artificially elongated would himself have a long head. A funerary monument that shows the practice, illustrated at Figure 4.17 shows that the custom was still practised in classical or post-classical times, and may have been referred to in the mythic world portrayed on the Parthenon.

258　The Commissioners allude to the notion, set out explicitly in a passage of Aristotle in his treatise on the movement of animals, iv, 706a. As elsewhere, 'nature' is set within the teleological emergence from brutishness narrative, with no implication that the presentations were copied from natural models as was to become a commonplace of western romanticism and of the custom of assuming that the ancient Athenians resembled the presentations. In hoplite warfare, as every ancient Athenian viewer knew, the notion that a citizen soldier might be permitted to choose to carry his shield on his right shoulder was militarily ludicrous, and any soldier who was inclined to prefer his left to his right hand, was a throwback who could not be tolerated.

259　The Commissioners repeat a point made by Aristotle in his treatise on the *Movement of Animals*, 12, 712a, where the problem was identified as overtiring the horses by their riders' misunderstandings of how horses actually move, whether walking or prancing, that caused them to refuse to obey their riders. There is, as with many points in the speech, a large learned literature on the numerous horses displayed on the Parthenon frieze. Most treat the horsemen as 'cavalry' although of course the real cavalry in classical Athens never appeared naked and I will call the figures presented simply as horsemen, the potential importance of to understanding what is displayed will be discussed in Chapter 3.

260　The Commissioners repeat the claim made by the Chorus in the *Oedipus at Colonus* Soph. OC 714. On the Parthenon frieze most of the bridles were rendered in paint, their presence can be easily restored from the actions of the riders and the heads of the horses pulled back. It was part of the discourse, perhaps related to the emergence from brutishness narrative, to assert that the Athenians were the first to apply useful new technologies. In the same passage the Chorus claim that the

Since the glorious time when we sacked the city of the Trojans, the best-bred of our youth have been ready to do their duty and to sack other cities and increase our wealth of possessions.[261] All over Hellas, the sons of Homer honour them in their rhapsodies.[262]

---

oar was an Athenian invention, and more plausibly the domestication of the olive tree as discussed in Chapter 1. The horses, like the dogs, and other domesticated animals, have advanced towards their 'natural' purpose by becoming members of the oikos.

261 The Commissioners refer to the ten four-horse chariots on the south and a similar number on the north frieze of the Parthenon that picture helmeted, semi-naked, but unarmed young men leaping off the war chariots as described as the way of fighting in the *Iliad*. The scenes interrupt the narrative of both friezes but are consistent with the convention designed into the composition that expects the events pictured to be encountered and perceived through the columns as episodes. As discussed further, with other examples, in Chapter 4. Those who, in modern times, have taken the view that, as an exception, the Parthenon frieze presented scenes from the contemporary festival of the Panathenaia (the 'Stuart conjecture') are able to interpret the episodes as references to the games that formed part of that festival. However, for those who are unconvinced by the Stuart conjecture, there is a ready explanation in the words of Joan Breton Connelly, in the more plausible 'Connelly conjecture', that what was shown were 'not Athenians taking part in the historical games but their legendary forebears who actually made war in this way.' Connelly, Joan Breton, *The Parthenon Enigma, A New Understanding of the World's Most Iconic Building and the People Who Made It* (New York: Alfred A. Knopf, 2014), 195. Only the wealthiest men, usually hereditary land-owners, were able to afford to keep horses, a status they proclaimed in the names that they gave themselves and their sons, Hippias, Hipparchos, Xanthippos and many more, including Hippothoon, one of the Eponymous Heroes pictured on the frieze, whose father was the god Poseidon. Noted with plentiful other examples, and confirmed by grave goods made over many centuries, by Camp, John McK. II, *Horses and Horsemanship in the Athenian Agora* (Athens: American School of Classical Studies, 1998). That even the most famous pan-hellenic games, and not just those associated with the Panathenaic festival were deemed to have existed in mythic times, another instance of jumping back across the ages about which the Greeks knew little, is exemplified by the ruse invented by the character of Orestes in the *Electra* of Sophocles, that has him make a slave swear that Orestes was killed falling from a chariot at the Pythian Games. Soph. El. 49. In the *Clouds* of Aristophanes, the play opens with the character of Strepsiades, pursued by creditors, telling the audience how he was persuaded into marrying a ruinously extravagant wife whose snobbish social pretensions include insisting that their son be given a name that includes 'horse.' The values that the Commissioners wish to present, such details suggest, are those of the privileged and that they were not universally accepted. Taken together with other indications of the discursive environment, notably the absence of weapons, we can be confident however, that the occasion that the horsemen are presented as attending a non-military celebration and that they are not soldiers but representatives of a privileged elite.

262 The Commissioners refer to members of the travelling guild of Homeridae, who seem to have started in Chios, the alleged birthplace of Homer, and who, as rhapsodes, in the classical periods and earlier travelled over Greece, including Athens, reciting selected passages in a particular style, in competitions. In Plato's *Ion*, Nestor's description of Homeric games is mentioned as an example. Plat. Ion 530a. As it happens, but this may be a coincidence, the dialogue is devoted

We mortals are, by our nature, moved by intellect, imagination, purpose, wishes, and appetites. And as we respond to our feelings, the objects of our desire move us to action.[263] And so we heed the wise advice of our guest and friend Pindar not to make images that stand idly on their pedestals and do nothing more, but they will [*the reciter signifies by tone of voice a quotation*] 'inspire men with impulses which urge to action, with judgments that lead them to what is useful'.[264] We will only choose the stories that will be useful to our own kin, including to our women, and not to strangers.[265] As our own god-inspired poet sings [*quotes*] 'Strange and wondrous is the power of kinship and companionship'. It is a power that even the gods themselves find and use for good or ill.[266]

---

to a discussion of the truth value of rhapsodies, a word rooted in weaving, and of the legitimacy of the strong emotions they brought about when sung well, and a comparison is made with static pictures, of which the Parthenon frieze was, in ancient terms, an example. No point about genealogy is explicitly made about the name of the character who is in conversation with the character of Socrates, Ion of Chios and its association with the mythic eponymous Ion may have been heard.

263 The Commissioners summarize a general theory set out by Aristotle in the *Movement of Animals*, 6, 700b, which, in accordance with what was then normal, makes no distinction between human and non-human animals, and justifies the use of erotic images as a means of persuading. It helps to explain the variety of male figures in various states of nudity presented on the Parthenon frieze, the diaphanous garments that reveal the female body underneath that were to become even more common later, and the particular case of the pubescent female as the ideal social body as presented on the central slab on the east frieze.

264 The Commissioners, use the authority of Pindar, quoting from a verse that was noted verbatim by Plutarch in his *Maxims of Philosophers*, Plut. Maxims 776c, turning it in a new direction. A discussion of how classical era viewers are noted as looking at the stories displayed on sacred buildings including the Parthenon is in Chapter 3.

265 The Commissioners use the phrase ἀνδράσιν ἀλλοφύλοις employed in the Thucydidean speech put into the mouth of Nikias who cautions against becoming involved with the city of Selinus in Sicily in Thuc 6.9.1. That the word excluded other Hellenes and not just barbarians is shown by the similar phrase put into the mouth of Athena as the spirit of Athens in the *Eumenides* by Aeschylus, line 851, ὑμεῖς δ' ἐς ἀλλόφυλον ἐλθοῦσαι χθόνα γῆς τῆσδ' ἐρασθήσεσθε, that shows both that the word was applicable to the people of Argos and, as with the rest of the play, was part of the self-fashioning of the classical city. From what we can tell from the fragmentary evidence, the stories presented on the Parthenon were in the event either pan-Hellenic, Ionian or locally Athenian.

266 The Commissioners quote the observation made by the character of Hephaistos, in the *Prometheus Bound* of Aeschylus τὸ συγγενές τοι δεινὸν ἤ θ' ὁμιλία. PB 39. In its context the phrase, with the ambiguous word 'deinon' whose meaning ranges from unusual and puzzling to admirable and terrifying, refers to the reluctance of the character of Hephaistos, that he overcomes, to bind his kinsman Prometheus. A similar sentiment, this time emphasizing that he is not acting out of kinship, is put into the mouth of the character of Ocean later in the play. PB 291.

And we will continue to send kinsmen to plant our seed overseas in places, such as Sicily, where none of the Hellenes are autochthonous, for unless we do so, we will lose those cities that we already hold.[267]

When our words have become deeds, when we visit our acropolis we are smitten as directly as Hippodameia is by Pelops, as if struck by a kind of lighting of the eyes, by which both are warmed and enflamed, and our minds are drawn to the images as directly as the craftsman's kanon goes straight.[268] And, as we all know: [*quotes*] 'he is no lover who does not love for ever'.[269] Just as a breeze or an echo rebounds from smooth rocks

---

267 The Commissioners anticipate statements about the history of the settlement of Sicily set out by Thucydides at the beginning of Book 6, 1 to 5, that as has often been pointed out is a resumption of the mythic history (the 'archaeology') in Book 1, that we can be confident formed part of the discursive environment long before the occasion of the reported debates on whether to invade and colonize Sicily. Like Thucydides, the Commissioners appear, for example, to endorse the element of that past that presents overseas colonization as part of a desirable stage in progress from brutishness, as one of the means by which in the Periclean Funeral speech, Athens is presented as 'the school of Hellas' overseas conquest being the military arm of what would later be called by modern European and American colonizers a 'civilizing mission.' The reported Thucydidean speeches bring out vividly the extent to which appeals to kinship were central to the question. And even when Thucydides, as narrator, offers his opinion that there was a 'real reason', he does not dismiss the kinship stories as untruthful, noting, for example, that some of the peoples were survivors from the fall of Troy, an aetiology claimed by several cities, such as the recently rediscovered Tenea, and later by Rome as celebrated by Virgil in the *Aeneid*. He also uses eponyms, such as Dorus as the father of the Dorians, presented as enemies of the Ionians, without noting that such names were a useful shorthand. The whole passage is, in my view, relevant to the mythic stories presented on the Parthenon, including my suggestion for the puzzle of the frieze as will be discussed in Chapter 3. The passage in Thucydides is commented on, mainly with respect to her discussion of money and resources, by Kallet, Lisa, *Money and the Corrosion of Power in Thucydides* (Berkeley: University of California Press, 2001), 24–31, https://doi.org/10.1525/9780520927421.

268 In referring to the ancient theories of what occurs in the act of seeing, 'extramission', as discussed in, for example, Plato's *Timaeus*, Aristotle's *On Sense and the Sensible*, and elsewhere back to the time of the Ionian Empedokles, the Commissioners quote faithfully from Sophocles's tragedy, Sophocles, 'Oenomaus', in his Fragments, edited and translated by Hugh Lloyd-Jones, Loeb Classical Library 483 (Cambridge, MA: Harvard University Press, 1996), pp. 242–248, fragment 274. They also imply, at the risk of falling into self-contradiction, that the visual does not need to be accompanied by the verbal ('ecphrasis') in order to be appreciated. An image of an actual kanon was given as Figure 1.8.

269 The Commissioners turn to the same maxim that Aristotle uses in the *Art of Rhetoric*, 2. 1394b5, to exemplify how to use [disputable] maxims as ways of pleasing and persuading an audience by telling them what they already believe to be true and generalizing it into a piece of accepted wisdom. This maxim, or gnomic utterance, is taken from Euripides, *Trojan Women*, 1051. The adding of one rhetorical trope to

and returns whence it came, so too the stream of useful stories passes through our eyes, the windows of our minds, and causes us inwardly to accept what they tell us.[270] And when our processions move amid the changing shadows cast by the Sun and by the Moon, turning the pictures into shadow pictures ('graphe' into 'skiagraphe'), they come alive in our minds. We take their stories shown on our buildings into our minds as we look at them and hold them there, perpetually renewed with every glance at the everlasting stone which the gods have bestowed on us.[271] The shining metal flashes, the mute stones speak, and the idols move and converse like living things.[272] When, as Orpheus sings, [*quotes*] 'the hour of delight arrives' [*ends quote*] I see each grasp the wrist of his nearest companion.[273] I see true Athenians joined together like the rings

---

another, piling Pelion on Ossa as they might have said, shows their inexperience and risked alienating the audience, many of whom, being trained in rhetoric themselves, understood what was happening.

270   The Commissioners turn to the metaphor for extramission used in Plato's *Phaedrus*, 245b–c, that, when combined with the erotic, as is also invoked in the same passage in the *Phaedrus*, helps to explain the aims of the producers of the Parthenon, not just by offering a rhetoric that they share with the consumers, but as an essential and unchanging characteristic of physiological perception and cognition. It is based on the same misunderstanding as was set out by Paul of Tarsus and Augustine of Hippo as discussed in St Clair, *WStP*, Chapter 22, https://doi.org/10.1164/obp.0136.22, although here widened to include warning against as well as inviting to imitate.

271   The Commissioners allude to the ways of seeing and of translating static visual images into explanatory and hortatory words, with the aid of the rhetorical devices known as 'enargeia' and 'ekphrasis', that had been practised since the age of Homer before the advent of writing, as discussed in Chapter 1 and of which actual examples are given and discussed in Chapter 3. They slip in a reference to the durability of Pentelic marble in the microclimate of Athens. The Commissioners only apply the modern distinction between 'sculpture' and 'painting' on occasions when it is needed, as it seldom was in the case of the images that formed part of the Parthenon and other temple sculpture, as distinct from free-standing works, preferring, as was more normal, to judge and categorize images by their expected effects.

272   Examples of actual ancient viewing of temple sculptures are given in Chapter 3.

273   This custom is explicitly mentioned in the Homeric Hymn to Apollo, HH 3 196, and shown on innumerable vase paintings. The ancients seem to have appreciated more than modern commentators until very recently that the skin is a sensitive organ of communicating pleasure, especially in places where hair grows, such as the wrist but not the palm of the hand. Discussed by Howes, David, 'The Skinscape: Reflections on the Dermatological Turn' in *Body and Society*, Vol 24 (1–2) (2018), 225–239, https://doi.org/10.1177%2F1357034X18766285. Some ideas that start from the presumption that the skin is a boundary are discussed by Grundmann, Steffi, *Haut und Haar: politische und soziale Bedeutungen des Körpers im klassischen Griechenland. Philippika, 133* (Wiesbaden: Harrassowitz Verlag, 2019) at present only known to me from the review in *Bryn Mawr Classical Review* dated 21 October 2020, https://bmcr.brynmawr.edu/2020/2020.10.21/.

of an iron chain, and the power of a Heraclean stone passing through every one.[274] The stories enter our minds both by our seeing and by our remembering.[275] As the heat rises in our bodies, the images are entering through the openings, ready to rise even when they are asleep, and are far from Athens.[276]

Our young children are given lessons ('paideia') by their parents and their nurses, and examples are shown to them in stories told in words. Even the youngest and least educated among us has eyes to see and can receive pictures, and the more often that they look upon them, the more the stories will live in their memories.[277] Some fortunate boys learn to

---

274 The Commissioners draw authority by referring to the ancient, almost mythic, poet even for a phrase that, by itself, appears to add little, but that to ancient listeners may have conjured up a memorable episode of climax. It is only known from having been used by Plat. Laws 2.669d. ὅσους φησὶν Ὀρφεὺς λαχεῖν ὥραν τῆς τέρψιος. The metaphor of a magnet and chain to describe the sense of a mutually-shared and self-reinforcing sense of shared excitement that occurs in crowds, attributed to Euripides, is used by the character of Socrates in Plat. Ion 535e, attributing it to Euripides as recorded in fragment 567 from the lost *Oeneus*.

275 The Commissioners use a phrase ὄψει καὶ μνήμη employed by Aristides in Oration 13, according to Dindorf's numbering, that describes how looking at built heritage, was thought to work, or was at least rhetorically commended as an explanation of how it might be deemed to work. Since 'seeing' carries all the justificatory force of extramission, that gave it primacy among the senses, it is likely that the phrase caught an aspect of the discursive environment that was long-lasting and not much contested. And that by looking, Aristides had in mind, not only individual viewing but the immersion of the collective experience of the movement, singing, dancing, smells etc. of festival processions and their associated rituals of communal eating and drinking. Elsewhere in his orations, for example in Dindorf number 20, Aristides employs the words for 'nature' and 'rationale' in their Greek senses, περὶ τῆς φύσεως τῆς αὐτοῦ τὰ μὲν ὄψει, τὰ δὲ καὶ λόγῳ.

276 The Commissioners refer to the theories of Democritus and others, summarised by later ancient authors, such as Plut. Quaest. Nat. 735a-b, that present the image-carrying particles, τὰ εἴδωλα, implied by extramission, as material objects, sometimes with their own mental agency. I record my thanks to Caterina Pellò whose paper 'Life and Lifeforms in early Greek Atomism' delivered online at the Institute of Classical Studies, London, on 18 January 2021, included a survey. And we have an example of how the psychology was thought to work in the *Athena* of Aelius Aristides Ael. Ar. Orat. 2 9. Although recorded centuries later and in the form of a meditation, the piece is firmly within the discursive environment which Aristides, who was not himself an Athenian, endorsed and prolonged in his Panathenaic oration. His reported dream takes the form of an imagined walk on the Acropolis of Athens, in which the statues, pictures, and the stories that they tell are all examples of the Acropolis as paideia. Athens, its history, its achievements, and its inventions, and Athena, its deity, are merged so as to be indistinguishable.

277 The speakers assume that the listeners share their understanding of extramission. In the key phrase of Aristides, whose Panathenaic oration reads in places like a tour of the Athenian Acropolis, they link sight with memory,

love 'arete' and wisdom ('sophia') by becoming the lovers of wise men, whose intensity of desire given by Eros surpasses the love of women and of family.[278] But, for the governing of our city all our people work must together in harmony and mutual trust. And to the end ('telos') that we are constantly reminded of what we share with one another, we follow the wise examples of Theseus and Solon when they brought us together into one city in former times. Just as a farm, when it is well tended, will yield crops for ever, and just as our Scythian slaves, when given food and shelter, will dutifully keep order at our meetings, so too, with foresight and care, our city will produce harvests of civic peace and harmony now and forever.[279]

An ability always to put our city first ('arete'), we all know, is not born in the nature of mortal men. It has to be learned and frequently practised like the skills that some men have in writing poetry, in making visual images, in performing music, or even in delivering [*the reciter here indicates by the modulation of his voice and his body language that the Commissioners are about to make a self-deprecating joke emphasizing the next phrase*] a 'useful' speech.[280] [*Pause for laughter*]. And as Prodikos reminds us, only a fool thinks he can acquire these skills just by praying to the gods.[281]

There are many paths to glory. As the eagle of Ceos sings: 'Each man seeks a different path on which to walk to attain conspicuous fame; and the forms of knowledge among men are countless. Indeed, a man

---

278 The Commissioners repeat the thought in the Thucydidean funeral oration by Pericles and in other authors as discussed by Azoulay, *Xenophon and the Graces of Power*.

279 The Commissioners take a moment to explain the economic concept of capital and streams of benefits as different from financial capital and the interest that money can earn if lent out. It was a distinction that, we can be confident, the Athenians were well aware of and that they practised in their personal as well as civic lives, although they do not appear to have had an overarching word for capital in this sense or, except by analogy, as here, the notion that the benefits from investment can take many forms.

280 The Commissioners summarize the dialogue between Socrates and others given in the imitation of a Platonic dialogue known as the *Eryxias*. Although not by Plato, the piece, that appears 'not to have been composed before the beginning of the third century B.C., belongs in tone to the previous age ... [and] is imagined to take place sometime between 431 and 421.' Laistner, M.L.W., M.A., Reader in Ancient History in the University of London; formerly Craven Student in the University of Cambridge, *Greek Economics* (London: Dent, 1923), ix. They include a touch of light humour, as is recommended in the rhetorical handbooks as part of the strategy of bringing the audience on to their side, known in Latin as 'captatio benevolentiae'.

281 *Eryxias*, 51.

is skilful if he has a share of honour from the 'Charites' and blooms with golden hope, or if he has some knowledge of the prophetic art; another man aims his artful bow at boys; others swell their spirits with fields and herds of cattle. The future begets unpredictable results: which way will fortune's scale incline?' [*Pause*]. But 'The finest thing is to be envied by many people as a noble man'.[282] The names of all those who have served their city by generously giving her a share of their surplus money will be commemorated for ever on the imperishable marble of our everlasting city.[283]

[*The reciter signals that the Commissioners are approaching the peroration*].

Look about you, men of Athens. The tables and tents are being taken out of storage. The servants hang fabrics on our buildings. The garlands of blossoms that the Charites love hang on the gates.[284] At Anagyra, at Acharnae, at Eleusis, at Rhamnos, at Piraeus, families rise before the sun. At Salamis the men are woken from their beds by their dutiful wives to make sure they do not miss the boat.[285] See our brothers and sisters putting on their coloured clothes and donning their flowered

---

282 The Commissioners quote from Ode 10 prepared by Bacchylides of Ceos for the winner of an Athenian footrace.

283 The Commissioners rhetorically conceal the contradiction between the notion of 'charis' as an obligation and as a gift given freely, and the *quid pro quo* that rich donors can expect. In the event only a few private donors were given the full marble treatment.

284 The Commissioners pick up a phrase, used, for example, in Pindar *Nemean* 5.53–54, reminding us again that, if we are to re-imagine the experience in a festival context, it is not only the paint and the metal that we have to include. The quotation, although referring to a festival at Nemea, also suggests that presentations of the Charites in some form as a reminder of the purpose of festivals were not unique to the Acropolis of Athens.

285 This example of enargeia by the Commissioners bears a close resemblance to the opening scene of the *Lysistrata* of Aristophanes. The saying aloud of the names of a selected list of typical localities in Attica is itself a contribution to unifying scattered real communities. Here, as in the *Lysistrata*, the mention of Salamis evoked not only the sea battle but the fact that, until the time of Solon, Salamis had been part of Dorian Megara, and its conquest by Athens marked the beginning of Athenian imperial expansion. Whether the people of Salamis had actually changed their kinship identity, assuming that they were the descendants of former Megarians and not settlers sent in to replace them, is not known.

chaplets.[286] Smell, men of Athens, the wild violets of the garlands.[287] Hear our Athenian women singing: 'Never will we divide the sisters of Charis from their sisters, the Muses, forever married in a sweet union / Never will we live among coarse men and women, but we swear always to be numbered among those who wear the crowns'.[288] The adulteresses, the criminals, and the oath breakers shrink away in shame, excluded from the glories of our city.[289] The pimps tremble with fear that they will be put to a deserved death.[290]

The men of Athens go to parts of our city that they seldom visit, full of wonder at our famous hills, at our agora (market place) where our goods as well as our news are exchanged. Those who seldom have

---

286 An explicit mention of those who are excluded by not being permitted to wear the chaplets in Xen Mem 2.7.22.

287 The Commissioners employ *enargeia*. According to Theophrastus, *On Odours,* 12, the smell of the flowers used in garlands could be felt at a great distance, and they were presumably chosen, like the music, so as to draw in outsiders. He discussed the same phenomenon in *De Causis* 6.17.1, with possible explanations, mentioning the difference between the wild and the domesticated varieties at 6.20.1. The famous lines by Pindar, on 'Athens the Violet Crowned', mentioned earlier as having become a kind of Athenian anthem, reminded audiences of the garlands as well as the violet of the sky. It is likely that the garlands shown on the Parthenon frieze were painted violet and saffron crocuses, another plant with the same property.

288 The Commissioners repeat the sentiment that unites the anonymous giving and social reciprocity of Charis with the arts associated with the nine muses, as sung by the Chorus in Euripides, *Heracles*, 675, in what was evidently a commonplace of the time and although a gentler phrase was used, μὴ ζῴην μετ᾽ ἀμουσίας, it was part of the self-affirming and excluding of others narrative of progress from brutishness. As an example of the longevity of the passage as catching the discourse of privilege and exclusion, and the need to distinguish themselves performatively from the vulgar and the boorish, it is quoted by Dio of Prusa in his discourse to the people of Alexandria. D.Chr. 32.100. Aristotle's view that 'charis' is a claim made by a civic elite that they are endowed with qualities that make them popular, including generosity, is noted by Azoulay, *Xenophon and the Graces of Power*, 28.

289 The primacy of sight in display and performance is assumed and implied by the Laconic saying attributed to king Agesilaos: 'When someone desired to know why Spartans do battle amidst the sound of fifes, he said, 'So that, as all keep step to the music, the cowardly and the brave may be plainly seen.' Plut. Apoph. 236.

290 Aeschines, *Against Timarchos*. Aeschin. 1 21. In his model speech 'on the Choreutes' the Orator Antiphon lists among the penalties for homicide, 'to be banished from his city, its temples, its games and its sacrifices, the greatest and most ancient of human laws.' Antiph. 6 4. For other lesser deviations from the norm to be excluded from the ceremonies in which the city performed its official self, was to be deprived of identity. An example of the official rhetoric being at odds with the real situation. Festivals, especially those that took place at night appear to have been the occasions for much transgressive behaviour, to the extent of that aspect becoming a standard plot of comedy and satire.

time visit our holy acropolis to see the latest decisions on treaties, on expenditures, on honours conferred, and stop womanly gossip and idle and vexatious [*emphasizes*] 'Rumour' from corrupting our democracy.[291] Some of the most useful wisdom began when groups of friends arranged to meet as they went together to see the new Thracian festival at the Piraeus, that, although still new, as all are agreed, is well arranged and orderly.[292] As we walk in the Panathenaic procession we see the young men of the Academy studying the secrets of Nature and acquiring useful knowledge, sometimes inviting wise men from abroad to help them.[293] As Herodicus says, they go to the city wall and back, and sometimes even to Megara [*laughter*].[294]

---

291 The Commissioners remind the audience of the role of the Acropolis as the site of many inscriptions, carefully placed in some cases so as to be near the buildings, that set out decisions by the city where they can be checked. As noted in Chapter 1, these inscriptions, that mostly record decisions already taken, although important for the record-keeping, the public information, and the audit and accountability aspects of democracy, tell little about the prior processes of proposing, deliberation, and decision taking. By using the neutral 'seeing' the Commissioners avoid embarrassing those who could not read but might have inscriptions read to them by others. They repeat the common belief that women were more guilty of spreading and believing rumours than men.

292 The hearers, in a passage that makes use of the licence given to authors of Thucydidean speeches to include references to the future, will be reminded on the opening scene-setting passage of Plato's *Republic*, a work that itself sets out ideas for promoting civic unity.

293 The Commissioners, in pointing to the incidental benefits of festivals in meeting the aim of unifying, and educating the various constituencies of the city, turn to the thought offered by Epicrates, the late fifth century comic dramatist, who reports that it was during the festival that he saw debates about what are now called the hard sciences and how they might be classified and defined, presented in comic terms, an aspect of the philosophical schools of Athens more often associated with Aristotle. Like Thucydides, the author/editor of the speech may have anticipated the future. Plato's Academy was not formally established until 387, although teaching of the kind mentioned is likely to have gone on long before that date. The fragment is embodied in Athenaeus 2.58. I am grateful to Dimitri El Murr for drawing attention to this passage and for other useful exchanges at a seminar at the Institute of Classical Studies in London on 25 November 2019.

294 The Commissioners anticipate what may already have been in the discursive environment as a rhetorical cliché, the description of a peripatetic walk round the city in Plato's *Phaedrus* 227d. The mention of Megara, a Dorian not an Ionian city on the land border of Attica, from whom Solon had, by using force and diplomacy, obtained possession of the island of Salamis, may imply that the walkers are so deeply engaged in their conversation that they forget where they are, or possibly that the Megarians are being told that they need to listen to the conversations as part of the mission of Athens to be, as in the Periclean Funeral Oration, the 'school of Hellas.'

We see our citizens and our kinsmen walking first in reverential silence and then, at the signal, the music starts at the bidding of the leaders, and they begin to dance and sing together.[295] As we all know, there is nothing more pleasing to the gods than to see, to hear, and to smell the processioning crowds, as the music-making flutes are mixed with the bleats of the doomed animals.[296] The gods, who have no need of our praises, joyfully join the mortals in the feast.[297] Listen to the crackle of the fire, smell the sizzling fat, hear the people sing and dance together with joy as the bursts of flame rise above the altars.[298] Happy too are those who watch and who smell the flowers of the garlands from afar.[299] They know that our city can be relied on to keep the gods on our side. Our festivals nourish the memories not only of those who see our Acropolis every day, but the dusty-footed workers in the fields who only come here on special occasions.[300] At our night festivals too, those who are travelling by land from our harbours see the Acropolis sparkling

---

295 Mentioning the ties of 'genos', a word that is liable to carry anachronistic associations if translated as 'race', is a reminder that many of the festivals were not confined to Athenians.

296 That different music was played for different gods is an implication of Aristotle, *Politics*, 1342 b3.

297 The Commissioners take care here and elsewhere to avoid implying that sacrificing to the gods was a form of bargaining, although it is evident from references in the ancient authors that many people understood the rites in those terms. It was a common joke that the gods were only given the parts of the dead animals that humans did not want.

298 The Commissioners resort to enargeia to make vivid for their audience the dramatic lighting of the fat-wrapped thigh bones of the slaughtered animals, which, as recent experiments have confirmed, sends a burst of flame about six minutes after the lighting, that lasts for about ten minutes before burning out. Discussed by Morton, Jacob, 'The experience of Greek sacrifice: investigating fat-wrapped thigh bones', in Miles, Margaret M., ed., *Autopsy in Athens: Recent Archaeological Research on Athens and Attica* (Oxford: Oxbow Books, 2015), 66–7. The Commissioners are careful not to claim that sacrifices encourage the gods to confer favours. But, they also allude to the civic trope that, if sacrifices were to be discontinued, the gods would desert the holy places. In the *Antigone* by Sophocles, the character of the wise Teiresias declares that the gods are no longer accepting the prayers that accompany the burning of the thigh bones, because Antigone's brother remains unburied. Soph. Ant. 1019–1022. The passage may imply that scavenging birds and animals congregated near sacred sites because of the leftovers from animal sacrifices, as part of the habitat and that an unburied body would quickly become carrion.

299 According to Theophrastus, *On Odours*, 12, the smell of the flowers used in garlands could be felt at a great distance, and they were presumably chosen, like the music, so as to draw in outsiders.

300 The phrase 'dusty-footed' was used by Plutarch to describe the country people of Epidauros, quoted from *Moralia* II, 291 d., by Burford, *Temple Builders*, 16.

with lights that match the stars.[301] Wisdom is lighting up in their minds with visions.[302] As the men, women, and children of our city live again the stories of the heroic deeds of our ancestors, the lessons are inscribed into the wax-tablets of their minds.[303] Our peoples are glued together as securely as one piece of wood is joined with another.[304]

In peace the images return to us in dreams that bring messages from the gods. In war too, when we stand together, hoplite by hoplite, horseman by horseman, oarsman by oarsman, we are united by a single Athenian mind.[305] As Homer tells us, Athena not only protects our city but gives us the means to sack the cities of others, whether Hellenes or barbarians, when they are mad enough to resist our just demands.[306]

---

301 The Commissioners pick out how the rites in the Acropolis could be seen from a distance, in much the same terms as the Christian rites were described by Lord Bute over two thousand years later, as noted in St Clair, *WStP*, Chapter 22, https://doi.org/10.1164/obp.0136.22.

302 Comparing the sudden realization of the truth of something not previously known with the kindling of a lamp is a rhetorical trope, found, for example, in Plato's *Epistles*, Plat. L. 7.341c, although Plato usually also presents it as the culmination of a sustained period of study, as do the Commissioners. It is also found in Plat. Sym. 210e.

303 Examples from the ancient authors for this common metaphor for memory are noted by Agócs, Peter, 'Speaking in the wax tablets of memory', in Castagnoli, Luca and Ceccarelli, Paola, eds, *Greek Memories, Theories and Practices* (Cambridge: CUP, 2019), 68–90, https://doi.org/10.1017/9781108559157.

304 The Commissioners turn to another image from the building industry, as it had been used by Pindar as quoted by Ath. 1.44.

305 A possible reference to the horsemen shown on the Parthenon frieze who show minimal individuality.

306 The Commissioners allude to *Homeric Hymn* 11. Although the hymns were almost certainly composed much later than the epics, from the seventh to the fifth centuries, they were accepted as having been composed by Homer by almost all ancient testimonies, including that of Thucydides at Thuc. 3 104. Although the texts from the classical period that have survived, especially the tragedies, suggest that a change in the treatment of refugees was being debated as part of the progress from brutishness narrative, we find little attempt to alter the conventions of war as such that brought about the miseries so vividly voiced by the female victims, both women and girls. On the contrary most authors uphold the view that if a city is captured by force, rather than by agreement under negotiated terms, everything belonged to the conqueror. For example, Xenophon puts into the mouth of the wise Cyrus addressing his troops an unequivocal claim that it is a universal law among Greeks and barbarians if a city is captured by force, everything, whether the bodies of the people or the useful things they possessed, belonged unconditionally to the conqueror. καὶ μηδείς γε ὑμῶν ἔχων ταῦτα νομισάτω ἀλλότρια ἔχειν: νόμος γὰρ ἐν πᾶσιν ἀνθρώποις ἀίδιός ἐστιν, ὅταν πολεμούντων πόλις ἁλῷ, τῶν ἑλόντων εἶναι καὶ τὰ σώματα τῶν ἐν τῇ πόλει καὶ τὰ χρήματα. Xen. Cyrop. 7.5.73. The notion that the conquered have no 'rights', to use a modern term, is put in the mouth of the character of Socrates in Plato's *Republic* in describing his ideal city, Plat. Rep.

See the battles in which all Ionians act together to defeat the arrogant Dorians who cannot forget that their ancestors conquered the lands that are now occupied by other Hellenes.[307] See the stupid and untrustworthy Thebans running like frightened sheep. Although we are far from home and meet many dangers, we know that Athens, the mother who bore us, always remains.[308] We will not rob our ancestors of the honours that they have won since the earliest times.[309] On the contrary we are glad when

---

1.327a, and is repeated in Aristotle's *Politics* as an example of the conventional law of slavery. Aristot. Pol. 1.1252a. When read against these indications of the norm, the decision of the Melians to resist and the subsequent action of the Athenians, which Thucydides reports but does not condemn or say is contrary to custom as he does for the enslaving of Naxos, appears less as an inevitable outcome than as the result of a conscious choice on the part of the Melians that, given their geographical as well as the political circumstances, was more than likely to be successful. During the classical period, the majority of assaults did nor succeed. According to the evidence gathered by Ducrey, Pierre, *Le Traitement des prisonniers de guerre dans la Grèce antique: des origines à la conquête romaine* (Paris: Boccard, new edition, revised and extended, 1999), xxii, sixteen sieges were successful, twenty-eight where the attack was abandoned, and fourteen when the situation was resolved by agreement. To Isocrates, the alleged cruelties committed by Athens on the people of Melos and other cities were slanders got up to sully the reputation of Athens by other cities, such as the Spartans under Lysander, who in modern terms had done worse, a defence that the historical record for other sackings tends to support. Isoc. 12 1, Ducrey, 125–127. Isocrates also claimed that it was an example of good government that Athens gave a public demonstration to cities already under Athenian control of the likely consequences if they were contemplating revolt, another situation in which the convention applied. Isoc. 4 1.

307 The Commissioners could not have known that what they hoped for was to occur (not quite as they had foreseen) during the Peloponnesian War: as Thucydides, at Thuc. 8.25.3, recounts, there was a battle in which the Argives, assuming that the Milesians would not stand their ground, made a sudden attack and were defeated, with the loss of three hundred men, who were then joined by the Athenians. It was one of the few historical examples in which the Parthenon project as advocated by the Commissioners led almost immediately to favourable results. Another was the decision by Lysander and the Spartans not to destroy Athens in 404 as already discussed.

308 The Commissioners repeat the sentiments, later committed to words, in the opening sentences of the treatise on war by the fourth century Greek writer known as Aeneas Tacticus. They know that war is normal, and that although the stories in stone of the Parthenon and other buildings all show the Hellenes as winning, the real viewerships would jib at such a rhetoric, and they offer a variation of, and practical application of the overriding thought that an essential Athenianness can survive the ups and downs of real events.

309 The Commissioners turn to the sentiment in the speech by Lycurgus against Leocrates Lyc. 1 110, that if those of the present day do not live up to the arete of the ancestors, they damage Athens by destroying its social capital, and they can only prevent that from happening, in this case, by putting Leocrates to death.

some god, out of admiration for our natural 'arete', has sent a war that shows that we are the equals of our fathers, and that, if we die, we too will be honoured for ever.[310]

Many here will also have heard your fathers speak of that other never-to-be-forgotten year when Phainippides was archon, when alone of the cities in Hellas apart from the gallant little Plataeans, our Athenian men of Marathon defeated forty six nations.[311] In that year we saved civilization itself.[312]

When your Commissioners first looked over the ruins of our shining city on the hill of Kecrops, with its broken dedications, kouroi and korai, forever young but now no longer able to bringing comfort or memory to the families who commissioned and visited them, we saw the shameless snakes slithering on paths along which our daughters used to dance and sing their music, hissing and spitting even at the wise bird of the night. We hear Solon, the founder of our modern Athenian constitution, cry out his immortal lament: 'How my breast fills with sorrow when I see Ionia's oldest land being done to death'.[313]

For thirty years, the effects of the barbarian invasion lay about for all to see, but as the metal crowns ('poloi') of the korai were stolen to be melted down, as the broken marble was used again for other building purposes, and as the serpents and the scorpions made their homes

---

310 Almost exactly the same words are used by Isocrates in *Panegyricus*, 84. The phenomenon of soldiers experiencing a sense of having missed out on the opportunities for fame and reputation open to those who survived a 'glorious' previous war is attested, notably for the philhellenes and for many other historical cases, notably in post-World-War-Two Britain, where the previous war has been mythographized in word, image, and performance. Isocrates's invoking of 'some god' exemplifies the common rhetorical practice of presenting events as occurring almost of their own accord, rather than as the result of human agency, and whose rhetorical tendency is to exculpate all concerned.

311 The claim to have defeated forty-six nations at Marathon is included in the speech put into the mouths of the Athenians by Herodotus when, before the land battle of Plataea, they claimed the right to be regarded as second only to the Lacedaimonians. Hdt. 9.27.

312 The dates of the archonates from Harding, *Atthidographers*, 102. For the convenience of readers, the editor has used the dates of the modern calendar.

313 The quotation, γιγνώσκω, καί μοι φρενὸς ἔνδοθεν ἄλγεα κεῖται,/ πρεσβυτάτην ἐσορῶν γαῖαν Ἰαονίας κλινομένην, preserved by Aristot. Const. Ath. 5, reminds us that a strong sense of Athenians being Ionian predated the Persian wars and their aftermath. The references to Ion in Attic cults and festivals are collected by Kearns, Emily, 'The Heroes of Attica' in *Bulletin Supplement* (*University of London. Institute of Classical Studies*), No. 57 (1989), 109–110, 174–175.

among the ruins, the memorials that had been living reminders of our glorious past became instead evidences of neglect and disrespect. And it was increasingly burdensome for us to have to explain the state of our holy places to our rising younger generations of future soldiers. Never again, our city decided, can our holiest places be put at risk.

Our ancestors, let us remind you, lived close to our life-giving spring when they first founded our city before they had even begun living together as households.[314] And it was not long afterwards, as we remember from the stories we learned in our boyhood, that the Hill of Kekrops became the Acro- [*the reciter pauses for emphasis*] -polis.[315] We will build to ensure that our clear water will always be plentiful on our Acropolis.[316] And, as in all the great cities of Hellas, we will welcome our new sons and daughters on their birthday, with water from our city's pure and cleansing stream.[317]

It was right to re-use the broken marble dedications to the practical task of repairing the Acropolis walls.[318] A memorial that does not carry a story or a memory, whether they are family members or others, is powerless painted stone and metal.[319] We are now at peace with the

---

314 The Commissioners refer to the development from brutishness account of the origins of their distinctive civilization in a polis. And as modern archaeology has confirmed, the caves on the Acropolis slopes near the water were settled in neo-lithic times. As discussed by Parsons, Arthur W., 'Klepsydra and the Paved Court of the Pythion' in *Hesperia*, Vol. 12 (3), The American Excavations in the Athenian Agora: Twenty-Fourth Report (July–September 1943), 191–267. How the Athenians of the classical period may have interpreted the remains of ancient settlement that turned up in their modern building works is not recorded in any ancient author, but it would have given empirical support to the brutishness narrative. The Athenians of the classical period also knew that many of the commemorative ceremonies associated with the caves, one of the main ways of preserving memory and identity across time in an age before the technologies of inscription, were built round gods and heroes that pre-dated the Olympian canon.

315 The Commissioners repeat the account by Thucydides in his account of the long past in Book 2.

316 The water carriers are shown on the Parthenon frieze.

317 The custom that, in Athens, water from the Enneacrounos spring was used to wash babies as part of the naming ceremonies, was described by Thucydides in Book 2, 13. 'Birthday' was not the day of physiological birth but of social birth that only occurred with the naming ceremony. The relevance of this observation to our interpretation of what story was told on the Parthenon frieze, where I offer a new conjecture, is discussed in Chapter 3.

318 As described in St Clair, *WStP*, Chapter 21, https://doi.org/10.1164/obp.0136.21.

319 The Commissioners here anticipate the bemused reactions of the Ottoman soldier to the western souvenir collectors, as described in Chapter 21 of my companion volume *Who Saved the Parthenon?*.

Great King, and do not need as many warships as in the past.[320] We have rebuilt our walls and our harbours, and our frontier forts too are well prepared. But the Great King, whose gods tell him that he rules the world, may come again one day, for who can foresee the future? The perennial struggle between Europa and Asia that began long before the war against Troy can never be over. Nor can we neglect the ambitions of the Lacedaimonians, the treacherous Thebans, and the luxury-loving Corinthians, who all look upon our city with envious eyes.[321]

We will employ craftsmen, carpenters, metal-workers, farmers, and men knowledgeable in numbers and in the management of households, and follow the advice of those with experience in commanding armies. Since the stone, the main material used by temple-builders, already belongs to us, most of the public money that we will spend will benefit you, men of Athens, and not flow away. For the cedar wood that we will obtain from other countries, we have the ships to bring it and the surpluses of fruits to give in exchange. We will learn too from those who understand the arts of divining for the deepest secrets that the gods reserve for themselves. You may plant a field; but you know not who shall gather the fruits: you may build a house well; but you know not who shall dwell in it. And although you are able to command, you cannot know whether it will turn out to be worthwhile to you to have accepted the honour. If you marry an attractive woman when she is still a girl, you cannot tell whether she will bring you sorrow.[322]No madman, out of impiety towards the gods or from a terror that his name will not be remembered, can destroy the holy buildings.[323] But nothing in human

---

320 A possible reference to the co-called Peace of Kallias of *c.* 449 at which the Achaemenid Empire accepted, at least for the time being, that it had lost control of the cities of Ionia.

321 In mentioning the threats from other Hellenic cities, the Commissioners remind the audience that the Thebans had taken the side of the invading Persians. By the time they come to their praise of Pindar later in the speech, they anticipate that the audience will have forgotten the earlier passage.

322 The Commissioners repeat, almost word for word sentiments set out in Xen. Mem. 1.1.7 and 8.

323 The Commissioners mention a fear of arson, as when in Euripides's play, the *Ion*, the character of old man suggests that the Delphic oracle has been so unreliable that it should be burned down Eur. Ion 974. This and other plays report many complaints against the gods. The Commissioners may have foreseen the danger, that occurred at Ephesos in the following century when Herostratus (Eratostratus) set fire to the temple at Ephesus, was put to the torture where he confessed to his motivation, and a decree was passed making it a criminal offence to mention his name. Since the

life is certain.[324] No man and no god can escape the changing winds of Tyche.[325] As the old Egyptian priest told our Solon [*quotes*] 'There have been and there will be many and divers destructions of mankind' in which the earth was burned up and all our ancient knowledge was lost.[326] And it was out of respect for that truth that the Commissioners for the design and construction of one of our images has, with the assent of the Assembly, inscribed their publicly-displayed accounts of the annual expenditures to 'Athena and Tyche'.[327]

---

story is well known and his name mentioned by the ancient historians the decree was evidently ineffective. The episode is referred to by Byron, in his satire *The Curse of Minerva*, lines 200ff.

'May hate pursue his sacrilegious lust!
Link'd with the fool that fired the Ephesian dome,
Shall vengeance follow far beyond the tomb,
And Eratostratus and Elgin shine
In many a branding page and burning line;
Alike reserved for aye to stand accursed,
Perchance the second blacker than the first.'

324 The Commissioners repeat the convention used, for example, in the Periclean Funeral Oration, 'Numberless are the chances to which, as they know, the life of man is subject.' Thuc. 2.44.1. Indeed it needs to be included in funeral orations and some alleviation offered. As, for example, 'But if, as a mortal being, [the soldier] meets his doom, what he has suffered is an incident caused by chance, but in spirit he remains unconquered by his opponents.' Demosthenes, *Funeral Oration*, Dem.60.19.

325 The Commissioners signal that they are reaching their peroration, that will link the past, the present, and the future to a notion of unchanging Athenianness as it will be instantiated in stone on the Acropolis. Whereas many writers after the end of antiquity until recently routinely invoked various forms of destinarianism, implying an ordered and sometimes a guided world, the authors of the classical period, especially Euripides when he presents the mainstream view in words attributed to the Chorus, draw attention to the arbitrariness and unpredictability. To present the gods themselves, as subject to Chance, as here, and in for example, the lost *Andromeda*, fragments 152, 153, and 154, Euripides, *Selected Fragmentary Plays*, Collard et al edition, ii, 155, is more rare.

326 The Commissioners refer to the story told at greater length in Plat. Tim. 21b.

327 The inscriptions are transcribed in Davison, *Pheidias*, ii, 1089 and 1094. The practice appears to have been discontinued perhaps because the Commissioners for the statue did not want to risk the charge that the character of Odysseus warns of in the *Cyclops* of Euripides, of having equated Tyche with the divine or implying that the divine was less powerful than the godly. My translation of ἢ τὴν τύχην μὲν δαίμον' ἡγεῖσθαι χρεών, τὰ δαιμόνων δὲ τῆς τύχης ἐλάσσονα Eur. Cycl. 606–607, that attempts to preserve something of the ambiguity of 'deeming' and of the generalizing word 'daimon.'An alternative explanation is that the Commissioners for the financial audit were setting up their excuses in advance if it turned out that valuables had been stolen or embezzled, or if the charge was brought as a political weapon, as is recorded as having happened as noted below. The received view that the accounts relate to the statue known as the Athena Promachos has recently been challenged by Foley, Elizabeth, and Stroud, Ronald S., 'A Reappraisal of the

When we travel to the land of Pelops and we ask what happened to Mycenae, rich in gold, the answer is that the name of the city of Agamemnon, which sent eighty men to fight at Thermopylae, is engraved with ours on the Brazen Serpent at Delphi.[328] The 'city of the walls' [Tiryns] too, whose men were with us at Plataea, is also honoured.[329] But the men of Argos who were cowards in the wars against the Medes and the Persians now see their runaway slaves take over the whole Argolid.[330] For some cities, there is everlasting glory, but to those who show themselves to be unworthy, the gods assign an endless shame.[331] Indeed, some wonder why Agamemnon and his [*implies contempt*] Argives took so long to win the war against the Trojans.[332]

Our children will always learn about the blind poet of Ionia. But we need no Homer to sing the praises of our city.[333] Our age too has its poets

---

Athena Promachos Accounts from the Acropolis (IG I³ 435)' in *Hesperia*, Vol. 88 (1) (2019), 87–153, https://doi.org/10.2972/hesperia.88.1.0087. It has been suggested that Tyche is amongst the figures presented on the pediments of the Parthenon, especially the female figure that has slots for wings. If ancient viewers could reasonably have thought that was the intention, we may have another indication that they were encouraged to regard the compositions as theatrical performances waiting to happen, in accordance with an ancient genre of seeing, as will be discussed in Chapter 3.

328   The Commissioners do not need to tell the audience that they are quoting from Homer, and are claiming an equality with, indeed a superiority to, the heroes of the mythic world of the Homeric epics.

329   Again the Commissioners do not need to say explicitly that they are quoting Homer.

330   As the audience know 'the Argives' was one of the phrases used by Homer to describe the whole Greek force. The humiliation of Argos in the classical period is described in Her. 6.83.

331   The Commissioners signal that they are reaching their peroration, that will link the past, the present, and future to a notion of a paideia whose aim of promoting an unchanging Athenianness will be instantiated on the Acropolis in the stories displayed and the rituals that take place in their vicinity.

332   The Commissioners trail an idea made explicit in the summary of early history at the beginning of Thucydides' work, at Thuc. 1.10.3, that suggests Homer as a poet had exaggerated, and probably distorted, what had really happened. The passage shows that what came to be called the Homeric question about the historicity of the Homeric poems, that began again in eighteenth century Europe, had also been considered in classical Athens.

333   The Commissioners use a trope employed, many have thought, to great effect in the Thucydidean funeral speech of Pericles, but that is likely to have been in use before, not coined for the first time for that occasion. Indeed it may have struck the audience as a cliché to be discounted as exaggerated rhetoric, as the Commissioners struggle to balance praise of Homer, as they must always do, with tentative attempts to criticize him or at least to gloss the works. Their own speech has itself been infused with Homeric echoes. And the listeners to the speech in contemporary classical

who carry our fame across Hellas and far beyond.[334] Our Athenian walls will not disappear like those that our ancestors, at Nestor's bidding, once built on the beach at Troy.[335] We have not destroyed these ancient walls that Heracles, maddened with grief and desire for vengeance, wanted to tear down with crow-bars and pickaxes. We Athenians will always sack cities, take plunder, and seize women unless there is good reason to do otherwise. But our enemies are men not stones.[336] We will leave many great signs of our power that will make Athens an object of wonder not only to the men of today but to those who come after us.[337]

---

times and later knew that classical Athens placed great weight on learning Homer, with competitions in reciting, and examples recorded of men allegedly knowing the poems by heart.

334 The Commissioners use a general term not city-specific, so as to be able to include Pindar, not an Athenian, although he was rewarded with a large sum of money and an honorary position as 'proxenos', an office that, in modern terms includes a notion of honorary citizenship. As the disgruntled Isocrates was to write not long afterwards: 'It would be even more absurd if, whereas Pindar, the poet, was so highly honored by our forefathers because of a single line of his in which he praises Athens as "the bulwark of Hellas" that he was made "proxenos" and given a present of ten thousand drachmas, I, on the other hand, who have glorified Athens and our ancestors with much ampler and nobler encomiums, should not even be privileged to end my days in peace.' Isoc. 15 166. The Commissioners have also, without naming him praised Simonides of Ceos, who, although from an offshore island of Attica, prepared celebratory epigraphs and epitaphs for other cities, including the Lacedaimonians. We have another reminder here that 'poets' of words, like the 'poets' of visual images, functioned within the political economy of the time and not outside it as rhetorics of romanticism imply.

335 The Commissioners refer to the passage in the *Iliad* which caused puzzlement in ancient times, in which the Achaeans are encouraged by Nestor to build walls which will protect their ships and bones of their dead, and the memory of their exploits in preparation for a return but which are then disappeared by Homer, leaving only the account by Homer as a memory of their fame. Discussed by Bassi, Karen, *Traces of the Past, Classics Between History and Archaeology* (Ann Arbor: University of Michigan Press, 2016), 40–63, https://doi.org/10.3998/mpub.8785930.

336 The Commissioners, reverting to the Homeric notion of hero may be referring to the story in the passage in Eur. Her. 945 where the messenger reports the cry by Heracles: 'I must take crow-bars and pick-axes, for I will shatter again with iron levers those city-walls which the Cyclopes squared with red plumb-line and mason's tools." Without quite saying so, they are moving the discourse away from monument cleansing as display to the need to protect the Parthenon from monument cleansing in the future, a policy implicit in the extent to which it is over-engineered and not easily dismantled, even for recycling the marble blocks, without incurring huge and disproportionate expense compared with the alternatives.

337 The Commissioners use the language of the Periclean Funeral Oration. The translator has left the awkward phrase 'signs' used there rather than more common rendering 'monuments' both to retain the continuity between past, present and

Our city gleams with radiance and our land is a garden. Our city is
a sacred fire that never goes out, but moves around from one time to
another, seen by some and then by others, a sight made more fair and
more just by the ways we live and have always lived, and we must pity
those who live outside our hegemony who are deprived of such gifts.[338]
Athens, favoured by Athena, will ensure that we and our children will
always preserve our sacred places and will add new memorials to our
glory just as our ancestors did, despite their misfortunes.[339] And our
holy places will be useful not only to the Athenians of today but to our
sons for always.[340]

But, as we approach the end of our speech, we say again that nothing
in human life is certain.[341] Mountains overwhelm cities with fire and the
earth itself is shaken.[342] As Homer teaches us, even the gods cannot see
the future.[343] But we know that, if a new Minos again invades our land
with swift ships, if Zeus and Poseidon again cover our land with water,

---

future and to include the implied thought that other forms of self-celebration are
included, such as historical works such as his own.

338 The Commissioners conjure up a mental image of what appears to have become
a cliché applicable to many cities. It was used by Aelius Aristides, noted for his
Panathenaic oration in praise of Athens but used in the words employed by the
Commissioners of Rome. Oliver, James Henry, *The Ruling Power: A Study of the
Roman Empire in the Second Century after Christ through the Roman Oration of Aelius
Aristides* (Philadelphia: American Philosophical Society, 1953), 99.

339 The Commissioners allude to a characteristic of rhetorics of heritage that the past
from which the narrative of essential continuity is compiled has, by selective puffing
up of some episodes and selective downplaying others, to include both triumphs
and disasters in a unifying narrative.

340 The Commissioners employ the phrase in which Thucydides described the purposes
of his history that also emphasises its own 'usefulness.' Thuc. 1.22. ἀνθρώπινον
τοιούτων καὶ παραπλησίων ἔσεσθαι, ὠφέλιμα κρίνειν αὐτὰ ἀρκούντως ἕξει.
κτῆμά τε ἐς αἰεὶ μᾶλλον ἢ ἀγώνισμα ἐς τὸ παραχρῆμα.

341 The Commissioners repeat the convention used, for example, in the Periclean
Funeral Oration, 'Numberless are the chances to which, as they know, the life of man
is subject.' Thuc. 2.44.1. Indeed the element of contingency needs to be included in
funeral orations and some alleviation offered for the general unfairness of life. As,
for example, 'But if, as a mortal being, [the soldier] meets his doom, what he has
suffered is an incident caused by chance, but in spirit he remains unconquered by
his opponents.' Demosthenes, *Funeral Oration*, Dem.60.19.

342 The destructive eruption of Etna in Sicily in 479/478 is referred to by Pindar, *Pythian*,
i. 21; and by Aeschylus in the *Prometheus Bound*, line 365.

343 The Commissioners anticipate a point made explicit by Isocrates in his speech
'Against the Sophists.' As the Commissioners and their audience knew there are
several passages in the Homeric epics where the gods are presented as debating what
to do.

as happened nine thousand years ago when Athens was in command in the long war against the huge island of Atlantis, then a new Deucalion, a new Hellen, and a new Ion will arise to repopulate our land.[344] And as the men of that time look at the ruins of our Acropolis, just as we today look on the ruins of the city of Agamemnon, they will say that here once stood the greatest city of Hellas and here lived its greatest men.[345]

---

344 There appears to be little sense of providentialism in classical Athens as distinct from a general sense of being at the mercy of fate ['moira'] or fortune ['tyche'], as something, usually unwelcome, that happens inexplicably and unavoidably. The instances in the surviving works of Euripides are collected by Mastronarde, *The Art of Euripides*, 188–189, https://doi.org/10.1017/CBO9780511676437. As the Commissioners and their audience knew there are several passages in the Homeric epics where the gods are presented as debating what to do. The possible existence of a king Minos of Cnossos who ruled the sea was dismissively mentioned also by Herodotus at Her. 3.122.2, incidentally providing more evidence that some memory, however hazy, had been maintained for over a thousand years, in stories passed orally as myths and/or renewed with the help of commemoration ceremonies. Stories of an invasion of Attica by the Cretans led by Minos were still being told in Athens another half millennium later at the time of Pausanias, and were memorialized in the tomb of Nisus, 'the red-haired', that stood near the site of Aristotle's Lykeion. Paus.1, 4, traditions that are easier to explain as by then established by all the technologies of inscription. The calendar date of the volcanic eruption on Thera/Santorini, and the subsequent tsunami that may have been decisive in bringing Minoan civilization to an end, has recently been dated, from the evidence of tree-ring patterns, by Charlotte Pearson and other members of a team, to 1506 BCE, as reported in the *Archaeology News Network* of 31 March 2020. The legends surrounding Deucalion as a variant of Middle Eastern myths of a Great Flood, of which the best known is that of Noah, were summarized from earlier accounts in Greek as well as from others, by Lucian, who was himself from Syria, in the text known in its Latinized version, as *De Dea Syria*, (on the *Syrian Goddess*), 12 and 13. The Commissioners refer to the story that, as usual, is presented as factual and that projects back notions of Athenian superiority and leadership into the deep past, put into the mouth of the character of Critias in Plat. Criti. 108e. By mentioning Deucalion, his son Hellen and his grandson Ion, the Commissioners reaffirm many of their earlier points including the autochthony story.

345 A similar point is in the Periclean speech at Thuc 1, 64. The Commissioners, without being explicit, point out that the post-479 Acropolis did not preserve much from the past; that their recent military and naval victories were at risk of being forgotten; and what was proposed by way of linking the past to the built heritage was, with exceptions, more artificial than organic. They then offer a version of the observation of Thucydides at 1.10.2 at which he explicitly links his difficulties as an evidence-led historian in finding reliable information about the past with what a future Thucydides might find, namely, that if Sparta were to become desolate, as Mycenae had become in his day, and all that remained were the holy places and the foundations of the public buildings, as time passed, posterity would greatly underestimate its power. If, by contrast, Athens 'were to suffer the same misfortune, I suppose that any inference from the appearance presented to the eye would make her power to have been twice as great as it is.' Although the Commissioners present

And now, men of Athens, it is time to sacrifice a sheep and pour a libation. And let us make a prayer that the gods will preserve all the right things that have been spoken today and punish us if we have sung out of tune.[346] Tomorrow all who have the right to speak will decide.[347] As our friend from Colonos reminds us, [*the reciter here gestures towards the Hill of Colonos*] 'In any question, the truth always has the greatest strength'.[348]

[*The president dismisses the Assembly*].

---

the planned and engineered longevity of the Parthenon as a reason for building it, and they were to be proved right in their prediction that it would endure, Thucydides uses the comparison as a warning to historians and others not to be misled by appearances, as he had declared at the very beginning of his work that one of the ways in which he intended that his work would be useful. Like the Commissioners, others have taken the idea not as a warning but as a measure of success. The risks of Athenocentrism in accounts of ancient Greece are now well understood, but even with the addition of archaeological evidence they remain hard to offset.

346   The Commissioners repeat what appears to have been a commonplace used in summing up, as, for example, at the start of Plato's *Critias*, Plat. Criti. 106a. If so, it is an example of the usefulness of 'the gods' as a coping stone holding together a public discourse, and that does not imply, nor even expect, the statement to be taken literally.

347   The Commissioners slip in the important qualification that not all those who were present and listening would be legally allowed to speak, not only women, metics, and slaves but the constituency of free Athenian men, who did not qualify as 'autochthonous' under the two-parent rule, among whom was included Antisthenes, who resented being a second-class citizen under the nativist rules, and the fictional Ion in the play by Euripides of that name, to be discussed in Chapter 4.

348   The Commissioners quote a remark of a character in one of the plays of Sophocles. Lloyd-Jones, Hugh, ed., *Sophocles, Fragments* (Cambridge, Mass: Harvard UP, 1996), number 955, page 412. Since Sophocles won, by far, the most prizes in the dramatic competitions, the Commissioners enlist his name on the side of their proposals. As a rhetorical practice, to quote what a character in a literary work is presented as saying as the opinion of the author, even when, as here as is common, it is deployed as a complement to the author, is of course, an appropriation that, by changing the boundaries of the context may change the meaning taken by listeners. In the case of an ancient dramatist, the practice is especially unfair since the opinions expressed by the character are frequently followed by a contrary opinion offered by another character. This rhetorical device, later called a 'chreia' by Theon of Alexandria, a writer of a rhetorical manual, although occasionally found in the classical period, with one example attributed to Plato, was to become more common, with other examples given in Chapter 4. Ancient authors, especially, Euripides, appear to have made a point of including what were later called in Latin 'sententiae;' in Renaissance English 'select sentences', but whether authors, subject to various limitations imposed by the city's institutions, saw it as part of their trade to provide pithy sentences and vivid metaphors, in modern terms 'sound-bites', cannot be ascertained from the record, but seems likely.

A Reflection on this Experiment

Since the Parthenon and the other buildings were actually built in record time, without interruption, we can be sure that all the necessary approvals were given by the institutions of the city and that any unforeseen problems were coped with. Although the process may have been more prolonged, untidy, and contested than the composers of the speech have suggested, the institutions were persuaded to accept the proposals. In the short term at least, we can therefore say that the Commissioners were successful, and also that it is likely that many of the cognitive, discursive, and rhetorical practices illustrated above were employed.

For resistance to the proposals that we can be certain occurred, although most of the evidence comes from non-contemporary authors, I will offer in Chapter 5 an attempted reconstruction of another ancient historiographical genre now seldom practised: a formal 'rhetorical exercise' composed with hindsight. I will use the opportunity to try to reconstruct what can be said about the opposition to the Commissioners' proposals for building the Parthenon, attempting to recover both the conventions and the substance of the contestation.

As for the potential value of the experiment, my initial aim was simply to see whether the discursive environment could be reconstructed from the inside looking out, and if so, what it might look like. I hoped that it might prove useful in treating the strangeness as a topic in its own right and as a caution against the unconscious biases to be found in much contemporary as well as past scholarly writings. As with scientific experiments, although it does not claim to be the only way the material can be presented, it offers an implicit challenge to others to try to replicate the results. Although obviously the weight attributed to each component could be altered, at the time of writing, I cannot think of any that has been omitted. What I had not expected to find was that the buildings were of less importance than the festivals that took place in their vicinity, that at the receiving of the officially endorsed mythic stories the media of performance were integrated with those of inscription. I was surprised to find the framing offered by kinship and Ionianism, the brutishness narrative, and the emphasis on success in aggressive war as the main collective aim of the city. I had not expected that, with the results of the experiment to hand, I would be able to make more authoritative suggestions on what stories were displayed on the Parthenon and how they were consumed.[349]

Meanwhile, in the following chapter, I revert to a normal modern voice to discuss how the Parthenon, when built, was encountered in classical times, with suggestions for the genres of seeing that were practised, for which the evidence is also patchy. And I will suggest my own solution to a long-standing question about the Parthenon frieze that, without implying that the speech offered above is more than a controlled experiment, is likely to prove more persuasive when it is set within a discursive context of the kind attempted above.

---

349 In Chapters 3 and 4.

3. Looking at the Parthenon in Classical Athens

How did the people of Athens of the classical period engage with the huge building that they, through their institutions, had caused to be designed and erected? The size of the building, with the statue of Athena Promachos towering above it, drawing eyes from the far and middle distance, has been noted in my companion volume, *Who Saved the Parthenon?*; so has its function as a focus for the 'famous hills of Athens'.[1] But how was the Parthenon seen, understood, and used from close up?

Who, we can first ask, had access to the Acropolis as a site? Later in antiquity, at some periods, it appears to have been open to citizens and others to be admitted by the guards at the entrance, and visitors are sometimes recorded as paying a small fee.[2] For the classical period, there are few contemporaneous mentions other than those concerned with protecting the monuments and the workshops from thieves, evidence in itself that the rhetoric offered by the building was not universally acted upon. We can, however, be sure that among the reasons an individual Athenian citizen might legitimately have for wanting to visit the Acropolis, other than temporarily to escape the interruptions of the town, was a wish to check on some point of law, contract, or treaty that had been set out on a marble inscription; to solemnize a contract; or to be present as a duty when a public or private dedication was made or an inscription formally endorsed as valid, by some ceremony equivalent to unveiling. Other citizens, whether as individuals or as civic officials or members of commissions, might need to inspect the financial accounts,

---

1   In St Clair, William, *Who Saved the Parthenon? A New History of the Acropolis Before, During and After the Greek Revolution* (Cambridge: Open Book Publishers, 2022) [hereafter *WStP*], https://doi.org/10.11647/OBP.0136, Chapters 2, https://doi.org/10.1164/obp.0136.2, and 22, https://doi.org/10.1164/obp.0136.22.
2   For example, several mentions in the works of Lucian of Samosata, some of which are best regarded as rhetorical exercises.

   https://doi.org/10.11647/OBP.0279.03

including those relating to building projects. Some office-holders, notably certain young women, were required to live on the Acropolis for fixed periods as part of their duties. The fragmentary inscription of 485/44 required that a physical audit should take place every ten days.[3]

As for what they saw when they arrived within the Acropolis, although it is now a place of buildings, in classical times it teemed with free-standing dedicated statues and with formal words inscribed on marble. Some contemporary inscriptions, such as one that listed the contributions to the budget of the cities of Ionia, were several metres high and unignorable. Taken together, however, although some secured the most conspicuous locations, they seem not to have been arranged in any geographical or chronological order. There were also, dotted around the Acropolis summit, a growing number of public and private dedications in the form of free-standing statues in the round, and especially of statue-groups, that presented stories, mostly mythic, as already discussed.[4] Since they could not be erected without the permission of the authorities, they too can be regarded as contributions to an official history in the form of a built heritage. As accretions occurred, the site offered a layered past, with each statue, statue group, or inscription composed in accordance with its own conventions that, taken together, told an officially approved history, not as a single narrative, but as a collection of primary visual documents from which a large part of the officially-approved civic history, both historic and mythic, could be constructed.

During the fourth century BCE, when the classical Parthenon was in full use for its intended purposes as part of a complex of buildings, the contemporaneous inscriptions suggest that there was a frequent to-ing and fro-ing of temple staff and others concerned with the safeguarding, the management, and the accounting for the portfolio of material assets that were kept behind locked doors within the Parthenon, as well as within other buildings on the summit and elsewhere. Architecturally, the building followed the main Hellenic convention of being divided into two compartments: the Hecatompedon ('hundred footer') at the west end, and the 'Parthenon' (room where the cult image of the virgin ('parthenos') goddess was housed and occasionally displayed) at the

---

3   Camp, John M., *The Archaeology of Athens* (New Haven: Yale UP, 2001), 52.
4   In Chapter 2.

east end.[5] In Aristophanes's comedy, the *Lysistrata*, first performed in 411 BCE, the Acropolis is taken over without difficulty by the chorus of women, who, as part of their plan to end the war, remove money from the public treasury.[6] With the topographical details given in the play, we can be sure that the ancient audience were invited to imagine the women entering through the west door behind the colonnade.

To judge from indications on the stonework, those who entered the building through the west door found themselves in a chamber, with little natural light, flanked on each side by Ionic columns, and a corridor to the inner dividing wall.[7] The chamber was arranged as a warehouse with stacks of shelves and boxes on the other sides of a corridor that may have led to a door through to the rear of the other chamber.[8] Even though, for a chamber used primarily for storage, something plainer would have met the purpose, the opportunity was taken to present a kinship feature that may have been designed to please both the Athenian families who claimed to be autochthonous Ionians, and the overseas Ionians whose contributions to the collective treasury were deposited there.

About two hundred ancient inscriptions carved on marble have been published in recent centuries; material that made the wording difficult to change and ensured both fixity and security against the tampering to which documents on perishable materials were exposed. This is a fragmentary sample, which is unlikely to be representative, of a much larger number that has since disappeared. In ancient times, one of the functions of these inscriptions, we can be confident from their wording, was to perform as publicly accessible inventories of items stored and safeguarded inside. Besides some denominated in monetary terms

---

5   The names were investigated by Schleisner, Steenberg, Brandes, and Heise, *De Parthenone eiusque partibus* (Hanover: Royal University publications, 1849), but doubts remain.

6   That temples were places where 'chremata' were kept is implied by the remark by the character of Polymestor in the *Hecuba* of Euripides, Eur. Hec 1019. Although some anachronism in pushing back the invention of 'money' to the mythic time of the Trojan war (that is, around half a millennium before the Athenians themselves estimated the calendar date of the introduction of coinage) was perhaps acceptable in Athenian tragedy, the word is used to connote what is referred to elsewhere in the play as gold and silver.

7   Discussed by Pedersen, Poul, *The Parthenon and the Origin of the Corinthian Capital* (Odense: Odense UP, 1989).

8   Discussed by Harris, Diane, *The Treasures of the Parthenon and Erechtheion* (Oxford: OUP, 1995), with transcriptions.

in drachmas and obols, the inscriptions refer to items made of silver and gold, such as wreaths, which are denominated by weight as well as in drachmas and obols—weight being a denominator more suited to inventory and audit than any monetary unit whose exchange value in terms of purchasing power was never steady. The wording reveals that objects made from these two metals were sometimes melted down if they became damaged, reverting to the status of bullion. As 'useful things' ('chremata'), both the 'signed', that is, the monetary, and non-monetary metal objects were convertible in both directions. By incurring a small manufacturing cost, bullion could be converted into coin, a process that, through seignorage, would normally produce a net profit for the Athenian state.

Judging from the wording, some items listed as held in the stores were awarded as prizes in festivals on condition that they were returned, and so became available to be awarded again on later occasions. As for objects not so described, it is not known the extent to which they were intended to be held permanently in the repositories as assets to be put to no further active use after the initial performance ceremony of dedication. If so, they continued to perform only on the occasions when the permanent inscriptions outside were encountered, read, and believed to be true, or untrue, by readers. In such cases, the permanent inscriptions were the equivalent of those still inscribed on modern banknotes that still purport to represent metal presented as intrinsically valuable, even when it cannot be exchanged for metal except among central banks, and its origin in metal is only deemed or 'nomismatic'.[9] Nor was deliberate deception a negligible risk. With plentiful resort to Thucydidean speeches that bring out the wider issues, Thucydides tells how the Egestans, as a way of drawing the Athenians into a war in which they had no stake as kinsmen, fooled them into believing that their temple, which was comparable in size to the Parthenon, contained more 'chremata' than it actually did.[10]

It seems likely, however, that many of the other items deposited in the Parthenon and other buildings were brought out from storage to be

---

9   The ancient notion of 'nomisma' was discussed in Chapter 1.
10   Summarized by, for example, Kallet, Lisa, *Money and the Corrosion of Power in Thucydides* (Berkeley: University of California Press, 2001), 27–31 and 69–75, https://doi.org/10.1525/9780520927421.

used in actual festivals. The 'tables' and 'couches' appear to be pieces of general-purpose furniture to which detachable specialized metal ornaments might be added. Among the smaller items inventoried are incense burners, trays, wine jugs, drinking cups, baskets, lamps, swords, shields, stools, musical instruments, wreaths, necklaces, bracelets, clothes, an iron knife presumably for the ritual slaughtering of animals, the standard paraphernalia of ancient processions and ceremonies, both real and as projected back to mythic times, as on the Parthenon frieze.[11] The lists also give evidence of wear and tear, or of theft or vandalism, such as parts of tables, parts of cauldrons, and parts broken from the doors. Among the unusual items listed are golden ornaments that include grasshoppers or cicadas, a symbol of the autochthony of the old Ionians of Athens, and an example of the Ionian origin and kinship claim whose role in the discursive environment is confirmed by the experiment.[12] As a public presentation of autochthony, the golden cicadas, as with other features of the Parthenon, linked the symbolism with the viewerly experience. As was noted by an ancient scholiast on Thucydides, and confirmed by modern observation, since the larvae of cicadas are buried underground, the emerging insects do appear, as Thucydides remarked, to be 'earth-born'.[13]

There are also records of documents written on perishable materials held in safe and accessible repositories.[14] The inventories for the Acropolis buildings, for example, note 'a writing tablet from the council ('boule') of the Areopagus sealed', evidently an official record of importance. The Athenian authorities were evidently well aware of the risks to which documents written on perishable materials were exposed from fire, forgery, and manipulation. In the *Clouds*, the comedy by Aristophanes, the character of Strepsiades, by turning a glass normally used for starting a fire by redirecting the suns rays, manages to melt the wax and destroy the words on a document that records the amount of his debt.[15] We may have here a glimpse of a tilt from memory held orally towards memory

---

11 To be discussed in Chapter 4.

12 Harris, *Treasures of the Parthenon*, no 372, item 373. χρυσίδια διάλιθα σύμμικτα πλινθίων καὶ τεττίγων σταθμὸν τούτων.

13 Noted by Hornblower, Simon, ed., *Lykophron: Alexandra: Greek Text, Translation, Commentary, and Introduction* (Oxford: OUP, 2015), 26.

14 Summarised by Harris, *Treasures of the Parthenon*, 15–17.

15 Aristoph. Cl. 768.

as checkable documentation that, in the case of Athens, accompanied the transition from an oikos economy, which produced its own means of subsistence internally as described by Thucydides, to one in which commodities, notably olive oil, were grown to be sold into markets, denominated in monetary terms, and mutual obligations recorded.[16]

But what, I now ask, occurred at festivals, to provide a backdrop for which, my experiment suggests, was the most important function of the Parthenon? What was the experience of arriving visitors when they were first able to make out for themselves the composition presented on the west pediment, the only part of the building that offered stories that were visible from ground level?[17]

In an influential book, *Architectural Space in Ancient Greece*, first published in 1972 but derived from researches done in pre-war Berlin and on the spot in Greece, the architect and planner Constantinos A. Doxiadis selected the now familiar iconic view of the Parthenon as seen from the west to exemplify his theory that the ancients had selected various stopping points on the Acropolis summit where the sightlines at which buildings were visually encountered were adapted to catch the attention of an ancient pedestrian.[18] Doxiades was among the first in modern times to understand that ancient cities, and their sacred sites, were built with a mobile rather than a static viewer in mind, and his book is doing much to correct the common assumption that ancient buildings achieved their effects because their geometric proportions acted directly on the minds of viewers looking at them face-to-face, as if

---

16   Harris, *Treasures of the Parthenon*, 144, no 168. They also give a glimpse of how Athens had developed a system of mobilising and deploying the savings of the economy for the purposes of investment, normally as loan capital, notably for financing trade, agriculture, and manufacturing, with the resulting economic surplus diverted to other purposes, and that also could provide a rate of return to the city as lender, which in financial terms, if not defaulted on, seems to have been around twelve per cent per annum.

17   The fact that, to the surprise of many visitors, the Parthenon was not visible from the Areopagus hill was discussed in St Clair, *WStP*, Chapter 22, https://doi.org/10.1164/obp.0136.22.

18   Doxiades, Constantinos A., *Architectural Space in Ancient Greece, Translated and Edited by Jacqueline Tyrwhitt* (Cambridge MA: MIT Press, 1972), especially the summary at 3–14. Based on the author's 1936 dissertation published in 1937 as *Raumordnung im griechischen Städtebau*. Doxiades presented his ideas as a 'discovery' and as a general theory, based on 'a natural system of coordinates', that was itself 'based on principles of human cognition'. His 1946 pamphlet on the damage done to Greece and its people during the Second World War was noted in St Clair, *WStP*, Chapter 23, https://doi.org/10.1164/obp.0136.23.

they were engravings printed in an architectural manual. However, by continuing to locate the site where meaning was made in the design of the building and its sightlines, rather than regarding acts of seeing and cognition as transactions that included the historically and culturally contingent expectations of viewers, Doxiades remained within the traditions of modern, object-centred, western art history.

As for the main viewing stations, although the ancient viewer arriving through the Propylaia would have had a clearer view of the west end of the Parthenon and of the stories presented there than was available from outside at ground level, he or she also knew that the main ceremonies took place at the eastern end of the Acropolis, and that the whole complex had been designed as an outdoor space where rites were performed. It was in the space between the east end of the Parthenon and the Erechtheion where the processions halted, where the culminating ceremonies occurred, and from where the processioners returned back through the Propylaia, and in some cases at least back along the peripatos before dispersing. The plentiful surviving descriptions and visual images of processions being performed in accordance with pre-arranged conventions and schedules, under the direction of leaders and marshals, suggest that the practices followed much the same general pattern for many centuries, before and after the classical period, until eventually being brought to an end or at least drastically reformed by the incoming Christian theocracy some time in the middle centuries of the first millennium CE.[19] The main ancient ceremonies included animal sacrifice, skinning, roasting, and communal eating of the meat, accompanied by music made with instruments, singing, dance, and invocations of the gods.

Standing in the pivotal eastern area of the Acropolis summit, the participants were overshadowed, often literally, as the sun or moon moved, by the two main sacred buildings, the Doric Parthenon and the Ionic Erechtheion, the former with a frieze such as was more common on Ionic buildings, and the latter out-Ionianizing the buildings of Asian Ionia in the richness of the coloured glass and the ceramic beads with

---

19   Discussed, as far as the classical period is concerned, by Parker, Robert, *Polytheism and Society at Athens* (Oxford: OUP, 2005), https://doi.org/10.1093/acprof: oso/9780199216116.001.0001, which systematically collected and presented the evidence and on which all subsequent work is reliant.

which it was bejewelled. This building was said to house the tomb of Erechtheus, so linking it to the myth of autochthony, and making it the earliest of the many tombs in the city and in the countryside where memory was officially deemed ('nomismatized') to be true, instituted, displayed, and occasionally performed.[20]

At the time the classical Parthenon and the other buildings on the Acropolis were being planned, the two main orders of Greek architecture, the Doric and the Ionic, appear already to have already been separated; the Parthenon and Propylaia being Doric, the Erechtheion and the small Nike temple added later, being Ionic. The Parthenon was unusual in having a frieze, an Ionic feature, although this was not unique nor an innovation, as is sometimes suggested, since friezes had formed part of Doric buildings elsewhere, mainly in cities in Ionia in Asia and on some islands.[21] And the 'pre-Parthenon' that was destroyed in the Persian invasions, and that later supplied some of the cut marble from which the classical Parthenon was built, or rather 'rebuilt', appears also to have included Ionic elements.[22]

Vitruvius, a Roman-era writer on architecture, in the Preface to his seventh book, recalling that the poet Zoilus, who had set himself up as a superior of Homer, and who, in the view of Vitruvius, had rightly been put to death for 'parricide' (in modern terms plagiarism) offers a long list of named predecessors who had written on architecture and on individual Doric and Ionic temples. Among these sources (Latin 'fontes', a word that retains its associations with water and fountains), which Vitruvius mentions that he has drawn on in making his compilation, is a work on the Parthenon written by its architectons, Iktinos, co-authored with an otherwise unrecorded Karpion.[23] Whether this composition, of which no trace survives, was confined to the broad design and engineering of the building, or whether it also discussed its displayed stories, is not known.

By the classical period, it seems that each architectural order had its own recognizable visual characteristics: the Doric plain and solid,

---

20 Discussed further in Chapter 4, that includes examples of real ancient viewers knowing explicitly that much of the built heritage was actively invented as a rhetoric.

21 Discussed by Castriota, David, *Myth, ethos, and actuality: official art in fifth-century B.C. Athens* (Madison, University of Wisconsin Press, 1992), 226 with a map.

22 Neils, Jenifer, *The Parthenon Frieze* (Cambridge; New York: CUP, 2001), 27.

23 Vitr. Praef. 7.12.

the Ionic lighter and more graceful. At some time not dated, each order had evidently been linked to myths of origin and to eponymous heroes, Doros for the Doric and Ion for the Ionic. Although the stories are only preserved in the work of Vitruvius, they appear to have been long established as components of a pan-Hellenic discourse and current at the time of the rebuilding programme. If so, the associations with the eponyms would have been present in the horizons that viewers brought to their seeing experience, acting—as was evidently a feature of eponyms—both as a mnemonic and a rhetoric, as has already been noted in the discussion of the interior of the building.

As for the main entrance at the east end of the Parthenon, only when the doors were opened, which may only have happened during festivals, perhaps as part of the culminating and concluding rites, was huge gold-and-ivory (chryselephantine) cult statue known as 'Athena Parthenos' visible only to a few people at a time, suggesting that processioners may have had to file past. The gold plates of that statue were designed to be detachable and therefore available to be useable, either uncoined or coined, as security for loans and guarantees denominated either in monetary or other terms. Both rooms of the Parthenon, therefore, served as strong-rooms for the most precious, and therefore the most at-risk material possessions of the city.[24]

When in use on collective festival occasions, the classical-era Acropolis was a place of bright and variegated colours to which participants contributed by their festival clothes, including wreaths and other markers of dress, some of which are likely to be the same as those shown mostly in two colours on ceramics and in full colour on the korai found in the nineteenth-century excavations. During the later classical period, when there were feasts or festivals every few days throughout the seasonal year, some at night, with many occurring in or near the Acropolis, there is a contemporary report that the east end was a place where grass grew, a remark which, if not just a euphemism for an area scuffed by human feet and animal hooves, may imply some cordoning and perhaps active watering and gardening.[25]

---

24   For completeness I note that there remains some doubt about the connotations of the various names and nicknames and it is possible that the hecatompedon was an adjoining building.

25   In the *Ion*, the rocky slopes of the Acropolis beside Pan's cave where the character of Kreousa alleges that she was made pregnant by Apollo are contrasted with the 'green acres' in front of the temples of Athena on the summit. στάδια χλοερὰ πρὸ

Stories Told in Stone

With so many claims on their senses, how did the processioners
look at the stories offered on the buildings? The *Ion* of Euripides is
unique among classical-era texts in presenting a scene of real viewers
looking at a real pediment on a real building, albeit in a fiction.[26] As
with Pausanias, it was formerly customary to scold Euripides for not
conforming to modern ways of seeing and their categories.[27] Instead,
I suggest, we can use the fictional scene and its place in the drama
to recover a fuller understanding of the practice ('praxis') and of the
conventions shared by producers and consumers, than any that can be
yielded by modern art criticism. In a scene in the play set in Delphi, the
chorus of women who are visiting as tourists make a direct reference to
the west pediment of the temple to Apollo there, which shows one of the
standard presentations on classical-era Hellenic temples including the
Parthenon: a battle of giants ('gigantomachy'). As a help to the audience
of the play, as well as to later readers, the women declare at the start that
some have looked at stories displayed on the buildings in Athens in the
same way.[28] The following is a translated extract from their conversation
as presented by Euripides:

> 'Look! come see, the son of Zeus is killing the Lernean Hydra with a
> golden sickle; my dear, look at it!
>
> I see it. And another near him, who is raising a fiery torch— is he the one
> whose story is told when I am at my loom, the warrior Iolaus, who joins
> with the son of Zeus in bearing his labours?
>
> And look at this one sitting on a winged horse; he is killing the mighty
> fire-breathing creature that has three bodies.

Παλλάδος ναῶν. *Eur.* Ion 497. Literally 'stades', a Greek measure of six hundred
English feet, from which the modern word stadium is derived. The fact that the
temples are in the plural tends to confirms that the character in the play is referring
to the open ground at the east end of the Acropolis.

26   It is difficult to infer much from the surviving lines and parts of lines of a satyr
     play by Aeschylus, called *The Festivalgoers* (*Theoroi*'), collected as Fragment 50,
     which include episodes of the satyrs looking at images of themselves displayed in a
     temple.

27   For example: '...his description of the temple at Delphi, which is even worse
     arranged than is usual with him'. Verrall, A. W., ed., *The Ion of Euripides, with a
     Translation into English Verse and an Introduction and Notes* (Cambridge: CUP, 1890),
     xlvii.

28   *Eur.* Ion 185 and following, not all of the text included in this excerpt.

I am glancing around everywhere. See the battle of the giants, on the stone walls.

I am looking at it, my friends. Do you see the one brandishing her gorgon shield against Enceladus?

I see Pallas [Athena], my own goddess. Now what? the mighty thunderbolt, blazing at both ends, in the far-shooting hands of Zeus?

I see it; he is burning the furious Mimas to ashes in the fire.

And Bacchus, the roarer, is killing another of the sons of Earth with his ivy staff, unfit for war.'

Although the audience of the *Ion* is given only a short passage, which has been fitted into the tight conventions of the tragic drama, Euripides has packed in many aspects of the ancient classical experience that are not normally practised by modern viewers. For example, the women immediately recognize the stories from having heard them told aloud as they worked at their looms. They fly in their imaginations to Chalcidike at the northern border of the Hellenic world where the war of the giants had taken place in mythic times, and which was now a place of recent Athenian settlement. Looking and seeing are presented as social experiences, conversational, interactive, and interrogatory, with the different characters of the composition on the building picked out, recognized, and made to move at the behest of the viewers.[29] As Katerina Zacharia has noticed, the women add details either from other compositions or from their own memories and imaginations.[30] And since the Ionians in the settlements in the northern Aegean were known as Chalcidians, the classical-era audience was invited to see parallels between the imagined world of myth and that of their own day.[31] To the women presented in Euripides's play, the pediment of the building in Delphi, over which they rapidly move their eyes, was not a static piece of sculpture nor a 'work of art', but a set of coloured pictures packed with episodes, in this case mostly violent, that could be rearranged, added to,

---

29 The marble fragments that were discovered in excavations are shown on the Perseus website: http://www.perseus.tufts.edu/hopper/artifact?name=Delphi,+Temple+of+Apollo,+West+Pediment&object=Sculpture

30 Zacharia, Katerina, *Converging Truths, Euripides Ion and the Athenian Quest for Self-Definition* (Leiden: Brill, 2003), 15, https://doi.org/10.1163/9789004349988.

31 Noted by Zacharia, *Converging Truths*, 3, https://doi.org/10.1163/9789004349988, referring to Thuc 4. 61. 2.

or subtracted from as they chose. Image and word were inseparable, and it was the women who collectively made the meanings.

A fragment of the *Hypsipyle*, a play by Euripides mostly lost, gives an indication of another of the ways in which the pictorial images on temples were encountered and used. As one of the characters declares: 'Look – run your eyes up towards the sky, and take a look at the written reliefs on the pediment'.[32] Although the lines have survived because they explain how the Greek word for 'pediment' was the same as that for 'eagle', they confirm features of the passage in the *Ion*, notably that looking at the pediments was an occasion for conversation, with no obligation to be hushed in reverence such as modern churches and museums enforce, and for the viewers to make and not just to receive meanings.

And there are other differences between the two ways of seeing offered in the two Euripidean plays. Besides drawing attention to the steep angle of viewing, the character, who is addressing the audience and not the other characters in the play, also makes clear that he sees the pieces as material manufactured objects, from which stories can be composed, as if in a play whose course is directed by the viewers. That some well-made images can be so like real life that a viewer cannot tell the difference is, of course, a rhetorical cliché found in much ancient as well as in modern writings. However, the more exact notion that static images are made to come alive in the imagination of the viewer is implied in a comment on the statues made by the mythic Daidalos reported by a later author, Diodoros of Sicily, who drew on earlier accounts and discursive conventions: '...they [the images] could see, they said, and walk and, in a word, they preserved so well the characteristics of the entire body that the beholder thought that the image made by him was a being endowed with life'.[33]

---

32 Collard, C., Cropp, M. J. and Gibert, J., eds, *Euripides, Selected Fragmentary Plays Volume II* (Warminster: Aris and Phillips, 2004), Fragment 752c, page 186. At the risk of introducing a new ambiguity, I have amended the translation of γραπτοὺς τύπους from 'painted reliefs' offered by the editors to avoid being too definite. I do not wish to exclude the possibility that the phrase may refer to words that identified the characters for viewers, as they have been found on the Treasury of the Siphnians at Delphi, and may have existed elsewhere, including on the Parthenon where, on the pediments, a large number of local mythic characters are shown, not all of which are likely to have been recognizable by even local viewers without the help of words, either inscribed, or performed by procession marshals and tour guides.

33 Diod. 4.76.2. According to Aristotle, a character in the lost *Cyprians* by Dicaeogenes, a fourth-century tragedian, weeps at the sight of an image. Noted by Wright,

As for the most visible stories presented on the Parthenon, those displayed in the two pediments, they imply a transaction with the ancient viewer that is specific both to the medium and to the occasions on which encounters normally occurred. The nature of the composition is necessarily limited by the triangular shape of the architectural space that, in both cases, presents an identifiable central episode from local myth, namely scenes relating to the birth of Athena in the east pediment, and a contest between Athena and Poseidon in the west. The fullest visual record of how the two pediments appeared in modern times was made in 1674 when the encounter with the classically educated western visitors had just begun, and before the destructive bombardment by the Venetian-led western European army of 1687 and the subsequent fire; it is shown as Figure 3.1.[34]

Figure 3.1. The pediments of the Parthenon as drawn on the spot in 1674. Engraving.[35]

Matthew, *The Lost Plays of Greek Tragedy, Volume 1, Neglected Authors* (London: Bloomsbury, 2016), 146, http://doi.org/10.5040/9781474297608, from Aristotle, *Poetics* 16, 1454b37–38, noting that 'graphe' may mean a piece of writing not a picture.

34   Only a general impression of the appearance can be gained from the drawing made by Cyriac of Ancona in the fifteenth century, shown and discussed in, for example, Bodnar, Edward W., *Cyriacus of Ancona and Athens* (Brussels: Latomus, 1960).

35   Included in *A Description of the Collection of Ancient Marbles in the British Museum* (London: British Museum, 1830), vi. Drawn by R. Corbould, engraved by H. Moses, published 8 November 1828.

The east pediment, shown at the top, had suffered more severely than the west underneath. The losses there, it now seems certain, had occurred when the Parthenon was adapted to serve as a Christian basilica with a Byzantine-style round-roofed apse at the east entrance, which took place at some time in the early centuries CE. In 1674 the western pediment was still largely complete, refuting later claims that the Ottoman Muslims, who at that time had controlled Athens for nearly two hundred years, deliberately destroyed figurative images as being inconsistent with Islam. Since, when the Ottoman forces first arrived in Athens in 1485, the Parthenon was a Christian church and was then to be converted into a Muslim mosque, it had benefited from the protection conferred on religious buildings by the *millet* system. The artist of the 1674 drawings, often referred to as Jacques Carrey although the attribution is doubtful, had prepared his record of the west pediment in chalk on two large sheets of paper, one for the parts under the apex on the viewer's right and the other for those on the viewer's left. When the two sheets were loosely joined, viewers of his work, and of copies of his work, were left with the impression that they were seeing a picture of the complete pediment.[36]

As for what the ancient producers of the west pediment intended to present to viewers, the tradition has been to rely on the brief remark by Pausanias that what was pictured was the contest between Athena and Poseidon for the land of Athens.[37] And most scholars have accepted that what was shown was a stand-off in which Poseidon was the loser.[38] However, even if Pausanias's remark were to be taken to imply that the contest was about which of the two deities could claim the greater honour or which had been the first, the notion of a contest that

---

36 Omont. Frequently reproduced, for example in the fine edition by Bowie, Theodore and Thimme, Diether, eds, *The Carrey Drawings of the Parthenon Sculptures* (Bloomington and London: Indiana UP, 1971), and earlier by Michaelis, Leake, and others. Modern photographs of the full set of drawings are viewable on Gallica, http://gallica.bnf.fr/ark:/12148/btv1b7200482m.r=.langEN, and a large selection in low resolution on Wikimedia Commons.

37 ὁπόσα ἐν τοῖς καλουμένοις ἀετοῖς κεῖται, πάντα ἐς τὴν Ἀθηνᾶς ἔχει γένεσιν, τὰ δὲ ὄπισθεν ἡ Ποσειδῶνος πρὸς Ἀθηνᾶν ἐστιν ἔρις ὑπὲρ τῆς γῆς. Paus. 1.24.5.

38 For example: 'One can hardly imagine a more fitting commemoration of Athena's victory over Poseidon than the thrilling composition at the very center of the gable, where god and goddess meet in the heat of the contest'. Connelly, Joan Breton, *The Parthenon Enigma, A New Understanding of the World's Most Iconic Building and the People Who Made It* (New York: Alfred A. Knopf, 2014), 107.

produced a triumphant winner and a disgruntled loser cannot be easily squared with the discursive environment within which the design of the classical Parthenon was decided upon and built.[39] There were plenty of offerings to Poseidon for his help in winning the sea battles of the Persian wars, both the immediate trophies by which after any battle the winner claimed victory, in this case dedications of wrecked enemy ships, and also permanent memorials built near the site. The remains of the classical-era temple dedicated to Poseidon on the promontory of Sounion still captures the attention of tourists and of ships at sea, and in Athens a shrine was set up to Boreas, the north wind that had disrupted the enemy's ships off Cape Artemisium.[40] It would be puzzling, incredible even, if, on the most often-seen story presented on the Parthenon, which is otherwise about promoting civic unity, inclusiveness, harmony, and mutual trust as the best way for the city's success in warfare to continue, the contribution of Poseidon had been omitted or presented in unfavourable or grudging terms.

There is, however, no need to rely on the ambiguous testimony of the phrase by Pausanias. What the modern tradition has recently forgotten is that we have a description written around two hundred years before Pausanias by a much more authoritative ancient author. Marcus Terentius Varro (116–27 BCE), who had studied in Athens around the same time as Cicero, held a string of the highest public offices in the late Roman Republic, and his portrait appears on a coin of the time. Despite his having served as a military commander in the Civil Wars of Pompey against Caesar, he was appointed to supervise the public library at Rome and served on various governmental commissions. He was the author of numerous books, a few of which survive in whole or in part, mainly in the form of well-researched encyclopedias that were highly respected and frequently quoted.[41] Varro's explanation is to be preferred

---

39 As restored in Chapter 2, including the explicit comment by the so-called Old Oligarch, Ps. Xen. Const. Ath. 4.6.

40 The evidence is collected and discussed by Shear, T. Leslie, Jnr., *Trophies of Victory: Public Building in Periklean Athens* (Princeton, N.J.: Department of Art and Archaeology, Princeton University in association with Princeton UP, 2016).

41 For example, Pausanias is referred to only once in the huge corpus of subsequent ancient writings, as noted in Georgopoulou, M., Guilmet, C., Pikoulas, Y. A., Staikos, K. S. and Tolias, G., eds, *Following Pausanias: The Quest for Greek Antiquity* (Kotinos: Oak Knoll Press, 2007), 19, whereas there are two volumes of fragments of Varro recovered from mentions in later authors, including many by Augustine.

to that of Pausanias, not just because he wrote two centuries before and his account matches what we should have expected from the discursive environment, but because he had better opportunities for knowing what was intended. Instead of regarding Varro's version as a later variant of Pausanias, Pausanias offers a variant of Varro, and an example of how, as in the Athenian tragic drama, the presented characters could perform more than one story, either advertently by a writer of plays, or in the minds of viewers listening to guides. A more elaborate version of the Varro fragment was offered by Aelius Aristides, in his Panathenaic oration in praise of Athens, one of the most formal of the occasions in which the official discourse was repeated, which is thought to have been composed around 155 CE, before Pausanias.[42] Since Aristides repeats most of the components first heard in the classical period, his work in this instance, as elsewhere, can be taken as yet another example of the longevity of the discourse.[43]

It now seems certain that some time before the chalk drawing was made, the centre of the composition was occupied by an image of an olive tree, picked out in painted marble or metal or some combination of the two. Indeed, since the image of the tree occupied what was, on normal as well as on festival days, the most prominent and most often-seen feature of the Parthenon, it may have been rendered in bronze or gilded bronze, making it a prime target for any thieves or mutilators who had the influence and infrastructure to be able to remove it. Low-denomination bronze coins made in Athens during the Roman imperial period often included views on prominent features to be seen in Athens.[44] The example shown as Figure 3.2 can be regarded as part of the discursive environment, not only recording a famous feature of the cityscape but commending to its users the ideologies that it instantiated.

---

42   The date favoured by Trapp, Michael, ed., *Aelius Aristides Orations. 1–2* (Cambridge, Mass and London: Loeb, 2017), 10.

43   The character of Aspasia in the *Menexenus* recommends that olive trees be explicitly mentioned, Plat. Menex. 238a. She comes near to suggesting that Athena was named after the land of Athens as an eponym rather than that Athena conferred the name.

44   Another, which showed the Acropolis and its caves, is shown as Figure 17.4 in St Clair, *WStP*, Chapter 17, https://doi.org/10.1164/obp.0136.17

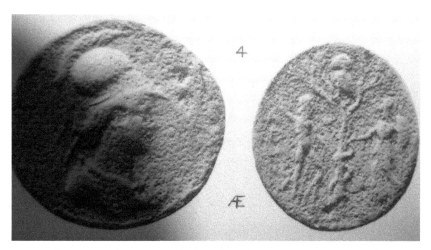

Figure 3.2. A bronze coin of Athens from the Roman imperial period.[45]

The mathematician Euclid, writing in the late fourth or third century BCE, but probably reporting observations made earlier, remarked that phenomena above eye level descend while those below ascend, something that the Commissioners are likely to have known about and might have chosen to build into the design and include in the contract with those commissioned to do the work.[46] However that may be, what seems certain is that an olive tree was depicted in the space most

---

45 Reproduced from Head, Barclay V., and edited by Poole, Reginald Stuart, *Catalogue of Greek Coins: Attica-Megaris-Aegina* (London: British Museum 1888), plate XVII. An example in good condition is photographed, with a description, by Kraay, C. M., *The Coins of Ancient Athens* (Newcastle: Minerva Numismatic Handbooks, 1968), viii, 3.
Another version reproduced in Frazer, J. G., trans., *Pausanias's Description of Greece* (London: Macmillan, 1898), ii, 300. Other examples, from various collections, noted by Beulé, E., Professeur de l'Archéologie à la Bibliothèque Impériale, *Les Monnaies d'Athènes* (Paris: 1858. Reprinted in facsimile by Forni of Bologna, 1967), 393.

46 Noted by Tanner, Jeremy, 'Sight and painting: optical theory and pictorial poetics in Classical Greek art', in Squire, Michael, ed., *Sight and the Ancient Senses* (London: Routledge, 2016), 110, https://doi.org/10.4324/9781315719238. Tanner also refers to a fragment of a work by Geminus, a writer of optics of the first century BCE, which gives practical advice, such as presenting circles as ellipses and foreshortening rectangular elements, which are necessary when picturing buildings so that they appear to be symmetrical and 'eurhythmic'. Discussed also by Senseney, John R., *The Art of Building in the Classical World: Vision, Craftsmanship, and Linear Perspective in Greek and Roman Architecture* (Cambridge: CUP, 2011), https://doi.org/10.1017/CBO9780511976711, who offers examples of what the drawings for the Parthenon may have looked like.

often looked at on the Parthenon, immediately below the apex of the pediment, to which all eyes were drawn.[47]

The scene presented on a fourth-century water jar (hydria), which may be a direct allusion to the west pediment, shows the olive tree centred between the two divinities, with a flying figure with what looks like Victory ('Nike') in the upper apex, and a guardian snake curled round its lower trunk.[48] The main features can be seen in the image at Figure 3.3, a flattened version of the composition prepared not long after the piece was excavated from a burial ground in the modern Crimea.

Figure 3.3. 'Athena and Poseidon contending for Attica; vase from Kertch (at Petersburg)'. Photograph of a flattened version.[49]

As was evidently the case on the west pediment, personages, divine and mythic, are shown on either side of the tree, arranged in groups in a variety of stances. Some pay attention to the central episode. Others

---

47   The desire of the designers to draw the eye upward to the key feature of the composition is also apparent on the central scene of the Parthenon frieze, to be discussed in Chapter 4.

48   Dated c. 360–350 in the Hermitage, St Petersburg from excavations in Kerch. Described, with photographs in colour, in Cohen, Beth with contributions by Lapatin, Kenneth [et al.], *The Colors of Clay; Special Techniques in Athenian Vases* (Los Angeles, Getty, 2006), 339–341, https://www.getty.edu/publications/resources/virtuallibrary/0892369426.pdf. Cited by Connelly, *Parthenon Enigma*, 107.

Reproduced in monochrome by Palagia, Olga, *The Pediments of the Parthenon*, second unrevised edition (Leiden: Brill, 1998), plate 10.

49   Walters, H. B., *History of Ancient Pottery: Greek, Etruscan, and Roman, Based on the Work of Samuel Birch* (London: Murray, 1905), ii, opposite 24.

are detached from the action and conversing. Some gaze directly at the viewer, inviting him or her to respond self-reflexively. And all, by their gestures and facial expressions, silently offer options to the viewer of how he or she might also choose to respond. They are mostly shown in attitudes of movement, of anticipation, of uncertainty, and of waiting for an event that lies in the future. As has been noted by Robin Osborne: 'Pediments ... manifest themselves to the viewer at once: any partial view is unstable: only the view of the whole can be satisfactory'.[50] As characters from various, mainly local Athenian, myths, they have no reason for being together other than as components of a discursive environment unconcerned with realism, time, or place, displaying what was needed to enable the characters to be recognized and their stories re-energized by a classical-era Athenian viewer in accordance with conventions that ignored geography and chronology. As with all vase paintings that I know of that depict an ancient temple, it is as incidental to the main action as the temporary structures used as scenery in performances of tragic drama, to the extent that it is often impossible to say whether a real event is being pictured or an allusion to a play.

Many attempts have been made to identify the personages displayed, mainly by trying to reconstruct who might have been expected, or 'deemed', by the classical Athenians to have been present. However, that enterprise may rest on an assumption that the aim of the designers was to present an actual event, albeit telescoped. Figure 3.4 pictures a nineteenth-century attempt at reconstruction of the west and east pediments, partly to exemplify the wide variety of speculations offered, but also because it includes a version by Giovanni Battista Lusieri, Elgin's artist and agent, republished here for the first time since 1845.[51] The pictures do not sufficiently bring out the extent to which some of the characters presented are bursting out of their pedimental frame as a form of *trompe l'oeil*.

---

50 Osborne, Robin, 'Temple sculpture and the viewer', in Rutter, N. Keith and Brian A. Sparkes, eds, *Word and Image in Ancient Greece* (Edinburgh: Edinburgh University Press, Leventis Studies, 2000), 230.

51 How it was obtained is not explained.

Figure 3.4. Reconstructions of the west pediment offering in the early nineteenth century. Copper engraving.[52]

Since studies of ancient visual images have become detached from studies of ancient drama, and both from studies of the practices of ceremonial display and performance, the high degree of commonality between the repertories has sometimes been lost from sight. For example, of the four or five hundred tragic dramas of which the titles have been preserved in lists and mentions, all but a handful appear to take their characters from the world of myth. And we have an explanation that was widely circulated in the classical period. According to Herodotus, when *The Fall*

52   Lucas, R. C., Sculptor. *Remarks on the Parthenon: Being the result of studies and inquiries connected with the production of two models of that noble building, each twelve feet in length, and near six in width. The one exhibiting the temple as it appeared in its dilapidated state, in the seventeenth century, and executed from the existing remains, or from authentic drawings; the other, being an attempt to restore it to the fulness of its original beauty and splendour. Also, a brief review of the statements and opinions of the principal Writers on the subject: viz. Spon and Wheler, Stuart and Revett, Visconti, Quatremere de Quincy, Col. Leake, the Chevalier Bronsted, Professor Cockerell, Mr E. Hawkins, Professor Welcker, &c. 'In the History of all Nations that have contributed to that greatness, and always adorning it; and in a commercial Nation, such as ours is, we may discern in the enlargement of Art an increase of our national prosperity* (Salisbury: Brodie, 1845), opposite 46.

of Miletus by Phrynichus, a prolific playwright, was first put on, and the audience wept with emotion, the author was heavily fined.[53] Soon afterwards, at some time after 492, no plays that dealt directly with current or recent events appear to have been permitted. Of the many hundreds of tragedies performed in classical Athens, only three are known to have presented contemporary subjects.[54] And we have an explanation of why a convention of excluding contemporary political questions from being directly discussed was introduced around 492 BCE.[55] The decision on where to set the boundary may have followed the convention already adhered to in sacred buildings all over the Hellenic world.

Since the content of both storytelling media was approved in advance by the institutions of the city, including those who provided or authorized the financing, the outer boundaries of permitted deviation from the civic norms appear to have been patrolled. We also have the story of how Mikon, son of Phanomathos, a contemporary of Pheidias, a master in the making of both two- and three-dimensional images who was responsible for executing commissions in Athens (including some offered on the Theseion) was accused because, in an image of the Battle of Marathon, he presented the Persians as taller than the Athenians. Like Phrynichus, in the medium of the performed drama, the crime with which alleged offenders were charged was that of departing from the terms of contracts approved by the Athenian assembly.[56]

The same cohort of Athenian citizens might recently have been exhorted from the Pnyx by a gesturing Pericles or his reciter to uphold the civic values set out in stone, metal, paint, and fabric on the physical Acropolis. Since many were also frequent viewers of the tragic drama, it would have been impossible in practice to prevent the interpretation

---

53 Her. 6.2.
54 Besides *The Fall of Miletus*, the exceptions are another play by Phrynichus called the *Phoenician Women*, and Aeschylus's *Persians* that is dated to 472, and can be explained as a permitted exception
55 Herodotus 6.21. Frequently discussed, most recently and with the contexts most fully explored, by Wright, *Neglected Authors*, 17–27, http://doi.org/10.5040/9781474297608. The Phrynichus episode as reported by Herodotus, even if it simplified a process into a single event, also explains how the near contemporary Persians by Aeschylus passed the filters, and how both Phrynichus and Aeschylus in their numerous subsequent plays used stories from myth as comments on contemporary events and questions.
56 This example, with others taken from rhetorical exercises, is given by Russell, D. A., *Greek Declamation* (Cambridge: CUP, 1983), 56.

of the stories in stone from being influenced by those offered by the characters in the drama. One discursive medium interacted with the other, with the result that over the course of a typical lifetime of a classical-era Athenian, numerous myths were dramatized. Some existed in half a dozen versions; all explored general questions without explicit reference to topical political questions. The producers of tragedies were permitted to invent new mythic characters to appear alongside those in the familiar repertoire, and in at least one play, the *Antheus* by Agathon, said by Aristotle to have been successful, an entirely new myth was allowed.[57]

Looked at from modern times, a convention of excluding the immediately political may appear to be a censoring restriction, an aberration from the freedom that is often thought of as a normal prerogative of a 'creative' artist. However, seen from the perspective of an ancient classical writer conscious that he was making his contribution to a long-run moral development from brutishness, a decision to deploy the ancient myths in performance may have seemed like a democratic solution, building on the past while looking to the dialogic needs of the present and the future: exactly the kind of useful innovation that was central to Athenian imaginative self-construction.

What is probably the best representation of the west pediment, showing the olive tree as the central feature, was made in white plaster as a model for a full-scale work by the Viennese sculptor Karl Schwerzek in the late 1890s, as shown in Figure 3.5.

Figure 3.5. Suggested reconstruction of the West Pediment by the professional Viennese sculptor Karl Schwerzek. Photograph.[58]

---

57 Aristot. Poet. 1451b.
58 Photograph inserted in Schwerzek, Karl, Bildhauer, *Erläuterungen zu der Rekonstruktion des Westgiebels des Parthenon* (Vienna: Selbstverlag des Verfassers, 1896). Private collection.

For his researches, besides talking with the leading scholars of the day, Schwerzek had visited the building and studied the detached pieces, including fragments held in museums elsewhere. In London he noticed that a fragmentary marble torso previously thought to have been a part of a metope had been carved in the round and it was reassigned to the west pediments.[59] If, as there is no reason to doubt, images of children were included on either side of the central scene with the olive tree, it is likely that what were presented to ancient viewers were family groups, not individuals, making the myths that they were invited to actualize easier to recognize and to identify with. If, as is also likely, as consumers they shared with the producers a belief in extramission, they may have thought that their looking experience helped to make them heroic in accordance with Athenian civic ideology.

As far as the pediments are concerned, although it would have been hard for even the most antiquarian-minded ancient viewer to identify all the personages in the packed composition—even if, as is possible, there were words on the architrave or elsewhere—the fact that what was presented on the west pediment is a contest would have been plain to see even from a distance. And, since the actual viewerships of both media largely coincided, it would have been impossible in practice to prevent interpretations of the stories in stone from being influenced by those offered by the drama, and vice-versa. Indeed, far from the producers trying to keep the media separate, we have occasional evidence of how they were deliberately offered to ancient viewers as mutually supporting, as when, for example, the leader of the chorus of women in the *Phoenician Women* by Euripides compares herself to the golden statues to be seen at Delphi.[60] Over the course of a typical adult male lifetime, and of those of some women and of other residents of the city too, few official ideologies were immunized against being converted into the more democratic conventions of dialogue.

Rather than thinking of the painted stone and metal figures presented on the pediments as statues fixed for ever in a historic moment like those photographed in a clicked moment by a still camera, it may be more fair to the ways of seeing recommended to ancient viewers to think of them

---

59   Noted by Smith, Cecil, 'Additions to the Greek Sculptures in the British Museum' in *The Classical Review*, Vol. 6 (10) (Dec., 1892), 475.

60   Eur. Phoen. 220.

as the assembled actors of a repertory company, already costumed, standing ready to perform (or already beginning) an old or a new play within a wide repertoire, whose broad scope was already familiar.[61] Such plays could be composed either by the viewer himself or herself, as was the case of the women at Delphi on the *Ion*, or invented for a range of occasions by a playwright, orator, or leader of a festival. Indeed, the women presented in the *Ion* not only make the images behave as actors in a play of their own making, but shrink the gap between themselves as viewers of the play and the players, so that they themselves become participants in the events that they are causing to unfold in their imaginations.[62]

With this way of seeing, there is no 'correct' nor 'original' version, nor any need for the plays to be speculatively arranged into a chronological sequence of development and divergence. Rather, I suggest, as with presentations on the tragic stage, the aim was to enable viewers to explore ideas within a genre they understood, and that needed only a few words of preface to remind the viewers of the characters and their mythic situation. To an extent every Athenian was encouraged to become his own dramatist, using the old stories not as a set of fixed texts that preserved quasi-historical information about the past but as an agenda for a not-yet-performed set of dialogic dramas of moral and political debate, many of which explored notions of civic 'arete.' Euripides, in particular, made plentiful use of the freedom that the conventions provided. In the *Erechtheus*, for example, the character of Athena demands that the character of Poseidon leaves Attica, having done damage enough with his earthquakes.[63] The speech then offers what is tantamount to a commentary on the scene pictured on the west pediment of the Parthenon. By subverting the usual story that Athena and Poseidon were reconciled, the play can treat the static images as able to move and to develop in new directions, as in a new dramatic version of an old myth. In Euripides' *Ion*, there are indications that the

---

61   That viewers who see either a real person who is standing still, or a [static] image of a real person, feel an urge to imagine them moving was noted by Plato in the Timaeus. Plat. Tim. 19b.

62   Discussed by Zeitlin, Froma, 'The Artful Eye: Vision, Ekphrasis, and Spectacle in Euripidean Drama', in Goldhill, Simon, and Osborne, Robin, *Art and Text in Ancient Greek Culture* (Cambridge: CUP, 1994), 138–196.

63   Euripides *Erechtheus* fragment 370 line 4 in Euripides, *Selected Fragmentary Plays*, Collard et al edition, i, 171.

characters, by appealing to 'pictures', are presented as having those on the Parthenon in mind, or at least they could reasonably have been assumed to have done so by the ancient attendee.

Making the Mute Stones Speak: The Role of the Viewer

We have only a few recorded examples of how the ancient individual viewer was encouraged to release, to revivify, and, as in terms of ancient rhetoric, to 're-enargize' the frozen figures; to make the mute stones speak; and to do so in new and sometimes in unexpected ways. Euripides imagined the conversations of the women looking at the pediment in Delphi on a special occasion. Under this way of seeing, which I will call 'Every man (or woman) his own dramatist', there is no 'correct' or 'original' version, nor need we attempt to recover a chronological stemma of commonality and divergence. As on the tragic stage, viewers are offered opportunities to explore ideas within a genre whose boundaries are understood, in which general questions are of greater importance than the characters who wrestle with them. Even in the brief phrase by Pausanias, one of the few real ancient viewers of whom we have records of his way of seeing, we can pick up this view, offered almost as an aside that scarcely needed to be mentioned, that the presentation is not one of a specific moment either before, during, or after an event. As George Mostratos translates Pausanias's remark on the east pediment: 'all the figures in the pediment over the entrance to the temple called the Parthenon *relate* to the birth of Athena'.[64]

Varro goes on to say that, in order 'to appease his [Poseidon's] wrath, the women should be visited by the Athenians with the three-fold punishment — that they should no longer have any vote; that none of their children should be named after their mothers; and that no one should call them Athenians.'[65] This too is fully consistent with the

---

64 Paus 1.24.5. ὁπόσα ἐν τοῖς καλουμένοις ἀετοῖς κεῖται, πάντα ἐς τὴν Ἀθηνᾶς ἔχει γένεσιν. Although Pausanias' main interest was in collecting and systematizing the old stories, in describing how the ivory of the cult statue in marshy Olympia needed to be preserved with olive oil, in contrast with the ivory of the cult statue on the Athenian Acropolis that had to be kept damp with water, he mentions as an aside, as something that everyone knew, that the reason why the Acropolis has no water is because its great height keeps it dry, a scientific explanation that related both the phenomenon and the visual rhetorical presentation to the microclimate.

65 Augustine of Hippo, *On the City of God Against the Pagans*, Book 18, Chapter 9. Again, the author is careful to enable the reader to separate his own voice, in which he

discourse. As Nicole Loraux has pointed out, although there are words for 'women of 'Boeotia, Lacedaimon, Corinth, and other cities, usually formed with the suffix –issai- that puts their native city as central to their identity. Although, as we might translate, there were 'Corinthiannesses,' there were no 'Atheniannesses'.[66] The separation of gender roles between the polis for men and the oikos for women is advocated by both Plato and Aristotle, and by characters in the tragic drama. In the classical period the claim provided much merriment in the *Lysistrata* and the *Birds* of Aristophanes, we can take it that this feature of the official ideology was contested.[67]

Here, it may be worth noting the reported experience of one real visitor of the pre-First-World-War era when in Britain and elsewhere a political campaign for votes for women was at its height. Mrs. R. C. Bosanquet, wife of an archaeologist resident in Athens, and a classical scholar in her own right, remembered the version recorded by Varro. As she noted: 'The vote was given on grounds of sex, the men voting for sea-power, the women for the goddess of wisdom and needlework. Then, as now, the women had the numerical majority and carried the business in hand. But the men had superior strength and punished the *suffragatrices* by the loss of the vote and otherwise'.[68] In the second, post-war, edition of her book, when the aims of the women's suffrage movement in Britain had been met in part, the story was omitted and, on the title page, Mrs Bosanquet now marked and aligned herself with the modest change in social and political attitudes by styling herself 'Ellen. S. Bosanquet'.[69]

However, although the Varro version may appear to validate some notion of the equality of the sexes, it is undermined, or at least dialogically responded to, by the remark of the character of Apollo, speaking with the authority of a divinity who takes a special interest in Athens in the

---

offers his own opinions, from that of Varro, from whose work he quotes in support of his own. It seems likely that Augustine's motive in riding on the authority of Varro was to help his own advocacy of the separation of gender roles that soon slipped into a claim that women were 'by nature' inferior.

66 Loraux, Nicole, *The Children of Athena, Athenian Ideas about Citizenship and the Division between the Sexes, Translated by Caroline Levine* (Princeton: Princeton UP, 1993), 153.
67 Loraux, *Children*, 153.
68 Bosanquet, Mrs R. C., *Days in Attica* (London: Methuen, 1914), 74. As an indication of the system of signs that Bosanquet shared with her expected readership, she described the land of Attica, at page 68, as 'not much bigger than a medium-sized Scotch shooting'.
69 Bosanquet, Ellen S., *The Tale of Athens* (London: Methuen, 1932).

Eumenides of Aeschylus, first performed in 458 when the Parthenon was under construction but when all its features had probably already been decided upon. In asserting that women are not the real parents of children but only steward-nurses of embryos brought into being by a male impregnation, the character of Apollo cites, 'as visible proof' of his words, the fact that Athena is shown emerging from the head of Zeus, as on the east pediment, a statement of the official ideology and paideia of the classical city.[70]

The custom of producing new versions for new times continued long after the classical period, without anyone protesting that the true or original meaning had been misunderstood, subverted, or misappropriated. Aelius Aristides, in his Panathenaic oration of 151 CE—one of the formal occasions on which the asserted ideological continuity of the city was renewed—offered his audience a version such as Euripides might have dramatized. The struggle presented, he declared, was a warning against attempts at political coups by seizing the Acropolis. The mythic story had ended in a reconciliation, showing that it was better to use Athens's tradition of courts and juries. As for Poseidon, presented on the pediment as the loser in the contest, that divinity had not, Aristides declared, ended his intense love for Athens, but had given her naval superiority in the wars of the classical period.[71] In what has been called 'visual theology', that is, the practice of attempting to access the unseeable gods through images of the gods, Aristides exposes the endless circularity of the argument. Men make images of gods as they imagine them to be, he says, and then, by a reverse cognition, 'deem' them to be real and available to be invoked.[72] It is tantamount to an admission that the gods are 'nomismatic' that is

---

70 Aeschylus *Eumenides*, passage beginning at 656, and especially the phrase in line 663: τεκμήριον δὲ τοῦδέ σοι δείξω λόγου.

71 Aristides, *Panathenaic*, 39, 42. I have amended Oliver's translation to bring out more clearly that Aristides uses the word 'eros' that was normally reserved for sexual desire, and its use as a metaphor in describing the exchange implied by the prevalent theory of extramission. Oliver, James Henry, 'The civilizing power: a study of the Panathenaic discourse of Aelius Aristides against the background of literature and cultural conflict, with text, translation, and commentary' in *Transactions of the American Philosophical Society*, Vol. 58 (1) (1968), 1–223, https://doi.org/10.2307/1005987.

72 The phrase 'visual theology' is from Israelowich, Ido, *Society, Medicine and Religion in the Sacred Tales of Aelius Aristides* (Leiden: Brill, 2012), 177, https://doi.org/10.1163/9789004229440.

needed to hold together the officially commended belief system, but, like the nomisma of treating money as a thing and not a convention, it does not have to have any existence outside the decisions of those who collaborate in the deeming.

4. A New Answer to
an Old Question

As for the frieze of the Parthenon, what experiences, I now ask, were offered to the ancient viewers when the building was first brought into use? What events and stories were pictured and commended? How, and in which contexts, were they encountered? What expectations did the men, women, and children of that time bring to the experiences? What emerges if we temporarily throw off the mind-forged manacles of western categories, traditions, and academic disciplines, and look instead for answers that fit comfortably, and even predictably, into the discursive and rhetorical environment?

The frieze presents many of the standard components of ancient Greek festival processions as described by ancient authors and pictured on ancient objects. Large numbers of men, women, and children are shown as coming together for an occasion that will involve the ritual slaughter of cattle and sheep, whose meat, the viewers of the composition will know, will be used in ritual feasting. Indeed, the fact that only large and highly prized animals are pictured, rather than the pigs, rabbits, and fowls that were more commonly used in real festivals, itself marks the pictured event as special. The bones and other inedible body parts of the slaughtered animals will, in the fiction as in real life, be ritually burned, in ways that ensure that the fire, the smoke, and the smells, including some specially contrived with odorous substances added to the fire, catch the attention of people within a wide local periphery. The participants in an actual festival were being invited by the frieze to imagine a fictional festival.

At many actual festivals, the participants were not performing for an audience external to themselves like actors in a drama, but within in sight of one another for long periods, with all the pressures to conform,

        https://doi.org/10.11647/OBP.0279.04

at least outwardly, that such practices bring about, and that in classical Athens were among their publicly acknowledged purposes.[1] It is however unlikely that it was always possible, however eagerly and sincerely the participants may have wished to transport themselves into an alterative immaterial world, that they could forget or ignore the material setting. Many rituals required long-term planning and careful organisation on the day, which inescapably entered the conscious minds of participants during the events as well as in the assembling and dispersing, before and after. Many ancient Athenians, we can also be certain, knew that what was presented to them had passed through all the stages of approval that marked the formal acceptance of the completed work by the client who commissioned it: the city of Athens through its institutions. Indeed, many of the citizens had personally participated in these processes, with changing cohorts of citizens sharing a responsibility for the vision of the imagined city that was displayed and commended.

Individuals, and members of constituencies at a community-building festival, might display and perform their acceptance, but to suggest that they all always believed in what was ritually spoken and sung, or followed the advice of the appointed or elected officials, would be to risk confusing the implied with the historic viewer or assuming that the rhetoric was always successful in persuading those who received it. Such an approach also ignores or downplays the plentiful evidence for playing along, for scepticism, and for resistance, including the ever-present risk of the theft of valuables, despite the heavy penalties. What we can say with confidence is that participants knew that what they were offered, including the stories presented and the desired responses, had been officially approved and commended by the institutions of the city. As a society marked by a keen sense of rhetoric, it had little need for the modern concept of 'propaganda', often assumed to be a deception of those who receive it rather than as a reassurance to would-be conformists that what was offered had been officially 'deemed' to be true or right.[2]

---

1   As noted in the discussion of the *Ion* in Chapter 3.
2   As in many other societies that put a high value on outward conformity, including the propaganda companies overtly attached to the invading German army in 1941 as noted in St Clair, William, *Who Saved the Parthenon? A New History of the Acropolis Before, During and After the Greek Revolution* (Cambridge: Open Book Publishers, 2022) [hereafter *WStP*], https://doi.org/10.11647/OBP.0136, Chapter 23, https://doi.org/10.11647/obp.0136.23.

On the Parthenon frieze, young women and men, seldom differentiated as individuals, are presented as carrying what appear to be containers of food and drink that, we can be confident, will also be consumed by the participants pictured in the composition in the forthcoming feasting. Others are leading large animals, notably much-prized heavy cattle and sheep, but no day-to-day items, such as rabbits or fowls, to be slaughtered in a ritual sacrifice. As part of such rituals, a share was invariably scattered or poured on to the ground as offerings to the gods, and although small as a proportion, the rituals themselves were sufficiently frequent to affect the local ecosystem of the Acropolis site and how it appeared both to participants and to observers within the local periphery. Indeed, the flocking birds were as much part of the Acropolis festival experience as the buildings and the people.[3]

The events shown are pictured as a series of episodes in broadly chronological order, like frozen frames in a film, that the viewers experienced either individually, or at the group level. They are guided by leaders ('marshals') who are directing the events and whose presence within the composition itself both helps viewers to see the images episodically and gives silent advice on what to expect. If a visitor or member of a festival procession attempted to see the whole frieze in chronological order, he or she would have had to break ranks and disrupt the implied script of a united community arriving at its ritual culmination.

When the marble blocks are rearranged in a gallery or in a book of photographs, the sense of encountering a succession of episodes is lost, and attempts to understand the ancient experience are made harder. However, even with the complete loss of large sections of the frieze, the export of many sections, the almost total disappearance of the colour and the metal, and the changes brought about by weathering, by casual damage, and, in the case of most of the pieces at present entrusted to the care of the British Museum trustees, by deliberate mutilation and whitening, there remain markers that, when situated within the discursive environment, can help to reduce the obstacles

---

3   As implied by the character of Teiresias in the *Antigone* of Sophocles Soph. Ant. 1000. The presence of the birds as part of the ecology and human experience of large sacralised sites was useful to the 'priests' who delivered advice based on observing them, as in this example. The fuller example of the *Ion* of Euripides is discussed later in the chapter.

to understanding brought about by the many modern anachronistic intrusions into the strangeness.

The frieze was only comprehensible as a totality if the ancient viewers walked round the whole building. If they did so, negotiating any internal walls, gates, and guards, they would have had to choose whether to try to follow with their eyes the part of the procession that moved eastwards along the north side of the building or, alternatively, the other part of the procession moving in the same direction along the south side. Unless he or she doubled back after seeing one section and then started again, he or she would have had to view one of the two as moving in reverse. But however predisposed an ancient viewer might have been to regard the Parthenon frieze as an aid to imagining the invisible, it is hard to envisage anyone, even in a festival context, being so rapturously transported by the magnetic force running through the bodies of the hand-linked crowds as to be unaware that they were in a setting invented by human decisions.[4]

And here we encounter a problem. Those who have studied the sculptural components as objects to be subjected to stylistic analysis have found themselves withholding some of their usual admiration, describing the frieze, for example, as 'decorative', 'ornamental, 'repetitive', 'monotonous'.[5] If, however, we regard the ancient viewer as at least an equal partner in the cognitive transaction with the ancient producer, we can see that it would have suited parties of ancient processioners and their guides to be able to halt simultaneously from time to time before an image of an episode.[6] In ancient times, however, in sharp contrast with the easily visible pediments and metopes, it was hard for anyone looking up from ground level to see the frieze at all, let alone comprehend it as a unified composition. Indeed, only if viewers kept close to the steps of the building, or entered the tight Parthenon colonnade (assuming they were permitted to do so) and then stood still, could they make out much of the composition at all. Insofar as they

---

4   The metaphor of the magnet that was used by both Euripides and Plato was noted in Chapter 2.

5   For example, Ridgway, Brunilde S., 'Notes on the Development of the Greek Frieze' in *Hesperia*, Vol. 35 (2) (April 1966), 188–204.

6   In the fictional procession at Delphi described by Heliodorus, the processioners divide into two equal groups who dance and sing their way along both sides of the temple and come together again at the far end. That temple had no frieze.

were able to follow the frieze through the columns, it was as a series of episodes. The extraordinarily steep angle, around forty degrees, that any ancient viewer would have had to contend with in looking up at any section of the frieze can be seen from Figure 4.1.

Figure 4.1. Walter Hege photographing the west frieze of the Parthenon, *c.* 1929.[7]

---

7   *Atlantis*, Heft 4, April 1930, 247. Private collection. The photographs of the frieze taken by Hege were published in a series of books that were published round the world, noted in the Bibliography. Since, in Hege's time, the Parthenon had lost its roof and the frieze was open to downward light, the eye-level photographs that he produced, which show the shadows in the wrong places, introduced another distortion compared with ancient times. A discussion of the ancient sightlines, with photographs from the Parthenon replica in Basel, although without any attempt to restore colour or metal or the other markers of identity such as head-pieces and bracelets now lost, was offered by Stillwell, Richard, 'The Panathenaic Frieze' in *Hesperia*, Vol. 38 (2) (Apr.–Jun., 1969), 231–241. Hege's style is discussed with biographical information by Harder, Matthias, *Walter Hege und Herbert List, Griechische Tempelarchitektur in photographischer Inszenierung* (Berlin: Reimer, 2003). The French photographer Frédéric Boissonas was allowed to erect ladders sixty or seventy feet long, from the top of which he made eye-level photographs from a few feet away, apparently also unaware that he was being unfair to the ancient viewers and to the ancient designers and craftsmen who had taken measures to present the frieze as it was seen from the ground. A photograph of him on his ladder is reproduced in Papageorgiou-Venetas, Αθήνα, ένα όραμα του Κλασικισμού (Athens: Kapon, 2001), 127.

A photograph taken in 1900, one of the first to show the portion of the frieze on the building, as shown as Figure 4.2, gives an indication of the scale of the frieze when seen close up.

Figure 4.2. Looking at the west frieze in 1900. Photograph.[8]

It was this section of the Parthenon frieze, within the west porch, that the agents of Lord Elgin had been ordered to leave on the building by the Ottoman vizieral letter ('firman') sent at the instigation of the French Ambassador Brune, and that, as a result, now gives us and

8   Bremond, Henri, de L'Académie française, *Le charme d'Athènes* (Paris: Pour la Société des Médecins Bibliophiles, 1924), frontispiece. The photograph was taken by a French student who must have positioned himself on a viewing station even higher on the building. The scaffolding had been hurriedly erected a few years earlier when the last section of building still standing was discovered on the verge of collapse as discussed in St Clair, *WStP*, Chapter 21, https://doi.org/10.11647/obp.0136.21. The figures shown are the French Academician, Henri Bremond, a former member of the Roman Catholic order of Jesuits, and author of numerous books on religion in France, and Maurice Barrès, another well-known author of the time, part of a group who preferred Sparta.

future generations the best chance we have of understanding the ancient experience.[9]

At the end of the twentieth century, when the air pollution and acid rain in Athens were severe, it was decided to bring the blocks of the west frieze indoors, replacing them with replicas. To the surprise of many, although damage had been done to the surfaces, the deposits of soot of recent times resting on older deposits had, to an extent, not only acted as a shield against erosion but brought out the sharpness of the carving, as shown in Figure 4.3.

Figure 4.3. The surface of part of the west frieze before the removal of the surface deposits. Photograph c. 1999.[10]

It is possible that, in ancient times, the oily deposits from the smoke of innumerable acts of burning the non-edible parts of sacrificial animals improved visibility from ground level. The removal of the surface deposits also showed how little the surface had deteriorated over

---

9 As discussed with new archival information in Appendix A of St Clair, *WStP*, https://doi.org/10.11647/obp.0136.

10 Reproduced by courtesy of the Greek Ministry of Culture.

the centuries. And it provided further proof that the frieze had been coloured, as shown in Figure 4.4.

Figure 4.4. The surface of part of the west frieze after the removal of the surface deposits, showing the remains of bright blue mineral. Photograph *c.* 1999.[11]

Some modern writers, aware of the difficulties faced by real ancient viewers looking up at a sharp angle, have suggested that it is 'a mistake' to think in such terms. Joan Breton Connelly, for example, has claimed that the intended and implied viewer was 'Athena, not the human visitors', giving renewed currency to what others had already suggested.[12] However, there is little or nothing in the ancient authors or in the wider discursive environment to support this suggestion. On

11 Reproduced by courtesy of the Greek Ministry of Culture.
12 Connelly, Joan Breton, *The Parthenon Enigma, A New Understanding of the World's Most Iconic Building and the People Who Made It* (New York: Alfred A. Knopf, 2014), 166. Others in modern times who have taken this view include Sokratis Mavrommatis: 'the certainty that the frieze served a higher purpose than to impress mortals' in Delivorrias, Angelos, and Mavrommatis, Sokrates, *The Parthenon Frieze, Problems, Challenges, Interpretations* (Athens: Melissa and Benaki, 2004). A translation into English by Alexandra Doumas of the Greek edition of 2004. Unnumbered preliminary pages, and 17. Another example is cited by Osborne, R. G., 'The viewing and obscuring of the Parthenon frieze' in *Journal of Hellenic Studies*, Vol.

the contrary, with the Parthenon, as with other buildings, the ancient designers and the craftsmen that they employed were evidently aware of the need to help human viewers to understand the compositions as they were visually encountered at the steep angle.

Nor was the fact that offsets were routinely designed into buildings a secret or a guild secret. As 'the stranger from Elea', a character in the Platonic dialogue, *The Sophist*, points out, if the makers of visual images reproduced the true proportions: 'the upper parts, you know, would seem smaller and the lower parts larger than they ought, because we see the former from a distance, the latter from near at hand'.[13] Since the character of the stranger, who is introduced as an educated philosopher, presents his point as something well known, we can be confident that knowledge about offsetting from the orthogonal was routine and expected. Indeed, without such an understanding, the changing cohorts of Athenian citizens who served on the various commissions, including those with responsibility for the design, execution, and acceptance of building projects, would not have been equipped to meet the responsibilities laid on them. Since optical devices that help the ground-level viewer are employed in many other classical-era buildings besides the Parthenon, we can have confidence that the techniques needed for making images appear more convincing to the human eye than if they were produced orthogonally formed part of the training of the guild, passed on by experience and tradition from master to pupil, perhaps also with the help of written handbooks and treatises.[14]

CVII (1987), 98, https://doi.org/10.2307/630073, from a booklet by Langlotz, Ernst, *Phidias und der Parthenonfries* (Stuttgart: Reclams, 1965).

13   Notably the passage at Plat. Soph. 236α: τὰ ἄνω, μείζω δὲ τὰ κάτω φαίνοιτ' ἂν διὰ τὸ τὰ μὲν πόρρωθεν, τὰ δ' ἐγγύθεν ὑφ' ἡμῶν ὁρᾶσθαι ...[and] ἆρ' οὖν οὐ χαίρειν τὸ ἀληθὲς ἐάσαντες οἱ δημιουργοὶ νῦν οὐ τὰς οὔσας συμμετρίας ἀλλὰ τὰς δοξούσας εἶναι καλὰς τοῖς εἰδώλοις ἐναπεργάζονται to which the other main character in the dialogue known as the *Theaetetus* is presented as giving his wholehearted assent. Also made explicit in Plat. Criti. 107d. Alluded to in Xen. Ec. 15.

14   Discussed in St Clair, *WStP*, Chapter 21, https://doi.org/10.11647/obp.0136.21. The last works in the tradition of searching for an orthogonal secret can be regarded as Hambidge, Jay, with a preface by L. D. Caskey, *The Parthenon and Other Greek Temples: Their Dynamic Symmetry* (New Haven: Yale UP, 1924); and Flagg, Ernest, Architect, *The Parthenon Naos from the author's forthcoming book entitled The Recovery of Art, the present sheets being a communication addressed to Charles Marie Vidor, Perpetual Secretary of the Institute of France* (New York: Scribner, 1928). Later circulated with an inserted personal letter from the author to his readers, dated 16 January 1937.

When the pan-Hellenic site of Delphi was excavated in the nineteenth century, it was discovered that the marble slabs of the frieze of the elaborate Treasury of the Siphnians had been designed to tilt from the perpendicular, being wider at the foot of the composition than at the top.[15] Some have thought that the same optical device was used in the frieze of the Parthenon.[16] What is, however, apparent to any modern visitor is that the composition is more deeply carved at the top than at the foot of the slabs. As was noted by the late Martin Robertson: 'a three-quartered face [is] given almost its sculptural value, a foreshortened foot hardly more than drawn in the marble'.[17] The general effect, as had been noticed earlier by Charles Waldstein (later Sir Charles Walston) who conducted experiments in the nineteenth century, was to pull the attention of the human viewer upwards to the top of the composition, making it appear larger and more 'realistic' than it would have appeared if it had been carved to a uniform depth.[18]

The details of the carving become more visible to a modern viewer when the pieces are presented close up in a gallery, but they detract from attempts to understand the ancient experience. The hair shown on the displayed persons and monsters, for example, that could be seen 'only as masses' at a distance, when it is re-presented at eye-level, wisp by wisp, curl by curl, misrepresents the experience of the ancient viewers.[19] The aim of the classical-era commissioners, we can be

---

15   Described by Demangel, R., *La Frise ionique* (Paris: de Boccard, 1932), 561, with a diagram.

16   Marconi, 5, commenting on the work of Haselberger and others, says the frieze is set at right angles and that there is no tilt. However, it is not impossible that there may have been differences in different parts of the building.

17   Robertson, Martin, and Franz, Alison, *The Parthenon Frieze* (London: Phaidon in association with British Museum Publications, 1975), 10. Cesare Brandi, who in a brief note in a specialist journal published in 1950 in Italy drew attention to the fact that many of the pieces of the Parthenon in London had been damaged by being scraped ('*grattate*') by the British Museum workmen at the behest of Lord Duveen, believed that chisels had been used on some pieces to deepen the relief. Brandi, Cesare, 'Nota sui Marmi del Partenone' in *Bollettino dell'Istituto Centrale del Restauro*, No. 3–4 (1950), 3–8.

18   Waldstein, Charles, Director of the Fitzwilliam Museum and Reader in Classical Archaeology in the University of Cambridge; Ph.D. Heidelberg; M.A. Columbia College, *Essays in the Art of Pheidias* (Cambridge: CUP, 1885), 204, 227–228.

19   A point made by Waldstein, Sir Charles, Litt.D., Ph.D., L.H.D., Fellow and Lecturer of King's College, Cambridge, Sometime Slade Professor of Fine Art, Reader in Classical Archaeology, Director of the Fitzwilliam Museum, Cambridge, and Director of the American School of Archaeology, Athens, Greek Sculpture and

confident, was not to give ground-level visitors a technical lesson in how skilled craftsmen executed an intermediate stage of their work when the surfaces of the stones were being given their last touches before being lifted into their appointed place on the building, but to seduce the eyes of viewers towards a fuller appreciation of what they were being invited to think was there. In an age when alternatives can be offered with digital technology, it seems perverse to offer only a version that is anachronistic and therefore unfair to those who commissioned and executed the work.

When the carved front parts of the marble blocks are cut out and hung like pictures in a picture gallery, or when they are re-presented as a continuum in a book of photographs, they do not form a single narrative even within the sections where the composition is at its most simple.[20] Some horses are presented as moving so fast that they would cause an immediate pile-up as soon as they reached the next horse. In some places the wind is shown as blowing so strongly that it causes the drapery of the costumes of the horsemen to stream out almost horizontally, but the cloaks of the adjoining horsemen on either side are unruffled. Seen through the columns, it was a series of discreet panels or episodes that the viewer might choose on focus on, as, for example, the breezes as among the features of the local microclimate.[21]

Modern Art, *Two lectures delivered to the students of the Royal Academy of London* (Cambridge: CUP, 1914), 10. At the time of the 2014 loan of one of the pieces of the Parthenon east pediment to Russia, the British Museum authorities sought to take credit for making it harder to imagine the ancient experience, by implying, in accordance with the rhetorics of western romanticism and of post-modern consumerism, that the way of seeing that they recommended was a characteristic of the objects themselves: 'A new life, with new meanings in different stories, had begun. For the first time they could be seen and studied at eye level'. Blog of the director of the British Museum dated 5 December 2014.

20 I refer only to the books that attempt to present and describe the pieces as they have survived without further manipulation. Of little value to a reader who wishes to try to understand how the Parthenon was seen and regarded in ancient Greece are the numerous books that employ unusual camera angles, strong spot-lighting, and other devices associated with retail shopping. Such volumes tend to reinforce the suspicion that some museum managers wish to withdraw from their educational role of trying to explain the ancient past in all its strangeness, in favour of a consumerist ethic of giving the public what they think the public wants or ought to want.

21 Noted by Marconi, Clemente, 'The Parthenon Frieze: Degrees of Visibility' in *RES: Anthropology and Aesthetics*, No. 55/56 (2009), 8, https://doi.org/10.1086/RESvn1ms25608841. I am grateful to Michael Squire for drawing this article to my attention. The breezes were noted in Chapter 2.

The events pictured are, in accordance with long-standing pan-Hellenic convention, evidently set in mythic time when, in contrast with the civic time of the classical era, men went naked or semi-naked, and women wore the clothes associated with festivals and ceremonies, and that were also presented in the words used in the tragic drama as normal in mythic times. Occasionally some mortals are shown as suffering the same mishaps as contemporary viewers, as, for example, in Figure 4.5, where one of the carriers has either stumbled under the weight of the heavy jar, or is resting, without breaking ranks. Some males appear to be carrying liquids in large jars balanced on their left shoulders, with others bringing goods that cannot be identified, in all cases invariably carried on their left shoulders.[22] It is likely that the jars were understood by viewers as containing fresh water, for pouring as well as for drinking and that the basins were for ritual washing. On the mythic Acropolis, as on the real, water was always a precious commodity.

Figure 4.5. Carriers of liquids, and, on the slab to the left of the viewer, an unidentified box-like object. Photogravure made at eye level before 1910.[23]

---

22   The significance of the left shoulder, with its alleged benefits of swaddling and its read across to hoplite warfare, was noted in Chapter 2. A real water carrier of the era before water could be pumped, bent under the weight of his jar, is pictured at Figure 2.3 in St Clair, *WStP*, Chapter 2, https://doi.org/10.11647/obp.0136.02, as part of a discussion of the lack of potable water on the site and the decisive military importance of that geological fact during the conflict and later. This gives an indication of how unrealistic are the unbending figures pictured as Figure 4.5.

23   Smith, Cecil, 'Additions to the Greek Sculptures in the British Museum' in *Classical Review*, Vol. 6 (10) (Dec., 1892), Plate 42. It was with this slab that the late Bernard

Such touches offered a hint of realism, part of a general assumption, shared with the conventions of the tragic drama, that the mythic world was inhabited by personages who were subject to the same contingencies as the humans who observed and dramatized them. Such touches encouraged viewers to see themselves, or rather their aspired-to-but-hard-to-attain better selves, self-reflexively. The temple dedicated to Zeus at Olympia, which is almost contemporaneous with the classical Parthenon, shows one of the Lapiths with a cauliflower ear like a then-contemporary boxer.[24] These details can be regarded as the equivalents in the static theatre of the Parthenon of the 'signs' that the character of the god Hermes in the Prologue to Euripides's play, the *Ion*, mentions in encouraging the audience of the performed theatre to be alert to contemporary parallels.[25]

The Scene Above the East Door

The central slab on the east side, the culminating scene towards which both processions are moving, is the crux of one of the longest-running questions about the classical Parthenon. Figure 4.6, reproduced from a photograph taken at eye level before 1910 when the slab retained more of its surface than it does now, shows a scene that has caused puzzlement since it was first noticed by those who in modern times wished to learn about ancient Athens from a study of its standing remains.[26]

Ashmole chose to illustrate the fact that all the slabs of the frieze are all more deeply carved at the top than at the foot, as discussed later in the chapter. Ashmole, Bernard, *Architect and Sculptor in Classical Greece* (New York: NYU Press, 1972), 118.

24 Noted by Barringer, Judith M., *Art, Myth, and Ritual in Classical Greece* (Cambridge: CUP, 2009), 29. From what is recorded of the violence tolerated in sporting competitions, the faces of successful sportsmen and women must often have been mauled to a far greater extent.

25 As discussed in Chapter 1.

26 A summary of the main interpretations offered since the mid-twentieth century until recently, but not including Connolly and Fehr, with some attempt to categorize them by Shear, T. Leslie, Jnr., *Trophies of Victory: Public Building in Periklean Athens* (Princeton, N.J.: Department of Art and Archaeology, Princeton University in association with Princeton UP, 2016), 401–404. Many more suggestions had been offered earlier, some of which were collected and commented on, sometimes contemptuously, by Davidson, Thomas, *The Parthenon Frieze, and Other Essays* (London: Kegan Paul, 1882). The phrase used by Loraux, *Children*, 20.

Figure 4.6. The central scene of the Parthenon frieze as presented above the east door. Photogravure made before 1910.[27]

In the eighteenth century the piece was built into the south wall of the Acropolis, facing inwards.[28] And, from its sheer length, weight, and size, its importance as an extraordinarily large piece of the Parthenon frieze that had required extraordinary feats of quarrying, transportation, and engineering, was quickly recognized.[29] Richard Chandler, for example, in many respects the best prepared of the eighteenth-century researchers, who saw it in 1765, realized that it was the slab that had 'ranged in the centre of the back front of the cell', that is, below the east

---

27　Smith, A. H., ed., *The Sculptures of the Parthenon with an Introduction and Commentary* (London: British Museum Trustees, 1910), part of plate 35. The other even earlier photograph in *Grecian Antiquities, Photographed by Stephen Thompson*, in 2 volumes (London: Mansell, 1872) is less clear.

28　Shown, for example, as part of a picturesque composition in the drawing by Thomas Hope, in Hope, Thomas, and Tsigakou, Fani-Maria, ed., *Thomas Hope (1769–1831) Pictures from 18th Century Greece* (Athens: Benaki Museum, British Council, Publishing House "Melissa", 1985), plate 29, probably sketched in 1799. I know of no other picture of the slab while it was built into the wall. If it was seen by the artist of the so-called Carrey drawings made in the 1670s, or if it was seen but not recognized, it was not copied.

29　'fourteen feet eight inches long.' *A Description of the Collection of Ancient Marbles in the British Museum* (London: British Museum, 1839), viii, 50. As with the lintel of the Propylaia, as discussed and pictured in St Clair, *WStP*, Chapter 4, https://doi.org/10.11647/obp.0136.04, for the ancients to have located such an unusual piece in the quarries and to have cut and transported it to the Acropolis implies that it had merited special attention at the time it was first made.

pediment that, as Pausanias had reported, displayed scenes from the birth of Athena.[30] Chandler could not, however, identify the event being pictured, suggesting that the display was of 'a venerable person with a beard reading in a large volume, which is partly supported by a boy'.[31] In the early 1750s, however, the architect James Stuart conjectured that the tall figure 'is a man who appears to examine with some attention a piece of cloth folded several times double: the other is a young girl who assists in supporting it: may we not suppose this folded cloth to represent the peplos?'[32]

The question of which story was presented on the frieze has been a matter of speculation and contention since the eighteenth century.[33] Among the suggestions that, in my view, are incompatible with the discursive environment are all those, such as the Stuart conjecture, that regard the frieze as reproducing pictorially a then-contemporary practice, such as the Panathenaic procession. Only a mythic story that looks back to a mythic past would pass the conditions applied to temples for hundreds of years across the Hellenic world. We should, I suggest, be searching for candidates from within the discursive tradition that shows an event already known to the main viewerships, and recognizable by them, as Loraux remarked, 'without any hesitation'.[34]

A display of a peplos ceremony, even if thought of as idealized version set in a mythic past—an Ur-peplos ceremony—would have been so exceptional that it is unlikely to have passed unnoticed in the plentiful

---

30 Chandler, Rev. Richard, *Travels in Greece* (Oxford: Clarendon Press, 1776), 51. Chandler, an academic of Oxford University, had been selected by the Society of Dilettanti partly because of his record of scholarly publications on ancient inscriptions.

31 *Ibid.*

32 Stuart, James, and Revett, Nicholas, *The Antiquities of Athens* (London: John Nichols, 1787), ii, 12.

33 A summary of the main interpretations offered since the mid-twentieth century until recently, but not including Connolly and Fehr, with some attempt to categorize them by Shear, *Trophies of Victory*, 401–404. Many more suggestions had been offered earlier, some of which were collected and commented on, sometimes contemptuously, by Davidson, *Parthenon Frieze.*
The phrase used by Loraux, *Children*, 20, that can serve to describe both the actual horizons of expectations existing in the actual viewerships, and the rhetorical conditions that the institutions of the city would feel the need to fulfill in approving the construction of heritage.

34 *Ibid.*

subsequent written record.[35] To commemorate the establishment of a commemoration would, in the discursive conventions of the time, I suggest, be almost as much a breach as displaying the commemorative ceremony.

In recent times, too, even those who have felt obliged, for lack of any more plausible explanation, to accept the Stuart conjecture as updated, have found it 'strangely anticlimactic'.[36] To Robin Osborne, writing in 1987, the central scene was 'an embarrassment', only explicable, if at all, as a preparation for looking at something else.[37] Some in the confident nineteenth century blamed the designers, which, since they assumed that the design was a matter for 'artists', implied that the Pheidias had misjudged. According to Thomas Davidson, even the best-known German scholars, Welcker and Michaelis, were of the opinion that the reason why the gods were presented with their backs turned was that the central scene was 'not specially worth looking at'.[38]

Are there better candidates? Are we obliged, for lack of anything better, to accept that all these gods and heroes, men, women, and children, three hundred and seventy-eight personages in all, plus two hundred and forty-five edible animals, have been brought together just so as to be present when a piece of cloth made in a local workshop is ceremonially folded in order to be put away in a cupboard?[39] The

---

35   The suggestion that what is presented is an Ur-Panathenaic was made by the late Brian Shefton at a conference in the University of London, 1998, at which I was present, when Connelly first began to present her critique of the Stuart conjecture and her own alternative.

36   The phrase used by Neils, Jenifer, *The Parthenon Frieze* (Cambridge; New York: CUP, 2001), 67.

37   Osborne, 'Viewing and obscuring', 101, https://doi.org/10.2307/630073. Osborne's article tried to enfranchise the historic viewer and to draw attention to the fact that damage is done to the prospects of understanding the Parthenon by altering the viewing context: 'by re-displaying the frieze in a totally alien manner, a new monument is created, and one which stands between the viewer and the original', 105.

38   Reported by Davidson, *Parthenon Frieze*, 44, 45.

39   The number as estimated by Neils, *Parthenon Frieze*, 33. In the *Hecuba* of Euripides, when the Chorus of women recently enslaved after the fall of Troy debate the degrees of misery that they might face when shipped to Greece, as between Sparta and other possible locations, their best hope is that they will be sent to Athens and be employed in the weaving of a ceremonial peplos for the Panathenaic festival, another example of the claim that Athens was the city in Hellas that was most advanced from brutishness, but also implying that the weaving was work suitable for slaves who had come from high-class families. Eur. Hec 466.

modern discussions too, that mostly take the Stuart conjecture as their starting point, have tended to suggest that 'peplos' is a term of art for the ceremony performed in the Panathenaic festival. There has also been modern writing about the alleged deep significance of the ceremony in the Panathenaic festival.[40] In the usage of classical Athens, however, a peplos meant festival or ceremonial clothes as distinct from those worn day to day, as when, in the *Suppliants* by Euripides, the character of Theseus is surprised that the women who are in distress at not being permitted to bury their dead relatives, and are tearing their skin with their nails, are not peplosed.[41] On an Attic funerary monument of the fourth century, a grieving widower, in praising the devotion of his dead wife to himself and to family values, declares that she was 'not impressed by peploses or gold'.[42] In the world of tragic drama, peplos could refer to the garments worn by a male, as when, in the *Orestes* by Euripides, the hero lies comatose after killing his mother and is described by the Chorus as coming back to life, stirring in his peploses.[43] And it is the same sense of a large piece of cloth that might, or might not, be cut and worn that is employed when the character of Agamemnon, recently returned from sacking Troy, was stepping out of his specially prepared bath when the character of his wife Clytemnestra, all smiles, wrapped him in an embroidered peplos before murdering him.[44]

The 'deep significance' suggestion, leaving aside that almost everything about the Parthenon and the mythic stories it presented could be so regarded, was evidently contested. In Plato's dialogue, the *Euthyphro*, the character of Socrates, who in the dialogue has already been indicted for spreading disbelief in the gods, is presented as confronting the credulous Euthyphro with the absurdity of believing that the story of the war between the gods and the giants is true. It also runs counter

---

40 For example by Sourvinou-Inwood, Christiane, *Athenian Myths and Festivals: Aglauros, Erechtheus, Plynteria, Panathenaia, Dionysia; Edited by Robert Parker* (Oxford: OUP, 2011), 263–311, https://doi.org/10.1093/acprof:oso/9780199592074.001.0001.

41 Eur. Supp. 97. κουραί τε καὶ πεπλώματ᾽ οὐ θεωρικά.

42 Discussed by González González, Marta, *Funerary Epigrams of Ancient Greece: Reflections on Literature, Society and Religion* (London: Bloomsbury Academic, 2019), 67, http://doi.org/10.5040/9781350062450. I have made a slight amendment to her translation.

43 ‹ὁρᾷς; ἐν πέπλοισι κινεῖ δέμας.› Eur. Orest. 166, recently translated by David Kovacs as 'he stirs in his blankets', replacing the 'robes' of the previous Loeb edition.

44 Aesch. Eum. 665.

to the remark of Aelius Aristides that the peplos was an 'ornament' used in that festival, the Greek word ('kosmos') being cognate with that used for the 'cosmetic', that is, he remarks, was deemed ('nomismatized') to be symbolic by those observing the spectacle.[45] In Xenophon's Socratic dialogue on the management of the household ('oikos') and of the city ('polis') the character of Ischomachos is set up as exemplifying the arguments whose incoherence Socrates is about to expose. Dutiful and rich, a man who pays his taxes and contributes voluntarily as examples of his 'charis', to the cost of festivals, Ischomachos is presented as well satisfied with the education he gave his wife whom he married when she was 'not yet fifteen'. Among the wifely qualities that he picks out for special praise is her care in looking after clothes and making sure that they are neatly folded away in the right places, along with 'the things that we use only for festivals or entertainments, or on rare occasions'.[46] That passage has been read as a comic exaggeration, although it need not be, but we can guess that if such a scene had been presented on the Parthenon frieze, it would also have raised wry smiles. The 'deep significance' of the peplos in the Panathenaic festival lay in the picture it exhibited, that is, as a reminder of the age at the beginning of the world when gods struggled with giants, one of a range of images that reminded viewers of an era when chaos reigned as were traditionally offered on Hellenic temples, such as the Telamons of Acrigas (modern Agrigento), and not in the soft fabric on which the picture was able to be carried and shown off by processioners.[47]

Can more be gleaned from the history of the slab in modern times? In 1801, acting under the authority of the Ottoman firman of May of that year, it was removed by Elgin's agents from its then setting on the inside of the Acropolis wall. Although the agents were astonished and

---

45   ὥσπερ ἀκρόπολίν τινα ἢ κορυφὴν νομίσαντας τῆς Ἑλλάδος καὶ τῶν ὁμοφύλων τὴν πόλιν καὶ ἔργῳ καὶ λόγῳ κοσμεῖν, καὶ μετέχειν τῆς δόξης, ἀλλ᾽ οὐκ ἀποστερεῖσθαι νομίζοντας. εἴργασται καὶ ἡμῖν ὁ λόγος ἀντὶ τοῦ πέπλου κόσμος Παναθηναίων τῇ θεωρίᾳ· δοῦναι δὲ χάριν τῆς αὐτῆς θεοῦ ἧσπερ καὶ ὁ λόγος καὶ ἡ πόλις. Ael. Ar. Orat. 13 197. The wordplay of repeated words provides evidence that Aristides was making a juxtaposing parallel between the static Acropolis as an object of vision, and the peplos as an object of vision in the parallel world of display and performance, which adds yet more to the many objections to the Stuart conjecture.

46   Xen. Ec. 9.

47   The long timescale within which such legends were fitted was summarized in Chapter 1.

impressed by its size, they did not at first realize that, when on the building, it had displayed the culmination of the composition presented by the frieze.[48] Since the slab was too heavy to be transported with the resources available to Elgin's agents in Athens, mainly ships' tackle, they had planned to cut it into two, but they seem to have changed their minds before the sawing was completed. However, as the slab was being moved, it broke down the middle.[49] Both pieces, which were separately packed, were included among the cargo of the brig, the *Mentor,* commissioned by Elgin that sank near Cerigo (Cythera) in the Arches in September 1802. They spent some months on the seabed before being brought to the surface, and were then stored under a temporary covering on the beach, from where they were shipped in another vessel to Malta in February 1805, and later to England, where they were put in store again, and a few years later gathered into the Elgin Collection.[50] If any paint or gilding had remained in Elgin's day when it was removed, as is possible given that colour survived on the west frieze that Elgin's agents had been obliged to leave on site, it is unlikely to have survived its months in the sea and on the beach.[51] When the broken slab was reassembled on its arrival in the British Museum in 1817, besides the empty holes for metal attachments that are found on many other pieces of the Parthenon, the traces of rust were thought to indicate that the two personages presented on the central scene on the viewer's right, had been shown wearing coronets or wreaths made of ferrous metal that had been painted or gilded, as is likely, from what we know of the general custom, to have been the case.[52]

An earlier photograph, made with a source of light that brings out more of the contours, is shown as Figure 4.7.

---

48   It is described variously in the Elgin documents of the time as 'a great bas-relief', 'a long piece of the Baso Relievo from ye Temple of Minerva', 'the great relief' and 'the great bas relief that was on the Acropolis walls', and 'one half ... taken from the South wall'. Smith, A. H., 'Lord Elgin and his Collection' in *Journal of Hellenic Studies*, Vol. 36 (Nov. 1916), 201, 217, 231, 233, 248, https://doi.org/10.2307/625773.

49   The jagged line caused by the sawing and the breakage can be seen on the piece on display in the British Museum.

50   Summarised from the documents transcribed in Smith, 'Lord Elgin', notably 231: 'Not being well sawn, for want of sufficiently fine saws, and being a little weak in the middle it parted in two in the course of transport, in spite of all the precautions taken'.

51   *Ibid.*

52   [British Museum] *Ancient Marbles* (1839), viii, 43.

Figure 4.7. Detail from the central scene. Photograph made before 1885.[53]

With low relief, even small differences in the position of the source of light affects where the shadows fall, and therefore the modern viewer's ability to re-imagine what was to be seen before the ancient surface was battered, bleached and stripped down to the layer below the epidermis of the marble.[54]

So how might the scene have appeared in ancient times? An example of looking at the slab through modern eyes, defended on the grounds that: '[T]he first law of iconography [is] that a depiction ought in some way to look like what it represents' was provided by the art historian Evelyn B. Harrison in 1996.[55] Harrison invited her readers to 'think of yourself folding up a sheet after you have taken it out of the dryer', noting that 'if you have a little helper it will be easier to get the edges

---

53   Inserted in Waldstein, *Essays*, after page 234. Not further identified.
54   The best photograph at present available, which shows the shape of what is carried in the wrapping peplos, albeit taken, as the photographer says, 'en face', are in Delivorrias and Mavrommatis, *The Parthenon Frieze*, 164 and 165, where the photographer waited for an opportunity for the distorting spotlights in the British Museum gallery to be temporarily turned off, and the image photographed in a downward, although not of course a natural, light.
55   Harrison, Evelyn B., 'The Web of History: A Conservative Reading of the Parthenon Frieze', in Neils, Jenifer, ed., *Worshipping Athena: Panathenaia and Parthenon* (Madison, Wis: University of Wisconsin Press, 1996), 198–214.

and corners even'.[56] She also addressed the question of the sex of the young person pictured on the viewer's right by looking at the surviving marble through modern eyes, suggesting, in leading a race to the bottom, that 'the bare buttocks of the child are obvious enough to identify the figure from a distance as a boy'.[57] When it was pointed out that in the Metropolitan Museum of Art, New York is a grave memorial to a girl shown in a similar pose that has been known since the eighteenth century, Harrison suggested, not without prudery, that on that piece, 'the bare flesh is very discreet', and 'this child is alone with her pets in the sheltered courtyard of her home'.[58]

What we can say with confidence is that the smaller figure on the viewer's right is wearing a peplos. Ancient costumes were mostly not

---

56   *Ibid.*

57   *Ibid.* 203–204.

58   MMA, 27.45. Fletcher Fund, 1927, found in 1785 in the island of Paros, a centre of marble production. It was held in a private collection in England until 1927, frequently reproduced since the nineteenth century. Harrison was participating in a western tradition of fear of nudity and its power to cause sexual arousal, which can be traced back to Paul, Augustine, to the Christian tradition, and to the long-exploded theories of extramission, as discussed in St Clair, *WStP*, Chapter 22, https://doi.org/10.11647/obp.0136.22. In 1817, as part of selling to the British public the idea that Elgin's collection of marbles was worth buying, Felicia Hemans had emphasized their 'chastity', an idea that we find repeated frequently into the twentieth century, including by Lord Duveen.

During the nineteenth century, there were calls, for example, by French historian Jules Michelet, that only married women should be allowed into the Elgin gallery of the British Museum. Younger women, he feared, were already at risk from reading novels that made adultery appear exciting. His visit in 1834 is noted by Seznec, Jean, 'Michelet devant les Elgin marbles' (Paris: *English Miscellanies*, Rome, 1860). I have not found any evidence that the authorities of the British Museum ever agreed to demands, of which there are reports, that figleaves should be fitted to conceal the male private parts, but in standard histories of the materiality of ancient Greek culture published in Germany in the nineteenth century, whose illustrations were sometimes photographs of casts, the so-called Ilissos from the east pediment of the Parthenon that in 2008 was sent to Russia, was fitted with a fig leaf. For example, in Baumgarten, Fritz, Poland, Franz, and Wagner, Richard, *Die Hellenische Kultur* (Leipzig and Berlin: Teubner, second edition, 1906), 359. This finely produced book, edited by the foremost scholars of the time, includes photographs of other statues or casts, similarly figleafed, including some from Athens, the bronze from Anticythera, the Apoxyomenos in Vienna, and the pieces of the Aegina pediments in Munich. As discussed in Chapter 2, such evidence as exists for classical Athens suggests that sexuality was not only not feared but was actively mobilized as a 'natural' power able to draw attention to images that promoted gendered 'arete' to both sexes as on the Parthenon frieze.

tailored but consisted of a folded piece of cloth, sometimes pinned at the shoulder, as reconstructed from presentations elsewhere in Figure 4.8.

Figure 4.8. 'Open peplos'. Wood engraving.[59]

The idealized female body presented by Athenian families in korai, the perfect 'social body' pictured on grave memorials, so that viewers can remember the dead at their best (or aspired-to best) is usually, in the case of classical Athens, physiologically young, with the shape of the back of the body presented in such a way that it is often impossible to tell from the surviving marble whether the figure was pictured as naked or as wearing a diaphanous garment that may have been rendered with paint.[60] Nor need we exclude the possibility that the young men and women, the boys and girls, and even the gods and goddesses, who are themselves mostly shown in varying degrees of dress and undress,

59   Studniczka, F., *Beiträge zur Geschichte der altgriechischen Tracht* (Vienna: O. Gerold's Sohn, 1886), 7.
60   Discussed by Stewart, Andrew, *Art, Desire, and the Body in Ancient Greece* (Cambridge: CUP, 1997). An image of a mythic adolescent girl, the shape of whose naked body beneath a finely pleated chiton is made plain, is presented on a large fifth-century cup from the pottery workshop of Euphronios. Obtained in Athens in 1871, now in the Louvre. G 104. Frequently reproduced and discussed, notably by Neils, Jenifer, *The Youthful Deeds of Theseus* (Rome: Bretschneider, 1987), 58–61.

were designed to attract an erotic, including a homoerotic, gaze.[61] Aristotle, discussing sexuality, says that a boy resembles a woman in shape.[62] In the ancient romance known as *Aethiopica*, written much later but preserving older conventions, albeit in fictional form, and perhaps mocking the official values and verities, a father introduces his seven-year-old daughter, who is 'as beautiful as a statue' and appears to her male admirer to be 'approaching marriageable age'.[63] What Harrison regarded as an objection may instead be evidence that ancient viewers were being shown a mythic scene relating to the women's sphere and to its rituals and customs.[64]

That an erotic gaze was discursively a valid way of generating extramissionary exchange with the imagined city emerges from an image of Aphrodite on the Acropolis, surrounded by scenes from olive cultivation and consumption, shown as Figure 4.9.

Figure 4.9. Aphrodite with Eros on the Acropolis. Engraving by Notor from a vase painting in the British Museum, not identified.[65]

---

61 In Plato's *Phaedrus*, 237b–241d, for example, the character of Socrates describes the advantages, as well as the risks, of certain types of homoerotic desire for boys, who are mainly presented as meeting a physical need on the part of the adult male in exchange for educational and career benefits. Sexual desire as a powerful force of 'nature' that can bring about change was discussed with reference to Aristotle's theories in Chapter 2.

62 Ἔοικε δὲ καὶ τὴν μορφὴν γυναικί παῖς Aristotle, *Generation of Animals* 728b, his word for 'woman' normally used to mean one who has reached the stage of marriage and childbearing that was often in mid teens, and presented as such as the perfected social body.

63 Heliodorus, *Aethiopica*, I. 30.6.

64 As, for example, in Figure 4.9, there can be no doubt that the figure shown to the viewer's right is a girl wearing a garment that reveals her bare bottom.

65 Aristophanes, *Lysistrata*, 20. The words in Greek, of which the first is not fully readable, are 'Reputation-building, good laws ('Eunomia'), Civic education

Notor may have over-adapted his source. However that suspicion cannot apply to a key moment presented on the Parthenon frieze that shows the gods sitting in a circle going about their normal activities when Aphrodite, with Eros, turns away from the others to point to the central scene as shown in Figure 4.10.

Figure 4.10. Aphrodite and Eros pointing to the central event. Line drawing.[66]

These two images suggest that the passage in the Thucydidean Funeral Oration in which the character of Pericles advises his audience to learn to love Athens sexually, in accordance with the conventions, social hierarchies, and reciprocities noted and discussed in Chapter 2, was not an invention of Pericles or of Thucydides but part of the mainstream discourse, here shown visually, and would have been regarded as such by the Athenian viewer. So: what was the event that could turn the heads even of the gods?

As was pointed out, with some impatience, by a nineteenth-century scholar, there is nothing in the ancient authors to connect the Parthenon

---

('Paideia'), Aphrodite, Persuasion ('Peitho'), and Well-being ('eudaimonia').

66   Carrey drawing of East Frieze see plate 62 Mark, Ira S., 'The Gods on the East Frieze of the Parthenon', in *Hesperia* Vol. 53, No. 3 (Jul.–Sep., 1984), pp. 289–342. Frequently reproduced, for example in the fine edition by Bowie, Theodore and Thimme, Diether, eds, *The Carrey Drawings of the Parthenon Sculptures* (Bloomington and London: Indiana UP, 1971), and earlier by Michaelis, Leake, and others. Modern photographs of the full set of drawings are viewable on Gallica, http://gallica.bnf.fr/ark:/12148/btv1b7200482m.r=.langEN, and a large selection in low resolution on Wikimedia Commons.

with the Panathenaic festival.[67] Nor is the building alluded to in formal written compositions where we might have expected to find it mentioned, for example in the long Panathenaic orations of Isocrates or Aristides, nor in any description of the festival during the subsequent half-millennium when it continued to be celebrated. On the contrary, as many have pointed out, the scene displayed on the Parthenon frieze does not match what is recorded about what occurred in the historical Panathenaic procession. Where are the hoplites, where is the ship, where are the allies?[68] Nor, when we read on an ancient public inscription how the duties were allocated according to ancient custom, does the washing and folding away of the ceremonial peplos, a commemoration of the establishment of a commemoration, to qualify for the place of honour.[69]

Far from being immediately recognizable by those who participated in the real event, it would have required an implausible stretch of imagination to see any resemblance.[70]

When we imaginatively restore the archaic costumes familiar from archaic korai, including the crowns, wreaths, and chaplets, the decorated garments, the nudity and semi-nudity and other markers that signal that a mythic scene was being offered to viewers, we should expect that what was presented on the central slab before it was stripped was more like the image shown as Figure 4.11, one of many scenes from myth pictured on ancient pottery. We have an opportunity then to imagine it bright with strange non-realistic colours and glittering in endless variations as the changing sunlight, and at some festivals the changing moonlight, was reflected from the metal.

---

67 Davidson, *Parthenon Frieze*, 19.

68 Discussed by many, including Castriota, David, *Myth, Ethos, and Actuality: Official Art in Fifth-Century B.C. Athens* (Madison, University of Wisconsin Press, 1992), 199, who provides a useful summary of the decrees by which the contributions of the allies to the Panathenaia were regulated.

69 I draw this inference from the discussion by Robertson, Noel, 'The Praxiergidae Decree (IG I3 7) and the Dressing of Athena's Statue with the Peplos' in *Greek, Roman, and Byzantine Studies*, Vol 44 (2) (2004), 111-161.

70 The evidence was collected by, for example, Holloway, R. Ross, 'The Archaic Acropolis and the Parthenon Frieze' in *The Art Bulletin*, Vol. 48 (2) (Jun., 1966), 223–226, https://doi.org/10.1080/00043079.1966.10788948.

Figure 4.11. Mythic scene with Pherephatta ('Persephone') and Triptolemos.
Engraving of a vase painting, flattened.[71]

Can we find a local myth, preferably one recognized across Hellas,
such as those shown on the metopes and the central figures in the
pediments that ancient viewers might have expected to see shown on
the Parthenon frieze? The suggestion that the frieze shows the sacrifice
of the daughters of Erechtheus, made by Joan Breton Connelly in the
1990s and later the subject of her book-length study, is the only one
offered so far that meets the requirement that what was pictured must
be a scene from myth, which had evidently become as inflexible as the
convention that only stories from myth should be allowed in the tragic
drama.[72] Connelly was the first to relate the composition to the speech
in the play by Euripides, the *Erechtheus* (of which fragments previously
unknown were first published in 1948, adding to a substantial passage
already known) and to suggest that what is displayed is the sacrifice of
the daughters of Erechtheus. In the story, Erechtheus, the king of Athens,
surrounded by enemies, saves the city by agreeing to sacrifice his eldest

---

71 Berlin Antikensammlung. Flattened image of a kyphos by Heiron in Notor, G.,
    *La Femme dans l'Antiquité Grecque, Texte et Dessins de G. Notor. Préface de M. Eugène
    Müntz, Membre de l'Institut, Trente-trois Reproductions en couleurs et 320 dessins en noir
    d'après les documents des Musées et collections particulières* (Paris: Renouard, Laurens,
    1901), 233.

72 I have been among those who have commended the Connelly conjecture in print,
    but now offer an alternative.

daughter, and the other two daughters proudly offer themselves too. What is presented, according to Connelly, is the sacramental dressing before death.

Human sacrifice, a means of appeasing, or negotiating with, supernatural forces, is common in Hellenic myth, Iphigeneia being the best-known example—and she was among many mythic characters whose actual tomb was allegedly situated in Attica—but human sacrifice is to be found in other religions practised in the Eastern Mediterranean region, with many instances found in the archaeological record, including some from prehistoric Greece. Connelly's conjecture, however, although the most plausible offered so far, has its own difficulties. The speech includes many of the features of the emergence-from-brutishness narrative familiar from the version offered by Thucydides; for example, that the inhabitants were only able to remain autochthonous because Attica, having poor-quality land, was not resettled as a result of successive conquests, re-conquests, and re-settlements, which are compared to moves in a board game, implying, as Thucydides does, that no justification other than a wish to seize 'useful things' was needed in mythic times. The passage reports the transition to living in families in an oikos-based economy, an episode in the brutishness narrative of which examples of the different stages were observable across Hellas and beyond. The speech includes a comparison with those brutes that have a well-developed culture, in this case, with bees. There is an emphasis on the mutual obligations of 'charis' that are directly linked with the mutual obligations of children and parents, with the word in its cognates being repeated in the same line, as 'useful'.[73] In all these respects, the Connelly conjecture meets expectations of what might have been offered to the viewer to picture and animate in his or her imagination. However, the notion of human sacrifice would set the occasion as a stage in the brutish narrative that had long been superseded. And there are remains of a countering speech to the anti-immigrant rhetoric that we would expect in a dialogic text, with its metaphor from the building industry, as when the character of Praxithea, the mythic queen, declares: 'a person who

---

73 As was done in the passage Milton misquoted from the *Suppliants* of Euripides discussed at the end of St Clair, *WStP*, Chapter 22, https://doi.org/10.11647/obp.0136.22.

moves from one city to another is like a peg badly fitted into a piece of wood, a citizen in name but not in action'.[74]

The story of the Eumolpides, one of the eponymous families by which the classical city was politically constituted, and among the core corpus of Athenian identity-constructing myths, grates in a community-building context. It would have had to be presented by the guides as a step in the brutishness narrative that, in the drama, was brought to an abrupt end when Athena causes an earthquake. Lycurgus, the orator, whose works have been preserved as examples of the arts of persuasion used in schools of rhetoric, who quotes the passage from the speech in making the case against a man on a capital charge of deserting Athens in its hour of danger, refers to it as having been 'composed' by Euripides, with the implication that the playwright had invented a variation.[75]

Although, in one sense, the saving of the city by a human sacrifice may be an event to be celebrated, it was also a horror to be mourned. In the *Agamemnon* by Aeschylus, the character of Iphigeneia does not go willingly to have her throat cut by her father, but protests and resists. And the Chorus, when inviting the audience to imagine the scene, refers them to 'pictures', appealed to as normalizing and legitimating that reaction—but the one visual image that has been found offers horror, not honour.[76] Nor does the character of Iphigeneia go willingly to her death in the *Iphigeneia in Aulis* by Euripides.

Moreover, in the rest of the composition of the frieze with which ancient viewers were presented, there is little to suggest an act of impending heroism. The figures identified as the Eponymous Heroes, who flank the gods on the east side, wear sandals and cloaks, an informal dress usually a sign of having travelled from a distance.[77] They stand

---

74 Collard, C., Cropp, M. J. and Lee, K. H., eds, *Euripides, Selected Fragmentary Plays Volume I* (Warminster: Aris and Phillips, 1995), 158, fragment 360, lines 12–13. Quoted by Connelly, *Parthenon Enigma*, 289. Whether the sentiment was answered by another character or by the Chorus, or it was a reply to a speech already delivered, as was normal in the tragic drama, is not known.

75 In the speech of Lycurgus in the criminal trial of Leocrates, which has evidently been edited and has some of the characteristics of a rhetorical discourse.

76 πρέπουσά θ' ὡς ἐν γραφαῖς. Aesch. Ag. 242. Discussed with examples by Woodford, Susan, *Images of Myths in Classical Antiquity* (Cambridge: CUP, 2003), 4–8. The role of pictures as 'nomismata', that is, as being deemed to confer authority, is discussed later in the chapter in the discussion of the *Ion* by Euripides.

77 Discussed by Morrow, Katherine Dohan, *Greek Footwear and the Dating of Sculpture* (Madison: University of Wisconsin Press, 1985), notably 47 and 55.

around, apparently chatting, scarcely appropriate for the imminent judicial killing of the three most highly privileged young women in the mythic city.[78] Although twelve, invisible, deities are shown seated, six male, six female, they are not the twelve Olympians. Hestia, the goddess of the hearth, whose role is to stay at home when the other gods go out, is omitted, her place being taken by Dionysus, the god of festivals.[79] Athena has taken off her helmet and left her shield behind. Described by the late Martin Robertson as 'relaxed and informal' and as having a 'casual gossipy air', the gods do not evince the solemnity required at a human sacrifice intended to placate their wrath.[80] Under the Stuart conjecture, what the female figures are carrying on their heads are cushions brought by slaves or temple servants, as they may appear to modern eyes, but scarcely, in ancient terms, worth noticing, let alone assigned spaces of honour on the most significant story pictured on the whole frieze. Under the Connelly conjecture, they are the shrouds of the daughters of Erechtheus who are about to die for the city. If, however, as I suggest, the ancient Athenians were being shown a scene of joy, the objects are gifts appropriate to a mythic rite of celebration, such as are shown as Figure 4.12.

In a telling detail, Aphrodite and Eros are shown pointing to the central scene, a neat example of how presenting the viewer in the picture can not only direct the gaze of the viewer but, as on the west pediment, recommend the appropriate response. None of the women are presented as having cut off their hair as signs of impending mourning. The horsemen have not cut off the manes of their horses, as was the custom in the mythic world as presented in the tragic drama, and the manes stream conspicuously behind the horses as part of an illusion that they are moving.[81]

---

78 Noted by Mattusch, Carol C., 'The Eponymous Heroes; the Idea of Sculptural Groups', in Coulson, W. D. E., Palagia, O., Shear, T. L., Jr., Shapiro, H. A., and Frost, F. J., eds, *The Archaeology of Athens and Attica under the Democracy: proceedings of an international conference celebrating 2500 years since the birth of democracy in Greece, held at the American School of Classical Studies at Athens, December 4–6, 1992* (Oxford: Oxbow, 1994), 74.

79 Noticed by Robertson and Frantz, *The Parthenon Frieze*, unnumbered, at IV.

80 *Ibid.*

81 The custom is alluded to in Eur. Alc. 427.

Figure 4.12. Woman carrying a basket on her head. Engraving.[82]

In the modern tradition, the naked and semi-naked horsemen are commonly said to be 'cavalry', but no weapons are depicted.[83] The fact that many are presented as naked by itself rules out any suggestion that a contemporaneous event is being pictured.[84] The horsemen display

---

82   From Aristophanes, in Zevort, Ch., ed., *Lysistrata Traduction nouvelle, avec une Introduction et des Notes de Ch. Zévort. Edition ornée de 107 gravures en couleurs par Notor, d'après des documents authentiques des musées d'Europe* (Paris: Eugène Fasquelle, éditeur, 1898), 98, said to be from the Museum at Naples, not identified. It would be tempting to push the idea further and suggest that the long ribbons are mythic-era swaddling bands, an appropriate gift for a new-born child.

83   Some supporters of the Stuart conjecture, aware of this difficulty, have suggested solutions to the apparent contradiction. Jeffrey M. Hurwit, for example, suggested that 'the martial character of the frieze is pervasive' by postulating that it shows 'preparations for the presentation of a representation of battle', by which he means the battle scene (gigantomachy) that was displayed on the 'peplos', although he also noted that 'few of the riders bear weapons or wear armor, and action is not imminent'. Hurwit, Jeffrey M., *The Acropolis in the Age of Pericles* (Cambridge: CUP, 2004), 249, 250.

84   That ancient viewers, from their understanding of genre and of markers, could scarcely have imagined that they were being shown a contemporary event in which human processioners were presented as naked did not need to be pointed out to the authors of older histories of ancient sculpture, who were familiar not only with

so wide a variety of combinations of dress, including of headgear and footwear, as to suggest not uniformity but diversity. If they were intended by the ancient designers to be seen as cavalrymen, they are not on duty.[85] As Thucydides says explicitly in his account of the Athenian development from brutishness, the decision not to carry arms, in which the Athenians of the past had set an example that others later followed, was only made possible by the trust that had been built up.[86] These features, taken together, we may reasonably conclude, not only signalled that viewers were being offered a procession on a non-military occasion, but that they asserted the values, including the practical usefulness, of the internal civic peace and mutual trust that Athenian civic and personal paideia was intended to promote.

So can we find another candidate that fits, in Connelly's phrase, the 'ultimately genealogical function of architectural sculpture' and that 'demands the telling of local versions of myths, grounding the formula in specific landscapes, cult places, family lines, and divine patronage'?[87] A point that has seldom, if ever, been noticed is that, whichever authority it was that first arranged for the huge central slab to be removed from its slots on the Parthenon without breaking it, performed a complex feat of engineering, almost as impressive as that of the ancient builders who

---

numerous examples but with what the ancient Roman authors—who had seen many more that are now lost—had written. James Dallaway, for example, who had lived in the Ottoman territories and who rushed out his book on ancient sculpture shortly after the publication of the Select Committee report in 1816, noted, as a matter of common knowledge that: 'Statues without drapery are confined to the representation of the deities male and female, heroes, Olympic victors, Genii, and the characters employed in the most ancient mythology or heroic fables'. Dallaway, James, *Of Statuary and Sculpture among the Antients: With some account of specimens preserved in England* (London: Murray, 1816), 67. Dallaway evidently drew on the work of Emeric-David, T. B., *Recherches sur l'art statuaire, considéré chez les anciens et chez les modernes, ou Mémoire sur cette question proposée par l'Institut national de France: Quelles ont été les causes de la perfection de la Sculpture antique, et quels seroient les moyens d'y atteindre?* (Paris: Nyon, an XIII, 1805). Dallaway's book, by situating Phidias as the 'zenith' in a long parade of sculptors in a narrative of rise and decline, may have encouraged the British Parliament to vote for the funds, although it is seldom mentioned in accounts of the episode.

85 Noted by Fehr, Burkhard, *Becoming Good Democrats and Wives: Civil Education and Female Socialization on the Parthenon Frieze.* Hephaistos Sonderband. Kritische Zeitschrift zu Theorie und Praxis der Archäologie und angrenzender Gebiete (Berlin, Münster, Vienna, Zürich, London: Lit Verlag, 2011), 36.

86 Thuc. 1.6.

87 Connelly, *Parthenon Enigma*, 184.

raised it into place in the first place. The modern suggestion that such a long slab could have 'fallen to the ground' whether accidentally or deliberately brought about, accelerating through a drop of nearly forty feet, without breaking up on impact, is next to impossible.[88] When that dismantling occurred is not noted in any surviving literary or epigraphic record, although a technology already exists that will enable the dates of breakage and mutilation to be estimated with greater precision, for example to the nearest century, and could be proposed as a project to the authorities responsible for the site.[89] From recent studies of the stones, it is already almost certain that this slab was taken down and repositioned at the time when the ancient Parthenon was adapted for use as a Christian basilica, sometime in the middle centuries of the first millennium CE. It is likely that the dismantling occurred at that same time as the changes authorized and financed by the ecclesiastical authorities, that the door at the west end, which had previously been the entrance to the part of the building, normally shut, where the city's possessions were kept secure, became the entrance to the building, having being adapted to receive a congregation inside and to align it along a Christian axis. At the same time, again in accordance with a top-down empire-wide decision to bring Christian ritual practice indoors, an apse was built into the east end, making the removal of the huge central slab of the frieze architecturally unavoidable.

The slab was, however, not actively destroyed, nor treated as marble waste to be recycled as building material, as seems to have happened with the private dedications on the Acropolis at that time. A more plausible explanation is that it was carefully taken down and then systematically mutilated, as had been the custom of the Romans and occasionally in classical Athens. In this case, as with other parts of the Parthenon frieze and figurative sculpture found in sanctuaries all over the ancient world, the mutilations were not intended to destroy the artefact outright and so remove it from the built memory altogether, but to commemorate the act of mutilation itself. The intention was to display to members of the then newly triumphant religion, and to others who might not have actively wanted to be Christianized, the fact that the 'idolatrous' images

---

88   The comment by Tsigakou in Hope and Tsigakou, *Thomas Hope,* 223.
89   For informal advice on this point, I record my thanks to Professor Yannis Lyzitzis of the University of the Aegean.

which their 'pagan' votaries had allegedly 'worshipped' had now lost their power. To these men, the Parthenon was, in modern terms, a dark heritage, that had a value as a building that made it worth preserving, but only provided it no longer exercised the power to persuade that it had done in former, now happily superseded, centuries.

When the piece was examined in preparation for the first formal publication, the museum managers thought that 'the heads of these figures, as of almost the whole line of the [east] frieze, appear to have been purposely defaced'.[90] The care given to the taking down and selective mutilation can be regarded as part of the slow, long-drawn out, step-by step, top-down policy of imperial Christianization.[91] Paradoxically, if this is what happened, it has not only brought about the survival of the slab but has had the incidental result of enabling us to offset the damage that was done at that time. We can also offset the distortion of presenting the composition at eye level. A recent photograph, as shown as Figure 4.13, taken from a more oblique angle, shows a bulge more clearly.

Even without the adjustment to the viewing angle, it is implausible that the lump of mutilated marble at the top of the composition is the left hand of the central male figure as many have assumed.[92] If

---

90   British Museum, *Ancient Marbles* (A series, of which engravings of the sculptured pieces from the Parthenon were published, after many delays, in expensive volumes (pediments 1830, metopes 1835, frieze 1839)), viii, 50. Indications of the actual practice of displaying the performance of mutilation are given in *The Reunification of the Parthenon Marbles, A Cultural Imperative* (Athens: Ministry of Culture and others, 2004), a catalogue of an exhibition showing the effects of the scattering of the sculptured pieces arranged by the Council of Europe, which show how some heads or parts of heads were apparently cleanly severed, and left among the débris, so enabling them to survive, while other heads and faces were defaced.

91   As discussed in St Clair, *WStP*, Chapter 4, https://doi.org/10.11647/obp.0136.04.

92   The speculation that the lump presents a hand and knuckles can be traced back to the engraving in British Museum, *Ancient Marbles* (1839), viii, opposite 41, which was designed by Corbould and engraved by Le Keux. This apparently authoritative representation was subsequently copied without discussion by Ellis, Sir Henry, *Elgin and Phigaleian Marbles* (London: Knight, 1833), i, 167, and repeated by others who relied on Corbould throughout the age of engraving, including, Le Normant/ Collas, Michaelis, Boetticher, Flasch, Lucas, and Davidson. Exceptions are the drawings offered by Waldstein, *Essays*, 198 and Perry, 296 who present the marble as a large, unexplained, lump without imposing this interpretation. Curiously, the guidebook to the British Museum, Vaux, W. S. W., *Handbook to the Antiquities in the British Museum* (London: Murray, 1851), whose paratext claimed that the central scene was illustrated in plates along with the rest of the frieze, does not include the scene at all. Since the pagination is continuous, and this is not therefore a case of a page having been torn out, it may be that the omission is deliberate, possibly

that had been the case, the left arm of the adult male figure under the cloth would be grotesquely long, and the knuckles of the hand implausibly disproportionate, even if some allowance were to be made for helping the ground level viewer. Nor is the lump likely to be some disproportionately large piece of a frame positioned in the most central spot of the central composition to which all eyes are drawn.

Figure 4.13. Detail of the slab in its state at the time of writing. Photograph by author taken from an oblique angle. CC BY.

As was pointed out in the nineteenth century, the action assumed by the Stuart conjecture to be the handing over a piece of cloth by the smaller figure to the tall bearded male figure on the viewer's left is better seen as the man who is looking at the viewer as he hands over or accepts something wrapped in the cloth to or from the smaller figure.[93] In 1975, the late Martin Robertson suggested that what was wrapped in the cloth

---

because the editor could see that the traditional image did not match the marble. A hand was, however, recently drawn in by Valavanis, Panos, *The Acropolis through its Museum* (Athens: Kapon, 2013), a translation into English by Alexandra Doumas of the Greek edition, 139.

93 For example, Davidson, *Parthenon Frieze*, 65. He attributes the suggestion to Dr Flasch, referring to Flasch, Adam, *Zum Parthenon-Fries* (Würzburg: Druck der Thein'schen Druckerei, 1877) and describing it as 'the one thing that redeems his pamphlet from utter worthlessness'.

might be the image made of olive wood ('xoanon') that had allegedly fallen from the skies at the time of Erechtheus. But, like the Stuart conjecture, it is open to the objection that it is not a mythic event.

When we adjust the viewing angle, the lump of marble becomes the feature of the composition to which the eyes of viewers are drawn. As Waldstein had noticed in another context, once we offset the distortion brought about by presenting the piece at eye level, the effect is to draw the eye of the viewer upward. From the most common angles at which the composition was seen in ancient times, that is, all those other than full frontal, the central male figure, even in its mutilated state, appears be looking at the viewer, exhibiting to him and her the object under the cloth, a pose encouraging the reflexivity that is to be expected in the central action of the composition of the frieze. A co-opting stance of this kind can be seen in Figure 4.14, a photograph of a plaster cast that also preserves only the contours of the marble sub-surface as it has come down to our time.

Figure 4.14. Cast of the central scene, Acropolis Museum. Photograph by the author of a cast taken from an angle, June 2018. CC BY.

The cast also preserves a line of holes, whose purpose is not clear, but which, if they are the remains of coloured ceramic studs of the kind that were prominent on the Erechtheion nearby, would have indicated to the ancient viewers both the shape and the importance of the covered object that is being displayed to them by the male figure. And, even in its mutilated state, and after over a thousand years without maintenance, unsheltered from wind and weather, and its surface cleansed by its months in the sea, the exposed marble subsurface may still retain traces of other identity markers. The figure on the viewer's right, for example, appears to be shown as wearing something on her wrist that was so pronounced that it has been picked out in marble and not just in paint or ceramic. The raised lump may be a survival of the 'golden snake' that was worn by those women of Athens who belonged to families who claimed to be autochthonous.[94] The puzzling incisions to the neck could be the remains of a golden snake necklace that, as is noted in the *Ion*, served the same identifying purpose.[95] If the heads of the older men depicted on the frieze had survived in better condition, with their paint and metal, it might have been possible to find traces of the golden cicadas or grasshoppers that Thucydides and others say were worn in the hair by old-fashioned Athenians as symbols of their Ionianism.[96] Among the objects listed in the inventories of valuables held in the Acropolis temples, alongside the special clothes, wreaths, brooches, necklaces,

---

94	Another close-up photograph of the hand and forearm, that also brings out the rounded piece of raised marble on the wrist was included by Lagerlöf, Margaretha Rossholm, *The Sculptures of the Parthenon: Aesthetics and Interpretation* (New Haven, Conn.; London: Yale UP, 2000), 121.

95	The late Martin Robertson, puzzled by the irregularities on the neck, speculated that they might be 'pronounced Venus rings,' although that seems unlikely for a figure that in its mutilated state appears as almost child-like. Robertson and Frantz, *The Parthenon Frieze*, unnumbered page following plate V.

96	'it was only recently that their [Athenian] older men of the wealthier class gave up wearing tunics of linen and fastening their hair in a knot held by a golden grasshopper as a brooch; and this same dress obtained for a long time among the elderly men of the Ionians also, owing to their kinship with the Athenians.' Thuc. 1.6. In the main manuscript tradition, the word for grasshopper is given in Ionic dialect that tends to confirm that Antisthenes is referring to the claims to autochthony in the Ionian brooches and not just the real creatures. Prince, 41. The force of his contempt is lessened if it is altered to Attic. Among the candidates are the figures depicted on the north frieze X in the Acropolis Museum. Delivorrias and Mavrommatis, *The Parthenon Frieze*, page 95.

and other paraphernalia used in festivals, are golden grasshoppers.[97] Whether they were made available to temple servants ('priests'), male or female, or to other participants in festivals in which Ionian kinship was remembered and re-enacted, is not recorded but seems likely.

The object wrapped in a cloth is, I suggest, a baby tightly wrapped in swaddling bands, a public display of a custom known to every Athenian family, even if not always practised.[98] Among the tens of thousands of visual images surviving from the ancient world, not one has been found that shows a man and a young person folding a piece of cloth.[99] By contrast images of tightly swaddled babies, of which a typical example is shown as Figure 4.15, are common.

---

97 Harris, Diane, *The Treasures of the Parthenon and Erechtheion* (Oxford: OUP, 1995), no 372, item 373. χρυσίδια διάλιθα σύμμικτα πλινθίων καὶ τεττίγων σταθμὸν τούτων.

98 A terracotta of a satyr shown holding a tightly wrapped baby is reproduced by Hall, Edith, *The Theatrical Cast of Athens; interactions between ancient Greek Drama and Society* (Oxford: OUP, 2006), 92, https://doi.org/10.1093/acprof: oso/9780199298891.001.0001. A tightly swaddled new-born infant is shown, with deities present, perhaps as a representation of the acceptance ceremony, on a votive stele in the Metropolitan Museum of Art, New York, MMA 24.97.92 discussed by Demand, Nancy H., *Birth, Death, and Motherhood in Classical Greece* (Baltimore; London: Johns Hopkins UP, 1994), 88, and viewable at http://exhibits.hsl.virginia. edu/antiqua/gynecology/. A birth scene with a baby apparently about to be wrapped in highly decorated cloth and swaddling bands is presented on a red-figure hydria in the British Museum, usually said to be the birth of Erichthonios, reproduced by Loraux, *Children*, plate 3. Swaddled babies are shown on the so-called Sigean relief, one of the first antiquities to be acquired, against the wishes of the local population, by Lord Elgin on his way to Constantinople in 1799. Illustrated in [British Museum] *Ancient Marbles*, ix, 1842, plate xi. It appears to show a procession in which women seek to put their children under the care of Athena. Since one woman is shown as mourning, the piece may have been part of a tomb. Two examples of swaddled babies pictured on funerary pottery are noted by Lewis, Sian, *The Athenian Woman: An Iconographic Handbook* (London: Routledge, 2002), 221, note 20, https://doi.org/10.4324/9780203351192.

Swaddling was assumed to have been practised in the mythic age, as for example, at Eur. Tro. 759. Even baby gods are put in swaddling bands, as is the character of Hermes in the passage in Homeric Hymn 4 beginning at 237, although, since he is presented as only one day old and yet is able to speak and argue coherently, play the lyre, and steal cattle, this may be an example of the playful nature of the text and of non-reverential attitudes towards the gods.

99 The only exceptions I know of, which tend to prove the rule, are scenes pictured on images in the Naples Museum, *Raccolta delle più interessanti Dipinture e de'più belli Mosaici rinvenuti negli scavi di Ercolano, di Pompei, e di Stabia che ammiransi nel Museo Reale Borbonico* (Naples: n.p., 1840), 43 and 76 where a lady is apparently shown as considering buying cloths from a tradesman.

Figure 4.15. Grave memorial apparently of a woman who died in childbirth or soon afterwards handing over the swaddled baby to be cared for by another woman. Author's photograph. CC BY.[100]

According to Hippocrates in his treatise on how climate, diet, and social customs affect the character of a people, those babies who were not swaddled were likely to grow up to be flabby, squat, and impotent.[101] In Plato's ideal state it was to be laid down in law that a child should be swaddled, 'moulded like wax', until the age of two, and to be carried by their nurses till the age of three to ensure that their legs were straight.[102] To present a baby tightly swaddled was therefore itself a recommendation to viewers, female as well as male, on how they ought to bring up their children to become useful to the city. Images of tightly swaddled babies made from terracotta, a material associated with personal votive offerings, look much the same.[103] Although there

---

100   Photograph taken at the British Museum, unprovenanced, probably made in Athens in the last quarter of the fifth century, GR 1894. 6–16.1 (Sculpture 2232). A similar image, apparently also of a baby surviving a mother's death in childbirth, is shown, tightly wrapped, with its face fully sculpted, on a grave memorial reproduced in Neils, Jenifer and Oakley, John H., eds, *Coming of Age in Ancient Greece: Images of Childhood from the Classical Past* (New Haven and London: Yale UP, 2003), 223, figure 3. Described as 'Attic marble grave stele ca 375–350 BCE. Houston, Museum of Fine Arts. Gift of Miss Annette Finnegan. From Athens.'

101   Hp. Aer. 20.

102   Plat. Laws 7.789e, although the idea is presented as an example of how some legislation would lead to ridicule among women and be unenforceable in practice.

103   One found in the sanctuary of Artemis at Munychia, dated to the late fourth century, now in the Archaeological Museum of Piraeus, 5383, is reproduced in Lee, Mireille M., *Body, Dress, and Identity in Ancient Greece* (Cambridge: CUP, 2015), 97, https://doi.org/10.1017/CBO9781107295261. Another, unprovenanced except as derived from a collection made in Corfu, presented as lying in a crib with a pillow, is reproduced in Walters, H. B., *Catalogue of the Terracottas in the Department of Greek*

are innumerable presentations of actual swaddling both in words and images over many hundreds of years, making it one of the most enduring and recognizable components of the discursive environment, only one image of an event set in the mythic age is known to me. Shown as Figure 4.16, as noticed and copied by Winckelmann, it is thought to picture the birth of Telephos and may refer to the play by Euripides, of which some fragments survive.

Figure 4.16. Birth of Telephos, , facsimile of an engraving from a bas relief in the Villa Borgese, with a similar image depicted in a mural from Heculaneum that was moved to the Museo Archeologico in Naples.

and Roman Antiquities, British Museum (London: Trustees of British Museum, 1903), B106. A terracotta of a satyr shown holding a tightly wrapped baby is reproduced by Hall, *Theatrical Cast*, 92. A tightly swaddled new-born infant is shown, with deities present, perhaps as a representation of the acceptance, on a votive stele in the Metropolitan Museum of Art, New York, MMA 24.97.92 discussed by Demand, *Birth, Death, and Motherhood*, 88, and viewable at http://exhibits.hsl.virginia.edu/antiqua/gynecology/
A birth scene with a highly decorated cloth and swaddling bands is presented on a red-figure hydria by the Oinanthe painter, British Museum, usually said to be the birth of Erichthonios, reproduced by Loraux, *Children*, plate 3.

The image, which appears to present the pregnancy of a mother and the presentation of the swaddled child, 'scenes from the birth of Telephos', shows the infant with even its head tightly swaddled, wrapped in a large peplos, as it is ceremonially handed over and accepted. What was shown positioned under the pediment that presented scenes surrounding the birth of the Athena, I suggest, were episodes relating to the birth and naming of a famous mythic child. Indeed, since both pediments offer myths of eponymous naming, we might even have guessed that the frieze would do the same.

In the custom of classical Athens, there was a time gap between the physiological birth of a child and the ceremony of accepting it as a member of the family.[104] Although there are differences in the record, it appears that on the fifth day, the nurse, in the presence of close family members, carried the infant round the family hearth in the middle of the room, hence the name 'amphidromia', literally 'walking round in a circle', a custom so well known to contemporary Athenians that the character of Socrates, in Plato's *Theaetetus*, used it to explain his method of arguing as a circular process.[105] On the tenth day the child was formally named. During that interval, from which males appear to have been excluded or to have excluded themselves, the baby was without identity, born physiologically but not yet socially.[106] One of the characters of Theophrastus, commonly called 'The Superstitious Man' but perhaps more accurately rendered as 'the man who pays excessive attention to customs', refuses to visit a woman when she has given birth for fear of pollution, which he regards as equivalent to the prohibition on touching a dead body.[107]

---

104 According to Aristotle's *History of Animals*, 7, 12: 'The majority of deaths in infancy occur before the child is a week old, hence it is customary to name the child at that age, from a belief that it has now a better chance of survival.'

105 *Ibid.*

106 The custom is described by Hall, *Theatrical Cast*, 62–67, https://doi.org/10.1093/acprof:oso/9780199298891.001.0001, drawing on the primary contemporary sources collected by Hamilton, Richard, 'Sources for the Athenian amphidromia' in *Greek, Roman, and Byzantine Studies*, Vol. 25 (1984), 243–251.

107 Theophrastus, Character 16. The Greek word, deisidaimonia, is cognate with that used by Paul of Tarsus in his initial complement to the men of Athens as discussed in St Clair, *WStP*, Chapter 22, https://doi.org/10.11647/obp.0136.22. The prohibition, many scholars have suggested, applied even to the biological father.

Nor was the interval between physiological and social birth a formality. Exposing an unwanted child to die seem to have been legal and acceptable during the first days of a child's life, both on grounds of physical unfitness, if, for example, the infant exhibited a disability, and also on moral and social grounds, as would be the case, for example, if it was not born legitimately according to the city's norms.[108] In archaeological excavations in the Athenian agora in the 1930s, a well was discovered near the so-called Theseion that contained the skeletal remains of about four hundred and fifty children as well as of dogs. Although dated to the Hellenistic period, it appears to give confirmation that infanticide whether active or passive was practised in Athens, as well as in Sparta, and probably in other Hellenic cities.[109] The autochthony claimed by certain Athenian families was not only a discourse, but ensuring racial purity was a current social practice.

When, however, as I suggest is the case here, the birth is entirely legitimate and a source of family and social celebration, the giving of gifts, of animal sacrifices and feasts, a birth scene fits well with the general storytelling function of the Parthenon and of the site. In Aristophanes's comedy, the *Birds*, the character of Euelpides, who boasts of how Athenian he is by birth, complains that his cloak was stolen when he was drunk at a tenth-day naming party. The dramatic purpose of the remark in the context of the play, other than to imply that Euelpides is a free-loader, is not obvious since it hangs without further explanation or follow up. The anecdote may have had a topicality not now recoverable, but its presence in the play shows that naming parties were a normal part of life in classical Athens.[110] Nor should we assume that kinship festivals took second place to civic, nor that attendance was optional.[111]

---

108 Noted by Swift, Laura, *Euripides, Ion* (London: Duckworth, 2008) referring to Patterson, Cynthia, '"Not Worth the Rearing": The Causes of Infant Exposure in Ancient Greece' in *Transactions of the American Philological Association*, Vol. 115 (1985), 103–123, and other works.

109 The evidence is revisited in Liston, Maria A., and Rotroff, Susan I., *The Agora Bone Well* (Boston: American School of Classical Studies, *Hesperia Supplement*, 2018).

110 Aristophanes, *Birds*, line 493. Nan Dunbar, in her authoritative edition, Dunbar, Nan, ed., *Aristophanes, Birds* (Oxford: Clarendon Press, 1995), https://doi.org/10.1093/actrade/9780198150831.book.1, adds a little more, notably that the amphidromia may have happened in the afternoon and continued into the night, which would account for the presence of many torches on the presentation of the procession.

111 Plutarch records that Pericles during his long period of ascendancy never accepted invitations from friends, with the exception of a wedding celebration given by

In the *Birds*, Aristophanes includes a parodic description of a naming ceremony with its procession, whose comic potential is exploited to great effect. Although it is usually overambitious to infer actuality from comedy, it is striking that when the scene is introduced, the first things that are called for, which serve as markers for the audience of the play, are a basket and a washing basin, both of which are presented among the objects being assembled on the Parthenon frieze.[112] In the *Clouds*, we are given a comic conversation between the character of Strepsiades and his wife about the choice of names and how the child would be affected by the alternatives.[113] At the naming ceremony, a birth tax that can also be regarded as a registration fee, consisting of a quart measure of barley and another quart of wheat, plus one obol in cash, was also payable by the father, as it had been since the age of the tyrants, so turning the ceremony of acceptance of a child into a public civic duty. The same tax was levied at death, so marking both the entrance to and the exit from the status of Athenian citizen.[114]

Figure 4.17, a detail of a nineteenth-century sepia photograph of an unidentified funerary monument appears to show a woman who has died soon after giving birth handing over responsibility for the infant to surviving family members. It conforms with a common theme, but also, unusually, provides visual evidence for the practice of swaddling an infant's head in order to turn him into a 'long-head' like Pericles.[115]

As Figure 4.17 showed, head swaddling was also presented as occurring in the mythic world. Although my suggestion does not depend upon the point, I note that if the image of the swaddled baby in the central scene of the Parthenon included such a head covering, it would situate its head even more prominently in the composition as

---

a kinsman. Plut. Per. 7.4. That expulsion from the community of the city meant exclusion from the family and not just from the civic festivals is explicitly stated in a speech put into the mouth of Oedipus in the *Oedipus Tyrannus* of Sophocles. Soph. OT 234–235.

112 Aristoph. Birds 850′ παῖ παῖ, τὸ κανοῦν αἴρεσθε καὶ τὴν χέρνιβα.

113 In the passage following Aristoph. Cl. 56.

114 Noted by Aristotle as payable to the priestess, that is, to a member of staff of the temple to Athena, at Aristot. Econ. 2.1347a. While it might be going too far to suggest that the central scene reminded viewers of their duty to pay their taxes, if more had survived, we might have been able to pick out the preamble to the act of payment in the composition, set back in time in the same way as recent customs were given an imagined ancient pedigree in, for example, the *Eumenides* of Aeschylus.

115 As discussed as part of the discursive environment in Chapter 2.

seen by viewers looking up, and make it an even stronger candidate to be mutilated. The same would be true of any other head-dress that acted as a marker.

Figure 4.17. A swaddled infant with a conical head covering. Detail from a nineteenth-century sepia photograph, perhaps by Constantinos, of a grave memorial in high relief.[116]

So, if viewers of the Parthenon were being shown a mythic baby being accepted into the community of the city, who is being pictured? One candidate jumps to mind. What was being shown, I suggest, are 'scenes relating to' the birth and naming of Ion, to adopt the phrase used by Pausanias for the stories presented by the pediments, 'birth' being understood as the social birth that did not occur until the naming ceremony. Ion, the eponymous father of all Ionians, was one of the most ancient of Athenian heroes, being mentioned in the eighth century in Hesiod's *Catalogue of Women* in a fragment not discovered till the twentieth century, and with an apparently unbroken tradition for over a thousand years.[117] According to Thucydides, the Ionian descendants

---

116 Loosely inserted in an album of nineteenth-century photographs of Greece, none labelled or dated. Private collection. I have been unable to identify the piece photographed in any collection. A swaddled baby with a similar head wrapping shown as highly decorated, is reproduced in a scene from myth from the Laborde collection in Notor, *La Femme dans l'Antiquité Grecque*, 91. Another image from a bas-relief from the Troad in the same volume, page 8, perhaps showing a farewell or a handing over scene, shows a mature and a young woman each holding a swaddled infant. That held by the younger, to judge from the reproduction, may also be hatted.

117 The Hesiod fragment noted, with transcription by Martin, Gunther, ed., *Euripides, Ion, Edition and Commentary* (Leiden: de Gruyter, 2018), 15, https://doi.org/10.1515/9783110523591.

of the Athenians who lived in Athens continued in his day to celebrate their (kinship) connexion annually on a special day in the month of Anthesterion as part of the 'ancient Dionysia'.[118] My suggestion therefore fits well with Nicole Loraux's suggested requirement, as well as that of Connelly already noted, that the mythic stories, if they were to fulfil their purpose, had to be recognizable by Athenians 'without any hesitation on their part, as if these identifications were self-evident'.[119]

The suggestion, unlike those suggested by others, is fully in line with the rhetoric of the building as a whole and with the discursive environment. Besides the allegedly welcoming attitude to foreigners presented by the character of Pericles in the Thucydidean funeral oration, there is plentiful evidence of a fear of hybridity.[120] To reassert the common kinship and the mutual obligations through the mythic figure of Ion was therefore not just a useful old story alongside others in the mythic past of Athens, but, as was the case in some tragedies, one with topical relevance. As Lisa Kallet has remarked about the classical period: 'They [the Athenians] also, through an increasing cultivation of the hero Ion and an emphasis on their connection to Ionians, marketed themselves as the mother city of all Ionians', an observation well attested in the contemporary authors who described the institutions of the classical city, the claims to antiquity, and the use of eponyms.[121]

---

118 Thuc. 2.15.
119 Loraux, *Children*, 20. Fehr's suggestion that the scene presents an idealized family, the domain of the 'oikos' a female space, as a parallel with the male world of the 'polis', is attractive and consistent with my suggestion, but except as part of a displayed myth, it is not enough to meet the postulate.
120 As evidenced by the examples in Chapter 2. Indeed, the fact that the character of Pericles was presenting his point suggests that it was not universally shared
121 Kallet, Lisa, 'Wealth, Power, and Prestige: Athens at Home and Abroad', in Neils, Jenifer, ed., *The Parthenon from Antiquity to the Present* (Cambridge: CUP, 2005), 61. In the *Persians* by Aeschylus, thought to have been produced for the first time in 472, a pitiless celebration of the misery inflicted on the leadership and people of the Achaemenid empire by the defeat of the invasion led by Xerxes, the characters frequently refer to the Athenians as 'Ionians'. The vital role accorded to Ion in the construction of Athenianness is referred to several times in the Aristotelian 'Athenian Constitution' [Ath Pol] and in the fragments preserved in the works of other authors, where, as is normal with eponyms, he is treated as a historical as well as a mythological personage. In 41.2, for example, Ion is credited along with others unnamed with having divided the recently unified people of Attica into the 'families' of which the four 'sons of Ion' described earlier by Herodotus, Her 5. 66, were the old Ionians. Even after the Athenian political domination ('arche') came to an end, the genealogical commonality of the Ionians continued be celebrated on formal occasions, as, for example, Aelius Aristides in his panegyric *Panathenaic*

And her comment is amply borne out not only by the experiment that brings out the plentiful references to Ion in the discursive environment, but by much other evidence. It was part of their self-fashioning that the Athenians were themselves Ionians, and that overseas Ionians as their 'children' owed them obedience, especially at a time when the original Ionians, the Athenians, had saved them in the still recent unsuccessful Persian invasion.[122]

But a presentation of scenes surrounding the birth of Ion offered even more. One of the biggest, the most regular, amongst the most ancient, and, at three days, the longest-lasting of all the festivals, the pan-Ionian Apatouria, which occurred in various sites in Attica every autumn, was not only a celebration of kinship, but the administrative occasion when new members were formally enrolled.[123] Although there appears not to have been any age limit after which a boy or man could not be enrolled, most enrolments appear to have been of infants born to the legitimate wives of existing members in the previous calendar year. The naming and enrolment displays not only enabled boys to proceed through later rites of passage to the privileges and duties of citizenship, but they determined private property and inheritance rights far into the future. As emerges from the corpus of legal speeches of the fourth century in which the details of the induction ceremonies were put under scrutiny, naming and enrolment were amongst the instruments by which the inter-generational continuity of the city was celebrated and performed.

Once modern assumptions are discarded and the lost paint and metal restored, the smaller figure can emerge as the mythic Kreousa, mother of the eponymous Ion. Since it is a social birth that is being celebrated, not the physiological, she is pictured as a girl at the moment of transition

---

Discourse, 57–58, tells the Athenians that 'at both ends of our [Mediterranean] world, there dwell children of your children'. The tomb of Ion at Potamoi, a small port town in Attica, was still a site of commemorative ceremonies at the time of Pausanias. Paus 1, 31.3, with a substantial passage on stories about Ion and the Ionians in Paus 7, 1–17.

122 In the *Persians* by Aeschylus, 591, the Chorus claims that the peoples of Ionia who were formerly under Achaemenid domination need no longer curb their tongues but can speak freely, a celebration of Athenian democracy.

123 What is known about the Apatouria is summarized by Parker, Robert, *Polytheism and Society at Athens* (Oxford: OUP, 2005), 458–461, https://doi.org/10.1093/acpr of:oso/9780199216116.001.0001. The study by Lambert, S. D., *The Phratries of Attica* (Ann Arbor, University of Michigan Press, 1991) adds more details especially about the enrolment of names.

to adulthood, as an ancient viewer would recognize.[124] And the male figure who is accepting the baby into the family can be identified as Xuthus, the husband of Kreousa, whose memory was also honoured in recurrent ceremonies, as testified by a fragmentary inscription of *c.* 430; one of many that regulate the calendar of sacrifices, it notes that an Attic 'trittys', one of the large constituencies of citizens into which the population had been divided in 506, records a duty to sacrifice 'a lamb to Xuthus'.[125] As for the female figure to the left of the tall male figure, she may be formally receiving the gifts associated with a naming ceremony, some of which are mentioned in ancient authors, brought to her by female kin and friends holding trays on their heads.[126]

Recovering the Ancient Meanings of the Ion Myth

If my suggestion is valid, can more can be said about the way the stories were likely to have been understood by real Athenians? Although the Parthenon frieze was part of the background experience of those participating in rituals on the Acropolis for around a thousand years, not a single author of the surviving corpus makes even a passing reference to it in the terms used by modern histories of sculpture, or even in those used by Pausanias as a collector of stories.[127] However, there are some indirect indications. In listing the benefits that a mother can give to her daughters that will be precluded by her voluntary death, for example, the character of Alcestis, in the play by Euripides of that name, declares that attending them in childbirth is the most caring.[128]

And we have a few reports of critiques of the discourses of autochthony and Ionianism. Antisthenes, for example, a learned and prolific author and friend of Plato, had a personal reason for resenting the backward-looking nativism of the two-parent decree. Although born in Athens,

---

124 'For Greek women, the first birth marked the transition from youth to adulthood.' Fehr, *Good Democrats and Wives*, 96.
125 LSCG 27. Because the inscription is incomplete, the trittys is unidentifiable.
126 As for example in the illustration from a vase in Naples reproduced by Notor, *La Femme dans l'Antiquité Grecque*, 237, which shows gifts appropriate to a funeral ceremony being carried on such trays. We might, for example, see what others have regarded as mere cushions, or in the case of the Connelly conjecture, as shrouds, as swaddling bands, or the long peploi in which babies were wrapped.
127 LSCG 27. Because the inscription is incomplete, the trittys is unidentifiable.
128 Eur. Alc. 319.

his mother had been born in Thrace, and he was therefore barred from participating in many aspects of public life, including speaking in the Assembly.[129] He was 'Attic' but not 'Athenian'. His sardonic remark that moving from Athens to Sparta was like moving from the women's quarters to the men's, a variation on a standard theme that Spartans were more manly than Athenians, is more pointed if he is alluding to scenes relating to the birth of Ion.[130] And when he said, in a sardonic phrase that owes its survival to its having been adopted as a moral tag ('chreia'), that the only autochthonous creatures on the Acropolis were the snails and the grasshoppers/cicadas, he was referring both to the creatures that appeared to hatch spontaneously and to the golden grasshopper brooches of the 'old Ionians' who wore them.[131]

As Jenifer Neils has pointed out: 'images of youths carrying troughs or baskets are not common'.[132] And the suggestions for what the receptacles might have been understood by viewers to contain, for example honeycombs, as well as other free-standing items, have tended to start from descriptions of the Panathenaic processions, despite the lack of any correspondence with what is pictured on the frieze in any of the main features. If, however, we start instead from a hypothesis that what are presented are scenes from the naming of Ion, in which all the elements presented are immediately recognizable as following the normal Athenian practices of birth ceremonies, the youths are explainable as male guests bringing gifts. Athenaeus, a later writer who gathered stories about the lore of food, preserves mentions of the customs of the naming festivals that he had extracted from works now otherwise lost: the *Geryones* by Ephippus; the *Parasite* by Antiphanes; the *Insatiable Man* by Diphilus; the *Palæstra* by Alcæus; and the *Birth of the Muses* by Polyzelus.[133] We also have a papyrus fragment that may come from the tragedy of Aeschylus known as *Semele, or the Water Carriers*, which seems to have been enacted by the Enneakrounos

---

129 Price, Susan, ed., *Antisthenes of Athens: Texts, Translations, and Commentary* (Ann Arbor: University of Michigan Press, 2015), https://doi.org/10.3998/mpub.5730060.
130 ἐκ τῆς γυναικωνίτιδος λέγειν εἰς τὴν ἀνδρωνῖτιν ἐπιέναι. Price item 7, page 39, from Theon.
131 *Antisthenes of Athens,* Price edition, 41, https://doi.org/10.3998/mpub.5730060.
132 Neils, *Parthenon Frieze,* 150.
133 Ath. 9.10.

('Nine Channels') spring.[134] The ceremony of inducting children into the community, real and imagined, by washing them in the local source of fresh water, thus linking them securely to the life-giving earth, is recorded for several ancient Greek cities, including Argos and Thebes, as well as for Athens. As familiar to every Athenian family of the classical period as the practice of swaddling new-born babies, it is referred to by Thucydides, and given authority by being pushed back in time to the heroic age as already noticed.[135]

Although there are many descriptions in words, visual images of the ceremony are rare. One, evidently drawing on a Greek model, was seen and pictured by Winckelmann in the collection of Cardinal Albani, as shown in Figure 4.18.

Figure 4.18. 'Bacchus raised by the nymphs of Dodona'. Engraving.[136]

If my suggestion is right, how should we regard the *Ion*, the play by Euripides? The first public production, which depended upon its having passed through the stages of obtaining approval and financing required of all works entered for dramatic festivals and competitions, can be reliably dated to some time in the latter part of the mid-fifth century when the main plans for the Parthenon had already been approved

---

134 Smyth, Herbert Weir, ed., *Aeschylus, with an English Translation* (London: Heinemann; Cambridge: Harvard UP, 1971, 1973). Appendix and Addendum to Vol. 2 edited by Hugh Lloyd-Jones. ii, 566–571.

135 In Chapter 2.

136 No 52 from Winckelmann, *Monumenti antichi inediti*. Private collection, showing some browning of the page. Reproduced in Winckelmann and Appelbaum, *Winckelmann's Images*, 24.

and some of the actual construction work had begun and perhaps been completed.[137] Since Euripides's career as a dramatist began in 455, there is no problem in relating one of its themes to the Periclean two-parent decree of 451/450. How, we can therefore ask, would an early audience of Athenians have regarded the play in the circumstances in which it was first performed?

In the play, a male baby who was found abandoned by some unfortunate local girl outside the perimeter of the holy site ('temenos') of Delphi, is taken in by one of the female temple servants, out of kindness and against the regulations, itself a critique of convention. Gradually the child learns to survive by living off scraps from the sacrifices. As he grows into a boy, he makes himself so useful by doing odd jobs that he is given permanent employment. Among those whom he meets as he goes about his temple duties is Xuthus, husband of the Kreousa, daughter of King Erechtheus of Athens who has come to seek advice. After many unexpected twists, it turns out that the boy is the same person as a baby whom Kreousa bore in secret in a cave of the Acropolis slopes and then she abandoned. When the boy's true history is eventually discovered, he is given his name 'Ion' in a belated ceremony, and taken to Athens where he is installed as heir to Xuthus and awaits his destiny as founding father of all Ionians.

My suggested answer has used the *Ion* as a source for contemporary Athenian customs of the classical era, such as the gold rings, bracelets, and other markers that signalled to viewers that a woman was from an autochthonous family. My suggestion is not however that the story offered on the Parthenon frieze shows any moment, episode, or set of scenes in the play, something we should not expect. It does, however, fit well into the discursive environment. Indeed, it fills a gap in the array of stories that my experiment suggests demand to be given prominence on the Parthenon.

As was common in the Athenian tragic theatre, especially in the plays of Euripides, the *Ion* took the myth in a new direction while maintaining many features of its predecessors. In the world of myth, it was not uncommon for characters to be abandoned as infants, brought up by shepherds or animals, and eventually recognized and either

---

137 The difficulties of establishing a more precise date are summarized by Swift, *Euripides, Ion*, 28–30.

rehabilitated into a normal social hierarchy, or, as in the case of Oedipus, made to confront an unwelcome truth.[138] In the *Ion*, Euripides offered a plotline full of mistaken identities, plans to kill family members, and of death by stoning narrowly averted. The drama, a work of astonishing poetic power and of narrative complexity, is held together by fantastical coincidences and by no less than three instances of dramatic reversal, of 'peripateia,' defined by Aristotle, who may have coined the term, with the peripatos road round the Athenian Acropolis in mind, as 'a change by which the action veers round to its opposite, subject always to our rule of probability or necessity'.[139] The skill of the playwright, presenting within a genre that in modern terms is more romance than tragedy, and that was shared with the implied and the actual audience, enabled the interlocking complexities and instances of implausibility to be fitted into the complex formal structure demanded by the rules of the dramatic festival competition into which the *Ion* was entered.[140]

In the *Wise Melanippe*, an earlier play by Euripides, of which fragments survive, the eponymous heroine notes, as an incidental contribution to the setting of the scene, that Ion had been born in Athens to Kreousa and her foreign-born husband Xuthus.[141] Indeed, in the new play, in order to display and draw attention to the change being made from the version of the Ion myth known to and expected by the first audiences, Euripides included a summary of the older version in the Prologue where it was reported under the allegedly unquestionable authority of the god Hermes and of the Delphic oracle.[142]

As a story, the *Ion* elaborated what had hitherto been an unremarkable foundation myth of a child born to a Athenian mother, Kreousa, and to her husband, the military hero Xuthus, into one in which Ion implausibly

---

138 *Ibid*, 88, mentions as examples Zeus, Paris, and Oedipus, as well as Cyrus, Moses, and Romulus and Remus. The fragmentary *Antiope* of Euripides also has some other similarities in its plots and surprises to the *Ion*, which tends to suggest that the Ion may have conformed with a genre that audience already knew; when Antiope claims that she was made pregnant by Zeus who took the form of a satyr, her sons do not believe her and decide to put her to death. Euripides, *Selected Fragmentary Plays*, Collard et al, ii, fragment 210. The foundling is also a common character in Menander and in the traditions of New Comedy.

139 Aristotle, *Poetics*, 1452a. Some of the reversals are attributed to Tyche.

140 Rehm, Rush, *Understanding Greek Tragic Theatre*, second edition (London and New York: Routledge, 2017), 149, https://doi.org/10.4324/9781315748696.

141 Euripides, *Selected Fragmentary Plays*, Collard et al edition, i, Fragment 491, 9–10, pages 251 and 267.

142 Eur. Ion 70.

turns out to have been fathered by the god Apollo, Kreousa having been impregnated against her will outside the Cave of Pan on the north slope.[143] In the *Ion*, as the story was recast, Ion therefore eventually turns out be Athenian by both parents, and to conform with the Periclean two-parent decree of 450, assuming that Apollo is a deity closely although not exclusively associated with Athens.

By the end, the mythic eponymous hero Ion has been culturally reconstructed to be in full compliance, with implications not only for his exercise of citizenship in the male public sphere of speaking in debates, participating in elections, and in his eligibility for holding public offices, but in the private and family sphere, especially in questions relating to inheritance. As Gunther Martin has written, the character of Ion 'who was formerly only half Athenian is turned into a "pure" citizen'.[144] And, as the character of Ion himself makes explicit, before he knows about the soon-to-be revealed circumstances of his birth and upbringing, if it had not been for the unexpected change in the story of his birth, he would be excluded from participating in public affairs. His tongue, he says, would have been enslaved.[145] If he did not satisfy the two-parent rule, he could not have passed the test set at the Ionian-wide festival of the Apatouria at which his name would be voted on and registered on a citizen list ('phratry'), a rite of passage that, for most male children occurred in their first year of adulthood but that had no age or time limit.[146] One of the many ironies in the old Ion story, which Euripides has the character of Ion himself point out, is that after the two-parent decree, Ion was not even an Ionian.[147]

---

143 It was from the evidence of the *Ion*, among other sources collected by Meursius, that Spon and the early topographers had been able to refute the local story that Pan's cave was the far larger one under the Monument of Thrassylos on the north slope as discussed in St Clair, *WStP*, Chapter 7, https://doi.org/10.11647/obp.0136.07.

144 Martin, *Euripides, Ion*, 22, https://doi.org/10.1515/9783110523591.

145 Eur. Ion 675. And Eur. Ion 585–589, with an even more explicit long passage that follows that has been omitted from some editions as a gloss that made its way into the text as manuscripts were copied.

146 Summarised by Garland, Robert, 'Children in Athenian Religion', in Grubbs, Judith Evans, and Parkin, Tim, eds, *The Oxford Handbook of Childhood and Education in the Classical World* (Oxford: OUP, 2013), 213, https://doi.org/10.1093/oxfordhb/9780199781546.013.010, with references to the ancient sources and modern discussions.

147 Among the other candidates for Athenian founders whose birth might have been presented is Theseus, but, as discussed in Chapter 2, Theseus, for all his importance in Athenian self-fashioning, does not appear to have been pictured on the Parthenon, being too important just to be one of the many presented on the

The *Ion* concludes with what Gunther Martin has called 'a glorifying twist' that asserts that all Ionians are the descendants of the autochthonous citizens of Athens, a point about an aspired-to future already trailed in the Prologue.[148] The implication is that the Ionians overseas, as 'kin' of the Athenians, owe obedience to the largest city in the Ionian world, a staple of the discursive environment. However, before the play reaches what Donald J. Mastronarde has called its 'veritable orgy of imperialistic genealogy', it has performed another function of the Athenian tragic drama. In a series of exchanges, the characters question the credibility of the implausible narrative of a series of events that the audiences, and later the readerships, of the play were being invited to believe. Surely Kreousa's story that she had been raped by a god, the character of Ion suggests, was just a tale commonly invented by women who become pregnant in circumstances they are unable or unwilling to explain?[149]

The women viewers of the frieze on the temple at Delphi were wrong to trust the stories and songs that they had heard from other women as they worked at their looms.[150] The knowledge of the future supposedly obtained from scrutinizing the entrails of sacrificed animals and bird omens is unreliable.[151] What the gods allegedly tell humans through the medium of the Delphic oracle also turns out to have been untrue.[152] With example after example, the characters in the play are presented as losing their confidence in the ways in which Athenians had been officially taught to regard their city.

The character of Kreousa presents herself as a victim of gender stereotyping when she asserts that women are all treated in the same way by men. But shortly afterwards her husband Xuthus not only

---

Parthenon pediments. Stories of his early life given by Plutarch in his *Life of Theseus*, apart from the killing of the Minotaur, consisted mainly of rapes and murders. Like the character of Ion, he would not have counted as an Athenian citizen under the Periclean two-parent decree, and, like that of Ion, his name was also derived from a groan-inducing pun. Theseus did, however, have his own cult in a site in the town.

148　Martin, *Euripides, Ion*, 22, https://doi.org/10.1515/9783110523591. The Prologue declares 'Apollo will cause his name throughout Greece to be called Ion, founder of the cities of Asia'. Eur. Ion 74.

149　Mastronarde, Donald J., *The Art of Euripides: Dramatic Technique and Social Context* (Cambridge: CUP, 2010), 184, https://doi.org/10.1017/CBO9780511676437. Another example of a god allegedly raping a girl during a festival is in the *Auge* of Euripides.

150　Eur. Ion 507.

151　Eur. Ion 369–380.

152　Eur. Ion 369–380.

declares that he is not interested in who was the biological father of Ion, whom he intends to treat as his son and heir, but shows himself to be considerate of Kreousa's feelings. Indeed, some audience members might have thought, he is remarkably forgiving of a wife who, in an earlier scene, had intended to kill him.[153] And not only is gender-stereotyping critiqued as a two-edged weapon. When the generous-minded Xuthus, in deciding to accept the temple boy Ion as his son and heir, reaches out to touch him as a member of his family, Ion thinks he is being subjected to a homoerotic advance and has to be reassured that, in this case, his normally useful working assumption did not apply.[154]

When the character of Ion, in repeating the official civic ideology of autochthony, says he was 'born from the earth', the character of Xuthus tells him that the earth does not give birth to children.'[155] In affirming his belief in the autochthony myth, the still un-disillusioned character of Ion quotes, as his evidence that the stories are true, the fact that they are validated by 'pictures.'[156] There are other examples in classical Athens of images of the half-man, half-serpent creature that personified autochthony, but none was more often seen nor more officially normative than the so-called Cecrops group presented on the west pediment of the Parthenon and on the base of the more rarely seen cult statue inside. If so, we have another example of the custom of inserting features of the classical-era built landscape into the mythic age of the tragic drama, and also of how, as with 'the gods', that does not shield them from discursive assault. By using a cognate of the Greek word 'nomizo', the character of Ion implies that the mythic stories and the gods that people them are also fictions, socially useful for those who benefit, but with nothing intrinsically valuable supporting them, other than the misplaced belief that they are true which is conventionally accorded to them.

There are other passages in the play in which the nature of what should count as evidence is discussed, drawing attention, for example, to the absurdity of judging individuals by their external markers and indicators ('gnorismata') rather than by their observable behaviour. In

---

153 Eur. Ion 655–657.
154 Eur. Ion 519–526.
155 Eur. Ion 542.
156 Eur. Ion 542. ὥσπερ ἐν γραφῇ νομίζεται, The almost identical phrase ὡς ἐν γραφαῖς is also used in *Iphigeneia in Aulis*, Eur. IA 265, to give vividness to the description in language of Iphigeneia's distress at her impending death.

the play, neither Kreousa nor Ion meets the standard of paideia, although the non-autochthonous Athenian Xuthus usually does. When the character of Xuthus performs the belated naming ceremony on the boy, he prophecies a good fortune ('Tyche') that any audience would have recognised as a reference to the future role of Ion as the eponymous hero and father of all Ionians. But that ceremonial speech act is immediately followed by what to modern ears is a groan-inducing pun: '... for I first met you when you were exiting ('exIONti') the sanctuary'.[157] The same word had already been used twice in the play where we can imagine the actors drawing attention to the pun in their diction and preparing the audience for the comic bathos of the naming ceremony.[158] By word play, more suited to comedy than to tragedy, the mythic characters, like the historic Antisthenes, dismiss the whole discourse of eponyms and of Ionianism, and suggest that the play may be giving currency to the ideas of Prodikos, who taught that the gods were in origin nothing more than names of useful things.[159]

As in Athenian tragedy generally, the *Ion* exposes moral questions to scrutiny and debate. Although, when he is a mere temple servant, the character of Ion has qualms about killing the birds 'that bring messages from the gods', he decides to be a slave to his human duties and never to 'cease serving him who feeds me', an unheroic and hypocritical pragmatic surrender to outward conformity and its system of economic beneficiaries, who include not only himself but the sections of the Athenian citizenry who made good money from building, supplying goods and services to, and promoting the official rhetoric.[160]

When the character of Kreousa is complimented on her illustrious ancestry, she replies that it has not been of any use to her, indeed has caused her three sisters to be put to death as sacrifices 'for the city', a riposte to those advocating conquering war and glorious death found in funeral orations and celebrated on the Parthenon.[161] The gods themselves

---

157 Eur. *Ion* 661. Ἴωνα δ' ὀνομάζω σε τῇ τύχῃ πρέπον, ὁθούνεκ' ἀδύτων ἐξιόντι μοι θεοῦ ἴχνος συνῆψας πρῶτος.

158 At lines 516, by the Chorus, and at 535 by Xuthus.

159 Other examples of appropriate punning names that were collected by Aristotle, *Rhetoric* 2.23 and by others are noted by Mayhew, Robert, ed., *Prodicus the Sophist: Texts, Translations, and Commentary* (Oxford: OUP, 2011), 37.

160 Eur. Ion 179–183.

161 Eur. Ion 264, 268. The playwright explicitly refers to the story of the sacrifice of the daughters of Erechtheus, which provided the topic for another play by Euripides

that claim to advise mortals on how to act do not practise what they are deemed to preach. Who can blame mortals if they copy the gods? It is the teachers who are to blame.[162] If the gods had to pay the fines that mortals are charged for their rapes, their temples would soon be empty, a reference to the role of buildings such as the Parthenon as strong-room repositories of a city's assets, including inflows of payments from fines.[163] Near the end of the play, the Chorus, who are not yet up to date with the civically reassuring raped-by-the-god explanation and are still xenophobic, pronounce their curse on the formal feast for the naming of Ion that is about to take place.[164]

In episode after episode, the play glories in pointing out quite how many and quite how implausible are the changes needed to the usual story if Ion is to be regarded as autochthonous. But the solution that the character of Athena, speaking as the personification of the city, offers in her *deus ex machina* culmination is straightforward. First, let there be no recriminations, and, second, maintain a silence. Let Xuthus continue to remain in ignorance of the 'true' story. And her advice appears to have been accepted. To Pausanias, writing hundreds of years later, as he listened to the stories being told elsewhere in Greece, Ion was the regular son of Kreousa and of her husband Xuthus, with no mention of the elaborate chains of coincidences, deceptions, plots, and surprises set out in the play.[165] In the list of genealogies and eponyms of the Athenian kings given by the learned Strabo, no alternatives to 'Ion, the son of Xuthus' was even mentioned.[166]

When, in 1890, on a stage in Cambridge, England, the play was publicly performed as a drama, not read as a literary text, perhaps for the first time for over two thousand years, Arthur Verrall, then a famous academic classicist who had helped make the arrangements, was horrified. Euripides, he declared, was a 'botcher', a 'bungler', and no 'true Greek'. He was 'morally a monster, intellectually a fool' and his works were 'unfit for our theatres'. Among the audience too, he

---

that tells a version of a myth that Joan Breton Connelly has conjectured is shown on the central slab of the Parthenon, as discussed above.

162 Eur. Ion 449.
163 Eur. Ion 447.
164 Eur. Ion 705–711.
165 Notably Paus.2.14.1; and 7.1.2.
166 Strab. 9.19.

reported: 'the revolting nature of the subject, unredeemed … by any serious purpose, provoked a merited disgust'. What sort of man', he thundered, deducing the personality of the author from the characters in his works, could proclaim that the oracles were frauds and that the gods do not exist? Only a 'rationalist' who hated 'embodied mystery'.[167]

A few years earlier, as part of the preparations, Verrall had published an edition and translation of the *Ion* with mainly respectful philological notes with no indication of the shock and sense of betrayal he was to experience after seeing it performed.[168] The 'men like ourselves' rhetoric had met its match. For if Euripides had pointed out to the classical Athenians that their gods were only a 'nomisma', a social convention that produced economic benefits for some, where did that leave the official religion of the audience? Unlike the DDs of Mars Hill who had mostly regarded the ancients as unfortunate pre-Christians doing their best with what they had, the intellectuals of Cambridge University, many of whom had lent their prestige to the Christian cause, were also now being forced into retreat, not by modern arguments but by ancient.

To return finally to the classical period, in attempting to reconstruct the interior mental experiences of real historic viewers of plays, the problem of evidence is almost insuperable, although I would suggest, made more imaginable by recovering the discursive environment within whose boundaries producers proffered and consumers received. Pausanias, the only sustained ancient observer of the interactions of images and stories whose work has survived, is more of an anthropologist looking in than a participant organising his experiences into words for his own memorializing purposes. We do however have another set of texts, the so-called 'Sacred Tales' of Aelius Aristides, a man much concerned about his own bodily health who, externally at least, took seriously the discourses of theism, of cognition, and of dreams prevalent in his own times and assembled into a long-lasting discursive environment.[169] One

---

167 All the quotations are from the chapter on the *Ion* in Verrall, A. W., Litt.D. Fellow of Trinity College, Cambridge, *Euripides, the Rationalist: A Study in the History of Art and Religion* (Cambridge: CUP, 1895), 129–165.

168 Verrall, A. W., ed., *The Ion of Euripides, with a Translation into English Verse and an Introduction and Notes* (Cambridge: CUP, 1890).

169 That Aristides was conventional is among the conclusions arrived at by Israelowich, Ido, *Society, Medicine and Religion in the Sacred Tales of Aelius Aristides* (Leiden: Brill, 2012), https://doi.org/10.1163/9789004229440.

of his works, the so-called 'Athena', although presented as a dream and a prayer, is an imagined walk among the monuments on the Acropolis of Athens, almost a companion to Pausanias, but one in which the statues, pictures, and the stories that they tell are integrated into a single paean of praise for the city, its history, its achievements, and its inventions, deeply internalised. Aristides begins, as is to be expected, with the birth of Athena on east pediment, interpreting it as a presentation of the indissolubility of the connection between Athens and the father of the gods, picking out a feature of the shield to allow his mind to remember Homer, with other authors, including Pindar, as infiltrating ('intertexualizing') his mind. He looks at the Gigantomachy of the metopes in much the same terms as the women at Delphi, and appears to let his mind meander to the stories on the west pediment, and other thoughts and interpretations that are unique to the occasion.

When in his peroration he addresses Athena, presented as an imagined presence on the Acropolis, he invokes a verse from a lost play by Aeschylus: '"Oh thou before the royal palace as sang the Chorus of Aeschylus" the heavenly palace and the greatest palace in our land, grant ... [etc]', and he reveals a mind so deeply infiltrated by traditions that, although a professional orator, he cannot compose his own words.[170] A prisoner of phrases removed from their first contexts to serve new rhetorical purposes, he may have thought that he was participating in a tradition that he was upholding and reinforcing, but he has become a reciter of words written by others to describe experiences allegedly felt by himself. The weight of the intermediate past, in modern terms, 'reception', has deprived him of independence and he has become a mere participant in a predictable ritual.

The waking dreamer does, however, sum up paideia as a series of hoped-for results, making explicit that the Acropolis is a visual equivalent of the long-enduring conventions of funeral orations and panegyrics. Banished are 'folly, wantonness, cowardice, disorder,

---

170 Ael. Ar. Orat. 2 16. My translation, with an amendment to Behr's translation, in Behr, Charles A., ed., *P. Aelius Aristides, The Complete Works* (Leiden: Brill, 1986), ii, 229 of 'phronesis' as 'intelligence' to accord more fully with the use of the word in the policy-making process noted in Chapter 1 from Aristotle's account of that process. The quotation is ἀλλ᾽ ὦ τῶν βασιλείων πρόδρομος μελάθρων Aeschylus fragment 216 renumbered from 388, apparently a description by Hekabe of the gates of Troy.

faction, scorn of the gods'. In comes 'rational consideration, moderation, courage, concord, good order, success, and honour of the gods and from the gods'.[171] Here we have a formal statement of why the Parthenon was built and of how those who commissioned and designed it intended that it would be seen and internalized by its users over the long term.

Isocrates had used the same phrase in an earlier speech, on the Areopagus: 'Yes, and who of my own generation does not remember that the democracy so adorned the city with temples and public buildings that even today visitors from other lands consider that she is worthy to rule not only over Hellas but over all the world'.[172] But then he had almost immediately undermined his implied claim that it had been rhetorically successful, by pointing out that the Thirty Tyrants who took over Athens after its defeat in the Peloponnese had plundered the temples and privatized the dockyards on which a thousand talents had been spent so that they could be destroyed and the land used for other purposes.

In the following chapter I offer another experiment in recovering the mentalities of the past by reviving another genre of ancient historiography that is also composed from the inside looking out. The 'rhetorical discourse' is offered as an example of those composed for the competitions at the philosophical schools in Athens during the first centuries CE.[173] The open-ended title allowed candidates a choice between opting for one of the more common and safer genres, such as panegyric or refutation of a well-known argument, and bolder alternatives, such as putting an argument into the mouth of a mythic or historic personage, a device much favoured by Libanius centuries later.

In the event, the speaker chose to follow the model attributed to Laurentius, a superintendent of temples and sacrifices, who

---

171 Aristides, *Complete Works*, Behr edition, ii, 228. ' δι' ἣν ἀφροσύνη μὲ καὶ ἀσέλγεια καὶ δειλία καὶ ἀταξία καὶ στάσις καὶ ὕβρις καὶ ὑπερηφανία θεῶν καὶ πάνθ' ὅσα τοιαῦτ' ἂν εἴποι τις ἐκχωρεῖ· φρόνησις δὲ καὶ σωφροσύνη καὶ ἀνδρεία καὶ ὁμόνοια καὶ εὐταξία καὶ εὐπραγία καὶ τιμὴ θεῶν τε καὶ ἐκ θεῶν ἀντεισέρχεται.› Ael. Ar. Orat. 2 16.

172 Isoc. 7 66.

173 A survey of what Simon Swain calls the 'discursive practice' of the period, including the heavy use of themes and examples from classical Athens and its past, is provided by Swain, Simon, *Hellenism and Empire, Language, Classicism, and Power in the Greek World AD 50–250* (Oxford: Clarendon, 1996). As he notes, the variety is wide, and, at page 93, drawing on earlier work, he notes that the titles of at least three hundred and fifty recorded in the writings have come down to us.

was described by Athenaeus as 'proposing questions deserving of investigation; and at other times asking for information himself; not suggesting subjects without examination, or in any random manner, but as far as was possible with a critical and Socratic discernment; so that every one admired the systematic character of his questions'.[174] Laurentius is recorded as having been as knowledgeable about the literature of the Greeks as he was of his own, and also as possessing a large collection of books.[175] However, as with the experiment in Chapter 2, despite the evidence of the many parallels referred to in the editorial footnotes, our Pseudo-Laurentius shows him to have been a clumsy imitator writing much later.

Like the Thucydidean speech, the rhetorical discourse offered here is an experiment in reclaiming an ancient discourse that prescribes, or reveals the boundaries of, the socially constructed norms of the age, a form of historiography, not a work of imaginative literature such as a modern historical novel. Its attempts to recover some of the conventions that were shared between speakers and listeners, producers and consumers may help to build an understanding of the mentalities, or at least of the publicly displayed values, of those who looked at the classical-era Parthenon half a millennium after it was first brought into use, that is, at a time when, besides continuing in its former roles, notably as a backdrop to processions, sacrifices, and other community-building religious rites, it had become a site of heritage.

As with the Thucydidean speech, it exemplifies some of the conventions of the times as evidenced by passages in the surviving texts and by the advice of rhetorical manuals. The speaker has, for example, caught some of the rhetorical tropes of the so-called 'Second Sophistic', a modern term derived from the *Lives of the Sophists* written by Philostratos

---

174 Ath. 1.4.

175 'a library of ancient Greek books, as to exceed in that respect all those who are remarkable for such collections; such as Polycrates of Samos, and Pisistratus who was tyrant of Athens, and Euclides who was himself also an Athenian, and Nicocrates the Samian, and even the kings of Pergamos, and Euripides the poet, and Aristotle the philosopher, and Nelius his librarian; from whom they say that our countryman Ptolemæus, surnamed Philadelphus, bought them all, and transported them with all those which he had collected at Athens and at Rhodes to his own beautiful Alexandria'. Ath. 1.4. Only known as a character in a Platonic dialogue written long after Plato's time, it is impossible to say whether he ever existed other than as a useful fiction in an exercise.

in the fifth century CE, that retrospectively imputed a cultural unity to a group of writers in Greek, some practicing in Athens, who, between the mid-first and the fifth centuries CE, revived the traditions of classical Athens for which they showed great respect.

5. 'On the Temple dedicated to the Divine Minerva, vulgarly called the Parthenon'

O Men of Athens.[1] It is a time-honoured custom for the traveller who sets out on a perilous journey by land or by sea to swear an oath that he will set up an offering to the gods if he arrives safely. When we walk round the Acropolis, we admire the dedication made by the great Nikias, although it has lost its gilding.[2] Your city, all men know, honours the gods more than any other.[3] And we have more [*the speaker by his tone of voice and gesturing toward the Acropolis, indicates that he is about to repeat a conventional phrase*] 'things worth looking at' than any city in the Greek-speaking regions of our Roman imperium, in which the two great cities of Rome and Athens have long been allies and friends, united by our shared past.[4]

---

1   The speaker repeats the standard exordium expected in an oration in Athens. However, he also reveals his inexperience. A study that compared the usage of the phrase 'Men of Athens' with the alternative version that uses the vocative adverb 'O Men of Athens' has revealed that the latter was almost always used by Plato and that there are over a thousand examples in the Attic orators that our author is studying. However, by the time our author was writing, the vocative adverb implied a deliberate archaizing, and since in his case it is evidently not parodic, it is also an example of the many hazards that faced practitioners of rhetoric as they attempted an artificial form. Summarized from Dickey, Eleanor, *Greek Forms of Address from Herodotus to Lucian* (Oxford: Clarendon Press, 1996), 177. Paul of Tarsus, as reported by the narrator of the Acts of the Apostles, omits the 'O', one of many indications that he was competent not only in the Greek language, but in the conventions in his time.

2   Plut. Nic. 3.3. The speaker confirms that, as with the Seated Athena of Endoios, the Acropolis presented images that together showed the astonishing continuity over many hundreds of years.

3   This too is part of the conventional exordium, and was also factual. See the list in Chapter 1.

4   The speaker is careful to note that, formally, Athens remained an independent city, not part of the Roman province of Graecia, and that its classical-era institutions

       https://doi.org/10.11647/OBP.0279.05

I am certain I will have the sympathy of all here when I say that the vow this poor apprentice sophist made when he embarked on his journey was that, as one who is still unversed in the arts of persuasion, he might survive the ordeal of making his oration.[5] No old woman in Athens is going to accuse me of not being an Athenian because my Greek is [*pause for quotation*] 'too Attic for Athens'. [*Polite laughter at an old joke*].[6] Let me say, however, that although I come from a land more cold and more distant than that of Anacharsis the Scythian, ever since I was a boy, I have studied your Attic ways, and although I will always be your guest, Athens is now my city too.[7]

My chosen topic today, men of Athens, is our magnificent although out-of-sight Parthenon that amazes all who come to our city, as we all see with our own eyes.[8] Today the great work of Pheidias is still in the

---

still functioned, in name at least. As discussed in St Clair, *WStP*, Chapter 7, https://doi.org/10.11647/obp.0136.07, in the context of the Roman-era inscription on the front of the Parthenon, although that had probably already been removed, but not forgotten, by the time of the speech.

5   Oliver, James Henry, *The Ruling Power: A Study of the Roman Empire in the Second Century after Christ through the Roman Oration of Aelius Aristides* (Philadelphia: American Philosophical Society, 1953), 1. The comparison is so disproportionate that a modern reader might think that the speaker is mocking the conventions of rhetoric, but the evidence suggests that the display and performance of what to modern ears is obsequiousness were in the speaker's time regarded as normal, while also becoming ever easier for audiences, who were themselves trained in rhetoric, to discount and ignore.

6   The speaker, shifting from the solemnity of referring to himself in the third person, repeats the joke told about Theophrastus, Aristotle's successor, noted by Kennerly, Michele, *Editorial Bodies: Perfection and Rejection in Ancient Rhetoric and Poetics. Studies in Rhetoric/Communication* (Columbia, S.C.: The University of South Carolina Press, 2018), 11, from Cicero, *Brutus*, and Quintilian 8.1.2. The audience had heard boasts pretending to be modesty before, and some may have used the device in their own compositions. Although apparently joking, the speaker reveals that he is worried that his attempt to use pure classical Attic Greek may let him down. In his time a number of lexica aimed at addressing the problem had been produced, of which one, known in modern times as *The Antiatticist*, has survived. Discussed by Valente, Stefano, *The Antiatticist: Introduction and Critical Edition* (Berlin: de Gruyter, 2015), https://doi.org/10.1515/9783110404937.

7   The speaker deploys the double meaning of the Greek word ('xenos') as both stranger and guest.

8   The speaker repeats sentiments made explicit by a later travel writer who was, it seems likely, himself not saying anything original, set out in Heraclides of Crete, 'A view of Athens.' A fragment by an author of the third century BCE, previously attributed to Dicaearchus of Messene of the fourth century BCE. Translated into English by Stambaugh, John E., in 'The Idea of the City: Three Views of Athens' in *The Classical Journal*, Vol. 69 (4) (Apr.–May, 1974), 309–321, from Pfister, Friedrich,

Parthenon and, since the year of destruction that father Herodotus recounts, our citadel has never been plundered. It was our own Cicero who taught us that, with images, [*he quotes*] 'their beauty puts them in danger, but their size keeps them safe'.[9]

It was one of our city's founders, Theseus, who decreed that Persuasion ('Peitho') should be honoured with an image dedicated to her on the Acropolis, and the sacred woman appointed to superintend her shrine and the ceremonies that take place there was assigned a seat of honour at the theatre.[10] I know, as one who has chosen to pursue my studies amongst so many ancient [*quotes*] 'things that make us remember', that I can never aspire to an oration that is worthy of the majesty of our city, as many famous men have done in the past and

---

Die Reisebilder des Herakleides (Vienna, Rohrer, 1951). I have altered Stambaugh's translation to avoid his word 'costly' that may imply that readers and others judged the building against the price of constructing it, I also suggest that the rare word ἀποψιον, that Stambaugh translates as 'conspicuous' refer to the fact that the building was not visible from the town but came into view on special occasions, such as festival processions. The Greek phrase is transcribed by Davison, Claire Cullen, with the collaboration of Birte Lundgreen, ed. by Geoffrey B. Waywell, *Pheidias: The Sculptures and Ancient Sources* (London: Institute of Classical Studies, 2009), ii, 794. The speaker, without implying that the building does not have other uses, notes that its former purpose in promoting Athenian arete, as discussed in Chapter 2, has largely gone and it is now 'heritage' with a tourist economy as a reference to the good inns in the full version also suggests. By adopting the device of appealing to the sense of sight, 'autopsy', as a way of coopting listeners and later of readers, partly in order to attempt a paradox, the speaker risks appearing to be trying too hard to impress. He was however commended for stating the subject right at the beginning as the rhetorical handbooks recommend.

9   The speaker repeats a phrase used by Cicero in his case against Verres who removed innumerable artworks from the sacred places where they were used in the celebration of the gods into his private possession in his own houses, but who found some too costly to remove. Pulchritudo periculo, amplitudo saluti fuit, quod eorum demolitio atque asportatio perdifficilis videbatur. Cic. Ver. 2.4.110. The thought, presented as a general truth, helps to explain why the Parthenon and other buildings were over-engineered, possibly something that Cicero had learned while a student in Athens.

10   The speaker repeats the story reported by Pausanias 1.22.3, that the art of rhetoric ('Peitho' {'Persuasion') had been established in Athens in mythic times by Theseus, a late example of the practice discussed in Chapter 2, of conferring antiquity and authority on institutions and practices by claiming that they already existed in mythic times, the ancient equivalent of the invention of tradition. Peitho had both a statue and at least one priestess to service what we can guess was some regular commemorative ceremony involving processions, prayers, and the communal consumption of the food and drink shared with the gods. The special seat is recorded in an inscription CIA, iii. 351.

others will do in the future.[11] And we have all learned how wise it was of Euripides to warn that [*quotes*] 'speaking well can be a terrible thing if it brings harm'.[12] I will not just say whatever occurs to me at this moment.[13]

The last and greatest of the many gifts that our teacher Isocrates gave to our city in the darkest days of war was his warning to the intellectual men of that never-to-be-forgotten classical age against employing their skill with words not for the public good, but for what they themselves, or their faction, might expect to gain.[14] And as we know from the great Aristides, who also learned his craft here in Athens, any speaker who aims to please his audience rather than to lead them to what is in their best interests, is guilty of profaning the sacred mysteries of our profession.[15]

---

11   The speaker refers to the long tradition of speeches in honour of Athens, delivered by prominent men by invitation, of which a number survive and of which many more were available to be read in the speaker's time. He reminds his audience that the numerous memorials to be seen in Athens were not just material objects that, if paid attention to, reminded potential viewers of famous historical figures and episodes in the past, but performed the rhetoric function of instantiating a civic ideology, as in the concluding phrase of the treatise on how to achieve dignity in rhetoric by Aelius Aristides περὶ σεμνότητος. 'ἐν τῷ τελευταίῳ ὀνόματι, ἵν' ἐκεῖναι τοῦ τῆς πόλεως ἤθους μνημεῖον ὦσιν.' By the time these speeches were composed, much of the purpose of images, namely to influence minds and behaviour as was assumed at the time of the Thucydidean speech in Chapter 2 was giving way to a Roman notion that they should be treated as mobile, plunderable, and copyable objects for displaying the 'taste' of the appropriator, an episode in the history of the modern western notion of ancient 'art' that was adopted from the Roman authors in the early years of the revival of interest in the fifteenth century CE and that, in a modern garb, continues to stand in the way of any attempt to understand the ancient past.

12   The candidate, quoting the remark of a character in Euripides fragment 253, earns approval for acknowledging that rhetoric is a dangerous skill, a thought that the judges always have to confront. The thought is made more explicitly in Euripides fragment 56, where the character notes that skill in rhetoric can lead to injustice.

13   The speaker shows that he knows the advice in rhetorical manuals as satirised by Lucian in the dialogue known in 'The Professor of Public speaking' by turning round the advice to appear spontaneous and therefore sincere, caught by a chreia of an unknown poet that was to become proverbial 'λέγε ὅττι κεν ἐπ' ἀκαιρίμαν γλῶτταν ἔλθῃ' Luc. Rh. Pr. 18, while in fact plastering the speech with conventional references to Marathon and so on. Again the speaker shows the judges of rhetorical skill that he understands the rhetorical devices for pretending not to be resorting to rhetoric.

14   The speaker invokes the long semi-autobiographical, at once self-pitying and pugnacious, defence of rhetoric as a truth-telling or as at least a sincere, discourse and of his own life as a successful member of the trade, that is itself an example of what he condemns, in the *Panathenaicus*, especially Isoc. 5 12.

15   The speaker refers to a remark in Oration 34, noted by Trapp, Michael, ed., *Aelius Aristides Orations. 1–2* (Cambridge, Mass and London: Loeb, 2017), xvi. Aristides

You will hear many say that the graphic and plastic arts are like the verses that we learn and that we recite. Like Aristodemus of Caria, they tell you how light and shade show whether a man is mad or in sorrow, and how the different colour of the garments of heroes match the trees and the mountains and shimmer in the clear or the misty air in which they are wrapped.[16] But I do not wish to offer just a display piece ('epideixis') but something that will be of benefit.[17] And here, O men of Athens, allow me to say that, though a stranger, in Athens I have found men – as Euripides wisely says, [*pause*] 'Able to inspire one, though he were speechless before, to eloquence and skill'.[18] [*Murmurs of approval that the speaker has got off to a good start with his exordium*].

---

appears to refer to the trade secrets of the guild of which one, in this case, is the need to persuade an audience to a particular point of view, even at the expense of truth. Since the Panathenaic teems with examples of exaggeration, fake history, and absurdity, the speaker's praise of spin over truth may not have played well with judges who disliked any remark that suggested that they employed tricks of their trade. According to the author of a rhetorical manual known as Menander Rhetor, the Panathenaic of Aelius Aristides was the best model for a eulogy of the city. Noted by Loraux, Nicole, *The Invention of Classical Athens, The Funeral Oration in the Classical City, translated by Alan Sheridan* (Cambridge Mass: Harvard UP, 1986), 256.

16   The speaker boldly distances himself from a type of rhetorical exercise that was gaining in popularity, a commentary on an image, sometimes on one that does not exist. His words follow or anticipate the defence of the genre offered by the elder Philostratos. To judge by the extant examples, these exercises in 'ekphrasis' were much like more elaborate versions of the stories that the women visitors to Delphi are reported as telling one another in the *Ion* of Euripides noted in Chapter 3 and they may have been appreciated by listeners who had few opportunities of seeing images of any complexity. The speaker may have been right that it was likely to have been chosen as the easiest option by other candidates but at the risk of boring the judges.

17   The speaker uses the formula that, on the surface, claims modesty but is also boastful, employed by Isocrates in his *Letter to the Children of Jason* Isoc. L. 6.5. Since the speech is intended to display the speaker's ability to compose a display piece, the contradiction is not made explicit. The speaker has adapted the rhetorical device of claiming not to be using rhetoric, as the judges might commend or dismiss but would certainly have noticed, with some even recognizing the source in a little-known work.

18   The speaker repeats in the same slightly archaic form sentiments deployed as the opening words of Aelius Aristides in his Roman oration that is, in some ways a companion piece to his oration in praise of Athens. Aristides, *Roman*, Oliver edition, 895, in which he adapts a quotation from a play of Euripides, now lost. As was becoming normal the speaker attributes the sentiments in his quotation to 'Euripides', rather than to a character in a play by Euripides. The speaker also lets slip that he has 'read' the quotation from Euripides not heard it in a live performance of the play, perhaps an indication that he may not even have read the whole play but

We who are privileged to be citizens of Rome as well as of Athens have much that makes us justly proud. As one of our own great poets who knew the history of our shared past declared... [*The speaker signals by his change of tone of voice that he is about to give a quotation in Latin*] 'Graecia capta ferum victorem cepit et artes intulit agresti Latio' ('Captured Greece took her savage conqueror captive and brought her artistic skills to rustic Latium').[19] And long before Horace, our priests had understood that the Greek Olympians are also our Roman gods, and that Athena and Minerva, Zeus and Jupiter, are only different names for the same deities. Today throughout our world we also all pay reverence to [*pauses*] 'Tyche' and to [*pauses*] 'Fortuna' and I am sure she will favour me today.

It was Marcus Tullius Cicero, the consul who saved Rome, who taught us that the laws of man must conform with the laws of [*he emphasizes*] 'Nature'.[20] To one of the greatest orators of all time, another man who learned his craft here in Athens, and who contests for the palm of glory with Aristotle, we owe the greatest work on the science of rhetoric, both for its theory and for its practical advice. One of the lessons he taught the world is that to be a great orator is not only a matter of learning skill with words, but of mastering all branches of knowledge.[21] I could mention, too, another of our sons, the great Marcus Terentius Varro, to whose works on divine antiquities we are all indebted.[22]

---

that he is repeating a tag ('chreia') from a repertoire he had learned as part of his training in rhetoric.

19   The speaker quotes in Latin the already famous tag from Horace, *Epistles*, 2.1.156 that celebrates how Roman writers, dramatists, architects, sculptors, painters, and others adopted Greek models, adapting them to their own circumstances and to their Roman verbal and visual languages and purposes. He demonstrates that he is familiar with both Greek and Latin, the two languages of the Roman Empire. And he makes a veiled allusion to the classical era development from brutishness narrative discussed in Chapter 1.

20   The speaker refers to Cicero's role in defeating the conspiracy of Catiline in 63 BCE and to his work *De Officiis* ('on Duties'). Discussed by Callanan, Keegan, *Montesquieu's Liberalism and the Problem of Universal Politics* (Cambridge: CUP, 2018), 54–61, https://doi.org/10.1017/9781108617277, as influencing Montesquieu's critique of Plato and Aristotle, and therefore on the search for a philosophy of history as discussed in St Clair, *WStP*, Chapter 8, https://doi.org/10.11647/obp.0136.08.

21   The speaker, flattering his audience, refers to Cic. de Orat. 1.20.

22   The speaker, who trails the topic of antiquities, had no need to mention Varro's description of the west pediment of the Parthenon that was mainstream, as discussed in Chapter 3.

[*Pauses and looks unhurriedly at the hour glass*] I could mention others, but none of us ever has enough time to perfect our discourse. I have therefore followed the wise practice of Demosthenes to lay out my thoughts like a moulder in clay who tries out his compositions to ensure that he chooses only the best version to be made into bronze or marble.[23] As we all know, the great Isocrates was still improving his matchless *Panegyric* in his ninety-first year, and when Plato died at the age of eighty, after a lifetime spent combing, curling, and his re-plaiting his dialogues, his heirs found a writing tablet in which he had arranged and rearranged the first words of his dialogue on government in deciding which would make the richest tapestry of effects.[24] But hear me, dear listeners, when I say that if I win the prize, I will devote the rest of my life to building on the sound foundation that Athens is giving me.

We Romans, like children who have been taught well by worthy parents, are now more Greek than the Greeks, more Athenian than Athens was at the height of her glory.[25] We owe a mutual debt ('charis') to those who rescued our divine art from the intruders from Asia who, like shameless whores, pushed their way into our households, took over our most precious possessions, and corrupted our ancient Attic purity.[26] You will not hear an untoward word from me, any more than

---

23   The speaker repeats a comment by Dionysius of Halicarnassus in his critical essay on Demosthenes, cited in the next footnote.

24   The speaker repeats the stories given by Dionysius of Halicarnassus in Usher, Stephen, trans., *Dionysius of Halicarnassus, Critical Essays* (London: Harvard UP, 1974, 1985), ii, 223–225, in which the art of rhetoric is compared to other arts, including music, not mentioned here. I have slightly altered Usher's translation to bring out the notion of multicoloured, as in the word ποικίλως. Whether the judges approved of the speaker suggesting that he could be the new Isocrates or Plato or thought that he was a pushy young man aiming for a political career is not known. It is possible that he was simply repeating a cliché of the schools, as the phrase, 'as is well known', that is used by Dionysius, may imply. Most probably, if we had information about how the speech was delivered, say with winks and gestures, he was playing safe in persuading the judges that he was 'one of us' who knew the conventions. The passage prides further evidence that the verbal and the visual were regarded as alternative or complementary types of rhetoric.

25   Discussed with especial reference to Dionysius of Halicarnassus by the essays contributed to Hunter, Richard, University of Cambridge, and de Jonge, Casper C., eds, *Dionysius of Halicarnassus and Augustan Rome: Rhetoric, Criticism and Historiography* (Cambridge: CUP, 2019), https://doi.org/10.1017/9781108647632. By jumping from you to we, the speaker presents himself as both Greek and Roman.

26   The speaker, besides flattering at least some of the judges, shows them that he is familiar with the works of Dionysius of Halicarnassus who, using the prostitution metaphor, postulated a narrative of moral degeneration and regeneration not

in the works of Isocrates. I have attempted, as Thucydides did, to read what was said at the time and the writings of our modern sophists who have increased our understanding. And although this is not the right occasion to list any weaknesses in style, in arrangement, and in choice of words, which are inevitable, and, we would all agree, forgivable when an author or speaker decides to break away from the traditions of his time, we are wary of any author or speaker who shows himself to be rough, inconsistent, and impure.[27] You will not hear me beginning a discourse by calling the Athenians the children of brutes, nor attributing to Pericles, unworthy words that our greatest statesman could never could have allowed to pass through the portals of his mouth.[28] As the

---

dissimilar to those devised by the philosophers of history in the long eighteenth century, and that was now being applied not only to the arts of rhetoric, including visual rhetoric, usually attributed, in part at least, as Dionysius in his writing does, to indulging in 'oriental' excess and luxury and to an accompanying commercialization of rhetoric, as leaders competed to mislead the masses in a competition for civic offices and honours as well as for money. It is, as he may have realized, a risky strategy, since by playing on fears of immigrants, he undermines his general position that the Athenians of the old days, whenever they were, were so deeply imbued with 'arete' that they would not have allowed the corruption to take a grip.

27 The speaker, attempting a balancing act, but veering towards the remarks of Dionysius of Halicarnassus, who at various points describes the writings of Thucydides as 'troublesome', 'affected', 'harsh', 'puerile', 'cold', 'less intelligible than the riddles and darker than the obscurities of Heraclitus', and 'as intricate as the windings of the labyrinth,' examples as translated from the Greek words that are also given, by Burges, George, A. M., late of Trinity College, Cambridge, ed., *Prolegomena on the peculiarities of Thucydidean phraseology, translated, abridged and criticized by G. Burges* ... (Cambridge: apparently privately printed, c. 1837), 1. In another passage, in his *Thucydides,* 34 that deals specifically with the Thucydidean speeches, Dionysius draws a distinction between native talent and skill in leaned rhetoric, reporting how educated opinion was sharply divided between fervid admirers who talked of 'divine inspiration' as a form of romanticism, and those, such as Dionysius himself who reserved the right to apply his own standards, that are mainly about judging the extent to which speeches and writings conform to rule-based conventions that are mainly linguistic. How far the author may have had access to primary fifth- and fourth-century documents that set out the justifications for building the Parthenon but have perished, is not knowable, but the remarks of Dionysius could, with justice, be levelled at the text of Chapter 2.

28 Like Dionysius, the speaker disowns the conventions of the Thucydidean speech, in effect advocating a polite and inoffensive blandness, such as Dionysius demonstrated in his suggested rewriting of some of the speeches and criticisms of the complex, uneven, and sometimes dense, style of Thucydides that does not conform to convention, that was now been being reduced to a set of rules and linguistic taboos. In fact Isocrates, who has become the most admired model to be followed makes plentiful use of the brutishness narrative, referring to it explicitly

poet said, among the Athenians there is nothing that cannot be talked about.[29]

Some of your speakers have been laughed at for repeating too much of what is already familiar, others for venturing too far into the new, and yet others for imitating the finches in the fields and the sparrows in the agora that pick up fallen seeds from here and there.[30] It is indeed presumptuous of me to bring, as they say, [*a pause signifies a famous phrase coming up*] 'owls to Athens', but, if you honour my discourse with a prize of a crown of olive, I will take some of them away.[31] And it

---

on at least three occasions, and it remains standard, even when the wording is slightly less in-your-face. It is perhaps in response to such criticisms, that are only linguistic, that Aelius Aristides in his Panathenaic oration of 155 CE, that retells the brutishness narrative in almost the same terms as it was offered by the character of Pericles, by Thucydides himself, and by many others as discussed in Chapter 1 and whose work is among the best evidence for the astonishing durability of the discursive and rhetorical environment over more than half a millennium and longer, and therefore excellent evidence for the validity of the data on which my two experiments are based, eschews the word 'brutish' and its cognates, contenting himself with saying that Athens was the first 'city', leaving the 'oikos' stage that preceded it unspoken. In his rhetorical speech to Athena, that also avoids the word, he speaks of Athena having persuaded the prehistoric, oikos-stage, Athenians to give up 'their solitary mountain life and to assemble and dwell together in the compass of a single, common settlement.' Behr, Charles A., ed., *P. Aelius Aristides, The Complete Works* (Leiden: Brill, 1986), ii, 223.

29   The speaker draws authority to criticize from a line from the classical era old comedy poet Eupolis, τί δ' ἔστ' Ἀθηναίοισι πρᾶγμ' ἀπώμοτον; The phrase was used as justification for saying something that needed to be said, however unwelcome, by Dio of Prusa in his thirty-second oration to the people of Alexandria, D. Chr. 32.6, and later by Aelius Aristides. It is another example of the longevity of the discursive environment. In practice, classical era politicians, notably Cleon, tried to limit the freedom that old comedy enjoyed, including being slanderous and unfair.

30   The Greek word 'spermologos' was used both literally as a bird that picks up seeds that fall from different bails of grain and other merchandise and, metaphorically, as a term of mild derision for those who hang about the agora picking up and repeating the overheard views of others without any coherence, what today might be called post-modern eclecticism. The word was used by the author of the Acts of the Apostles, imprecisely translated in the King James version as 'babbler,' in his reported summary of how the members of one of the philosophical schools described Paul of Tarsus after hearing his speech at the Areopagus.

31   The speaker, in an attempt at humour such as is recommended by the rhetorical handbooks, makes a play on the saying 'taking owls to Athens', that means both a waste of time, because there are already so many owls there, juxtaposed with the other meaning of owls, also implied by the proverb, as the silver coins he will receive if he wins the prize. It was probably already an old joke when it was made by Euelpides, a character in the *Birds* by Aristophanes, line 301, first produced in 415 BCE. Since the coins were no longer in use, his humour may have appeared forced, old-fashioned, and donnish. The ancient listeners may however also have heard an

was the same master, who after considering the many different ways in
verse and in prose in which men have chosen to write, such as histories
of wars, genealogies of demi-gods, and dialogues, decided that for
discussing the affairs of Hellas, the discourse is superior to all others.[32]
As he taught us, listening to a speech that is read from a prepared text
enables orators to set forth facts in a lofty style with striking figures
of speech and modulations of voice, but I promise you, honoured sirs,
I will not to burst into song.[33] [*Polite laughter but also some murmurs of
impatience that the speaker is devoting too much time to showing that he knows
the conventions of the exordium before getting on to the arguments*].

And today I myself follow the advice of the masters to give examples
of my argument not only with Greek poetry and history but with
antiquities.[34] As our teacher Isocrates, whose wisdom grew deeper the
longer he lived, has advised: [*quotes*] in any school of rhetoric the first
question is 'what is the object of the discourse as a whole and of its
parts' and, as he taught us [*quotes again*] 'it is necessary to aim direct
at the mark'.[35] Although some experienced men have suggested that

---

implied compliment to themselves as wise owls. The speaker's joke asserts that he
wishes to be taken seriously as a promising trainee who knows something of the
discursive world of the Second Sophistic. By showing that he is 'one of them', he
sets up a bond as in an aside by an actor to the audience in a theatrical performance.
He also signals to the audience that he knows that they will discount much of what
he has already said as mere display. And like the Commissioners, to whom his
speech is in the nature of a reply informed by long hindsight, he too sometimes
tries too hard. But he also prepares the ground for his critique of Phidias later in
his discourse.

32   Isocrates, *Antidosis*, 15. 46. It is not known whether the judges were impressed that
      the candidate had found such an apposite quotation that flattered their profession
      or marked him down for repeating a tired cliché that every student at the rhetoric
      school had learned on the first day if not before and repeated *ad nauseam*.

33   The judges realize that the speaker has set them up for a joke in which they can
      share, by alluding to the remark by Isocrates in the same passage that a good
      rhetorical discourse was as enchanting as listening to a sung poem. The speaker, far
      from being a dutiful plodder had evidently understood that, in the game in which
      they were all engaged, he had to show that he understood the rule that a parodist
      must always signal that he is being playful.

34   The speaker refers to Cicero's *De Oratore* ('on the orator') that includes what he
      says, although he could be accused of exaggerating the advice to bring antiquities
      into a speech.

35   The speaker refers to the discourse by Isocrates known as *To the Children of Jason*,
      7. The judges, who were themselves teachers, were flattered at the notion that
      age brings wisdom which Isocrates, who lived into his nineties, often claimed as
      applicable to himself.

occasionally, the master was inclined to exaggerate, and may even, like Homer, have sometimes nodded.[36] Nor do I want to appear to speak on both sides of the question like the former pupil at our school who was invited to praise the beauty of Helen's womanhood but was lured into defending the actions of the scheming Lacedaimonian whore.[37] But it was the same great master, who after considering the many ways in verse and in prose in which men have chosen to write, such as histories of wars, genealogies of demi-gods, and dialogues, decided that for discussing the affairs of Hellas, the discourse is superior to all others.[38] As he taught us, one that is read enables us to set forth facts in a lofty style, but I promise you, honoured sirs, I do not intend to sing. [*Some laughter but also relief that he has now sidled up to the main question*].

Isocrates, whose works we study as models ('paradeigmata'), declared towards the end of his long life, that Pericles [*here the speaker again signals that he is quoting*] 'because he was both a good leader of the people and skilled in the arts of rhetoric, beautified the city with so many temples, dedications, and all manner of other things, that even today visitors who come to Athens think her worthy of ruling not only the Hellenes but the whole world'.[39] And it becomes a duty laid on us,

---

36 The speaker shows that he knows that the style of Isocrates was criticized by Dionysius of Halicarnassus, but since he wants to avoid offending anyone in his audience, or being drawn into making a judgment, he does not go into detail, but carries on, knowing that, with his minimum qualificatory phrase, he has protected himself against a range of comebacks.

37 The speaker refers to the story recounted by Isocrates in his rhetorical exercise known as 'To Helen' 1 and then 14. As teachers of rhetoric and admirers of Isocrates the judges appreciated the skill with which the speaker had managed to take his discourse on to the unfamiliar ground of criticising the makers of the Parthenon, a transition that other competitors had been unable to negotiate, as those set the subject for the competition had foreseen. He at last revealed that he had boldly chosen the rhetorical genres known to the ancients as protrepsis or paraenesis.

38 Isocrates, *Antidosis*, 15. 46. It is not known whether the judges were impressed that the candidate had found such an apposite quotation that flattered their profession, or, as is more probable, they marked him down for repeating a tired cliché that every student at the rhetoric school had learned on the first day and repeated *ad nauseam*.

39 By repeating the vocative, the speaker signals that he is again serious and indeed makes one of the most important claims in the whole piece. Isoc. 15 234. τὸ δὲ τελευταῖον Περικλῆς καὶ δημαγωγὸς ὢν ἀγαθὸς καὶ ῥήτωρ ἄριστος οὕτως ἐκόσμησε τὴν πόλιν καὶ τοῖς ἱεροῖς καὶ τοῖς ἀναθήμασι καὶ τοῖς ἄλλοις ἅπασιν, ὥστ' ἔτι καὶ νῦν τοὺς εἰσαφικνουμένους εἰς αὐτὴν νομίζειν μὴ μόνον ἄρχειν ἀξίαν εἶναι τῶν Ἑλλήνων ἀλλὰ καὶ τῶν ἄλλων ἁπάντων, καὶ πρὸς τούτοις εἰς τὴν ἀκρόπολιν οὐκ ἐλάττω μυρίων ταλάντων ἀνήνεγκε. I have modified

who are men of today, to consider, as truthfully as we can, and without
falling into the conventions of a competition work, how far the success
that the Parthenon was intended to encourage by word, did achieve
in deed.[40] As their own wise and elegant writer pointed out when the
building was still new, the Athenians of that time did not come together
as a united people.[41] As the historians whom we study, and especially
Xenophon, whom many regard as the greatest of them all, have shown
with their well-evidenced writings, it is questionable whether the great
men of that age entirely succeeded in bringing about what was intended
by their much-vaunted [*he stresses*] 'paideia'. As Thucydides tells us, the
demos of Athens, before they had even completed the Parthenon and
the other buildings on the Acropolis, was so incensed at the desecration
of some priapic old herms in the town, that they almost reverted to
brutishness, an example of the wisdom of Plato and Aristotle and also,
O men of Athens, a warning to us all.[42] It is a mistake that the demos of
today will never make.[43]

---

the translations that take the passage at face value as commending the Periclean
building programme for its effectiveness. Its throwaway tone however and its
choice of the word ἐκόσμησε, which implies that the changes are cosmetic and
superficial, suggest that he is not inventing a notion of 'beauty' in the western
romantic sense as often appears to be the case in modern translations, but is setting
up a proposition to be knocked down, in which he is followed by the author of the
rhetorical discourse. The translation of the phrase ῥήτωρ ἄριστος, that can also
be read as disdainful, is usually taken to refer to his effectiveness as a speaker in
persuading the institutions of Athens to support his plans; I have also modified it to
give him credit for the visual rhetoric that influenced the visitors when the project
was implemented.

40   At this point, with his absurd claim that he was not offering a rhetorical exercise,
some of the judges began to worry that this candidate was at risk of copying a
magician who explains his tricks, if not quite mocking the arts of rhetoric as such.
The speaker and the judges however also knew that Isocrates, whose works were
almost all rhetorical exercises, had claimed that they were not. For example, in *To the
Children of Jason*, 4.

41   The speaker refers to Xenophon's *Hellenica*, a continuation of Thucydides, who
suggested that the lack of military success was the fault of the Athenians themselves.
The speaker reveals himself as a promoter of mainstream opinions, and as finding
Xenophon who wrote on many subjects as easier to read than Thucydides.

42   The speaker refers to the episode recounted by Thucydides in which he endorses the
brutishness narrative. ἀλλὰ καθ᾽ ἡμέραν ἐπεδίδοσαν μᾶλλον ἐς τὸ ἀγριώτερόν
Thuc. 6.60.1 and 2.

43   The speaker knows that the accommodation that the demos of his day and
earlier made with the Romans, that many commentators later presented as a

The classical Athenians thought they could turn every metic into an Anacharsis by telling them stories, showing them pictures, and allowing some to participate in some festivals. But, sadly, as we all know, they failed to turn the most talented, the richest, the most beautiful, and the most highly favoured of all the great men of that time into a well-paideia-ed Athenian.[44] But what, I ask you, could the Athenians have expected from a man who had been brought up by a Lacedaimonian nurse?[45] And although the Athenians liked to say that Themistocles, the victor of Salamis, was a hero who took our paideia to the tyrants of the East, he traitorously clothed himself in garments of gold and he smelled of frankincense and myrrh. He even ceased to speak our incomparable Attic language but babbled like a Mede.[46] He may have lived as the saviour of Hellas, but he died a satrap in an oriental court.

As we look out from our Acropolis through the Propylaia to our matchless harbour, we also remember, my dear friends, that we cannot trust images to tell the truth. And just as our historians are showing that old stories cannot be believed, so too our poets tell us that even the memories preserved in the tombs dug into our land, which we were taught when we were boys were the best ways of preserving a memory of the past, were intended to persuade us to believe that what they

---

sell-out incompatible with the civic values presented on the Parthenon and in the self-fashioning literary texts of the classical period could itself be fitted into the development from brutishness story as a worthwhile new stage.

44   As his audience knew from the description, the speaker refers to Alcibiades.

45   The speaker recalls that, according to Plutarch's *Life of Lycurgus*, 16.3, Alcibiades, as a baby, had been brought up in the Spartan custom without swaddling bands. Although some Athenians evidently saw that babies who were allowed to move their bodies were more content, the speaker upholds the traditional Athenian preference for tight constriction, as leading to a disciplined life, as shown on many images and possibly on the Parthenon. He also alludes to the standard convention, associated with geodeterminism, that the land itself was a wet nurse.

46   The speaker repeats points made in an ecphrastic rhetorical exercise composed, on allegedly looking at a statue of Themistocles, by Philostratos the Younger in his *Imagines*, ii, number 31. Gold, frankincense and myrrh, were the gifts that the Magi from the east are said to have brought to the infant Jesus in the Christian biblical story. As used by Philostratos, frankincense and myrrh are not, however, welcome gifts implying respect but oriental smells that 'pollute the air' and that, by implication in the Exercise, reveal anxieties about immigrants and the destabilizing non-Athenian, and non-Hellenic ideas and customs that they bring, that were more pronounced in Hellenistic and Roman times than in the classical era.

appeared to say was true and useful, as I am obliged to do today with the words of my mouth, although with sadness in my breast.[47]

The old Athenians paid no attention to the signs sent to warn them, the outbreak of plague described by Thucydides in one of his better passages that showed what he was capable of, in which he described how many of the common people, and some who ought to have known better, in their fear abandoned their belief that the gods could help them.[48] And even when, less than a quinquennium later, the temple itself was struck by the Earthshaker, the men of that time turned away their eyes from a proper understanding.[49] Within a generation our city had to accept a Spartan garrison into our acropolis and to submit to the rule of the Thirty Tyrants.

An outward show of grandeur, O men of Athens, when its skin is easily peeled away, turns into mere bombast. As Euripides asked the men of that age, of all the ills that Hellas has to suffer, are any men more useless to a city than the overpaid athletes whose bodies shine like the statues of heroes but who have none of the skills needed in war?[50] Our ancestors should have listened to Diodotos who told them never to

---

47		The speaker appears here to have some knowledge of the work of Dictys of Crete, long thought to have been composed in the fourth century, until the discovery of a fragment of papyrus reused as a tax record in 208 implied that it already existed in the second, and is picking up on ideas already current in the discursive environment.

48		While appearing to praise Thucydides, the speaker implies that his achievement was only as a stylist in the Greek language which was mainly how his work was kept current not only in the Roman period but in Byzantium.

49		Korres, Manolis, 'The Parthenon from Antiquity to the 19th Century', in Tournikiotis, Panayotis, ed., *The Parthenon and its Impact in Modern Times* (Athens: Melissa, 1994), 138.

50		The speaker summarizes a long passage thought to be from the *Autolycus*, a lost play by Euripides, preserved by Athenaeus, X 413 ff. The judges could not fault him for attributing the sentiment to Euripides rather than to a character in a play by Euripides nor for failing to mention that the sentiment was almost certainly spoken in the play as part of a dialogue in which another character offered an opposing argument. Indeed it was as a chreia that Athenaeus preserved it. And, although the point was well made that the skills that the athletes were honoured for, running, boxing, wrestling, and throwing the discus, were of little value in war, some of the judges who understood the huge contribution that such games made to the economy, including to their own incomes as suppliers of commodities, such as olive oil, and who themselves enjoyed watching the brutality and wounding to be seen in such contests, are thought to have murmured against the continuing influence of Euripides as against the direct moralizing of Seneca.

forget what it was they were aiming to do.[51] Instead of giving the people clear and consistent lessons, their rich, out-of-touch, and pampered politicians reverted, as usual, to showing off in front of one another, competing in the complexity of the images they commissioned and the stories that they presented.[52] The birth of Athena was a good choice for one of the Parthenon pediments, but, as for the other pediment, even Pausanias, who has been so diligent in collecting the stories that the cities of Hellas tell themselves, understood that the Athenians of former times, in commissioning the picture of Theseus bestowing democracy on our city, went too far. As he notes, they departed so far from picturing our true past that it could not be accepted even by the common people whose only knowledge comes from having seen plays or hearing stories from their childhood nurses and womenfolk.[53] And, unlike those who lived and studied here, he made mistakes that are difficult to correct.[54] Only when a work pleases people from different walks of life and of different ages can it bring about the needed unanimity.[55]

None of the Athenian generals who were appointed in accordance with their [*pause*] 'democratic' customs [*signifies some disdain, although many of these customs were still being adhered to in form*] was successful, except occasionally and only for a short time. They had no Lysander who,

---

51   Diodotos, the otherwise unknown citizen, who successfully urged the Athenians to have second thoughts about putting the whole population of Mytilene to death in the debate recorded in the Thucydidean speech offered by Thuc. 3.36–49.

52   A point arrived at independently on general stylistic grounds by Ashmole, Bernard, *Architect and Sculptor in Classical Greece* (New York: NYU Press, 1972), 116. '… induces the uneasy feeling… that it was dictated by a kind of artistic *hybris*.'

53   The speaker refers almost verbatim to the remark by Pausanias in Paus. 1.3.1, one of many indications that Pausanias understood that the role of stories as nomismata, a word he occasionally uses in its many cognates and that, in modern translations is sometimes inadequately translated as 'believed.' The judges may have agreed with the implication that Pausanias was often naïve and uncritical, as when, for example, he declared that the Persian force that was repulsed at Marathon had brought a piece of Parian marble from which they had intended to make a monument to their victory that was used by Phidias in the making of the cult image at Rhamnous. Paus. 1.33. 2.

54   The speaker may refer to what Pausanias wrote about the west pediment of the Parthenon, discussed in Chapter 4, comparing him unfavourably with Varro who had been a contemporary of Cicero, albeit at the Academy founded by Plato, a different school from that where Cicero studied.

55   A point made by Longinus, 183, referring to verbal rhetoric, although the image that he conjures up, from *Odyssey* 11.315, is visual. It is unusual for an ancient author to criticize Homer.

over his long career as a leader of Sparta, showed the common soldiers what war must be by personally killing hundreds of enemies with his own hands. The Athenians, who followed the men of Marathon, for all their boasts about being worthy sons, produced no great conquerors like our Sulla, a new son of Peleus like our great sacker of cities, who destroyed the luxury-loving corrupted city of Corinth, famous then only for its harlots, lawfully killing, enslaving, and carrying off a great booty.[56] Sulla, although he was unfairly criticised by some jealous Greeklings at the time, ensured that statues by famous Greek sculptors now decorate the houses of rich men in Rome, not only proclaiming their wealth to the vulgar mob but giving themselves a well-deserved reputation for discernment and civility. For these noble Romans, only the best of the best age of Greece would do, whether to take them away and set them up far from here or to copy them in marble so that many more men and women can enjoy them.[57] And although Sulla has been criticized for taking too much, he left much undestroyed, including [*he gestures*] the stories on the temple of Minerva that were, some say, made by the hands of Pheidias himself.[58]

56　The speaker alludes to the opening line of the *Iliad*, where Achilles, son of Peleus, is celebrated for having sacked many cities.

57　The remark helps to explain why the many copies of Greek statues made in Roman workshops, for which we are dependent for imagining many lost 'masterpieces' that are recorded in the literary record did not include any examples of what is today often called archaic art. The Romans evidently shared the view of Socrates reported in the Hippias Major, noted in Chapter 2, that the archaic style would attract ridicule. Why the Roman versions whether of works first made in marble, apparently did not add the colour that the works being replicated mostly did, has not yet been satisfactorily explained, although it is easy to think of possible reasons. I am grateful to Antonio Corso for his advice on the first part of this note.

58　The decision of Sulla not to destroy the Parthenon could be regarded as a success for the Periclean programme of rebuilding the Acropolis that put visuality and display or permanence at its centre. As Plutarch reported: 'But after a long time, at last, with much ado, he [Sulla] sent out two or three of his fellow-revellers to treat for peace, to whom Sulla, when they made no demands which could save the city, but talked in lofty strains about Theseus and Eumolpus and the Persian wars, said: "Be off, my dear Sirs, and take these speeches with you; for I was not sent to Athens by the Romans to learn its history, but to subdue its rebels." Plut. Sull. 13.4. Although Sulla did not sack the Acropolis, a decision that the ancient historians had no difficulty in explaining, his armies pursued their normal policies of killing, rape, pillage, and destruction of monuments in the town and in Piraeus.

Some great conquerors did not live by the normal laws of men but, as Euripides teaches us: 'If one must needs do wrong, far best it were to do it for a kingdom's sake.[59] Our monuments in Rome, like those of all good rulers, are honest in displaying the sufferings of foolish peoples who, instead of recognizing our superiority and enjoying the benefits of our rule, have had to be forced to submit to our will at the point of a sword.[60] Athens, the mother and the nurse of the arts and sciences, has had excellent makers of images of battles and of wars, both the old and the more recent. I need not mention Plistaenetus, the brother of Pheidias, nor Apollodorus, who invented the mixing of colours and the virtues of shadow. We remember and honour Euphranor, who in comparing his Theseus with that of Parrhasius, declared that while his rival's dainty version only ate roses, his had fed upon beef. [*Polite laughter*] And yet I do not believe that any one will want to compare the skill of an image maker with that of a general or would seriously believe that we should prefer the image to the real trophies of war, nor admire the imitation more than the truth.[61]

The Athenians who built the incomparable Parthenon liked to think that they had an empire ('arche'), but it was never more than a few islands and peninsulas, the claws of the land not the whole body, an

---

The archaeologists who excavated the Athenian agora in the twentieth century were able to identify a layer of ash and broken fragments of buildings that confirmed the fact of the destruction ordered by Sulla in 86 BCE. Noted by Miles, Margaret, M., *Art as Plunder: The Ancient Origins of Debate about Cultural Property* (Cambridge: CUP, 2008), 24, from personal observation. The providentialist explanation offered by Charles Lévêque was noted in St Clair, *WStP*, Chapter 16, https://doi.org/10.11647/obp.0136.16.

59   Quoted by Plutarch in Plut. Adolescens 3.

60   The speaker refers to images such as those that were to be displayed on the narrative column of Trajan. He may also have in mind the publicly displayed images of men having their tongues cut out shown in the British Museum 'BP-sponsored exhibition, I Am Ashurbanipal', which ran from 8 November to 24 February 2019, that invited viewers to regard Assyria as 'a great civilization', presenting it mainly in its own top-down, self-fashioning terms, with minimal reference to the Greek, Jewish, and other authors who offered a different story based on their own observations and experience.

61   The same sentiments were offered almost verbatim in Plutarch's On the Glory of the Athenians. Plut. De Gloria 2. The speaker, without causing offence, shows that he understands the debate that had worried practitioners of rhetoric, whether in words or images, since the time of Plato.

empire that existed more in their dreams than in any reality of power.[62] They thought that they would ensure the loyalty of the Ionians overseas by celebrating the Ionianness of the mother city, by including the overseas Ionians in their festivals, and by making them use the Athenian law-courts and Athenian currency, all measures that were intended for their mutual benefit. But the ships taking the overseas Ionians to Athens passed the ships going in the other direction, which were bringing in new colonists and extracting what they regarded as tribute, sometimes even in mid-year as new requirements arose.[63] They put the Ionian acropolises into the hands of their own men so that the people themselves gained no benefit from Athenian rule and even turned again to the Lacedaimonians.[64] In all these actions, they tried to rule by passing laws and decrees without sufficient understanding of the natural pride of their clients.

With our better knowledge, we can today all agree that, in many important ways, the old Athenians were right.[65] As our own master wrote,

---

62   A point made explicitly by Aristides, *Roman*, Oliver edition, 43.

63   *Ibid.* 45. The phrase that Aristides uses παρὰ τοὺς φόρους ἀργυρολόγων, appears to imply that they collected actual silver coins rather than that they incurred an obligation that could be met by altering the book entry for credit and liability. If so such an imposition would have played havoc with the local economies as the price of silver is likely to have risen sharply, relative to, say, olive oil or wine, as numerous small economies producing the same products scrambled to raise the cash. Over time, even allowing for economic benefits of increasing the money supply by credit, guarantees, and other non-cash forms of money, the tribute, however it was levied, is likely to have changed the terms of trade with harmful effects on the Ionian economies especially if the Athenian treasurers did not take active steps to recycle their surpluses, by, for example buying more of their production. We may have an example here of merchantilist thinking, of which there are many examples in the modern scholarly literature that tends to equate the 'wealth' of a jurisdiction such as the city-state of Athens by the amount of precious metal it holds in its treasury.

64   Aristides, *Roman*, Oliver edition, 46.

65   At this point the judges, sensing condescension, and that a but is on the way, assume that the formal exordium is over and that the author is sidling up to points he wishes to make on the substantial issues, although in practice, again showing that he knows his craft, the author postpones that moment with some more substantive, and indeed more interesting, words aimed at 'capturing benevolence' as the Latin writers on rhetoric called devices for encouraging the listeners to give a sympathetic hearing. The opening words of the speech of Paul of Tarsus, that were misunderstood and mistranslated by contemporaries and successors who were evidently not as fully immersed in the conventions as Paul was, not only exemplifies

in discussing how our minds can be influenced by associations: 'whether it is a natural instinct or a mere illusion I cannot say but one's emotions are more strongly aroused by seeing the places that tradition records to have been the favourite resort of men in former days than by hearing their deeds or reading their writings'.[66] The Athenians did right to hang the shields of their dead enemies on the Parthenon for all to see. The visitors who now flock there like sparrows following a hay cart, rushing about here and there with guides who tell them the silly stories that have been collected by Pausanias and his ilk, are impressed when they see the sword of Mardonius, although, if I am being completely honest, I cannot say that it really was the one taken from the Persian general.[67] The porch of the Caryatids is a fine building but, as was predictable, in all their temples the old Athenians were more interested in showing off the skill of their designers, managers, and workers than in striking terror into enemies and rebels, actual and potential. The Athenians chose well in showing the so-called Caryatids of the Erechtheum, who represent the women of the city of Caryes in Arcadia who treacherously sided with the Persians. As we all know, the men of that city were justly put to death and their city razed to the ground, and the womenfolk, who were justly condemned to slavery, are shown as wearing the long robes of mourning, condemned for ever to carry the burden of shame on their heads.[68] But again the old Athenians thought only of themselves. Our

---

the risks of assuming that words that are innocuous and appropriate, even intended to flatter, for one occasion, are easily misapprehended when repeated in another, but provides confirmation that all verbal utterances, including written utterances, are best regarded as speech acts delivered on a particular occasion for an implied audience. As discussed in St Clair, *WStP*, Chapter 22, Debates on Mars Hill, https://doi.org/10.11647/obp.0136.22.

66   The author, since he wishes his audience to assume that he assumes that they know the name of the famous man, and that they will be flattered at being co-opted into his illustrious company, quotes from Cicero *de Finibus* 5.1.2.

67   The judges marked down our author here, not for his celebration of state and imperial violence, which they commended but for his rhetorical mistake in trying to curry favour by apparently offering something in confidence, a rhetoric that implied that he was sometimes not honest with his audiences.

68   The author repeats the story made famous by Vitruvius, Vitr. 1.1.5. Modern authors, uncomfortable with the thought that the demos could have approved such a presentation have offered alternatives.

monuments in Rome display the sufferings of the foolish peoples who, instead of recognizing our superiority and enjoying the benefits of our rule, have had to be forced to submit to our will. Indeed, our practice is the same as that of all people who successfully hold sway over extensive territories and seas, including the kings beyond the eastern frontier.[69] The classical Athenians showed scenes of what happens to those who lose wars in their metopes but so did most other cities, and such images had already lost their power to shock or influence viewers.

It was that great philhellene, King Attalos of Pergamon, a second Maecenas, who recently showed us Athenians how educational stories can be told in stone. As we look up to our acropolis, we see a series of modern statues on our walls, that the king has generously dedicated, and that remind all visitors to our city and not just the ignorant tourists who flock to our acropolis from all over our sea, of the penalties of rebellion.[70] [*The audience can see or can remember seeing a number of human figures in the agonies of death, some of which were found during the Italian Renaissance, were unrecognized for what they were, and that made their way to a number of museums as shown in Figures 5.1 and 5.2. In the words of Andrew F. Stewart, who has recovered their history, 'they kneel, cower, sink, or sprawl in attitudes of corporeal abandon, pain, despair and death … Several are naked or half clothed … brute strength and savagery, gaping wounds, screams, snarls, gasps in pain frozen in death, blood spurts'*].[71]

---

69   The speaker refers to images such as those that were to be displayed on the narrative column of Trajan. He may also have in mind the publicly displayed images of men having their tongues cut out shown in the British Museum 'BP-sponsored exhibition, I Am Ashurbanipal', which ran from 8 November to 24 February 2019, that invited viewers to regard Assyria as 'a great civilization', presenting it mainly in its own top-down, self-fashioning terms, with minimal reference to the Greek, Jewish, and other authors who offered a different story based on their own observations and experience.

70   See note 61.

71   *Ibid.* 1.

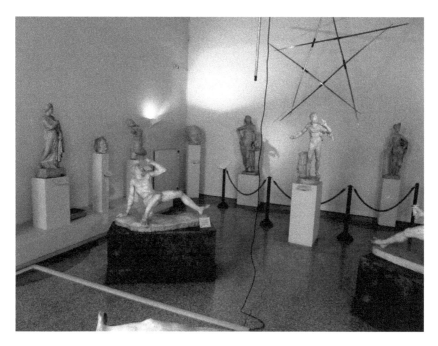

Figure 5.1. 'Little Barbarians' from the Acropolis of Athens, among other ancient statues, as foils for a modernist installation. Author's photograph at Venice Biennale, 2013. CC BY.

Figure 5.2. One of the Little Barbarians, known as 'The Persian'. Vatican Museum, Galleria dei Candelabri, 2749 no 32. Author's photograph, 17 October 2016. CC BY.

So what, I hear the judges ask, were the underlying causes that brought about the failure of the Parthenon? What, you all now want to know, was the 'truest reason'?[72] Men may change the law when it is appropriate to do so but we do not admit discussion of what Nature has made immutable. For, like old boundary stones and set-up inscriptions ('stelai'), they tell us only of the first decisions.[73] It is right to respect the ancients, but we should not be afraid of them nor appear to honour those who are famous for giving us their wisdom rather than honour the ideas themselves. I am not another Timaeus, who corrected the stylistic faults of Plato and Aristotle, for to be jealous of writers who are beyond all imitation is both undignified and stupid.[74] If someone disagrees with Plato, let him be listened to unless his arguments do not stand up in a dialogue, for as Plato himself told us, nothing comes before the truth.[75]

What I am now about to say may seem unpleasant, and if I had made my own choice, I would have remained silent, but friends who heard me conversing urged me to enter the competition and so ensure that my views are made public.[76] And now, since [*he pauses*] 'Necessity' obliges me, I am certain from what I have already learned here that I will have no difficulty in persuading you.[77] There can be much glory in making

---

72   The speaker quotes the famous words of Thucydides as his audience would immediately recognize, not only for themselves, but as a rhetorical signal that he is now approaching the main point of his argument.

73   The speaker reminds the audience that inscriptions in stone have their own rhetoric offered at the moment they were set up in accordance with the aims of those who authorized them, and as Socrates told Phaedrus, they do not go on saying the same things for ever. Plat. Phaedrus 275d already noted in St Clair, *WStP*, Chapter 1, https://doi.org/10.11647/obp.0136.01.

74   The speaker repeats the sentiment of Plut. Nic. 1.4.

75   The speaker upholds the tradition of critical engagement as against hero-worship or celebrity, using almost the same wards as those employed by Aristides in his *Defence of Oratory* 2D. An example of an actual boundary stone is shown as Figure 21.18 in St Clair, *WStP*, Chapter 21, https://doi.org/10.11647/obp.0136.21. His words anticipate later traditions of sacralizing selected texts and attempting to discover timeless meanings by hermeneutics.

76   Putting the responsibility on to unnamed friends and so claiming modesty and providing an exit if the views turn out to be unwelcome is one of the oldest devices in the rhetorician's repertoire, used, for example by Isocrates, Isoc. 5 7. We can be sure that members of the audience were not taken in, and indeed the speaker may have indicated with his tone that he was not claiming sincerity or spontaneity, staples of romanticism. Discussed by Kennerly, *Editorial Bodies*, Chapter 1.

77   The speaker shows that he has understood the rhetorical convention by which a transition is made from praise to criticism, a problem of 'prooemia' to which the authors of rhetorical manuals devoted much ink. The speaker here follows the

fine words and in making fine images, but only when they match the actions themselves and do not deceive. As Homer sang of Odysseus, a man of many wiles [*quotes*]:

> And many falsities he did unfold,
> That looked like truth, so smoothly were they told.[78] [*Ends quote*]

Pheidias was a great sculptor, as was Polycrates, two of the greatest makers before the hegemony of that divine art moved to Rhodes, where the Laocoon, the best of all works was made for us in Rome, as is universally acknowledged. But, as Antisthenes remarked when he was told that Ismenias, as a [*emphasises*] 'musician', played the pipes to the highest standard... [*Here the speaker adapts his tone to show he is quoting, with a pregnant pause in which a laugh can be raised and milked*] 'I agree with you but, as a [*emphasises*] 'man', he was useless [*pause*] ... for if it had been otherwise he could not have been a good piper'.[79] Those who, like his contemporary and also a master of the arts of persuasion, the venerable Isocrates, said that Pheidias was a mere doll-maker, were

---

advice of Apsines of Gaza, 81 and 69, as edited by Dilts, Mervyn R. and Kennedy, George A., *Two Greek Rhetorical Treatises from the Roman Empire: Introduction, Text, and Translation of the Arts of Rhetoric, Attributed to Anonymous Seguerianus and to Apsines of Gadara* (Leiden: Brill, 1997), 81 and 88, https://doi.org/10.1163/9789004330313.

78 The speaker turns to *Odyssey* XIX. 203, as Plutarch does to make the same point in his essay on the glories of the Athenians, itself an example of a rhetorical exercise.

79 The speaker, who takes the anecdote from Plutarch's *Life of Pericles,* politely lays the rhetorical foundations for making two related points, first that skill at making music could not be achieved without much training and practice, and secondly, that achieving a high level of skill must necessarily have been at the expense, in terms of time and opportunity cost, of the musician's knowledge of other matters, including education in paideia. The first observation provides an apparent justification for a sneering remark that, under the apparent cover of humour, attempts to coopt the audience into sharing his social-class-based, condescension and contempt, or at least to endorse and legitimate such attitudes. The advice of the rhetorical manuals that it is gross, and ineffectual, to sneer at whole groups has been ignored here, a slip for which the judges may have marked him down. The second argument, that Phidias was highly proficient as a worker in stone but that his technical expertise did not mean he had any wider understanding, was among the arguments used, without social sneering, by Aristotle in his general theory offered in the *Eudemian Ethics,* v, 7, in Kenny, Anthony, trans., *Aristotle: Eudemian Ethics, A New Translation* (Oxford: World's Classics, 2011), 80, https://doi.org/10.1093/actrade/9780199586431.book.1. Aristotle's argument may be an attempt to forestall a proto-romantic emerging notion of artist as seer, although his appeal to Euripides as a chreia in the same work, as noted in Chapter 2, suggests either that he was inconsistent or that he gave more weight to poets, 'makers', of words, than poets of images.

unfair, and all good men will condemn attempts by Envy to chip away at Fame.[80] Pheidias, to give him his due, was always careful to respect the laws and customs of the Athenians in small matters.[81] As an artisan and a manager of workmen, Pheidias was one of the best, but as a man of Athens, I shudder as I say it, Pheidias was not to be admired. Who, indeed, would want to be Pheidias, a man who for most of his life had to stand around in a filthy apron, bossed about by uncles, never leaving home, and like all banausics, obliged by his trade to fawn over clients and bend the truth like a slave? Socrates himself, and [*emphasizes*] he knew from his own experience, that makers of statues, like carpenters and shoemakers, suffer more than other craftsmen from illnesses to their eyes.[82] Even when Pheidias became rich and famous, he was a mere artisan, compelled to do whatever the Commissioners demanded, forever excluded from the company of the well-educated. Pheidias, we could have told him, should have done what Socrates did, and give up the fashioning of bronze and stone for the fashioning of fine words that benefit all mankind.[83]

---

80 'as one might have the effrontery to call Phidias, who made our statue of Athena, a doll-maker ...' Isoc. 15 2. The speaker resorts to the common rhetorical device of mentioning a derogatory remark with the apparent intention of disowning it, but which gives it as much currency as if he had said that he agreed with it.

81 The speaker may have had in mind the incident noted in Chapter 3 in which Phidias is reported as having obtained the approval of the Assembly to include references to owls.

82 The speaker quotes from Plat. Alc. 1 140a, not distinguishing the character of Socrates presented in the dialogue from the historic Socrates whose father had been commissioned to make the group statue of the three Charites and would have wanted to bring his sons into the guild. The dangers the three crafts shared might be those from using sharp tools, but more probably the character of Socrates had flying fragments and marble chippings in mind, as well as marble dust. Since the word employed for 'maker of statue' is normally used for portraits, Socrates may also have had the dangers of bronze casting in mind.

83 The speaker, while flattering his audience, sneering at those who work with their hands, and repeating the observation that goes back long before the classical period that those who have to pitch for sales in a commercial relationship cannot be trusted, makes the same points as are set out in the dialogue by Lucian known as *Lucian's Dream*, especially Luc. Somn. 12 and 13, a text that, incidentally, confirms the existence at that time, imputed without risk of contradiction back to the age of Phidias, of a guild system in which kinship was an almost indispensable requirement for entry. Lucian, from what is known of his life, also abandoned the trade of stone worker for that of travelling sophist. And his piece is itself a rhetorical exercise.

As Plutarch, the greatest historian of our age and perhaps of all time, has established from his many years of careful research work among the old books of that time that we now preserve in our libraries, Pheidias broke the laws that forbid making direct allusions to contemporary politics on sacred buildings.[84] For any who have not visited the Acropolis recently, I have ordered a sketch to be prepared that shows Pheidias and Pericles depicted as taking part in the mythic battle between Giants and Amazons.[85] [*A sketch on the lines of Figure 5.3 is passed round*].

Figure 5.3. Sketch made from a detail in the 'Strangford Shield'. Line drawing.[86]

---

84 The texts that the speaker refers to are collected by Davison. They are discussed by Pernot, Laurence, 'Phidias à la Barre', in Pernot, Laurence, ed., *La rhétorique des arts: actes du colloque tenu au Collège de France sous la présidence de Marc Fumaroli, de l'Académie française* (Paris: PUF, 2011), 11–44. The speaker praises Plutarch, an author of his own age, who in his account of Pericles seems to have uncritically repeated satires in the comic dramatists of the 'Old Comedy' such as Aristophanes, as if they could be used as direct evidence. Like others, including some in modern times, he evidently does not sufficiently appreciate how serious a charge was being made, as discussed in Chapter 1.

85 The many ancient authors who repeat the story are noted by Davison, *Pheidias*, iii, 1081.

86 Michaelis, Adolf, *Der Parthenon* (Leipzig: Breitkopf and Härtnel, 1871), illustrations volume, 34b on page 15. A photograph of the 'Strangford Shield' was given as Figure 21.10 in St Clair, *WStP*, Chapter 21, https://doi.org/10.11647/obp.0136.21.

'Is this a picture of Pheidias?' I ask. Or even more shameful, is it a portrait of the living Pericles? How could Pheidias imagine that any depictions he made of Pericles, let alone of himself, would not—horrible to relate— be noticed by the [*signifies contempt*] 'sophisticated' Athenians of that time?[87] Set at eye level it distracts pious viewers from looking upwards towards the god-like image, and prevents its divine essence entering their minds even when they stand in the presence of the gods.[88] Did Pheidias forget that the gods punish deceivers and those who pollute their shrines?

Why did the great Pericles befriend such a man, a mere travelling foreman of craft-workers, who used his skills not for the glory of his city but who made himself available to be hired for pay by any city who wanted to show itself off and promote its foolish stories? How could Pericles have been so deceived? For myself, I have never believed the story that Pheidias pimped Athenian married ladies for his friend Pericles who happened to have control of the budget from the disbursements of which he grew rich.[89] But who, I ask you, men of Athens, would ever want to be a Pheidias or want his son to become a Pheidias? A worker in a trade as dirty and as despicable as that of the dyers, their arms and hands never clean, who are paid to make fine clothes for other people to

---

87 The speaker repeats a stadial narrative of decline, that, while Plato and Aristotle were real 'philosophers', their successors, who were more overly aware of the rhetorical element in all speech acts, as were their audiences and readers, were mere 'sophists.'

88 The speaker alludes to the mental experience that was expected by those who adhered to the cognitive theory of extramission as was still mainstream at the time

89 As on other occasions the speaker gives renewed currency to a story by appearing to dismiss it, gathering credit from his auditors for his fair-mindedness. The story is only known from a scholiast to Philostratos that suggests either that the composition is from a much later date than may at first appear, or that the story by the scholiast was circulating much earlier. A later example of a similar rhetorical device, that spreads an idea attributed to expert opinion without naming names or accepting responsibility, is in the anonymous pamphlet that was used to advance Elgin's claims when he offered to sell his collection of antiquities to the British state, where one sentence appears to have been drafted so as to appeal to those who, whether as commissioners of public works or those who accepted the commissions, were thinking of what might be included as possible content, declared: 'Some antiquaries who have examined the [Parthenon] frieze with minute attention, seem to think it contained portraits of many of the leading characters at Athens, who lived during the Peloponnesian War, particularly of Pericles, Phidias, Socrates, Alcibiades, Aspasia, &c.' *Memorandum on the Subject of the Earl of Elgin's Pursuits in Greece.—Second Edition, Corrected* (London: John Murray, 1815), 12.

wear?[90] The Athenians of that time forgot the lesson that we all learned as boys so that we would all know how to act when we became men. [*Quotes, perhaps putting on an archaic accent and gesturing*]

> Oft-times a whole city suffers from one bad man
> whose deeds are wrong and whose aims are arrogant;
> On them from the skies Kronion launches
> dire plague and famine together joined;
> and the people perish.[91]

And it was his own actions that brought about his deserved downfall. Our best historians still discuss some points of disagreement that I need not repeat, but Pheidias used his position to embezzle from the plates of gold that had been entrusted to his care so that his men could make the statues look as if they were made entirely of gold, a deception of the kind that Thucydides and Plato had condemned. The Athenians of that time, inclined to trust too much, which as the great Pericles says was one of the characteristics of which they were so proud, should have expected no less from a mere tradesman who will tell whatever story he thinks will please the client, however exaggerated, if he thinks that his words will secure a contract. As Anacharsis said, the market place is where men go to deceive and cheat one another.[92]

But, as we learned from the great dramatists of Athens, a story does not have to be true for it to be useful. At our philosophical schools here in Athens, we learn wisdom as well as rhetoric by studying the questions raised by the life of Pheidias. Were the people of Elis right to

---

90   Paraphrased from Plutarch, *Life of Pericles*, i, 1–4, where he makes the same point about literature. The key passage, as elsewhere, limits the type of viewer able to appreciate what is offered: καὶ οὐδεὶς εὐφυὴς νέος ἢ τὸν ἐν Πίσῃ θεασάμενος Δία γενέσθαι Φειδίας ἐπεθύμησεν ἢ τὴν Ἥραν τὴν ἐν Ἄργει Πολύκλειτος, οὐδ' Ἀνακρέων ἢ Φιλητᾶς ἢ Ἀρχίλοχος ἡσθεὶς αὐτῶν τοῖς ποιήμασιν.

91   The speaker takes as authority a quotation from Hesiod, *Works and Days*, 240, perhaps knowing that it had been deployed earlier by Aeschines, an orator that was studied in the schools, in his speech against Ctesiphon, 135.

92   A typical chreia quoted by Hock, Ronald F., and O'Neil, Edward N., *The Chreia in Ancient Rhetoric, Volume 1. The Progymnasmata* (Atlanta: Scholars Press, 1986), 4, from Diogenes Laertius, i.105. The speaker is taking a risk in making this point since he, the judges, and most of his audience know that the training they are receiving in the philosophical school is, to a large extent, aimed at enabling them to compete successfully for commissions in a market for various types of speeches. He may have already learned that contradiction is not an obstacle to success in rhetoric since the audience will generally have forgotten the point as another is made.

cut off his hands when he was found to be stealing the gold intended for the statue? Should he have been put to death as some say the Athenians decided, for blasphemously robbing the gods?[93]

There have been many cases where conquerors decided not to destroy holy places and others where they have given back holy objects that they or their ancestors have taken. Such men, even when they are barbarians, understand the meaning of 'charis' and of 'philanthropy' and are justly honoured. This much you all know. But recently we have heard a new thought and seen new practices that it is our duty to consider. The Rhodians, kinsmen of the Athenians, who had many memorials overturned by the Earthshaker, began to turn the old into new, a practice that now is becoming normal. We have even seen cases here in Athens.[94] Some say that a city that has paid for its statues has a right to do what it likes with them, provided only that the correct legal procedures have been followed and the magistrates then in office have given their consent.[95] But, we should ask ourselves, are we being just when we alter our idols to fit the needs of today by recarving the inscriptions? Our colleague Dio of Prusa raised an interesting point when he delivered a speech to the Rhodians. By changing the value that was accorded to images, he suggested, did they not convert a true currency ('nomisma') that was accepted by all into a counterfeit coin that no wise man would accept? By agreeing that the monuments that the great men of the past built long ago can be turned to any purpose that the Rhodians now choose, do they not destroy both memory and honour? Have the Rhodians forgotten, Dio asked, that the majority of men regard the 'Charites' as divine, and that if anyone mutilates their statues or overturns their altars, we justly regard him as guilty of impiety, destroying the very charis from which these goddesses received their

---

93 The speaker refers to the custom of which the first recorded example is the 'Controversies' of the Elder Seneca, in which, without implying that an actual past is being referred to except as a convention, such moral questions are set as topics for training exercises. Although called schools of 'philosophy' purporting to teach how truth can be searched for, by the time of the speaker they were mainly concerned with attracting fee-paying pupils who wanted to learn the arts of persuasion.

94 Examples in Athens, statues of Miltiades and Themistocles, where the names had been altered into 'those of a Roman and a Thracian', were noticed by Pausanias, at Paus. 1.18.3.

95 The speaker alludes to the practice of deliberately authorizing a new meaning discussed in Chapter 1 as 'nomismatic.'

name? What would we say, he asks, to a man who puts on his festival wreath and leads the same goat from one holy place after another, and pretends to sacrifice it to Zeus, to Apollo, and then to Athena? Is not he also a counterfeiter?[96]

These are questions that, in my view deserve to be considered at our philosophical schools and on which your opinions will be valued around our world from the snows of Scythia to the deserts of Libya, from Syria, where the chariot of the suns rises, to Gades [*modern Cadiz*] where he returns to the Ocean.[97] Let me therefore also say, since, unlike Dio, I am invited to give an opinion, in my judgement a free city must always keep control of what is seen and remembered.[98] If we had paid attention to these new ideas of Dio, we would still have statues of the rebel Marcus Antoninus and his Egyptian whore occupying the most visible site of our sacred hill, shaming us every day.[99] And it was even more recently that our Areopagus and Demos had to damn the memory of a successor to Augustus that cannot be named who falsely claimed to be a [*shows contempt*] 'philhellene'.[100]

---

96   The speaker, like Dio of Prusa in his long oration to the Rhodians, the thirty-first, whose key points the speaker summarises, seems itself to have been prepared as a rhetorical exercise. In his exordium Dio says that he volunteers the advice and it is not given by invitation. At times the speech is almost explicit in saying that 'the gods' are useful inventions, 'fiat gods' equivalent to 'fiat currency.' His essay raises questions that have become common in the twenty-first century. It is notable however that although he claims rights for monuments and for those who have been accorded official responsibility for looking after them, he makes no claims on behalf of artists.

97   The speaker hopes that his clichéd venture into poetic language will remind his audiences of similar expressions to be commonly found in tragedy. Setting a time and place and implying that viewers are able to see the passage of time if they choose is part of the rhetoric on the display in the pediments of the Parthenon.

98   The speaker refers to the formal political position of the Athens of his day as a free city allied with Rome, that maintained its ancient institutions, although in practice Athens was little different from a province. He uses the formulation ('opsei kai mneme') of Aelius Aristides to describe how a built heritage was thought to work. Oliver, James Henry, 'The civilizing power: a study of the Panathenaic discourse of Aelius Aristides against the background of literature and cultural conflict, with text, translation, and commentary' in *Transactions of the American Philosophical Society*, Vol. 58 (1) (1968), 15, https://doi.org/10.2307/1005987.

99   The speaker refers to the episode in which Antony and Cleopatra, before the decisive defeat of their armies by Octavian, later Augustus, had caused statues of themselves to be erected on the pedestal shown as Figure 24.3, Volume 1.

100   The speaker, choosing his words carefully to avoid making the embarrassments, humiliations, and contradictions too obvious, refers to the episode in 61 CE when the emperor Nero, or his local representatives, persuaded the institutions of Athens

And what of today, I hear you ask? As our own Euripides has justly proclaimed:

> Now, in our time, the deep has ceased resistance and submits utterly to law; no famous Argo, framed by a hand of Pallas, with princes to man its oars, is sought for; any little craft now wanders at will upon the deep. All bounds have been removed, cities have set their walls in new lands, and the world is now passable throughout its length and breadth. The Indian drinks of the cold Arazes, the Persians quaff the Elbe and the Rhine. There will come an age in the far-off years when Ocean shall unloose the bonds of things, when the whole broad earth shall be revealed, when Tethys shall disclose new worlds and Thule not be the limit of the lands.[101]

There is more that could be said. And as Dio tells us, although if a foreigner or a metic offers you a gift of money even when you have no need of any more, and the world would be improved if he had less, you accept his gift with thanks, pay him honours, and listen to his advice, for all men, as we know, have need of good advice.[102] But, as I see the sand running down, let me say in conclusion that, in my opinion, the true reason why the Parthenon failed was that the Athenians of those days thought they could make the people think and act as one.[103] And they

---

to permit an inscription in his honour to be attached in bronze letters to the east pediment of the Parthenon, the most visible sight during festivals, and which was taken down some time after 68 when Nero was overthrown and disgraced. The story of how the text's inscription was recovered by the American archaeological student Eugene P. Andrews in 1906 from a study of the holes in the marble is related by Carroll, Kevin K., *The Parthenon Inscription*, Greek, Roman and Byzantine Monographs No. 9 (Durham, N. C.: Duke University, 1982).

101 The speaker quotes from the Latin version of *Medea*, beginning at line 364, written by Seneca the Younger, a play, as are most of his others, not dialogic and opening up questions like those of Euripides on whose reputation he and the speaker take an unfair rhetorical free ride, but more a series of consumerist declamations that endorse the official ideologies of his day.

102 The speaker, running some risks, repeats a sentiment in almost the same words as were used by Dio of Prusa in his Rhodian, the twelfth, oration, sheltering behind the name of a famous man who was himself a direct beneficiary of the system and whose fame enabled him occasionally to depart from the expected.

103 The speaker is so eager to show that he knows the phrase, the 'truest and most logical underlying cause, (τὴν μὲν γὰρ ἀληθεστάτην πρόφασιν, ἀφανεστάτην δὲ λόγῳ) in Thuc.1.23.6, in the summary of his findings that he, in effect, offers two, albeit related. His strictures about the ignorance of common people also echo Thucydides, who speaks of the return of old irrational ways of thinking almost immediately after the outbreak of the war.

thought they could change them by showing them pictures and telling them moralizing stories.

When we are being truthful, we have to admit that the 'demos' of that time did not consist, as the saying goes, of 'men like ourselves'.[104] Parrhasius, the greatest painter of classical Greece, who could paint cherries to look so sweet that even the birds pecked at them thinking they were real, could have told them so. In his picture, the men of Athens were shown as the they truly were, capricious, passionate, unjust, inconstant, inexorable, forgiving, compassionate, magnanimous, boastful, abject, brave, and cowardly, all at the same time.[105] Fortunately, under the guidance of the divine Sebastos [*Greek for Augustus*] and his wise successors who have loved this city and its history, those sad and shameful days are gone for ever.[106]

My speech is now approaching its ending. I know that good judges will never hand over responsibility to make their choices to others any more than a good doctor would yield the judgment of an illness to another.[107] And although many matters have come before you in the past, you have never been assembled to judge a contest as important as this.[108] Now is the time, men of Athens, to register your decision for

---

104   The speaker, employing the commonplace popularized later by Mahaffy, takes care not to imply that the demos of Athens of his own day were not the same as those of the past. As before, however, he shows his inexperience, sycophancy, and lack of sincerity, by suggesting that he does not normally tell the truth but is making an exception for this particular audience. They, we need hardly say, being men trained in the arts of rhetoric, are likely to have winced and marked him down as unworthy of the prize.

105   The speaker quotes from the description of the picture now lost as it was described by Pliny, *Natural History,* xxxv, 10. By the time of Pliny, painters were being lexically distinguished from sculptors, perhaps partly as a result of the Roman habit of collecting 'works of art' from the sites that gave them meaning, as a form of displaying their status, anticipating the dilettanti of the eighteenth century.

106   The speaker narrowly avoids the condescension that would have been rhetorically counterproductive for praising Athens not for what it was, but for its attractiveness to educated tourists, among whom the emperor might be included.

107   The speaker appears to be familiar with the sentiment offered by Ajax in a rhetorical exercise attributed to Antisthenes of Athens but probably prepared later. Translated by Price, Susan, ed., *Antisthenes of Athens: Texts, Translations, and Commentary* (Ann Arbor: University of Michigan Press, 2015), 190, https://doi.org/10.3998/mpub.5730060.

108   The speaker, although again by his exaggerations he shares the thought with the judges that they all know that they are engaged in a game, shows that he knows the rhetorical conventions of the game, such as the 'prooemia' that aimed at making the audience more receptive, as discussed by, for example, *Anonymous Seguerianus*

better or for worse.[109] Honoured sirs, I trust myself to Fortune, to the gods, and to your good and wise judgment. I will always pray that this city will continue to flourish until stones float upon the sea and trees cease to send forth new shoots.[110]

A Note on the Second Experiment

It is not known what the judges decided. It is thought that since they were professionally not much interested in either the substance of the argument or in its conclusions, but only in the speaker's skill in the arts of rhetoric, they commended the way in which he had linked the end of his speech with the beginning, but wondered whether he yet knew enough about how what they called the 'game', was played.[111] However in some respects the speaker does seem to have picked up an intellectual reaction against promoting a certain kind of local civic arete by resort to myth-making. As the Roman Empire faced incursions from peoples from far away, perhaps tribes forced to move as a result of climate change and population pressures in the Euro-Asian continent, classical-era paideia may have become even less trusted than it had been in the classical era itself. Half a millennium of sacrificing to 'Athena the Protector' or to 'Zeus the Savour' had not made any difference that could be historically evidenced, and arguments that, without them, things would have been even worse might have begun to sound as forced and as sophistical as some of the rhetorical contortions resorted to by the Christian apologists

---

at 7, with examples from famous masters. Dilts and Kennedy, *Greek Rhetorical Treatises*, 1–5, https://doi.org/10.1163/9789004330313. Anonymous Seguerianus also discusses how the issues in the (invented) trial of Phidias outlined by Seneca the Elder should be summarized at the end of a speech, implying that it may have been a standard case used in training.

109 The speaker's peroration follows closely that of the Roman oration of Aristides, 109.

110 The speaker turns to what appears to be a conventional farewell, used, for example as the peroration of the Roman oration of Aelius Aristides. As rhetorical constructions of permanence, the first is human: it can be associated with the custom of ceremonially throwing the material of allegedly everlasting and un-rescindable treaties into the sea. The second links permanence to the seasonal cycles of the natural world (although it looks inadequate in an era of climate change) and shows that it was possible to imagine that the local microclimate could last for ever. Consequently, the decision to build the Parthenon (which would rely on this microclimate) had a sound basis.

111 They were following almost to the letter the comment made by the character of Clinias in Plato's Laws. Plat. Laws 6.768.

on Mars Hill.[112]In 1920, in the excavations in the Agora of Athens, a fragmentary ancient inscription dated to the time of the rebuilding of the town wall in the third century CE was found.[113] As with the many other rebuildings in ancient as in modern times, the new 'Valerian' wall made use of existing carved blocks. The inscription, consisting of two diptychs in verse, declares: 'Not by the [?singing] of Aimon were these [walls] raised, nor by the strong hand of the Cyclops, but [unreadable phrase but we can postulate "by the people of Athens"]'.[114] Although inscribed on a memorial that was made centuries after the classical period, it may derive from a famous quotation, or 'chreia', perhaps from something said by a character in a lost play by Euripides. Whatever its status, it appears to show that, by the time the wall was raised, and probably for a long time before, the old myths of the classical period had not only lost whatever power they may once have possessed over minds and behaviours, but they were being actively superseded, historical experience having continued to show the limitations of rhetoric when confronted by actuality.

---

112 As discussed in St Clair, *WStP*, Chapter 22, https://doi.org/10.11647/obp.0136.22.

113 Described by Setton, Kenneth M., 'The Archaeology of Medieval Athens', in Mundy, John Hine, Emery, Richard W., and Nelson, Benjamin J., eds, *Essays in Medieval Life and Thought: Presented in Honor of Austin Patterson Evans* (New York: Columbia University Press, 1955), 241.

114 οὐ τάδε θελξιμελὴς Ἀμφιονὶς ἤρα[ρε φόρμιγξ/ οὐδὲ Κυκλωπείας χειρὸς ἔδ[ειμε βία]. My translation, unlike Setton's, leads with the 'Not'. Quoted in *Inscriptiones Graecae* vols. II–III², Part III: *Inscriptiones Atticae Euclidis anno posteriores*, fasc. 1 (Berlin, 1935), no 5200a.

6. Heritage[1]

Can the long history of the ways that the Parthenon has been put to use over thousands of years improve our understanding of built heritage as such? Can we discern patterns that are common to different epochs, including our own, that might serve as explanatory models or frameworks? And, if so, could they help to improve our understanding not only of eras and episodes in the past and their long aftermaths, but to help to inform current choices facing policy-makers and to equip those who are the consumers of the rhetoric of heritage with the tools needed to critique it?

In recent times, many monuments previously regarded as sites of collective memory have become objects of contestation, with demands, for example, in some countries to remove statues of colonial-era soldiers and governors, slave owners, and political and religious leaders whose recorded opinions on such matters as gender, race, sexual mores, and human rights, are out of line with those of vocal modern constituencies. For me the most depressing feature of these episodes has been to see those who have most responsibility for maintaining values in the public arena lining up to kick the ball into their own goal. 'You cannot rewrite history', has been the cry. What the speakers meant is that you cannot change the past, a very different idea. Of course, when we re-examine what the past has left us, we can, and we should rewrite history and, I would say, we should also make it available to be read.

We also see proposals to build new memorials to those who were previously marginalized or victimized and who are mostly absent from the built social memory. Old buildings are renamed and museum labels rewritten in an untidy process of changing the stories that the mute stones are deemed to be telling. Memorials to individuals are condemned

---

1   See Editor's Note on the inclusion of this chapter.

    https://doi.org/10.11647/OBP.0279.06

even if what they are found to have said or done was praiseworthy, unremarkable, or incidental to their contribution in their own times. We see the raising of new memorials to those previously omitted, forgotten, marginalized, or victimized. Conservation and cleansing increasingly appear to be opposite ends of a long spectrum in an ongoing political debate about the public display of memory and therefore of identity.

In the case of the Parthenon, even with the extraordinary advantages of being set in a geographical cognitive frame, and the fact that all substantial changes have been the result of the explicit intentions on the part of those who were in political control of the site, there is no unifying grand narrative.[2] The history can be arranged in accordance with the official uses to which the building has been put (ancient Athenian temple, Christian church, first Byzantine Orthodox and then Roman Catholic, Suni Muslim mosque, Greek national heritage site, and so on) on the analogy of a biography of an individual person. Nor do broad calendar chronologies of production (Mycenaean, archaic, classical Hellenic, Hellenistic, Roman, Byzantine, Ottoman, Modern Greece) adequately cope with fact that the things that were actually seen, even in ancient eras, were the productions of different times. Furthermore, all tidy, object-centred chronological narratives risk underestimating the contribution made by consumers to the cognitive transaction, whether in the past or now. No monument, I suggest, and perhaps especially the classical Parthenon, can be understood without giving due weight not only to the pull of then officially-imagined pasts and aspired-to futures, but also to how the aims of the producers for their consumers can only be understood within the then-prevailing theories of cognition and explanatory paradigms, some of which, including the many varieties of providentialism, few modern persons are able to accept.

The long history cautions against the circularities of romanticism, and of the notion that 'art' can reveal the minds of the societies that brought objects into being (so-called 'emanationism'), rather than of those individuals and institutions that were able to commission, finance, and cause the objects to be built and their rhetoric to be commended.[3] The

---

2   The extraordinary advantages of the site, including the historical particularity that the potential effects on the viewer were never absent, were discussed in St Clair, *WStP*, Chapter 1, https://doi.org/10.11647/obp.0136.01.

3   Joan Breton Connelly has, for example, described the Parthenon frieze as 'the largest and most detailed revelation of Athenian consciousness we have.' Connelly,

succession of physical Parthenons, including the classical-era building and its predecessors and successors, have all been part of the political economy of their time in which various considerations were brought together. The discursive environment, too, within which meanings were recommended and perhaps accepted and acted upon, has always itself been part of a political economy which, even in an age of social media, gives disproportionate advantages to some voices compared with others. We also see that in the long past there never seems to have been a time when the officially presented meaning was not contested, and that for a modern writer to imply that there were such times, not only risks being unfair but surrenders to the fallacy that actual reactions of live human beings to a cultural object can be deduced from a study of the rhetorical tendency of the object itself.

Regime changes too are now often marked by removing memorials, as when in the case of the late Saddam Hussein of Iraq, the staged performance of the act of knocking down a statue of the former leader was pictured on the news, a symbolic destruction of the past presented as a prelude to a new and better future. Revolutionary insurgencies frequently target buildings for their symbolic rather than their direct military value, as for example in the 2001 attacks on the World Trade Center in New York and the Pentagon in Washington, D.C., and individuals and transient political groups try to harm their perceived opponents by desecrating their valued buildings and the graves of their dead, actions seen as surrogates for, and sometimes threatening preliminaries to, the cleansing of people. An urge to destroy can show the symbolic power of a monument as much as an urge to save and preserve it.

History warns us of the risks and circularities of emanationism, a practice that attempts to deduce the mentalities prevalent in societies by a study of their most valued, often sacralized artefacts, without giving sufficient consideration to the governing political and economic structures, including theocratic monopoly, and the power to award contracts and supply finance, without which monuments could not have come into existence in the form that they did. Those who practice emanationism may think that they are recovering the mentalities of a

Joan Breton, *The Parthenon Enigma, A New Understanding of the World's Most Iconic Building and the People Who Made It* (New York: Alfred A. Knopf, 2014), xix.

society, but are often, even for a democratic society such as classical Athens, mainly recovering a production history of the methods employed by leaderships to influence the minds of the people over whom they exercised power. Emanationism too therefore is always at risk of giving the producers what they wanted, namely to influence the minds and actions of contemporaries and of later generations in ways that suit their own rhetorical and political agenda.

So, what remedies can be suggested? Some modern governments of nation states, a category that often presents itself as 'natural' 'permanent' and 'ancient', frequently practice monument cleansing, as the newly independent Greek state did in the nineteenth century, even if not so blatantly, attempting to change perceptions of the future by changing the visual landscape and the continuities with various pasts that this had previously implied, a form of memory cleansing. We also see many examples of the invention of an imaginary past or civic imaginary, however unhistorical, being promoted as a good thing in itself, for example by UNESCO, as a contribution to nation-building, which is still often regarded as a desirable activity despite the geographical and observable fact that there is scarcely a city, town, or village, from Ireland to the Urals that does not boast a war memorial, and that many in Europe have several from the twentieth century alone—let alone in the rest of the world, where memories were less often turned into materiality, even rhetorical materiality, and were allowed to fade into oblivion. Just as the champions of the active conservation of monuments sometimes deploy discourses that claim timeless value and universal applicability ('common heritage of mankind'), so too those who destroy usually call on other allegedly timeless, universal, and often theistic, discourses ('carrying out God's will') to justify their actions. It is now almost routine to describe the destruction of ancient monuments as a 'war crime', equating the destruction of things with the killing of people; by contrast, others argue that by leaving certain monuments intact one is in effect collaborating with those who had the power to build them in the first place, enabling them to prolong their rhetoric into our own time.[4] Today, when the visual is at least as influential as words

---

4   A recent example is Meskell, Lynn, *A Future in Ruins, UNESCO, World Heritage, and the Dream of Peace* (New York: OUP, 2018), xviii, 'war crimes against cultural property'.

in constituting and changing mentalities, such trends can be expected to continue and to intensify. Rather than regarding the built heritage as a sideshow in conflicts, perhaps the time has now come when it should be re-categorized as among the causes and the weapons?

The Parthenon, by providing a well-documented historical example of monument cleansing as well as of monument conservation, in the service of many of the most common forms of imagined community and of their universalizing and normalizing justificatory discourses, has a strong claim to be regarded as heritage in a more general sense: namely, as a store of retrievable experience that, by its very variety and its strangeness from modern assumptions, can help to inform understanding and choice today. The fact that so many people took an interest in the building and recorded their experiences is, I would say, itself a heritage. However, what is also striking is the extent to which traditional historiography has found it difficult to cope with the complexities without ignoring or severely downplaying what, in my view, constitutes the central question, namely, how to integrate the material world of the Parthenon stones with the contested immaterial worlds of ideas, memories, ideologies, imagined pasts and aspired-to futures that brought about the changes. Even in the last few centuries, a fraction of the thousands of years during which the Acropolis was a heritage as well as active site, we encounter examples of contestation across the whole spectrum from admiration, through indifference, to hatred. And we also see huge changes, both physical and in the attribution of value.

Although there is probably a developing unanimity about the nature of the problem, none of the main intellectual approaches for addressing it seem to me to be adequate. The history of the Parthenon can be told as a parade of the changing physicality, or as a set of parades of imputed meanings that then took on lives of their own with an astonishing capacity for adaptation, survival and revival that resulted in patterns and trajectories that cannot easily be fitted into the linearity of traditional historiography. But it can also be told as a story of the coining and re-use of sets of rhetorical tropes that became available to be deployed and that took on lives of their own. If, as I suggest, we regard the Parthenon as a uniquely full and well-documented store of experience, it is also a treasure-house of the rhetoric within whose conventions actual experiences of looking at the building, whether to admire, despise, or treat with indifference have been turned into words and deployed. As this generation increasingly understands that there is no determinist plan or pattern, and the future lies in the hands of successive generations looking forward as well as backwards with as much honesty and sincerity as can be mustered within the knowledge available at the time, the opportunity that the Parthenon offers to engage critically with its unrivalled collection of rhetorics, as a means of engaging with rhetoric itself, may turn out to be a heritage as precious, or as the classical Athenians might have said, as useful as the marble.

Bibliography

[n.a.], *The Reunification of the Parthenon Marbles, A Cultural Imperative* (Athens: Ministry of Culture and others, 2004)

[Aeschylus fragments] *Aeschylus, with an English Translation by Herbert Weir Smyth* (London: Heinemann; Cambridge: Harvard University Press, 1971, 1973). *Appendix and Addendum to Volume 2 Fragments* ed. by Hugh Lloyd-Jones

Agócs, Peter, 'Speaking in the Wax Tablets of Memory', in *Greek Memories, Theories and Practices*, ed. by Luca Castagnoli and Paola Ceccarelli (Cambridge: Cambridge University Press, 2019), pp. 68–90 https://doi.org/10.1017/9781108559157

Alty, John, 'Dorians and Ionians', *The Journal of Hellenic Studies*, 102 (1982), 1–14, https://doi.org/10.2307/631122

Ancey, George, *Athènes couronnée de Violettes* (Paris: Charpentier and Pasquelle, 1908)

Appelbaum, Stanley, ed., *Winckelmann's Images from the Ancient World: Greek, Roman, Etruscan and Egyptian* (New York: Dover, 2010)

Aristophanes, *Lysistrata*, trans. by C. Zevort (Paris: Librarie Charpentier et Fasquelle, 1898)

Aristophanes, *Birds, Edited with Introduction and Commentary by Nan Dunbar* (Oxford: Clarendon, 1995)

Aristophanes, *Fragments,* ed. by Jeffrey Henderson (London: Harvard University Press, 2007)

Aristotle, *Eudemian Ethics, trans. by Anthony Kenny* (Oxford: World Classics, 2011)

Arnott, W. G., ed., *Menander* (Cambridge, MA and London: Harvard University Press, 1979–2000)

Arnott, W. G., *Birds in the Ancient World from A to Z* (London: Routledge, 2007), https://doi.org/10.4324/9780203946626

Ashmole, Bernard, *Architect and Sculptor in Classical Greece* (New York: New York University Press, 1972)

Athenagoras, *Legatio and De Resurrectione*, ed. and trans. by William R. Schoedel (Oxford: Oxford University Press, 1972)

Azoulay, Vincent, *Xenophon and the Graces of Power: A Greek Guide to Political Manipulation*, trans. by Angela Krieger from the French edition of 2004 (Swansea: Classical Press of Wales, 2018)

Barringer, Judith M., *Art, Myth, and Ritual in Classical Greece* (Cambridge: Cambridge University Press, 2009)

Bassi, Karen, *Traces of the Past: Classics Between History and Archaeology* (Ann Arbor: University of Michigan Press, 2016), https://doi.org/10.3998/mpub.8785930

Baumgarten, Fritz, Franz Poland, and Richard Wagner, *Die Hellenische Kultur*, 2nd edn (Leipzig and Berlin: Teubner, 1906)

Behr, Charles A., ed., *P. Aelius Aristides, The Complete Works* (Leiden: Brill, 1986)

Beulé, E., *Phidias, Drame Antique* (Paris: Didier, second edition, 1869)

Beulé, E., *Journal de mes Fouilles* (Paris: Claye, 1872)

Bodnar, Edward W., *Cyriacus of Ancona and Athens* (Brussels: Latomus, 1960)

Bodnar, Edward W., ed. and trans., *Cyriac of Ancona, Later Travels* (Cambridge Mass: I Tatti Renaissance Library, 2003)

Boeckh, Augustus, *The Public Economy of Athens: In Four Books; To Which is Added, A Dissertation on the Silver-mines of Laurion. Translated from the German of Augustus Boeckh* (London: Murray, 1828)

Boersma, Johannes S., *Athenian Building Policy from 561/0 to 405/4 B.C.* (Groningen: Wolters-Noordhoff, 1970)

Bosanquet, R.C., *Days in Attica* (London: Methuen, 1914)

Bowie, Theodore, and Diether Thimme, eds, *The Carrey Drawings of the Parthenon Sculptures* (Bloomington and London: Indiana University Press, 1971)

Boyajian, Zabelle C., *In Greece with Pen and Palette* (London: Dent, 1938)

Brandi, Cesare, 'Nota sui Marmi del Partenone', *Bollettino dell'Istituto Centrale del Restauro*, 3–4 (1950), 3–8

Bremond, Henri, *Le charme d'Athènes* (Paris: Société des Médecins Bibliophiles, 1924)

Bresson, Alain, T*he Making of the Ancient Greek Economy: Institutions, Markets, and Growth in the City-States*, trans. by Steven Rendall (Princeton; Oxford: Princeton University Press, 2016), https://doi.org/10.23943/princeton/9780691183411.001.0001

[British Museum] *A Description of the Collection of Ancient Marbles in the British Museum* (London: British Museum, 1818)

Brock, Roger, *Greek Political Imagery from Homer to Aristotle* (London; New York: Bloomsbury, 2013), http://doi.org/10.5040/9781472555694

Burford, Alison, *The Greek Temple Builders at Epidauros: A Social and Economic Study of Building in the Asklepian Sanctuary, During the Fourth and Early Third Centuries B.C.* (Liverpool: Liverpool University Press, 1969)

Burges, George, ed., *Prolegomena on the Peculiarities of Thucydidean Phraseology, Translated, Abridged and Criticized by G. Burges* (Cambridge: apparently privately printed, c. 1837). A translation, with many additions, of Poppo, E. F., *Observationes criticae in Thucydidem* (London: Priestley, 1819)

Burr, Rev. E.F., *Dio, the Athenian; or, From Olympus to Calvary* (New York: Phillips, 1880)

Butler, Howard C., *The Story of Athens: A Record of the Life and Art of the City of the Violet Crown Read in its Ruins and in the Lives of Great Athenians* (New York: Century Company, 1902)

Callanan, Keegan, *Montesquieu's Liberalism and the Problem of Universal Politics* (Cambridge: Cambridge University Press, 2018), https://doi.org/10.1017/9781108617277

Camp, John M., *Horses and Horsemanship in the Athenian Agora* (Athens: American School of Classical Studies, 1998)

Camp, John M., *The Archaeology of Athens* (New Haven: Yale University Press, 2001)

Carbon, Jan-Mathieu, Saskia Peels, and Vinciane Pirenne-Delforge, eds, [CGRN] *A Collection of Greek Ritual Norms* (Liège: 2016), http://cgrn.ulg.ac.be/

Carroll, Kevin K., *The Parthenon Inscription, Greek, Roman and Byzantine Monographs No. 9* (Durham, N. C.: Duke University, 1982)

Castagnoli, Luca, and Paola Ceccarelli, eds, *Greek Memories, Theories and Practices* (Cambridge: Cambridge University Press, 2019)

Castriota, David, *Myth, Ethos, and Actuality: Official Art in Fifth-Century B.C. Athens* (Madison: University of Wisconsin Press, 1992)

Chandler, Rev. Richard, *Travels in Greece* (Oxford: Clarendon Press, 1776)

Chryssoulaki, Stella, 'The Excavations at Phaleron Cemetery 2012–2017: An Introduction', in *Rethinking Athens Before the Persian Wars, Proceedings of the International Workshop at the Ludwig-Maximilians-Universität München (Munich, 23rd-24th February 2017)*, ed. by Constanze Graml, Annarita Doronzio, and Vincenzo Capozzoli (München: Utzverlag, 2019), pp. 103–113

Cohen, Beth, with contributions by Kenneth Lapatin et al., *The Colors of Clay: Special Techniques in Athenian Vases* (Los Angeles: Getty, 2006), https://www.getty.edu/publications/virtuallibrary/0892369426.html

Collard, C., M. J. Cropp, and J. Gibert, eds, *Euripides, Selected Fragmentary Plays Volume II* (Warminster: Aris and Phillips, 2004)

Collard, C., M. J. Cropp, and K. H. Lee, trans. and eds, *Euripides, Selected Fragmentary Plays Volume I* (Warminster: Aris and Phillips, 1995)

Connelly, Joan B., *Portrait of a Priestess, Women and Ritual in Ancient Greece* (Princeton: Princeton University Press, 2007)

Connelly, Joan B., *The Parthenon Enigma: A New Understanding of the World's Most Iconic Building and the People Who Made It* (New York: Alfred A. Knopf, 2014)

Cornford, Francis M., *Thucydides Mythistoricus* (London: Arnold, 1907)

Coulton, J. J., *Ancient Greek Architects at Work: Problems of Structure and Design* (London: Elek, 1977)

Craik, Elizabeth M., *The 'Hippocratic' Corpus: Content and Context* (London: Routledge, 2015), https://doi.org/10.4324/9781315736723

Cromey, Robert D., 'The Penelope Painter's Akropolis (Louvre G372 and 480/79 BC): History and Image', *Journal of Hellenic Studies*, 111 (1991), 165–174, https://doi.org/10.2307/631894

Dallaway, James, *Of Statuary and Sculpture Among the Antients: With Some Account of Specimens Preserved in England* (London: Murray, 1816)

Davidson, Thomas, *The Parthenon Frieze, and Other Essays* (London: Kegan Paul, 1882)

Davison, Claire C., with the collaboration of Birte Lundgreen, *Pheidias: The Sculptures and Ancient Sources*, ed. by Geoffrey B. Waywell (London: Institute of Classical Studies, 2009)

de Moüy, Charles, *Lettres Athéniennes* (Paris: Plon, 1887)

Delivorrias, Angelos, and Sokrates Mavrommatis, *The Parthenon Frieze: Problems, Challenges, Interpretations* (Athens: Melissa and Benaki, 2004)

Demand, Nancy H., *Birth, Death, and Motherhood in Classical Greece* (Baltimore; London: Johns Hopkins University Press, 1994), http://exhibits.hsl.virginia.edu/antiqua/gynecology/

Demangel, R., *La Frise ionique* (Paris: de Boccard, 1932)

Detienne, Marcel, *L'invention de la mythologie* (Paris: Gallimard, 1981)

Dickey, Eleanor, *Greek Forms of Address from Herodotus to Lucian* (Oxford: Clarendon Press, 1996)

Dilts, Mervyn, and George Kennedy, eds, *Two Greek Rhetorical Treatises From the Roman Empire: Introduction, Text, and Translation of the Arts of Rhetoric, Attributed to Anonymous Seguerianus and to Apsines of Gadara* (Leiden: Brill, 1997), https://doi.org/10.1163/9789004330313

Dinsmoor, William B., *The Propylaia to the Athenian Akropolis* (Princeton: American School of Classical Studies at Athens, 1980 and 2004)

Dodds, E.R., *The Greeks and the Irrational* (Berkeley: University of California Press, 1951)

Dodwell, Edward, *Views and Descriptions of Cyclopean, or Pelasgic Remains, in Greece and Italy, with Constructions of a Later Period, Intended as a Supplement to his Classical and Topographical Tour through Greece during the Years 1801, 1805 and 1806* (London: Rodwell and Martin, 1834)

Doxiades, Constantinos A., *Architectural Space in Ancient Greece,* trans. and ed. by Jacqueline Tyrwhitt (Cambridge MA: MIT Press, 1972). Based on the author's 1936 dissertation published in 1937 as *Raumordnung im griechischen Städtebau.*

Ducrey, Pierre, *Le Traitement des prisonniers de guerre dans la Grèce antique: des origines à la conquête romaine* (Paris: Boccard, 1999)

Dunbar, Nan, ed., *Aristophanes, Birds* (Oxford: Clarendon Press, 1995), https://doi.org/10.1093/actrade/9780198150831.book.1

Ellis, Sir Henry, *Elgin and Phigaleian Marbles* (London: Knight, 1833)

Emeric-David, T.B., *Recherches sur l'art statuaire, considéré chez les anciens et chez les modernes, ou Mémoire sur cette question proposée par l'Institut national de France: Quelles ont été les causes de la perfection de la Sculpture antique, et quels seroient les moyens d'y atteindre?* (Paris: Nyon, 1805)

Falkener, Edward, *Daedalus: Or, The Causes and Principles of the Excellence of Greek Sculpture* (London: Longman, 1860)

Fehr, Burkhard, *Becoming Good Democrats and Wives: Civil Education and Female Socialization on the Parthenon Frieze. Hephaistos. Kritische Zeitschrift zu Theorie und Praxis der Archäologie und angrenzender Gebiete* (Berlin, Münster, Vienna, Zürich, London: Lit Verlag, 2011)

Figueira, Thomas, and Carmen Soares, eds., *Ethnicity and Identity in Herodotus* (London: Routledge, 2020), https://doi.org/10.4324/9781315209081

FitzGerald, Augustine, ed., *The Letters of Synesius of Cyrene* (London: Oxford University Press, 1926)

Flagg, Ernest, *The Parthenon Naos From the Author's Forthcoming Book Entitled The Recovery of Art, the Present Sheets Being a Communication Addressed to Charles Marie Vidor, Perpetual Secretary of the Institute of France* (New York: Scribner, 1928)

Flasch, Adam, *Zum Parthenon-Fries* (Würzburg: Druck der Thein'schen Druckerei, 1877)

Foley, Elizabeth, and Ronald S. Stroud, 'A Reappraisal of the Athena Promachos Accounts from the Acropolis (IG I3 435)', *Hesperia: The Journal of the American School of Classical Studies at Athens*, 88.1 (2019), 87–153, https://doi.org/10.2972/hesperia.88.1.0087

Fortenbaugh, William W., and Eckart Schütrumpf, eds, *Demetrius of Phalerum: Text, Translation and Discussion* (Oxford: Routledge, 2018)

Foxhall, Lin, *Olive Cultivation in Ancient Greece: Seeking the Ancient Economy* (Oxford: Oxford University Press, 2007)

Frazer, J. G., trans., *Pausanias's Description of Greece* (London: Macmillan, 1898)

Fulleylove, John, *Greece Painted by John Fulleylove. Described by Right Rev. J.A. McClymont* (London: A. and C. Black, 1906)

Galt, John, *Letters from the Levant* (London: Cadell and Davies, 1813)

Gardner, Percy, *Sculptured Tombs of Hellas* (London: Macmillan, 1896)

Garland, Robert, 'Children in Athenian Religion', in *The Oxford Handbook of Childhood and Education in the Classical World*, ed. by Judith E. Grubbs and Tim Parkin (Oxford: Oxford University Press, 2013)

Garston, Edgar, *Greece Revisited and Sketches in Lower Egypt in 1840, with Thirty-Six Hours of a Campaign in Greece in 1825* (London: Saunders and Ottley, 1842)

Geoffrey B. Waywell, ed., *Pheidias: The Sculptures and Ancient Sources* (London: Institute of Classical Studies, 2009)

Georgopoulou, M., and others, eds, *Following Pausanias: The Quest for Greek Antiquity* (Kotinos: Oak Knoll Press, 2007)

Gladstone, William E., *Studies on Homer and the Homeric Age*, 3 vols (Oxford: Oxford University Press, 1858)

González González, Marta, *Funerary Epigrams of Ancient Greece: Reflections on Literature, Society and Religion* (London: Bloomsbury Academic, 2019), http://doi.org/10.5040/9781350062450

Grand-Clément, Adeline, *La fabrique des couleurs: histoire du paysage sensible des Grecs anciens: VIIIe-début du Ve s. av. N. è.* (Paris: De Boccard, 2011)

Greer, Carl Richard, *The Glories of Greece* (Philadelphia, PA: Penn Publishing Company, 1936)

Grundmann, Steffi, *Haut und Haar: politische und soziale Bedeutungen des Körpers im klassischen Griechenland. Philippika, 133* (Wiesbaden: Harrassowitz Verlag, 2019)

Güthenke, Constanze, *Feeling and Classical Philology: Knowing Antiquity in German Scholarship, 1770–1920* (Cambridge: Cambridge University Press, 2020), https://doi.org/10.1017/9781316219331

Hall, Edith, *The Theatrical Cast of Athens: Interactions between Ancient Greek Drama and Society* (Oxford: Oxford University Press, 2006)

Hall, Herman J., *Two Travelers in Europe: A Unique Story Told by One of Them, What They Saw and How They Lived While Traveling Among the Half-Civilized People of Morocco, the Peasants of Italy and France, As Well As the Educated Classes of Spain, Greece, and Other Countries* (Springfield: Hampden Publishing Company, 1898)

Hambidge, Jay, *The Parthenon and Other Greek Temples: Their Dynamic Symmetry* (New Haven: Yale University Press, 1924)

Hamilton, Richard, 'Sources for the Athenian amphidromia', *Greek, Roman, and Byzantine Studies*, 25 (1984), 243–251

Hamilton, William R., *Memorandum on the Subject of the Earl of Elgin's Pursuits in Greece*, 2nd edn, corrected (London: John Murray, 1815)

Hammond, N.G.L., 'The Narrative of Herodotus VII and the Decree of Themistocles at Troezen', *Journal of Hellenic Studies*, 102 (1982), 75–93, https://doi.org/10.2307/631127

Hanink, Johanna, *The Classical Debt: Greek Antiquity in an Era of Austerity* (Cambridge, Massachusetts; London: Harvard University Press, 2017), https://doi.org/10.4159/9780674978249

Hanink, Johanna, trans., *Thucydides. How to Think about War: An Ancient Guide to Foreign Policy* (Princeton: Princeton University Press, 2019), https://doi.org/10.1515/9780691193847

Hanson, Charles H., *The Land of Greece Described and Illustrated. With 44 Illustrations and Three Maps* (London: Nelson, 1886)

Harder, Matthias, *Walter Hege und Herbert List, Griechische Tempelarchitektur in photographischer Inszenierung* (Berlin: Reimer, 2003)

Harding, Phillip, ed. and trans., *The Story of Athens: The Fragments of the Local Chronicles of Attika* (London: Routledge, 2008), https://doi.org/10.4324/9780203448342

Harris, Diane, *The Treasures of the Parthenon and Erechtheion* (Oxford: Oxford University Press, 1995)

Harrison, Evelyn B., 'The Web of History: A Conservative Reading of the Parthenon Frieze', in *Worshipping Athena: Panathenaia and Parthenon*, ed. by Jenifer Neils (Madison, WI: University of Wisconsin Press, 1996), pp. 198–214

Harrison, Jane E., *Primitive Athens as Described by Thucydides* (Cambridge: Cambridge University Press, 1906)

Henderson, Jeffrey, ed., *Aristophanes, Fragments* (London: Harvard University Press, 2007)

Heracleides of Crete, 'A view of Athens.' A fragment by an author of the third century BCE, previously attributed to Dicaearchus of Messene of the fourth century BCE. Translated into English by Stambaugh, John E., in 'The Idea of the City: Three Views of Athens', *Classical Journal*, 69.4 (1974), 309–321, from Pfister, Friedrich, *Die Reisebilder des Herakleides* (Vienna, Rohrer, 1951)

Hichens, Robert, *The Near East, Dalmatia, Greece, and Constantinople, Illustrated By Jules Guérin and With Photographs* (London and New York: Hodder and Stoughton, 1913)

Hobsbawm, Eric, 'Inventing Traditions' in *The Invention of Tradition, ed. by* Eric Hobsbawm and Terence Ranger (Cambridge: Cambridge University Press, 1992), pp. 1–14

Hock, Ronald F., and Edward N. O'Neil, *The Chreia in Ancient Rhetoric, Volume 1. The Progymnasmata* (Atlanta: Scholars Press, 1986)

Hock, Ronald F., and Edward N. O'Neil, *The Chreia and Ancient Rhetoric: Classroom Exercises, trans. and ed. by Ronald F. Hock and Edward N. O'Neil* (Atlanta: Society of Biblical Literature, 2002)

Holloway, R. Ross, 'The Mutilation of Statuary in Classical Greece', in *Miscellanea Mediterranea*, ed. by R. Ross Holloway (Providence, R.I.: Center for Old World Archaeology and Art, Brown University, 2000), pp. 77–82

Holloway, R. Ross, 'The Archaic Acropolis and the Parthenon Frieze', *The Art Bulletin*, 48.2 (1966), 223–226, https://doi.org/10.1080/00043079.1966.10788 948

Hölscher, Tonio, *Visual Power in Ancient Greece and Rome: Between Art and Social Reality* (Oakland, CA: University of California Press, 2018), https://doi.org/10.1525/california/9780520294936.001.0001

Hope, Thomas, and Fani-Maria Tsigakou, eds, *Thomas Hope (1769–1831) Pictures from 18th Century Greece* (Athens: Benaki Museum, British Council, Publishing House "Melissa", 1985)

Hopper, R. J., 'Athena and the early Acropolis', *Greece & Rome*, 10, *Parthenos and Parthenon* (1963), 1–16

Hornblower, Simon, ed., *Lykophron: Alexandra: Greek Text, Translation, Commentary, and Introduction* (Oxford: Oxford University Press, 2015)

Howes, David, 'The Skinscape: Reflections on the Dermatological Turn', *Body and Society*, 24 (2018), 225–239, https://doi.org/10.1177%2F1357034X18766285

Hunter, Richard, and Casper C. de Jonge, eds, *Dionysius of Halicarnassus and Augustan Rome: Rhetoric, Criticism and Historiography* (Cambridge: Cambridge University Press, 2019), https://doi.org/10.1017/9781108647632

Hurwit, Jeffrey M., *The Acropolis in the Age of Pericles* (Cambridge: Cambridge University Press, 2004)

Iakovidis, Spyros E., *The Mycenaean Acropolis of Athens* (Athens: Archaeological Society of Athens, 2006)

Iser, Wolfgang, *How to Do Theory* (Oxford: Blackwell, 2006)

Israelowich, Ido, *Society, Medicine and Religion in the Sacred Tales of Aelius Aristides* (Leiden: Brill, 2012), https://doi.org/10.1163/9789004229440

Izdebski, Adam, and others, 'Landscape Change and Trade in Ancient Greece: Evidence from Pollen Data', *The Economic Journal*, 130 (2020), 2596–2618, https://doi.org/10.1093/ej/ueaa026

Jeffery, L. H., 'The Inscribed Gravestones of Archaic Attica', *The Annual of the British School at Athens*, 57 (1962), 115–153, https://doi.org/10.1017/S0068245400013666

Jones, H. Stuart, *Select Passages from Ancient Writers Illustrative of the History of Greek Sculpture* (London, New York: Macmillan, 1895)

Kaldellis, Anthony, *The Christian Parthenon, Classicism and Pilgrimage in Byzantine Athens* (Cambridge: Cambridge University Press, 2009)

Kaldellis, Anthony, *Byzantine Readings of Ancient Historians: Texts in Translation with Introductions and Notes* (London and New York: Routledge, 2015)

Kallet, Lisa, 'Acccounting for Culture in Fifth-century Athens', *in Democracy, Empire, and the Arts in Fifth-century Athens, ed. by Deborah Boedeker and Kurt A. Raaflaub* (Cambridge, MA: Harvard University Press, 1998), pp. 43–58

Kallet, Lisa, *Money and the Corrosion of Power in Thucydides* (Berkeley: University of California Press, 2001), https://doi.org/10.1525/9780520927421

Kallet, Lisa, 'Wealth, Power, and Prestige: Athens at Home and Abroad', in *The Parthenon from Antiquity to the Present*, ed. by Jenifer Neils (Cambridge: Cambridge University Press, 2005), pp. 35–65

Kaltsas, Nikolaos, and Alan Shapiro, eds, *Worshipping Women: Ritual and Reality in Classical Athens* (New York: Onassis Foundation, and Athens: Hellenic Ministry of Culture and National Archaeological Museum, 2008)

Karamanou, Ioanna, 'Fragments of Euripidean Rhetoric', in *Poet and Orator: A Symbiotic Relationship in Democratic Athens*, ed. by Andreas Markantonatos and Eleni Volonaki (Berlin: Walter de Gruyter, 2019), pp. 83–99

Kearns, Emily, 'The Heroes of Attica', *Bulletin Supplement* (*University of London. Institute of Classical Studies*), 57 (1989), 109–110, 174–175.

Kennerly, Michele, *Editorial Bodies: Perfection and Rejection in Ancient Rhetoric and Poetics* (*Studies in Rhetoric/Communication*) (Columbia, SC: The University of South Carolina Press, 2018)

Kenny, Anthony, trans., *Aristotle: Eudemian Ethics, A New Translation* (Oxford: World's Classics, 2011), https://doi.org/10.1093/actrade/9780199586431.book.1

Kondaratos, Savas, 'The Parthenon as Cultural Ideal', in *The Parthenon and its Impact in Modern Times,* ed. by Panayotis Tournikiotis (Athens: Melissa, 1994), 20–28.

Korres, Manolis, 'The Parthenon from Antiquity to the 19th Century', in *The Parthenon and its Impact in Modern Times*, ed. by Panayotis Tournikiotis (Athens: Melissa, 1994), pp. 136–161

Korres, Manolis, 'Topographic Examination of the Acropolis at Athens', *Brewminate*, 1 June 2017, https://brewminate.com/topographic-examination-of-the-acropolis-at-athens/

Kousser, Rachel, *The Afterlives of Greek Sculpture, Interaction, Transformation and Destruction* (Cambridge: Cambridge University Press, 2017)

Kowerski, Lawrence M., *Simonides on the Persian Wars: A Study of the Elegiac Verses of the "New Simonides"* (New York; London: Routledge, 2005), https://doi.org/10.4324/9780203958452

Kovacs, David, *Euripides: Troades: Edited with Introduction and Commentary* (Oxford: Oxford University Press, 2018)

Kraay, C.M., *The Coins of Ancient Athens* (Newcastle: Minerva Numismatic Handbooks, 1968)

Lagerlöf, Margaretha R., *The Sculptures of the Parthenon: Aesthetics and Interpretation* (New Haven, CT.; London: Yale University Press, 2000)

Laistner, M.L.W., *Greek Economics* (London: J. M. Dent & Co., 1923)

Lambert, S. D., *The Phratries of Attica* (Ann Arbor: University of Michigan Press, 1991)

Lapatin, Kenneth, and Beth Cohen, *The Colors of Clay; Special Techniques in Athenian Vases* (Los Angeles, Getty, 2006)

Leão, Delfim F., and P. J. Rhodes, eds, *The Laws of Solon* (London: I.B. Tauris, 2015), http://doi.org/10.5040/9780755626281

Lee, Mireille M., *Body, Dress, and Identity in Ancient Greece* (Cambridge: Cambridge University Press, 2015), https://doi.org/10.1017/CBO9781107295261

Lefkowitz, Mary R., *Euripides and the Gods* (New York: Oxford University Press, 2016), https://doi.org/10.1093/acprof:oso/9780199752058.001.0001

[Lehnerdt's Canabutzes] *Ioannis Canabutzae magistri Ad principem Aeni et Samothraces in Dionysium Halicarnassensem commentarium primum edidit atque praefatus est Maximilianus Lehnerdt* (Leipzig 'Lipsiae': Teubner, 1890)

Lewis, Sian, *The Athenian Woman: An Iconographic Handbook* (London: Routledge, 2002), https://doi.org/10.4324/9780203351192

Liston, Maria A., and Susan I. Rotroff, *The Agora Bone Well* (Boston: American School of Classical Studies, 2018)

Lloyd, W.W., 'The Central Group of the Panathenaic Frieze', *Transactions of the Royal Society of Literature*, 5 (1854), 1–36

Lloyd, William W., *On the General Theory of Proportion in Architectural Design and its Exemplification in Detail in the Parthenon. Read at the Royal Institution of British Architects, June 13th, 1859* (London: Weale, 1863)

Loraux, Nicole, *The Invention of Classical Athens: The Funeral Oration in the Classical City*, trans. by Alan Sheridan (Cambridge Mass: Harvard University Press, 1986)

Loraux, Nicole, *The Children of Athena: Athenian Ideas about Citizenship and the Division between the Sexes*, trans. by Caroline Levine (Princeton: Princeton University Press, 1993)

Lorenz, Katharina, *Ancient Mythological Images and their Interpretation: An Introduction to Iconology, Semiotics, and Image Studies in Classical Art History* (Cambridge: Cambridge University Press, 2016)

Lucas, R.C., *Remarks on The Parthenon: Being the Result of Studies and Inquiries Connected with the Production of Two Models of That Noble Building, Each Twelve Feet in Length, and Near Six in Width. The One, Exhibiting The Temple as it Appeared in its Dilapidated State, in The Seventeenth Century, and Executed From the Existing Remains, or From Authentic Drawings; The Other, Being an Attempt to Restore it to the Fulness of its Original Beauty And Splendour.—Also, a Brief View of The Statements and Opinions of the Principal Writers on the Subject: Viz., Spon And Wheler, Stuart And Revett, Visconti, Quatremere De Quincy, Col. Leake, The Chevalier Brondsted, Professor Cockerell, Mr. E. Hawkins, Professor Welcker, &c* (Salisbury: Brodie, 1845)

Lykophron, *Alexandra: Greek Text, Translation, Commentary, and Introduction*, ed. by Simon Hornblower (Oxford: Oxford University Press, 2015)

Maggidis, Christofilis, 'ΜΑΓΙΚΟΙ ΚΑΤΑΔΕΣΜΟΙ or Binding Curse Tablets: A Journey on the Greek Dark Side', in *Miscellanea Mediterranea*, ed. by R. Ross Holloway (Providence, R.I.: Center for Old World Archaeology and Art, Brown University, 2000)

Mahaffy, Rev. J. P., *Social Life in Greece from Homer to Menander* (London: Macmillan, 1874)

Mantis, Alexandros, *Disjecta Membra: The Plunder and Dispersion of the Antiquities of the Acropolis*, trans. by Miriam Caskey (Athens: Anthemion, 2000)

Marconi, Clemente, 'The Parthenon Frieze: Degrees of Visibility', *RES: Anthropology and Aesthetics*, 55/56 (2009), 156–173, https://doi.org/10.1086/RESvn1ms25608841

Mark, Ira S., 'The Gods on the East Frieze of the Parthenon', *Hesperia*, 53.3 (1984), 289–342

Markantonatos, Andreas and Eleni Volonaki, eds, *Poet and Orator: A Symbiotic Relationship in Democratic Athens* (Berlin; Boston: De Gruyter, 2019), https://doi.org/10.1515/9783110629729

Martin, Gunther, ed., *Euripides, Ion, Edition and Commentary* (Leiden: de Gruyter, 2018), https://doi.org/10.1515/9783110523591

Marx, Patricia A., 'Acropolis 625 (Endoios Athena) and the Rediscovery of its Findspot', *Hesperia*, 70.2 (2001), 221–254

Mastronarde, Donald J., *The Art of Euripides: Dramatic Technique and Social Context* (Cambridge: Cambridge University Press, 2010), https://doi.org/10.1017/CBO9780511676437

Mattusch, Carol C., 'The Eponymous Heroes: the Idea of Sculptural Groups', in William D.E. Coulson, ed., *The Archaeology of Athens and Attica Under the Democracy: Proceedings of an International Conference Celebrating 2500 Years Since the Birth of Democracy in Greece, Held at the American School of Classical Studies at Athens, December 4–6, 1992* (Oxford: Oxbow Books, 1994), pp. 73–81

Mayhew, Robert, ed., *Prodicus the Sophist: Texts, Translations, and Commentary* (Oxford: Oxford University Press, 2011)

Meskell, Lynn, *A Future in Ruins, UNESCO, World Heritage, and the Dream of Peace* (New York: Oxford University Press, 2018)

Michaelis, Adolf, *Der Parthenon* (Leipzig: Breitkopf and Härtnel, 1871), https://doi.org/10.11647/obp.0136.21

Miles, Margaret M., *Art as Plunder: The Ancient Origins of Debate about Cultural Property* (Cambridge: Cambridge University Press, 2008)

Miles, Margaret M., 'Burnt Temples in the Landscape of the Past', in *Valuing the Past in the Greco-Roman World: Proceedings from the Penn-Leiden Colloquia on Ancient Values VII*, ed. by James Ker and Christoph Pieper (Leiden, Boston: Brill, 2014), pp. 111–145

Miles, Margaret M., ed., *Autopsy in Athens: Recent Archaeological Research on Athens and Attica* (Oxford: Oxbow Books, 2015)

Miller, Col. Jonathan P., of Vermont, *The condition of Greece, in 1827 and 1828; being an exposition of the poverty, distress, and misery, to which the inhabitants have been reduced by the destruction of their towns and villages and the ravages of their country, by a merciless Turkish foe* (New York: Harper, 1828)

Monoson, S. Sara, 'Citizen as *Erastes*: Erotic Imagery and the Idea of Reciprocity in the Periclean Funeral Oration', *Political Theory*, 22.2 (1994), 253–276

Monoson, S. Sara, *Plato's Democratic Entanglements: Athenian Politics and the Practice of Philosophy* (Princeton, NJ: Princeton University Press, 2000)

Morrow, Katherine D., *Greek Footwear and the Dating of Sculpture* (Madison, WI: University of Wisconsin Press, 1985)

Morton, Jacob, 'The Experience of Greek Sacrifice: Investigating Fat-Wrapped Thigh Bones', in *Autopsy in Athens: Recent Archaeological Research on Athens and Attica*, ed. by Margaret M. Miles (Oxford: Oxbow Books, 2015), pp. 66–67

Muir, J. V., ed., *Alcidamas, The Works and Fragment* (London: Bristol Classical Press, 2001)

[Naples Museum] *Raccolta delle più interessanti Dipinture e de' più belli Mosaici rinvenuti negli scavi di Ercolano, di Pompei, e di Stabia che ammiransi nel Museo Reale Borbonico* (Naples: [n.p.], 1840). One hundred and twenty-one outline copper engravings, untitled and unnumbered, although some copies have a manuscript index.

Neils, Jenifer, *The Parthenon Frieze* (Cambridge and New York: Cambridge University Press, 2001)

Neils, Jenifer, and John H. Oakley, eds, *Coming of Age in Ancient Greece: Images of Childhood from the Classical Past* (New Haven and London: Yale University Press, 2003)

Notor, G., *La Femme dans l'Antiquité Grecque, Texte et Dessins de G. Notor. Préface de M. Eugène Müntz, Membre de l'Institut, Trente-trois Reproductions en couleurs et 320 dessins en noir d'après les documents des Musées et collections particulières* (Paris: Renouard, Laurens, 1901)

O'Quinn, Daniel, *Engaging the Ottoman Empire, Vexed Mediations, 1690–1815* (Philadelphia, PA: University of Pennsylvania Press, 2019)

Oliver, James H., *The Ruling Power: A Study of the Roman Empire in the Second Century after Christ Through the Roman Oration of Aelius Aristides* (Philadelphia, PA: American Philosophical Society, 1953)

Oliver, James Henry, 'The Civilizing Power: A Study of the Panathenaic Discourse of Aelius Aristides Against the Background of Literature and Cultural Conflict, with Text, Translation, and Commentary', *Transactions of the American Philosophical Society*, 58.1 (1968), 1–223, https://doi.org/10.2307/1005987

Omont, Henri, ed., *Athènes au XVIIe siècle. Dessins des sculptures du Parthénon attribués à J. Carrey et conservés à la Bibliothèque nationale, accompagnés de vues et plans d'Athènes et de l'Acropole* (Paris: Leroux, 1898)

[Omont Missions], *Missions archéologiques françaises en Orient aux XVIIe et XVIIIe siècles. Documents publiés par H. Omont* (Paris: Collection de documents inédits, 1902)

Osborne, Robin, *Classical Landscape with Figures: The Ancient Greek City and its Countryside* (London: George Philip, 1987)

Osborne, R.G., 'The Viewing and Obscuring of the Parthenon Frieze', *Journal of Hellenic Studies*, 107 (1987), 98–105

Osborne, Robin, 'Archaic and Classical Greek Temple Sculpture and the Viewer', in *Word and Image in Ancient Greece*, ed. by Keith Rutter and Brian Sparkes (Edinburgh: Edinburgh University Press, 2000), pp. 228–246

Osborne, Robin, 'Classical Presentism', *Past and Present*, 234.1 (2017), 217–226, https://doi.org/10.1093/pastj/gtw055

Osborne, Robin, *The Transformation of Athens: Painted Pottery and the Creation of Classical Greece* (Princeton: Princeton University Press, 2018)

Osborne, Robin, and P.J. Rhodes, eds, *Greek Historical Inscriptions, 478–404 BC* (Oxford: Oxford University Press, 2017)

Owens, Ron, *Solon of Athens: Poet, Philosopher, Soldier, Statesman* (Brighton: Sussex Academic Press, 2010)

Palagia, Olga, *The Pediments of the Parthenon*, 2nd unrevised edn (Leiden: Brill, 1998)

Palagia, Olga, 'Fire from Heaven: Pediments and Akroteria of the Parthenon', in Neils, *Parthenon*, pp. 225–259

Palagia, Olga, 'Women in the Cult of Athena', in Nikos Kaltsas and H.A. Shapiro, *Worshiping Women: Ritual and Reality in Classical Athens* (New York: Alexander S. Onassis Public Benefit Foundation in collaboration with the National Archaeological Museum, Athens, 2008) pp. 31–37

Papageorgiou-Venetas, Alexander, Αθήνα, ένα όραμα του Κλασικισμού (Athens: Kapon, 2001)

Parker, Robert, 'Law and Religion', in *The Cambridge Companion to Ancient Greek Law*, ed. by Michael Gagarin and David Cohen (Cambridge: Cambridge University Press, 2005), https://doi.org/10.1017/CCOL0521818400.004

Parker, Robert, *Polytheism and Society at Athens* (Oxford: Oxford University Press, 2005), https://doi.org/10.1093/acprof:oso/9780199216116.001.0001

Parsons, Arthur W., 'Klepsydra and the Paved Court of the Pythion', *Hesperia*, 12.3, (1943), 191–267

Parsons, Mikeal C., and Michael W. Martin, *Ancient Rhetoric and the New Testament: The Influence of Elementary Greek Composition* (Waco, TX: Baylor University Press, 2018)

Patterson, Cynthia, '"Not Worth the Rearing": The Causes of Infant Exposure in Ancient Greece', *Transactions of the American Philological Association*, 115 (1985), 103–123

Pedersen, Poul, *The Parthenon and the Origin of the Corinthian Capital* (Odense: Odense University Press, 1989)

Pelling, Christopher, *Literary Texts and the Greek Historian* (London: Routledge, 1999)

Perdicaris, G. A., *The Greece of the Greeks* (Boston: Paine and Burgess, 1845)

Pernot, Laurence, ed., *La rhétorique des arts: actes du colloque tenu au Collège de France sous la présidence de Marc Fumaroli, de l'Académie française* (Paris: Presses Universitaires de France, 2011)

Pernot, Laurence, 'Phidias à la Barre', in *La rhétorique des arts: actes du colloque tenu au Collège de France sous la présidence de Marc Fumaroli, de l'Académie française*, ed. by Laurence Pernot (Paris: Presses Universitaires de France, 2011), pp. 11–44

Pfister, Friedrich, *Die Reisebilder des Herakleides* (Vienna: Rohrer, 1951)

Pollitt, J. J., *The Ancient View of Greek Art: Criticism, History, and Terminology* (New Haven, CT: Yale University Press, 1974)

Poole, Reginald S., *Catalogue of Greek Coins: Attica-Megaris-Aegina* (London: British Museum 1888)

Pope, Spencer A., 'Financing and Design: The Development of the Parthenon Program and the Parthenon Building Account', in *Miscellanea Mediterranea,* ed. by R. Ross Holloway (Providence, R.I.: Center for Old World Archaeology and Art, Brown University, 2000), pp. 61–69

Porter, James, *Observations on the Religion, Law, Government, and Manners of the Turks. The Second edition, Corrected and Enlarged by the Author* (London: Nourse, 1771)

Porter, James, *The Origins of Aesthetic Thought in Ancient Greece: Matter, Sensation, and Experience* (Cambridge: Cambridge University Press, 2010)

Price, Susan, ed., *Antisthenes of Athens: Texts, Translations, and Commentary* (Ann Arbor: University of Michigan Press, 2015), https://doi.org/10.3998/mpub.5730060

Pritchard, David, *Public Spending and Democracy in Classical Athens* (Austin: University of Texas Press, 2015)

Race, William H., ed., *Menander Rhetor: Dionysius of Halicarnassus, Ars Rhetorica* (Harvard: Harvard University Press, 2019)

Rehm, Rush, *Understanding Greek Tragic Theatre*, 2nd edn (London and New York: Routledge, 2017), https://doi.org/10.4324/9781315748696

Reinach, Salomon, *Peintures de vases antiques recueillies par Millin, 1808, et Millingen, 1813. Publiées et commentées par S. Reinach* (Paris: Firmin-Didot, 1891)

Rhodes, P. J., *The Greek City States: A Source Book,* 2nd edn (Cambridge: Cambridge University Press, 2007), https://doi.org/10.1017/CBO9780511818035

Richter, Gisela M. Augusta, *The Archaic Gravestones of Attica* (London: Phaidon, 1961)

Ridgway, Brunilde S., 'Notes on the Development of the Greek Frieze', *Hesperia*, 35.2 (1966), 188–204

Robertson, Martin, *The Parthenon Frieze: Text: Martin Robertson; Photographs: Alison Frantz* (London: Phaidon in association with British Museum Publications, 1975)

Robertson, Noel, 'Athena's Shrines and Festivals', in Jenifer Neils, *Worshipping Athena* (Madison, WI; London: University of Wisconsin Press, 1996), pp. 27–77

Robertson, Noel, 'The Praxiergidae Decree (IG I3 7) and the Dressing of Athena's Statue with the Peplos', *Greek, Roman, and Byzantine Studies*, 44.2 (2004), 111–161

Rodd, Rennell, *The Violet Crown, and Songs of England* (London: D. Scott, 1891)

Rous, Sarah A., *Reset in Stone: Memory and Reuse in Ancient Athens* (Madison: University of Wisconsin Press, 2019)

Russell, D.A., *Greek Declamation* (Cambridge: Cambridge University Press, 1983)

Russell, D.A., ed., *Dio Chrysostom, Speeches. Selections. Orations VII, XII, and XXXVI* (Cambridge: Cambridge University Press, 1992)

Schanz, Holly L., *Greek Sculptural Groups: Archaic and Classical* (New York: Garland, 1980)

Schleisner, Steenberg, and Heise Brandes, *De Parthenone eiusque partibus* (Hanover: Royal University publications, 1849)

Schoedel, William R., ed., *Athenagoras, Legatio and De Resurrectione* (Oxford: Oxford University Press, 1972)

Schwab, Gustav H., *An Archaeological Cruise in the Levant: A Diary of a Trip to the Ancient Art-Centres of Greece, Asia Minor, the Aegean Islands and Sicily* (New York: privately printed, 1904)

Schwab, Katherine A., 'Celebrations of Victory: The Metopes of the Parthenon', in Neils, *Parthenon*, pp. 159–197

Schwab, Katherine A., 'The Parthenon East Metopes, the Gigantomachy, and Digital Technology', in *Parthenon and its Sculptures*, ed. by Michael B. Cosmopoulos (Cambridge: Cambridge University Press, 2004), pp. 150–165

Schwerzek, Karl, *Erläuterungen zu der Rekonstruktion des Westgiebels des Parthenon* (Vienna: Selbstverlag des Verfassers, 1896)

Schwerzek, Karl, *Erläuterungen zu dem Versuch einer Rekonstruktion des Östlichen Parthenongiebels* (Vienna: Selbstverlag des Verfassers, 1904)

Senseney, John R., *The Art of Building in the Classical World: Vision, Craftsmanship, and Linear Perspective in Greek and Roman Architecture* (Cambridge: Cambridge University Press, 2011), https://doi.org/10.1017/CBO9780511976711

Setton, Kenneth M., 'The Archaeology of Medieval Athens', in *Essays in Medieval Life and Thought: Presented in Honor of Austin Patterson Evans*, ed. by John Hine Mundy, Richard W. Emery and Benjamin J. Nelson (New York: Columbia University Press, 1955), pp. 227–258

Seznec, Jean, 'Michelet devant les Elgin marbles', *English Miscellany* (Rome: [n.p.], 1960), 223–230

Shapiro, H. Alan, 'Autochthony and the Visual Arts in Fifth-Century Athens', in *Democracy, Empire, and the Arts in Fifth-Century Athens*, ed. by Deborah Boedeker and Kurt A. Raaflaub (Cambridge, MA: Harvard University Press, 1998), pp. 127–151

Shear, Ione Mylonas, 'The Western Approach to the Athenian Akropolis', *Journal of Hellenic Studies*, 119 (1999), 86–127, https://doi.org/10.2307/632313

Shear, T. Leslie, Jnr., *Trophies of Victory: Public Building in Periklean Athens* (Princeton, NJ: Department of Art and Archaeology, Princeton University in association with Princeton University Press, 2016)

Skiadas, P.K., and J.G. Lascaratos, 'Dietetics in Ancient Greek Philosophy: Plato's Concepts of Healthy Diet', *European Journal of Clinical Nutrition*, 55 (2001), 532–537, https://doi.org/10.1038/sj.ejcn.1601179

Smith, A.H., ed., *The Sculptures of the Parthenon with an Introduction and Commentary* (London: British Museum Trustees, 1910)

Smith, A.H., 'Lord Elgin and his Collection', *Journal of Hellenic Studies*, 36 (1916), 163–372, https://doi.org/10.2307/625773

Smith, Cecil, 'Additions to the Greek Sculptures in the British Museum', *The Classical Review*, 6.10 (1892)

Smith, Martin F., 'New Fragments of Diogenes of Oenoanda', *American Journal of Archaeology*, 75.4 (1971), 357–389

Smyth, Herbert Weir, ed., *Aeschylus, with an English Translation* (London: Heinemann; Cambridge: Harvard University Press, 1971, 1973)

Sophocles, *Fragments*, ed. and trans. by Hugh Lloyd-Jones (Cambridge Mass: Harvard University Press, 1996)

Sophocles, 'Oenomaus', in his *Fragments*, ed. and trans. by Hugh Lloyd-Jones (Cambridge, MA: Harvard University Press, 1996), pp. 242–248.

Sourvinou-Inwood, Christiane, *Athenian Myths and Festivals: Aglauros, Erechtheus, Plynteria, Panathenaia, Dionysia*, ed. by Robert Parker (Oxford: Oxford University Press, 2011), https://doi.org/10.1093/acprof:oso/9780199592074.001.0001

St Clair, William, *The Reading Nation in the Romantic Period* (Cambridge: Cambridge University Press, 2004)

St Clair, William, *Who Saved the Parthenon? A New History of the Acropolis Before, During and After the Greek Revolution* (Cambridge: Open Book Publishers, 2022), https://doi.org/10.11647/OBP.0136

Stadter, Philip, ed., *The Speeches in Thucydides: A Collection of Original Studies, With a Bibliography* (Chapel Hill: University of North Carolina Press, 1973)

Stambaugh, John E., 'The Idea of the City: Three Views of Athens', *The Classical Journal*, 69.4 (1974), 309–321

Steinbock, Bernd, *Social Memory in Athenian Public Discourse: Uses and Meanings of the Past* (Ann Arbor: University of Michigan Press, 2013), https://doi.org/10.3998/mpub.1897162

Stewart, Andrew, *Art, Desire, and the Body in Ancient Greece* (Cambridge: Cambridge University Press, 1997)

Stewart, Andrew, *Attalos, Athens, and the Akropolis, the Pergamene 'Little Barbarians' and their Roman and Renaissance Legacy* (Cambridge: Cambridge University Press, 2004)

Stewart, Andrew, 'Pheidias: The Sculptures & Ancient Sources', *American Journal of Archaeology*, 115.3 (2011), https://doi.org/10.3764/ajaonline1153.Stewart

Stillwell, Richard, 'The Panathenaic Frieze', *Hesperia*, 38.2 (1969), 231–241

Storey, Ian C., *Eupolis Poet of Old Comedy* (Oxford: Oxford University Press, 2003), https://doi.org/10.1093/acprof:oso/9780199259922.001.0001

Storey, Ian C., *Aristophanes: Peace* (London: Bloomsbury Academic, 2019), http://doi.org/10.5040/9781350020252

Stuart, James, and Nicholas Revett, *The Antiquities of Athens* (London: John Nichols, 1787)

Studniczka, F., *Beiträge zur Geschichte der altgriechischen Tracht* (Vienna: O. Gerold's Sohn, 1886)

Suksi, Aara, 'The Poet at Colonus: Nightingales in Sophocles', *Mnemosyne*, 54.6 (2001), 646–658, https://doi.org/10.1163/15685250152952121

Swain, Simon, *Hellenism and Empire, Language, Classicism, and Power in the Greek world AD 50–250* (Oxford: Clarendon, 1996)

Swift, Laura, *Euripides, Ion* (London: Duckworth, 2008), referring to Cynthia Patterson, '"Not Worth the Rearing": The Causes of Infant Exposure in Ancient Greece', in *Transactions of the American Philological Association*, 115 (1985), 103–123

Synesius of Cyrene, *The Letters of Synesius of Cyrene, Translated into English with Introduction and Notes by Augustine FitzGerald* (London: Oxford University Press, 1926)

Tanner, Jeremy, 'Social Structure, Cultural Rationalization and Aesthetic Judgment in Classical Greece', in *Word and Image in Ancient Greece*, ed. by N. Keith Rutter and Brian Sparkes (Edinburgh: Edinburgh University Press, 2000), pp. 183–205

Tanner, Jeremy, *The Invention of Art History in Ancient Greece: Religion, Society and Artistic Rationalisation* (Cambridge: Cambridge University Press, 2006)

Tanner, Jeremy, 'Sight and Painting: Optical Theory and Pictorial Poetics in Classical Greek Art', in *Sight and the Ancient Senses*, ed. by Michael Squire (London: Routledge, 2016), pp. 107–114, https://doi.org/10.4324/9781315719238

The Reunification of the Parthenon Marbles, A Cultural Imperative [exhibition showing the effects of the scattering of the pieces arranged by the Council of Europe] (Athens: Ministry of Culture and others, 2004)

Thomas, Rosalind, *Literacy and Orality in Ancient Greece* (Cambridge: Cambridge University Press, 1992)

Trapp, Michael, ed., *Aelius Aristides Orations. 1–2* (Cambridge, MA and London: Loeb, 2017)

Ullucci, Daniel C., *The Christian Rejection of Animal Sacrifice* (Oxford: Oxford University Press, 2012)

Usher, Stephen, trans., *Dionysius of Halicarnassus, Critical Essays* (London: Harvard University Press, 1974, 1985)

Valavanis, Panos, *The Acropolis Through its Museum* (Athens: Kapon, 2013)

Valente, Stefano, *The Antiatticist: Introduction and Critical Edition* (Berlin: de Gruyter, 2015), https://doi.org/10.1515/9783110404937

Verrall, A.W., *Euripides, the Rationalist: A Study in the History of Art and Religion* (Cambridge: Cambridge University Press, 1895)

Waldstein, Charles, *Essays in the Art of Pheidias* (Cambridge: Cambridge University Press, 1885)

Waldstein, Charles, 'Τραπεζώ and Κοσμώ in the Frieze of the Parthenon', *Journal of Hellenic Studies*, 11 (1890), 143–145

Waldstein, Charles, *Greek Sculpture and Modern Art: Two Lectures Delivered to the Students of the Royal Academy of London* (Cambridge: Cambridge University Press, 1914)

Walters, H. B., *Catalogue of the Terracottas in the Department of Greek and Roman Antiquities, British Museum* (London: Trustees of British Museum, 1903)

Walters, H. B., *History of Ancient Pottery: Greek, Etruscan, and Roman, Based on the Work of Samuel Birch* (London: Murray, 1905)

Whiting, Lilian, *Athens the Violet-Crowned, Illustrated from Photographs* (Boston: Little Brown, 1913)

Whitmarsh, Tim, *Beyond the Second Sophistic: Adventures in Greek Postclassicism* (Berkeley; Los Angeles, London: University of California Press, 2013)

Whitmarsh, Tim, *Battling the Gods: Atheism in the Ancient World* (London: Faber, 2016)

Wilkins, Henry Musgrave, *Speeches from Thucydides Third Edition Revised and Corrected* (London: Longman, 1881)

Winckelmann, Giovanni, *Monumenti antichi inediti, spiegati ed illustrati da Giovanni Winckelmann, Prefetto delle antiquità di Roma* (Rome: at the author's expense, 1767)

Woodford, Susan, *Images of Myths in Classical Antiquity* (Cambridge: Cambridge University Press, 2003)

Wright, Matthew, *The Lost Plays of Greek Tragedy, Volume 1, Neglected Authors* (London: Bloomsbury, 2016), http://doi.org/10.5040/9781474297608

Wright, Matthew, *The Lost Plays of Greek Tragedy, Volume 2, Aeschylus, Sophocles and Euripides* (London: Bloomsbury, 2019), http://doi.org/10.5040/9781474276450

Zacharia, Katerina, *Converging Truths, Euripides Ion and the Athenian Quest for Self-Definition* (Leiden: Brill, 2003), https://doi.org/10.1163/9789004349988

Zeitlin, Froma, 'The Artful Eye: Vision, Ekphrasis, and Spectacle in Euripidean Drama', in *Art and Text in Ancient Greek Culture*, ed. by Simon Goldhill and Robin Osborne (Cambridge: Cambridge University Press, 1994), pp. 138–196

Zevort, Ch., ed., *Lysistrata Traduction nouvelle, avec une Introduction et des Notes de Ch. Zévort. Edition ornée de 107 gravures en couleurs par Notor, d'après des documents authentiques des musées d'Europe* (Paris: Eugène Fasquelle, 1898)

Zuckerberg, Donna, *Not All Dead White Men: Classics and Misogyny in the Digital Age* (Cambridge, MA: Harvard University Press, 2018)

Illustrations

Index

About the Team

Alessandra Tosi was the managing editor for this book.

Lucy Barnes, Sam Noble and Cameron Baillie performed the copy-editing and proofreading.

Lucy Barnes indexed the book.

Anna Gatti designed the cover. The cover was produced in InDesign using the Fontin font.

Luca Baffa typeset the book in InDesign and produced the paperback and hardback editions. The text font is Tex Gyre Pagella; the heading font is Californian FB. Luca produced the EPUB, AZW3, PDF, HTML, and XML editions — the conversion is performed with open source software such as pandoc (https://pandoc.org/) created by John MacFarlane and other tools freely available on our GitHub page (https://github.com/OpenBookPublishers).

This book need not end here...

Share

All our books — including the one you have just read — are free to access online so that students, researchers and members of the public who can't afford a printed edition will have access to the same ideas. This title will be accessed online by hundreds of readers each month across the globe: why not share the link so that someone you know is one of them?

This book and additional content is available at:

https://doi.org/10.11647/OBP.0279

Donate

Open Book Publishers is an award-winning, scholar-led, not-for-profit press making knowledge freely available one book at a time. We don't charge authors to publish with us: instead, our work is supported by our library members and by donations from people who believe that research shouldn't be locked behind paywalls.

Why not join them in freeing knowledge by supporting us: https://www.openbookpublishers.com/support-us

Like Open Book Publishers

Follow @OpenBookPublish

Read more at the Open Book Publishers BLOG

You may also be interested in:

Who Saved the Parthenon?
A New History of the Acropolis Before, During and After the Greek Revolution
William St Clair

https://doi.org/10.11647/OBP.0136

That Greece Might Still Be Free
The Philhellenes in the War of Independence
William St Clair

https://doi.org/10.11647/OBP.0001

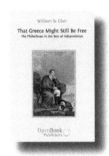

Cultural Heritage Ethics
Between Theory and Practice
Sandis Constantine

https://doi.org/10.11647/OBP.0047

CPSIA information can be obtained
at www.ICGtesting.com
Printed in the USA
LVHW071915180223
739851LV00022B/234